THE TIBETAN BOOK
OF THE
GREAT LIBERATION

OR THE METHOD OF
REALIZING *NIRVĀṆA* THROUGH
KNOWING THE MIND

THE GREAT *GURU* PADMA-SAMBHAVA

Described on pages xv–xvi

THE TIBETAN BOOK OF THE GREAT LIBERATION

OR

The Method of Realizing *Nirvāṇa*
Through Knowing the Mind

Preceded by an Epitome of
Padma-Sambhava's Biography
and Followed by
Guru Phadampa Sangay's Teachings
According to English Renderings by
Sardar Bahādur S. W. Laden La and
by the Lāmas Karma Sumdhon Paul
Lobzang Mingyur Dorje, and
Kazi Dawa-Samdup

Introductions, Annotations and Editing by
W. Y. Evans-Wentz

With Psychological Commentary by
Dr. C. G. Jung

With a new Foreword by
Donald S. Lopez, Jr.

OXFORD
UNIVERSITY PRESS
2000

OXFORD
UNIVERSITY PRESS

Oxford New York

Athens Auckland Bangkok Bogotá Buenos Aires Calcutta
Cape Town Chennai Dar es Salaam Delhi Florence Hong Kong
Istanbul Karachi Kuala Lumpur Madrid Melbourne Mexico City Mumbai
Nairobi Paris São Paulo Singapore Taipei Tokyo Toronto Warsaw

and associated companies in
Berlin Ibadan

Copyright © 1954, 2000 by W. Y. Evans-Wentz

First published by Oxford University Press, London, 1954

First issued as an Oxford University Press paperback, 1968

New Foreword copyright © 2000 by Donald S. Lopez, Jr.

Published by Oxford University Press, Inc.,
198 Madison Avenue, New York, New York 10016

Oxford is a registered trademark of Oxford University Press

Library of Congress Cataloging-in-Publication Data

The Tibetan book of the great liberation, or, The method of realizing nirvana through
knowing the mind ; preceeded by an epitome of Padma-Sambhava's biography and
followed by Guru Phadampa Sangay's teachings, according to English renderings by
Sardar Bahadur S.W. Laden La and by the Lamas Karma Sumdhon Paul Lobzang
Mingyur Dorje, and Kazi Dawa-Samdup ; introductions, annotations, and editing by
W.Y. Evans-Wentz ; with psychological commentary by C.G. Jung ; with a new
foreword by Donald S. Lopez, Jr.
    p. cm.
    ISBN-13 978-0-19-513315-8
    ISBN 0-19-513315-3

    1. Spiritual life—Buddhism—Early works to 1800. 2. Padma Sambhava, ca. 717-ca. 762.
3. Rdzogs-chen (Räiç-ma-pa)—Early works to 1800. 4. Buddhism—China—Tibet—Early
works to 1800. I. Title: The Tibetan book of the great liberation. II. Title: Method of
realizing nirvana through knowing the mind. III. Laden La, Sonam Wangfel, sardar
bahadur, 1876-1936? IV. Lobzang Mingyur Dorje. V. Zla-ba-bsam-'grub, Kazi,
1868-1922. VI. Evans-Wentz, W.Y. (Walter Yeeling), 1878-1965. VII. Jung, C.G. (Carl
Gustav), 1875-1961.

BQ7800.T53 2000
294.3'923—dc21   00-022483

3 5 7 9 8 6 4
Printed in the United States of America

IN GRATEFUL REMEMBRANCE OF
THE *GURUS*
WHO INSPIRED THE
TRANSMISSION OF THIS BOOK AND
THE TWO PRECEDING BOOKS
IN THIS SERIES
TO THE PEOPLES OF THE
WESTERN WORLD

DEDICATED
TO THOSE
SEEKING WISDOM

Bondage and Liberation

I: BONDAGE

Upon Ignorance dependeth *karma*;
Upon *karma* dependeth consciousness;
Upon consciousness depend name and form;
Upon name and form depend the six organs of sense;
Upon the six organs of sense dependeth contact;
Upon contact dependeth sensation;
Upon sensation dependeth desire;
Upon desire dependeth attachment;
Upon attachment dependeth existence;
Upon existence dependeth birth;
Upon birth depend old age and death, sorrow, lamentation, misery, grief, and despair. Thus doth this entire aggregation of misery arise.

II: LIBERATION

But upon the complete fading out and cessation of Ignorance ceaseth *karma*;
Upon the cessation of *karma* ceaseth consciousness;
Upon the cessation of consciousness cease name and form;
Upon the cessation of name and form cease the six organs of sense;
Upon the cessation of the six organs of sense ceaseth contact;
Upon the cessation of contact ceaseth sensation;
Upon the cessation of sensation ceaseth desire;
Upon the cessation of desire ceaseth attachment;
Upon the cessation of attachment ceaseth existence;
Upon the cessation of existence ceaseth birth;
Upon the cessation of birth cease old age and death, sorrow, lamentation, misery, grief, and despair. Thus doth this entire aggregation of misery cease.

The Buddha, *Samyutta Nikāya*, xxii. 90[16]
(based upon H. C. Warren's Translation).

PLATE II

THE TRANSLATORS AND THE EDITOR
Described on page xvii

FOREWORD

Donald S. Lopez, Jr.

A certain trepidation attends the decision to accept an invitation to write a foreword to new editions, published in 2000, of the four books of W. Y. Evans-Wentz: *The Tibetan Book of the Dead, Tibet's Great Yogī Milarepa, Tibetan Yoga and Secret Doctrines,* and *The Tibetan Book of the Great Liberation.* The four books in their old editions are already burdened with numerous prefaces, commentaries, and introductions, causing one to wonder what another preface could possibly add. It seems inevitable that the four books of Evans-Wentz will continue to outlive yet another generation of commentators, such that anything that a scholar might add today will only serve as material for a scholar some fifty years from now, who will demonstrate the biases and misunderstandings of a preface written fifty years ago, a preface that merely offers evidence of the fin de siècle zeitgeist of those who once called themselves postmoderns.

The four books of Evans-Wentz are surely ground-breaking works, the first to bring translations of Tibetan Buddhist texts to the English-speaking public. Evans-Wentz was equally avant garde in his method, collaborating closely with Tibetan scholars, a practice that would not become common for another four decades, after the Tibetan diaspora began in 1959. Yet, for the scholar of the present day, looking back now more than seventy years to the publication of the first volume of the series, *The Tibetan Book of the Dead*, in 1927, the Tibetan tetralogy of W. Y. Evans-Wentz, although a product of our century, seems to have originated in another age. All four books assume the undifferentiated dichotomy of the materialist West and the mystic East, an East that holds the secret to the West's redemption. Few of the concerns of scholars—such as language or culture or history—are to be found in the books. Instead, the volumes are presented as repositories of a timeless wisdom preserved by the East, a wisdom that will someday save the West, ultimately overcoming the duality of the hemispheres to culminate in the Unity of Mankind. This apparently beatific vision has since been shown to be the product of a romantic Orientalism that viewed the traditions of Asia as a natural resource to be extracted and refined for the consumption of the West; the books thus mark a moment in the history of colonialism.

Yet the four books of Evans-Wentz, especially the first, represent an important moment in that history. The products of a chance encounter between a Sikkimese school teacher and an American eccentric traveling in British India in 1919, the books have proved to be among the most durable products of the century's romance of Tibet, radiating their influence far beyond what might be expected from such an unlikely beginning.

Walter Wentz was born in Trenton, New Jersey, in 1878, the son of a German immigrant and an American Quaker. The late nineteenth century was a period of great fascination with spiritualism, the belief that spirits of the dead could be contacted through seances, materialization, automatic writing, and other techniques. Walter took an early interest in the books on spiritualism in his father's library, reading as a teen both *Isis Unveiled* and *The Secret Doctrine* by Madame Blavatsky of the Theosophical Society. These works were to have a profound effect on Walter Wentz. Indeed, it is impossible to appreciate his tetralogy without recognizing his lifelong commitment to Theosophy.

The Theosophical Society had been founded in New York in 1875 by Madame Helena Petrovna Blavatsky, a Russian émigré, and Colonel Henry Steel Olcott, a journalist and veteran of the Union Army during the Civil War. The goals of their Society were "to diffuse among men a knowledge of the laws inherent in the universe; to promulgate the knowledge of the essential unity of all that is, and to determine that this unity is fundamental in nature; to form an active brotherhood among men; to study ancient and modern religion, science, and philosophy; and to investigate the powers innate in man." The Theosophical Society represented one of several responses to Darwin's theory of evolution during the late nineteenth century. Rather than seeking a refuge from science in religion, Blavatsky and Olcott attempted to found a scientific religion, one that accepted the new discoveries in geology and archaeology while proclaiming an ancient and esoteric system of spiritual evolution more sophisticated than Darwin's theory.

Madame Blavatsky claimed to have spent seven years in Tibet as an initiate of a secret order of enlightened masters called the Great White Brotherhood. These masters, whom she called Mahatmas ("great souls"), lived in Tibet but were not themselves Tibetan. In fact, the very presence of the Mahatmas in Tibet was unknown to ordinary Tibetans. These masters had once lived throughout the world, but had congregated in Tibet to escape the onslaught of civilization. The Mahatmas had instructed her in Theosophy, which she also referred to as "Esoteric Buddhism," of which the Buddhism being practiced in Asia, including Tibet, was a corruption.

Throughout her career, she (and later, other members of the society) claimed to be in esoteric communication with the Mahatmas, sometimes through dreams and visions, but most commonly through letters that either materialized in a cabinet in Madame Blavatsky's room or that she transcribed through automatic writing. The Mahatmas' literary output was prodigious, conveying instructions on the most mundane matters of the Society's functions, as well as providing the content of the canonical texts of the Society, such as A. P. Sinnett's *Esoteric Buddhism* (1885) and Madame Blavatsky's *The Secret Doctrine* (1888).

The Theosophical Society enjoyed great popularity in America, Europe, and India (despite repeated scandals and a report by the Society of Psychical Research that denounced Madame Blavatsky as a fraud), playing an important but ambiguous role in the Hindu renaissance in India and the Buddhist renaissance in Sri Lanka (where Henry Olcott was particularly active). Its popularity continued after the death of the founders and into the twentieth century, when Blavatsky's heir, the former British suffragette Annie Besant, selected a young Hindu boy in 1909 as the messiah, the World Teacher, Krishnamurti. He renounced his divine status and broke with the Society in 1930. The death of Besant and other leaders followed soon after and the Society never regained the widespread popularity it once enjoyed, although it remains active, with its international headquarters in Pasadena,

California. The Theosophical Society has had a profound effect on the reception of Asian religions, especially Hinduism and Buddhism, in Europe and America during the twentieth century, inspiring, among other works, the Evans-Wentz tetralogy.

Walter Wentz moved to California at the turn of the century, where he joined the American Section of the Theosophical Society in 1901 at its headquarters in Point Loma, headed by Katherine Tingley, who established there the Raja-Yoga School and College, Theosophical University, and the School for the Revival of the Lost Mysteries of Antiquity. At Tingley's urging, Wentz enrolled at Stanford University, where he studied with William James and William Butler Yeats. After graduating, Wentz went to Jesus College at Oxford in 1907, where he studied Celtic folklore. It was there that he added a family name from his mother's side to his surname and became Walter Evans-Wentz. After completing his thesis, later published as *The Fairy Faith in Celtic Countries* (1911), he began a world tour financed by the income he received from rental properties in Florida. He was in Greece when the First World War broke out, and spent most of the war in Egypt.

From Egypt, he traveled to Sri Lanka and then on to India, gaining permission to travel from the British military authorities on the recommendation of a former classmate from Oxford, T. E. Lawrence. Evans-Wentz visited the Theosophical Society headquarters at Adyar and met with Annie Besant. In north India, he studied with various Hindu gurus, especially Swami Satyananda. In 1919 he arrived in the British hill station of Darjeeling on the southern slopes of the Himalayas, where he acquired a worn manuscript of a Tibetan text from a monk (some sources indicate that he acquired it in the bazaar). It was a portion of *The Profound Doctrine of Self-Liberation of the Mind [through Encountering] the Peaceful and Wrathful Deities,* (*Zab chos zhi khro dgongs pa rang grol*) said to have been discovered in the fourteenth century by Karma gling pa (1352–1405). The text is also known as the *Peaceful and Wrathful Deities According to Karmalingpa* or *Kar gling zhi khro* and as the *Bar do thos grol chen mo, The Great Liberation in the Intermediate State through Hearing.* Provided with a letter of introduction from the local superintendent of police, Sardar Bahadur Laden La (with whom he would later collaborate on the final volume in his series), Evans-Wentz, who could not read Tibetan, took the text to the English teacher at the Maharaja's Boy's School in Gangtok, named Kazi Dawa Samdup (1868–1922). Dawa Samdup was already acquainted with western enthusiasts of Buddhism, having served as translator for Alexandra David-Neel. She described him in *Magic and Mystery in Tibet*: "Dawasandup was an occultist and even, in a certain way, a mystic. He sought for secret intercourse with the Dâkinîs and the dreadful gods hoping to gain supernormal powers. Everything that concerned the mysterious world of beings generally invisible strongly attracted him, but the necessity of earning his living made it impossible for him to devote much time to his favourite study.... Drink, a failing frequent among his countrymen, had been the curse of his life.... But, peace to his memory. I do not wish to belittle him. Having acquired real erudition by persevering efforts, he was sympathetic and interesting."[1]

Kazi Dawa Samdup agreed to provide a translation, and over the course of the next two months he met with Evans-Wentz each morning before his school day began. The translations that Kazi Dawa Samdup made for Evans-Wentz would eventually appear in three books: *The Tibetan Book of the Dead* (1927), *Tibetan Yoga and Secret Doctrines* (1935), and *The Tibetan Book of the Great Liberation* (1954). Their time together was brief, however, with Evans-Wentz soon moving back to the ashram of Swami Satyananda to practice yoga. He returned to Gangtok to visit Kazi Dawa Samdup in 1920, shortly before the latter's appointment to the post of Lecturer in Tibetan at the University of Calcutta. This was to be their last meeting; Kazi Dawa Samdup died in 1922. In 1924, Evans-Wentz visited Kazi Dawa Samdup's family in Kalimpong, from whom he received a manuscript translation of the *Rje btsun bka' 'bum* (*The Hundred Thousand Words of the Master*), which Evans-Wentz subsequently edited and published as *Tibet's Great Yogī Milarepa* (1928). Of his relationship with Kazi Dawa Samdup, Evans-Wentz's biographer writes: "The few letters that have survived that they exchanged show a surprisingly distant and formal tone. Even in Dawa Samdup's diaries there is no word to suggest otherwise. There is nothing at all foreshadowing the later declarations that the Lama was the guru

---

[1] Alexandra David-Neel, *Magic and Mystery in Tibet* (New York: Dover Publications, 1971), pp. 15, 17, 19.

of Walter Evans-Wentz, nothing about the 'teachings' the American was supposed to have received."[2]

There is little testimony as to precisely how their collaboration took place. Kazi Dawa Samdup's English was presumably adequate to the task of producing rough translations. Evans-Wentz describes himself as having served as the lama's "living English dictionary." One can thus assume that much of the terminology derived from Evans-Wentz. And Evans-Wentz provided the lengthy introductions and copious annotations, which together provide the four books with his unmistakable stamp. He did not claim that they were scholarly works; he noted presciently that a critical study of the texts from the perspectives of philology, history, and philosophy was a task for scholars of the future. Instead, he described his works as "anthropological," taking anthropology to mean, "the Knowing, or Knowledge, of Man."

Evans-Wentz made several trips to India in the 1920s and 30s, studying yoga with several prominent neo-Vedantin teachers of the day, including Sri Yukteswar and Ramana Maharshi. He returned to Darjeeling in 1935 and employed two Sikkimese monks to translate another work from the same cycle of texts as the *Bar do thos grol*, entitled *Self-Liberation through Naked Vision Recognizing Awareness* (*Rig pa ngo sprod gcer mthong rang grol*). During the same visit, he received a summary of a famous biography of Padmasambhava, prepared by Sardar Bahadur Laden La, who had introduced him to Kazi Dawa Samdup some sixteen years before. These works would form the last work in the series, *The Tibetan Book of the Great Liberation*, eventually published in 1954.

Evans-Wentz returned to the United States in 1941, and spent the final twenty-three years of his life at the Keystone Hotel in San Diego. He spent his final months at the Self-Realization Fellowship of Swami Yogananda (a disciple of Sri Yukteswar and author of the popular *Autobiography of a Yogi*) in Encinitas, California. Walter Evans-Wentz died in 1965.

Evans-Wentz was apparently never a devotee of Tibetan

---

[2] Ken Winkler, *Pilgrim of the Clear Light* (Berkeley, Calif.: Dawnfire Books, 1982), p. 44. The other biographical information on Evans-Wentz here is drawn from Winkler's book. A useful summary is provided by John Myrdhin Reynolds in *Self-Liberation Through Seeing with Naked Awareness* (Barrytown, N.Y.: Station Hill Press, 1989), pp. 71–78.

Buddhism, considering himself instead a practitioner of Hindu yoga. His last contact with a Tibetan teacher seems to have been his collaboration with the two monks at the monastery of Ghoom, near Darjeeling, in 1935. Because his collaboration with Kazi Dawa Samdup was so brief, it is difficult to accept his claim that he was "the recognized disciple" of a Tibetan lama. Indeed, Kazi Dawa Samdup seems only to have been regarded as a "lama" by Evans-Wentz himself. Evans-Wentz remained a Theosophist and wrote for various Theosophical publications throughout the rest of his life. He never learned to read Tibetan; perhaps he did not feel it necessary, almost as if he already knew what the texts must say. And if they did not seem to say that, there was always recourse to their esoteric meaning, something he discusses at length in his introduction to *The Tibetan Book of the Dead*. Still, each of his four books holds an important place in the history of Tibetan Buddhism in the West and they must be regarded as pioneering works, not only in the texts chosen but in the mode of their creation; after the Tibetan diaspora that began in 1959, it became common for Western scholars to consult with Tibetan scholars in their translations of Buddhist texts, just as Evans-Wentz had done decades before.

From the perspective of the modern scholar of Tibetan Buddhism, the four books are fraught with problems: errors in translation, inaccurate dates, misattributions of authorship, misstatements of fact, unjustified flights of interpretation. (Referring to himself in the introduction, Evans-Wentz writes on page 79 of *The Tibetan Book of the Dead*, "The editor himself cannot expect, in a book of this nature, that his own interpretations of controversial problems will meet with universal acceptance; nor can he hope to have escaped all error.") With many decades of hindsight, each of the books seems somehow premature, translations attempted at a time when the requisite scholarly resources were not yet available. Still, Evans-Wentz makes little attempt to place them in their Tibetan literary and religious context. Indeed, there is very little that is "Tibetan" about the books, despite their titles. One wonders whether the adjective carried above all a Theosophical meaning for Evans-Wentz.

There is a certain audacity about the books; Evans-Wentz thought that he understood what he read, reading, as he did, through his bifocals of Theosophy and Hindu Yoga. But if Evans-Wentz had not been so audacious, we would not have had the books and their wide influence; even today, few scholars would feel competent to take on the task of translating and annotating all of the works found in *Tibetan Yoga and Secret Doctrines*, for example, and even if such a book were to be produced, the scholarly apparatus itself would render it esoteric to all but the initiates of Tibetology.

Evans-Wentz had a different, and much larger, audience of initiates in mind for his esoteric wisdom. The four books of Walter Evans-Wentz are, then, the products of another age, an age when there was little talk of cultural relativism, of radical incommensurability, of historicism, of identity politics, of Orientalism, of colonialism, of local histories, or of the late formation of the "world religions." Instead, in these texts, Evans-Wentz finds endless evidence of an ancient and universal wisdom, whose truth is not mediated by language or history or culture, but which is self-evident to all peoples of all races who will seek it. This may strike some as a rather quaint notion in 2000. Yet the books are about to enter their second century in print.

The Tibetan Book of the Great Liberation (published in 1954), is the fourth and final volume of a series that was intended as a trilogy. With Lama Kazi Dawa Samdup dead, Evans-Wentz turned to new translators to produce a book that is, in many ways, a companion volume to the first, *The Tibetan Book of the Dead* (published in 1927). Evans-Wentz considered it the most important work in the series. Here, Evans-Wentz returns to important texts of the Nyingma sect, texts in some ways more important than the *Bar do thos grol*, *Liberation in the Intermediate State Through Hearing*. As with his most famous work, Evans-Wentz provides a title of his own making; the full title of the work, *The Tibetan Book of the Great Liberation or the Method of Realizing Nirvāṇa Through Knowing the Mind*, is not the title of any of the three works translated in the volume. And once again, as with *The Tibetan Book of the Dead*, C. G. Jung provided a psychological commentary.

In 1935, during his final trip to India, Evans-Wentz returned to the Himalayas, where he again visited Darjeeling. There, he met with Sardar Bahadur S. W. Laden La (1876–1936), whom he had first encountered in 1919 when Laden La was the chief of police in Darjeeling. It was Laden La who had provided Evans-Wentz with a letter of introduction to Lama Kazi Dawa Samdup. Laden La had previously served in the Younghusband Expedition that had invaded Tibet in 1903–1904. He had gone on to an active career in diplomacy, continuing to serve the British until he was sent to England as an envoy of the thirteenth Dalai Lama, accompanying four Tibetan boys who were to receive training in science. He later served as the personal assistant to Sir Charles Bell in Lhasa (for Evans-Wentz's biographical sketch of Laden La, see pp. 87–89). By 1935, Laden La had retired to Darjeeling. Between November 22, 1935 and January 21, 1936, Laden La, assisted by a Sakya (Sa skya) monk named Bsod nams seng ge, and Evans-Wentz prepared an English summary of portions of a work entitled the *Injunctions of Padma* (*Padma bka'i thang yig*), the most extensive of the biographies of Padmasambhava, the Indian tantric yogin credited with establishing Buddhism in Tibet in the eighth century and with the authorship of many texts, including the *Bar do thos grol*. Laden La died in Kalimpong later that year. Their translation would form Book I, the first of the three texts to be included in *The Tibetan Book of the Great Liberation*. Evans-Wentz called it "An Epitome of the Life and Teachings of Tibet's Great *Guru* Padma-sambhava."

During the same stay in the Darjeeling district of West Bengal in 1935, Evans-Wentz visited the small town of Ghoom, the site of a Geluk (Dge lugs) monastery, where he collaborated with two monks, Karma Sumdhon Paul and Lobzang Mingyur Dorje. Karma Sumdhon Paul had served as translator for the sixth Panchen Lama during his tour of India. He later was headmaster of the Ghoom Middle English School before being appointed as Instructor for Research in Tibetan at the University of Calcutta, a post previously held by Kazi Dawa Samdup. By 1935, he had returned to Darjeeling where he was head lama of the government high school. Lobzang Mingyur Dorje had been a chief collaborator in the compilation of the *Tibetan-English Dictionary* by Sarat Chandra Das, first published in 1902 and still in wide use. He later succeeded Karma Sumdhom Paul at the University of Calcutta. Both monks had been students of the Mongolian monk, Sherab Gyatso, founder of the Ghoom monastery. The work that Evans-Wentz asked them to translate was not a Geluk text but a

Nyingma text also credited to Padmasambhava, an important work on the Great Perfection (*rdzogs chen*) from the larger work that contained the *Bar do thos grol*. The work is entitled *Zab chos zhi khro dgongs pa rang grol las rig pa ngo sprod gcer mthong rang grol*, *Self-Liberation through Naked Vision Recognizing Awareness* from *The Profound Doctrine of Self-Liberation of the Mind [through Encountering] the Peaceful and Wrathful Deities* said to have been discovered in the fourteenth century by Karma gling pa. Its translation composes Book II of *The Tibetan Book of the Great Liberation*, entitled "The [Yoga of] Knowing the Mind, the Seeing of Reality, called Self-Liberation, from 'The Profound Doctrine of Self-Liberation by Meditation Upon the Peaceful and Wrathful Deities."

The third and final text to be included here provided yet another link to *The Tibetan Book of the Dead*, because it was translated by Kazi Dawa Samdup. In 1919, prior to his first meeting with Evans-Wentz, Kazi Dawa Samdup had translated a work attributed to the Indian yogin Pha dam pa sangs rgyas, who is said to have visited Tibet in the twelfth century. He is regarded as the founder of one of the minor sects of Tibetan Buddhism, the Zhi byed pa ("Pacification"). Among his most famous works is a series of aphorisms, addressed to the people of Ding ri, a region in southern Tibet near Mount Everest. The work is entitled, *Pha dam pa sangs rgyas kyis zhal gdams ding ri brgya rtsa ma*, the *One Hundred Instructions of Pha dam pa sang rgyas to [the People of] Ding ri*. After the death of Kazi Dawa Samdup, Evans-Wentz received, presumably from his family, Dawa Samdup's translation of the text. Unfortunately, the last page or pages were missing. From this incomplete translation, Evans-Wentz selected and edited seventy-two stanzas and made them Book III of *The Tibetan Book of the Great Liberation*, entitled, "The Last Testamentary Teachings of the Guru Phadampa Sangay."

As with *The Tibetan Book of the Dead*, these translations by others were heavily annotated and commented upon by Evans-Wentz, making them very much his own. Once again, his own words came to both outweigh and circumscribe the translations, dwarfing them within a context very different from that of the culture that produced them.

The first text is a summary of the massive biography of

Padmasambhava, the *Padma bka'i thang yig*. Like the *Bar do thos sgrol*, it is a treasure text (*gter ma*), one of the thousands of works that Padmasambhava is said to have dictated to his Tibetan consort, the queen Ye shes mtsho rgyal, and then secreted in the Tibetan landscape, to be discovered at a time in the future when Tibet was prepared to receive its teachings. The *Padma bka'i thang yig* was found by the great text discoverer (*gter ston*) O rgyan gling pa in 1352. He is said to have extracted it from the heart of a stone image of a deity guarding the entrance to the Crystal Rock Cave in the Yarlung Valley. Modern scholars generally regard this text, and other treasure texts, as originating not at the time of Padmasambhava, who is said to have visited Tibet at the end of the eighth century, but rather at the time of their discovery; the discoverers of the treasure texts are considered to be either the authors or compilers of the works. The motives of the ascription of the works to Padmasambhava are debated; there is no doubt, however, that crediting the great Indian yogin with the authorship of the works lends them great legitimacy.

Regardless of its true origins as either Padmasambhava's dictation or O rgyan gling pa's composition, the *Padma bka'i thang yig* is a remarkable work in 108 chapters, recounting Padmasambhava's glorious lineage as an emanation of the Buddha of Infinite Light, Amitābha; the Buddha's prophecy, as he is about to pass into nirvāṇa, that twelve years hence he would appear as Padmasambhava to teach the secret mantras; his miraculous appearance as a beautiful eight-year-old child in the middle of a lotus blossom in the middle of Dhanakośa Lake (hence his name Padmasambhava, "Lotus Born"); his life as a prince, in which, like the Buddha, he excels at all sports and marries a beautiful princess, before deciding to renounce the world; his mastery of astrology, medicine, and all worldly arts; his tutelage under the Buddha's attendant Ānanda; his meditation in cemeteries; his taking of Princess Mandārāva as his consort; his defeat of the opponents of Buddhism; some thousand years later, his invitation to Tibet to subdue the demons and establish the first monastery at Bsam yas; and his departure to the land of the rākṣasas. In the course of the story, there are long excurses into Buddhist doctrine, as well as descriptions of the qualifications necessary for the future discoverers of Padmasambhava's hidden treasure texts.

The work is beloved by Tibetans for its effulgent description of their great culture hero and for the captivating description of his great and miraculous deeds. For scholars, the work provides a trove of information on Buddhist literature, Indian astrology and geography, tantric practice and its pantheon. The account of Padmasambhava's visit to Tibet is one of the most detailed accounts of the establishment of Buddhism in the Land of Snows, composed (if one accepts O rgyan gling pa as author) some five centuries after the fact. The text is all the more remarkable if one considers the opinion of some scholars that Padmasambhava may have been an entirely legendary figure.

In *The Tibetan Book of the Great Liberation*, Evans-Wentz provides a summary rather than a translation of the major events of the biography, in his words, "a brief synopsis of the very extensive and frequently verbose mass of matter." (94) He omits much of the beginning, commencing with the Buddha's prophecy in the eleventh chapter, and much of the end, with the instructions to the treasure discoverers. Evans-Wentz does not seem to have made use of Gustave-Charles Toussaint's remarkable French translation, *Le Dict de Padma*, published in Paris in 1933, more recently made available in English.[3] Nonetheless, Evans-Wentz's work remains a useful summary until a scholarly translation into English of the entire work can be made, certainly still a daunting task six decades after Evans-Wentz's pioneering work.

Book II of *The Tibetan Book of the Great Liberation* is more problematic. The text translated by the two Geluk monks of Ghoom Monastery is an important treasure text of the Nyingma sect, also said to have been composed and hidden by Padmasambhava. It was discovered in a cave by Karma gling pa (1356–1405) as one in a cycle of texts known as *Bar do thos grol chen mo, The Great Liberation in the Intermediate State through Hearing* or, more precisely, *Zab chos zhi khro dgong pa rang grol, The Profound Doctrine of Self-Liberation of the Mind [through Encountering] the Peaceful and Wrathful Deities, (Zab chos zhi khro dgongs pa rang grol)*, known more commonly simply as the *Kar gling zhi khro, The Peaceful and Wrathful Deities [According to] Karma gling pa.* The text translated

[3] See *The Life and Liberation of Padmasambhava*, 2 vols., trans. by Kenneth Douglas and Gwendolyn Bays (Emeryville, California: Dharma Publishing, 1978).

here is the tenth of seventeen chapters of this large work. Seven other chapters had been translated in *The Tibetan Book of the Dead*.

The text, entitled *Rig pa ngo sprod gcer mthong rang grol, Self-Liberation through Naked Vision Recognizing Awareness*, is an important text of the Great Perfection. In the Nyingma sect, Buddhist teachings are organized into nine vehicles, the highest of which is known as Atiyoga or, more commonly, the Great Perfection (*rdzogs chen*). These teachings, found also in Bon, describe the mind as the primordial basis, characterized with qualities such as presence, spontaneity, luminosity, original purity, unobstructed freedom, expanse, clarity, self-liberation, openness, effortlessness, and intrinsic awareness. This awareness, called *rig pa*, is not accessible through conceptual elaboration or logical analysis. Rather, the primordial basis is an eternally pure state free from the dualism of subject and object, infinite and perfect from beginning, ever complete. For this reason, some scholars prefer to translate the term *rdzogs chen* as "Great Completeness" rather than Great Perfection, because the latter term suggests that at some point the intrinsic awareness became perfect; in fact, it has always been so. The Great Perfection tradition shares with certain Indian Buddhist schools the view that mind creates the appearances of the world, the arena of human suffering. All of these appearances are said to be illusory, however. The ignorant mind believes that its own creations are real, forgetting its true nature of original purity. For the mind willfully to seek to liberate itself is both inappropriate and futile because it is already self-liberated. The technique for the discovery of the ubiquitous original purity and of self-liberation is to engage in a variety of practices designed to eliminate karmic obstacles, at which point the mind eliminates all thought and experiences itself, thereby recognizing its true nature. Like a mirror, it reflects whatever object stands before it, without being affected in the least by the object.

The Great Perfection doctrine does not seem to be directly derived from any of the Indian philosophical schools; its precise connections to the Indian Buddhist tradition have yet to be established. Some scholars (Evans-Wentz being perhaps the first) have claimed an historical link and doctrinal affinity between the Great Perfection and the Chan or Zen traditions of China and Japan, but the precise relationship between the two remains to be fully investigated. It is noteworthy that certain of the earliest extant Great Perfection texts specifically contrast their own tradition with that of Chan.

There are several problems with Evans-Wentz's rendering of the text. First, it is remarkable that he selected two Geluk monks to translate this Nyingma work. The literature of the Great Perfection is renowned for its specialized vocabulary, employing archaic Tibetan terms and giving different denotations and connotations to otherwise standard Buddhist vocabulary. There is no reason to expect that Geluk monks would be familiar with the specialized terminology of the Great Perfection. Indeed, the Geluk has historically been antagonistic to the Nyingma (and to Padmasambhava, as Evan-Wentz notes on page 25), with some Geluk authors dismissing the treasure texts as forgeries. This antagonism has ebbed and flowed over the centuries of Tibetan history; one of periods of flow occurred in the 1930s, led by the most influential Geluk monk of the period, Pha bong kha pa (1878–1943). It is difficult to say whether such antipathy extended to the monastery of Ghoom in 1935. We do know that Lama Govinda encountered a close disciple of Pha bong kha pa, Tromo Geshe Rinpoche, at Ghoom in 1936.

Exacerbating the problems with the translators is the now familiar problem of the Editor (as Evans-Wentz calls himself), who once again reads the text through his bifocals of Theosophy and neo-Vedanta. Evans-Wentz is at his best as a storyteller, explaining and annotating the life of Milarepa or Padmasambhava. He is less adept as a commentator on Buddhist philosophical texts, like the *Self-Liberation through Naked Vision Recognizing Awareness*. He clearly recognizes the importance of the text; for him it is *The Tibetan Book of the Great Liberation*, and he is both passionate and eloquent in his exposition. But he is misguided in his interpretation, appealing more often to Plotinus or Ramana Maharshi than to any Tibetan, or even Buddhist, source. For him, awareness (*rig pa*) is "the One Mind ... the Universal Mind, the Over-Mind, the Cosmic Consciousness." Such language is foreign to Buddhist thought in general and to the Great Perfection in particular.

The combination of inappropriate translators and an editor prepared to make the text say what he wants it to say results in a translation that is, sadly, unreliable. To give one example, chosen at random, Evans-Wentz's version reads on page 228:

> The impatient, ordinary person when dwelling in
> his fleshly body calls this very clear Wisdom 'com-
> mon intelligence.'
>
> Regardless of whatever elegant and varied names
> be given to this Wisdom as the result of thorough
> study, what Wisdom other than it, as here revealed,
> can one really desire?
>
> To desire more than this Wisdom is to be like one
> who seeks an elephant by following its footprints
> when the elephant itself has been found.

A more accurate translation might read as follows:

> Because it is undistinguished, ordinary, and remains
> where it is, this clear and lucid knowing is called "the
> ordinary mind." No matter what auspicious and po-
> etic names are used, it is, in fact, nothing other than
> this present awareness. Whoever wants more is like
> someone searching for an elephant's track when the
> elephant has been found.[4]

Apart from errors in translation, the rendering of Evans-Wentz
misses the simple and direct locution of the text, interpolating instead a vague and exalted notion of "Wisdom."

Book III of *The Tibetan Book of the Great Liberation* is composed
of Evan-Wentz's selections from an unfinished translation left by
Kazi Dawa Samdup. The text is a collection of aphorisms attributed to the Indian yogin Pha dam pa sangs rgyas, who is said to
have visited Tibet several times in the late eleventh and early

---

[4] The Tibetan reads, *bzang med tha mal rang mkhar gnas dus kyis / shes pa
gsal le hrig ge 'di nyid la / tha mal shes pa zhes pa'i ming 'di btags / bzang rtog snyan
ming mang po ci btags kyang / don la da lta'i shes rig 'di ka las / 'di man gzhan las
lhag pa su 'dod pa / glang po rnyed kyang rjes 'tshol ji bzhin no*. Recognizing the in-
adequacies of Evans-Wentz's version of this important text, it has been completely retranslated, with extensive commentary by John Myrdhin Reynolds,
Self-Liberation Through Seeing with Naked Awareness (Barrytown, N.Y.: Station
Hill Press, 1989). The translation above is my own, drawn from Reynolds edition of the text on p. 124.

twelfth centuries, prior to his death in 1117. He is remembered above all as the teacher who brought the Zhi byed pa or "pacification" practice to Tibet, a tantric tradition with strong links to the Perfection of Wisdom sūtras. The sūtras make repeated reference of the power of wisdom to destroy demons, four of whom are traditionally listed: the demon of death, the demon of the afflictions, the demon of the unenlightened mind and body (*skandhas*), and the demon Māra. The central practice of the pacification system is known as "the demon to be severed" (*bdud kyi gcod yul*) or, more commonly, simply *gcod*. Pha dam pa sangs rgyas is said to have been the teacher of the female *gcod* adept Ma gcig lab sgron (1055–1152?). The *gcod* practice is discussed at some length in *Tibetan Yoga and Secret Doctrines*.

The text translated here makes no explicit reference to these teachings, but is instead a collection of aphorisms directed to the people of Ding ri, where Pha dam pa sangs rgyas founded a monastery. It contains traditional Buddhist teachings on impermanence and the uncertainty of the time of death, on the importance of virtuous deeds such as pilgrimage and prayer, and admonitions to have faith in the guru, interspersed with instructions on meditation.

There remains, of course, Evans-Wentz's own introductions and notes, again outweighing, as in *The Tibetan Book of the Dead*, the translations themselves. Although the translations included here were made in 1935, Evans-Wentz did not publish *The Tibetan Book of the Great Liberation* until 1954. He spent most of the intervening years living in San Diego, California, conducting his research in the public library.

Although published twenty-seven years after *The Tibetan Book of the Dead*, his views here remain consistent with those expressed in his most famous work. There are the thinly veiled references to Theosophy: he mentions the "Secret Tibetan Brotherhood of Initiates of the Occult Sciences," (p. xviii), to what the Great Perfection text holds in common with "all Schools of the Oriental Occult Sciences" (p. 1); he fears that India, the last domain of the Great Masters of Wisdom, will fall with the rest of the planet to the Barbarism of the West, "until those who seek to guide, but who cannot guide when guidance is refused, send a new Messenger, a new Culture Hero, shall the Sacred Fire be rekindled in the hearts of men" (p. 20). It is noteworthy that Evans-Wentz seems much more concerned about India in 1952 than he does about Tibet, so recently invaded and occupied by the People's Liberation Army. His concern for the East as a source of inspiration for the universal benefit of mankind seems not to have extended to the political fates of nations. Tibet, which Evans-Wentz never visited in his travels, may have forever remained an ethereal abode for him, despite the plight of its people.

There is perhaps an even greater tendency than in the other volumes to read the Tibetan texts, especially *Self–Liberation through Naked Vision Recognizing Awareness*, as if it were a Vedanta work, with repeated references to Brahma, Māyā, and the One Cosmic Mind. In the intervening years, he had become a close associate of Yogananda Paramhansa and his Self-Realization Fellowship in Encinitas, California.

Although rarely related to the content of the texts at hand, Evans-Wentz's words are, as always, eloquent in expression and fascinating in content. His notes often provide references to psychic research, much of it long forgotten; in a long note on page 151 he mentions the study of two American physicians who found that a body weighs two or three ounces less immediately after death. Perhaps his most sustained and interesting discussion here is the social commentary he provides in his long analysis of the relative nature of the categories of good and evil (pp. 35–57), illustrated by the example of pederasty, which, he says, was regarded as having spiritual value by the ancient Greeks but condemned in modern America (pp. 47–48). Arguing that it is unwise to accept without question, "the verdict of the people, whether expressed by a jury in a court of law or through the ballot box, as to what is justice, right or wrong, good or evil," he asks that men see that the moral standards of the multitude are illogical, as the gurus teach. If this is done, "human society will speedily advance beyond the mental status of brute creatures and transcend the law of the jungle" (pp. 50–51).

Space does not allow any detailed consideration of Jung's "Psychological Commentary," composed in 1939. One finds here the same misreading of the *Self-Liberation through Naked Vision Recognizing Awareness* (admittedly hindered by Evans-Wentz's translation) that one found in his commentary to *The Tibetan Book of the*

Dead. There are the same gross cultural stereotypes of East and West, the same admonitions that Europeans not practice yoga, the same unsuccessful attempt to interpret "Eastern" consciousness in light of his theory of the unconscious. And even here, Jung cannot resist a jibe at Freud, claiming that Freud's negative valuation of introversion is something that he shares with National Socialism. This is a shocking comment to make in 1939; Freud, who died that year at the age of 83, had fled to London from the Gestapo in Vienna the previous year. A thorough study of Jung's misreadings, willful and otherwise, of "Eastern Religions" remains to be written.

One can say in conclusion that *The Tibetan Book of the Great Liberation* is perhaps the least successful volume in the tetralogy, at least as a representation of Tibetan Buddhism. Like the *Tibetan Book of the Dead*, it is a book that occupies two separate worlds, the world of Evans-Wentz, with his unique blending of Theosophy and Vedanta, and the world of the translated texts, that is, the world of Tibetan Buddhism. However, in this case, Evans-Wentz was deprived of the services of his trusted collaborator, the excellent translator Kazi Dawa Samdup, who had died in 1922. Evans-Wentz was thus forced to turn to others, who produced translations less reliable, and hence less lasting than those of the late Lama.

PREFACE

IN this volume, the fourth of my Tibetan Series, I have placed on record, in a manner intended to appeal equally to the learned and to the unlearned, to the philosopher and to the scientist, some of the most recondite teachings of Oriental Sages. In doing so, I have had the right guidance of an original text, heretofore unknown to Europe, the authorship of which is attributed to Tibet's Precious *Guru* Padma-Sambhava, the illustrious master of the Tantric Occult Sciences, of whose life-history an epitome is herein presented.

Inasmuch as this volume sets forth the very quintessence of the Great Path, the Māhāyana, it not only supplements the three previous volumes, but is, in some respects, the most important member of the Series. At the time of the publication of *Tibetan Yoga and Secret Doctrines*, I did not, however, foresee that it was my destiny to be the transmitter of this additional volume.

In the General Introduction and the textual annotations there have been incorporated, to serve as a very necessary commentary, complementary teachings which were orally transmitted through a long line of *Gurus* of the Kargyütpa School to my own Tibetan *Guru*, the late Lāma Kazi Dawa-Samdup. Also, in Book III, the teachings of the *Guru* Pha-dampa Sangay supplement those of the other *Gurus*.

Thanks to the kindly assistance of Lāma Karma Sumdhon Paul and Lāma Lobzang Mingyur Dorje, the first two successors of the late Lāma Kazi Dawa-Samdup in the University of Calcutta, Book II, the essential part of this volume, has been rendered into English.

All who read this volume will join with me in offering homage to the late Sardar Bahādur S. W. Laden La, whom I had the great joy of assisting, in my capacity as scribe and editor, when he translated the excerpts from the Lotus-Born One's Biography, upon which the epitome of it, comprising Book I, is based.

I am especially grateful to Dr. C. G. Jung, the distinguished dean of Western psychologists, for his erudite Foreword, which serves as a bridge between the best thought of Occident and Orient. Today, even more than in the days of the Greek philosophers, East and West not only are meeting, but are recognizing their inherent and inseparable oneness. Only the vulgar notice and advocate racial and religious differentiation. To the clear-seeing, Humanity is One Family, eternally transcending geographical demarcations, national limitations, and every fettering concept born of the unenlightened mind.

To the late Dr. R. R. Marett, Rector of Exeter College, and formerly Reader in Social Anthropology in the University of Oxford, whose encouragement of my anthropological research is well known to readers of other books bearing my name, I am indebted for his having critically examined the matter herein contained before it took final shape. I owe a similar debt to Dr. F. W. Thomas, Emeritus Boden Professor of Sanskrit in the University of Oxford, more particularly for his assistance with certain of the Tibetan transliterations and place-names; and to Mr. E. T. Sturdy, translator of the *Nārada Sūtra*, for his no less timely help with the Sanskrit transliterations. I am, also, very greatly indebted to Mr. R. F. C. Hull, translator of the forthcoming Collected Edition of the works of Dr. C. G. Jung, for having constructively read the proofs of this book as a whole.

My thanks are likewise due to each of the translators who in Germany and in France have made the results of my Tibetan studies available in their several languages. In this connexion I cannot omit the names of Madame Marguerite La Fuente, of Paris, who, under the extreme stress of economic conditions, arranged for the production of *Le Yoga Tibétain et les Doctrines Secrètes* (Paris, 1938); and of Miss Constant Lounsbery, author of *Buddhist Meditation in the Southern School* and also President of *Les Amis du Bouddhisme*, of Paris, who aided Madame La Fuente in the arduous task of making the translation.

I acknowledge, too, the encouragement and aid rendered by many other helpers, friends, and correspondents hail-ing from all the continents—who, like myself, are earnestly striving to overthrow every barrier born of Ignorance that separates race from race, nation from nation, and religion from religion.

May this book afford added courage and strength to those many helpers and friends. May that Universal Good Will of the Great Teachers of Wisdom, such as is herein set forth, speedily prevail, so that mankind may recognize their divine at-one-ment.

W. Y. E.-W.

SAN DIEGO, CALIFORNIA
All Saints' Day, 1952

It Were Better to Live One Single Day

'It were better to live one single day in the development of a good life of meditation than to live a hundred years evilly and with undisciplined mind.

'It were better to live one single day in the pursuit of understanding and meditation than to live a hundred years in ignorance and unrestraint.

'It were better to live one single day in the commencement of earnest endeavour than to live a hundred years in sloth and effortlessness.

'It were better to live one single day giving thought to the origin and cessation of that which is composite than to live a hundred years giving no thought to such origin and cessation.

'It were better to live one single day in the realization of the Deathless State than to live a hundred years without such realization.

'It were better to live one single day knowing the Excellent Doctrine than to live a hundred years without knowing the Excellent Doctrine.'

The Buddha, from the *Dhammapada*, vv. 110–15
(based upon N. K. Bhagwat's Translation).

CONTENTS

BOOK I

AN EPITOME OF THE LIFE AND TEACHINGS OF TIBET'S GREAT *GURU* PADMA–SAMBHAVA

BOOK II

THE *YOGA* OF KNOWING THE MIND, THE SEEING OF REALITY, CALLED SELF–LIBERATION

BOOK III

THE LAST TESTAMENTARY TEACHINGS OF THE *GURU* PHADAMPA SANGAY

The Buddha's Sermon on What is True Blessedness?

Praise be to the Blessed One, the Holy One, the Author of all Truth.

Thus I have heard. On a certain day dwelt the Blessed One at Srāvastī, at the Jetavana Monastery, in the Garden of Anathapindaka. And when the night was far advanced, a certain radiant celestial being, illuminating the whole of Jetavana, approached the Blessed One and saluted Him, and standing aside, and remaining so, addressed Him with these words: 'Many gods and men, yearning after good, have held diverse things to be blessings; declare Thou, What is true blessedness?'

'To serve wise men rather than fools, to give honour to whom honour is due; this is true blessedness.

'To dwell in a pleasant land, to have done virtuous deeds in a former existence, to have a heart filled with right desires; this is true blessedness.

'Much wisdom and much science, the discipline of a well-trained mind, and right speech; this is true blessedness.

'To wait on father and mother, to cherish wife and child, to follow a peaceful calling; this is true blessedness.

'To give alms, to live piously, to protect kinsfolk, to perform blameless deeds; this is true blessedness.

'To cease doing evil, to abstain from strong drink, to persevere in right conduct; this is true blessedness.

'Reverence and humility, contentment and gratitude, the hearing of the Law of Righteousness at due seasons; this is true blessedness.

'Patience and pleasing speech, association with holy men, to hold religious discourse at fitting moments; this is true blessedness.

'Penance and chastity, discernment of the Four Noble Truths and the realization of peace; this is true blessedness.

'A mind unshaken by the vicissitudes of this life, inaccessible to sorrow, passionless, secure; this is true blessedness.

'They that observe these things are invincible on every side, on every side they walk in safety; yea, their's is the true blessedness.'—*Maṅgala Sūtra*.[1]

[1] A recension by the Editor, based on Professor Childer's Translation and on that by Irving Babbitt in *The Dhammapāda* (Oxford University Press, New York and London, 1936), page 76.

DESCRIPTION OF ILLUSTRATIONS

I. THE GREAT *GURU* PADMA-SAMBHAVA   *Frontispiece*

A photographic reproduction (about one-fifth of the original size) of a modern Tibetan painting in colour, on cotton cloth, acquired in Nepal, representing Padma-Sambhava, robed in his royal robes as a King of Sahor, India, sitting in kingly posture on a lotus-lunar throne. The *dorje* (described on p. 107[1]), in his right hand, is held in the posture (or *mudrā*) called in Tibetan the *Dorje Dik-dzup* (*Rdo-rje-sdigs-mdzub*), i.e. the Indomitable (or *Vajra*) Finger-pointing *Mudrā*, to guard against all evils which might affect the *Dharma*, and to place the Three Realms of Existence (described on p. 205[1]) under his dominion. The human-skull cup in his left hand is filled with the nectar of immortality (Skt. *amrita*); and superimposed upon the nectar is the urn of longevity and immortal life, also filled with the ambrosia of the gods, of which his devotees are privileged to drink. The skull cup itself symbolizes renunciation of the world. The trident-pointed staff (Skt. *trīshūla*) which he holds in the folds of his left arm is highly symbolical. The trident at the top symbolizes the Three Realms of Existence (in Sanskrit, the *Trailokya*), and suggests his dominion over them and over the three chief evils, lust, anger (or ill will), and sloth (or stupidity). It also symbolizes the Three Times, the past, present, and future. The flames emanating from the middle point of the trident are the Flames of Divine Wisdom which consume Ignorance (Skt. *avidyā*). The skull underneath the trident symbolizes the *Dharma-Kāya*; the first of the two human heads below the skull symbolizes the *Sambhoga-Kāya*, and the second the *Nirmāṇa-Kāya*. (The Three *Kāyas* are described on pp. 3–4, 178[1]). The golden urn below the heads is filled with the essence of transcendent blessings and perfections. The golden double-*dorje* below the urn is described by the *lāmas* thus: the southern (or lower) point represents Peace; the western point Multiplicity; the northern (or upper) point (hidden by the urn) Initiatory Power; the eastern point Fearfulness; and the centre the at-one-ment of all spiritual endowments and perfections. The white silk ribbon-like banner below the double-*dorje*, resembling a Banner of Victory, of which it is an abbreviated form, symbolizes the Great *Guru*'s Victory over the *Sangsāra*. The staff itself symbolizes the Divine *Shakti*.

The Great *Guru* wears as his head-dress what Tantrics call the lotus-cap. The crescent moon and the sun, on the front of it, signify, as does the lotus-cap itself, that he is crowned with all initiatory powers. The feather surmounting the lotus-cap being that of a vulture, regarded as the highest and mightiest of fliers among birds, symbolizes that his Doctrine of the Great Perfection is the most aspiring, noblest, and loftiest of spiritual doctrines. His blue and purple and priestly yellow inner dress is the dress of a Tibetan *Nyag-pa* (*Sngags-pa*), or one who is a Master of Tantric Occultism.

Kneeling on a smaller lotus-lunar throne, to the left of the Great *Guru*, is the figure of Bhāsadhara, his Queen when he was the King of Sahor, offering to him *amrita* in a bowl made of a human skull; and on his right, similarly enthroned and kneeling and making a like offering, that of Mandāravā, his most faithful and beloved disciple.

Immediately above the head of the Great *Guru* is shown the Buddha Shākya Muni, sitting in *Padmāsana*, or Buddha posture, on a lotus-lunar throne, holding in His left hand the begging-bowl, symbolical of His being a religious mendicant, and with His right hand touching, and thus calling, the Earth to bear witness to the truth of His Doctrine. The Buddha is so placed above the Great *Guru* because He is his spiritual Predecessor and Ancestor; the Great *Guru* representing on Earth the Tantric, or Esoteric, Emanation of the Buddha.

On either side of the Buddha, posed as He is, but on the simpler throne of a disciple or *Bodhisattva*, are two *Arhants*, each holding a mendicant's begging-bowl and alarm-staff. The Sun (red) to the left and the Moon (white) to the right of the Buddha, the clouds, the blue sky, the land and mountains and waters below, the blossoms and the fruits, signify, as in other of the Illustrations, the *Sangsāra*, and, therefore, that the Teachers are still active therein and ever striving for the salvation of mankind.

The Great *Guru*, the Buddha, and the two *Arhants* are enhaloed in rainbow-like radiance. The Great *Guru* and the Buddha have nimbi of green, indicating the eternity of the Bodhic Essence manifested through Them. The nimbi of the other four figures are orangered, suggestive of their possessors not yet being wholly free from worldly or *sangsāric* bondage.

Directly below the Great *Guru* are the insignia of the Five Objects of Enjoyment, offerings made to him by his devotees: (1) luscious food substances, symbolical of pleasing taste, in the blue receptacle at the centre surmounted by a red *chorten*; (2) the white conch-shell filled with perfume, symbolical of pleasing smell, resting on two sweet-smelling fruits; (3) the mirror on the opposite side, symbolizing pleasing form or sight; (4) the pair of cymbals (resting against the mirror), symbolical of pleasing sound or hearing; and (5) the red Chinese silk (binding the two cymbals together), symbolical of pleasing touch or feelings. In the Hindu system, whence they appear to have been derived, these Five Objects of Enjoyment correspond in symbolism, in their order as here given, to the Sanskrit *Rasa* (Taste), *Gandha* (Smell), *Rūpa* (Form or Sight), *Shabda* (Sound or Hearing), and *Sparsha* (Touch or Feelings).

II. THE TRANSLATORS AND THE EDITOR   *facing p.* vii

Upper: A reproduction of a group photograph, showing the Editor in the centre, in Tibetan dress, holding a copy of the *Bardo Thödol* block-print series of texts containing the text employed in producing the translation of the ' *Yoga* of Knowing the Mind in Its Nakedness'; to the Editor's right the Lāma Karma Sumdhon Paul, and to the Editor's left the Lāma Lobzang Mingyur Dorje. This photograph was taken during October 1935 in front of the Temple of the coming Buddha Maitreya, which appears in the background and forms a part of the Ghoom Monastery, Darjeeling. Three Tibetan prayer-flags (*Dhar-chok*), mounted on tall poles, appear to the left of the Temple. Such prayer-flags, made of cotton cloth printed on both sides with Tibetan prayers and *mantras*, usually bear verses ending with 'May the Doctrine of the Buddha prosper'.

Lower: A reproduction of a photograph of the late Sardar Bahādur S. W. Laden La, of Darjeeling, in the yellow silk dress of a Tibetan Peer (*Dzasa*) and wearing the black travelling-hat called *Chhok-sed* (*Mchhog-sred*) and some of the insignia of the various high honours conferred upon him by the British Government and the Government of Tibet.

Brief biographies of the late Sardar Bahādur and of the two Lāmas are given on pages 86–92.

III. MAÑJUSHRĪ'S BOOK OF DIVINE WISDOM   *facing p.* xxiii

A reproduction of a photograph of a rare manuscript copy of the *Phak-pa-Jam-pal-gi-Tsa-way-Gyud* (*Hphags-pa-Hjam-dpal-gyi-Rtsa-wahi-Rgyud*): Skt. *Ārya Mañjushrī Mūla Tantra*: Eng. 'The Original [or Root] Treatise [or Book] of the God of Wisdom', concerning the Kālachakra Doctrine as taught originally by the Lord Buddha, and forming a part of the *Kanjur* (*Bkah-'gyur*), 'The Translated Commandments', the canon of Tibetan Buddhism. The exposition and guardianship of this Doctrine, because of its profound esotericism, is entrusted to the Tashi Lāma, who is otherwise known, among the Tibetans, as 'The Precious Great Doctor', or 'Great Gem of Learning' (*Pan-chen Rin-po-ch'e*), and also as 'The Precious Lordly Victor' (*Kyap-gön-Rin-po-ch'e*). The text is written in gold and silver on lacquered Tibetan-made paper, each folio of which measures 25⅜ inches by 6⅛ inches. The first page of the text is shown underneath the volume.

In order to safeguard it, the manuscript was given over to the custody of one of the officials accompanying the late Tashi Lāma at the time His Holiness fled from Tibet. It was then seized, along with other goods of the fleeing Tashi Lāma, by the Tibetan Government and sold, and afterwards came into the possession of Mr. Tharchin, editor of *The Tibetan Newspaper*, Kalimpong, from whom we acquired it. The manuscript was probably one of the Tashi Lāma's most treasured books that he wished to carry with him and, as the incarnate guardian of its secret teachings, to preserve inviolate.

The manuscript, which is about two hundred years old, was examined by Lāma Lobzang Mingyur Dorje, who submitted to the Editor the following report. 'This, rightfully, is the Book which Mañjushrī holds on the lotus blossom. According to tradition, the King of Shambhala having been the chief listener when the Kālachakra Doctrine was taught by the Buddha, committed the Doctrine to writing for the first time; and, inasmuch as he was the incarnation of Mañjushrī, it is said that Mañjushrī himself was its compiler. In the *Saṃ-bha-la-hi-Lam-yik*, or *Journey to Shambhala*, is contained the prophecy that the twenty-fifth Tashi Lāma will be the incarnation of the King of Shambhala and attain dominion over the whole world.'

The Book is largely astrological; and no one save a master of classical Tibetan and an adept in the esotericism and initiatory *mantras* of Mañjushrī could intelligibly translate it as a whole. There is no treatise in Tibet, or elsewhere among men, more sacred and occult. Lāma Karma Sumdhon Paul has rendered the text of the page shown, as follows:

'In the Sanskrit language [this treatise is called] *Ārya Mañjushrī Mūla Tantra*; in the Tibetan language, *Phak-pa-Jam-pal-gi-Tsa-way-Gyud (Hphags-pa-Hjam-dpal-gyi-Rtsa-wahi-Rgyud)*.

'Homage I render to all the Buddhas and *Bodhisattvas*.

'Thus have I heard: Once upon a time, the Bhagavat, in the celestial pure region above, where the *Bodhisattvas*, in their own ineffable excellent various *maṇḍalas* [or divine conclaves], had assembled, preached [this doctrine] to the sons of the gods of that pure realm in the following manner: "O ye sons of the divine ones, give ear to me".'

The Kālachakra (Tib. *Dus-kyi Khor-lo*: pron. Dü-kyi *Khor-lo*), meaning 'Circle of Time', is an esoteric system of *yoga*, to which tradition assigns a primeval origin antedating the advent of the Buddha Gautama and therefore associates it with the *Ādi* (or Primordial)-Buddha. The prophecy, that the King of Shambhala, who is sometimes called the Chief of the Secret Tibetan Brotherhood of Initiates of the Occult Sciences, shall govern mankind, implies the coming of a Golden Age and the enthronement of Divine Wisdom on Earth. Further reference to the Kālachakra and to Shambhala is made on pages 59, 122³, 117, following.

Initiates consider the Kālachakra to be the most important doctrine contained in the *Kan-jur*, wherein it is expounded in the first of the twenty-two volumes of *Tantra*. The mention made by the editors of the Peking edition of *The Voice of the Silence* (excerpts by H. P. Blavatsky from *The Book of the Golden Precepts*), that they were presented by the late Tashi Lāma 'with a small treatise in Tibetan on the Kālachakra, entitled *The Communion of Mystic Adepts* (Tü Kor-la *deń-pä la-mä niń-jor*)',[1] suggests the deeply esoteric character of this Tantric doctrine, the teaching of which is a prerogative of the Tashi Lāma Dynasty of *Gurus*.

IV. MAÑJUSHRĪ, THE GOD OF DIVINE WISDOM *facing p.* lxiv

A photographic reproduction (about one-quarter of the original size) of an old monastic painting in colour, on heavy cotton cloth, painted in Lhāsa (or 'The Place of the Divine One'). The central figure represents the princely and youthful *Bodhisattva* Mañjushrī (Tib. *Hjam-dpal*: pron. *Jam-pay*), the 'Gently Beautiful One', also called, in Sanskrit, Mañjughosha, or, in Tibetan, Jam-yang (*Hjam-dyang*), the 'Melodious Voiced One'. Quite in musical keeping with this character of Mañjughosha is his mellifluous *mantra*: '*Om! a-ra-pa-ca-na-ḍhi!*' As the 'God of Divine Wisdom' (Tib. *Shes-rab-kyi-lha*) he is the Secret Presence presiding over this volume, especially over Book II. His worship confers Divine Wisdom, mastery of the *Dharma*, retentive memory, mental perfection, and eloquence; even by uttering his *mantras* one attains enlightenment. He is the third of the *Dhyānī Bodhisattvas*. According to the Nepalese *Svayambhū Purāna*, Mañjushrī came from the Five-peaked Mountain in China (mentioned, herein, in Book I), and with his sword cleft asunder the southern barrier of hills in Nepal, and the water rushed out, and the broad fertile valley of Nepal emerged. Thus he appears to have been a Chinese culture hero who brought culture to Nepal.[2] In his right hand he holds aloft the all-victorious flaming Sword of Wisdom and Light, with which he cuts off Ignorance and Darkness. In his left hand he holds, on a blue lotus blossom, the Book of Divine Wisdom,[3] shown in Illustration III and described above, by virtue of which his devotees attain the Great Liberation of the Other Shore.

In the Tibetan canonical *Kanjur* more books or treatises are dedicated to Mañjushrī, as the Divine Protector of the *Dharma*, than to any other *Bodhisattva*; and the *lāmas* place him first in the list of *Bodhisattvas*. He is, in some of the *Tantras*, the listener, or one receiving the *yogic* instruction. There are attributed to him discourses with the Buddha, and a discussion with Shāriputra on the problem of how the world came to exist.

Esoterically, Mañjushrī is the *Logos*, which, in the Wisdom Teachings of ancient Egypt, was personified as Thoth, a form of Hermes. In ancient Greece he was the beautiful young sun-god Apollo, who

---

[1] Cf. *The Voice of the Silence*, edited with notes and comments by Alice Cleather and Basil Crump (Peking, 1927), p. 105.

[2] Cf. B. Bhattacharyya, *Indian Buddhist Iconography* (Oxford University Press, 1924), pp. 15–16.

[3] It is sometimes said that this Book represents the *Prajñā-Pāramitā* (or 'Transcendental Wisdom'), referred to on pp. 129, 157[2], following.

enlightened the mind of those initiated into the Mysteries; or, under another manifestation, the youthful Mercury, with winged feet, bearing the mystic staff of intertwined serpents, who, being the messenger of the gods, brought to men the Heavenly Wisdom.

In the earliest Mahāyāna Buddhism, Mañjushrī is the only Tantric deity represented without a *shakti* (or feminine counterpart), in signification of his perfect state of *brahmachāri* (or sexual continence) and adeptship of the occult sciences. In later Mahāyāna Buddhism there was assigned to him as his *shakti* the Hindu Goddess of Learning, Sarasvati.

Mañjushrī also presides over the law of righteousness; and all knotty problems of law he cuts with his sword. He is particularly associated with Astrology; and astrologers make him their chief tutelary and patron. There are a number of special forms or aspects of Mañjushrī, some of which receive mention in the Biography of Padma-Sambhava. Various Sages, too, in India, Nepal, Tibet, and China have been regarded as incarnations of Mañjushrī. Among these is Ātisha (A.D. 980–1052), who, in the year 1038, when almost sixty years of age, set out for Tibet from the Vikramashīla Monastery in Maghada to begin his great pioneer reformation of Lāmaism which resulted in the Gelugpa or Established Church. Tsong-Khapa, who, at the beginning of the fifteenth century, went to Tibet from the Amdo Province, China, and completed Ātisha's work of establishing the Gelugpa Order, in A.D. 1417, is believed to be another of these incarnations, and, as such, the reincarnation of Ātisha. In Sikkim, the founder of the present dynasty of kings has also been canonized as one of Mañjushrī's earthly manifestations.

In his ordinary aspect, Mañjushrī is a deity of the Peaceful Order (Tib. *Zhi-wa*). When represented as of the Wrathful Order (Tib. *Thowo*), he is Bhairava-Vajra, or 'The Awesome Thunderbolt One'.

In this Illustration, Mañjushrī sits in the Buddha posture on a lotus-lunar throne. His loose-flowing garments of silk, his bodily adornments of gold inset with precious gems, and his richly bejewelled golden head-dress indicate that he is a royal prince. His body emanates a rainbow-hued halo; and his nimbus, of the mystic colour green edged with dark crimson, indicates his immutable and everlasting spirituality.

At the bottom of the painting is depicted the Jewel Lake of Wisdom. The radiance of the jewels emanates from the water; and on either corner of the upper shore are the Three Jewels, or Three Values (Skt. *Tri-Ratna*), of the Buddhist Faith, symbolizing the Buddha, the Doctrine, and the Priesthood. A miniature figure, amidst the lotus leaves above the lake, represents the deceased devotee of Mañjushrī in whose honour the painting was made by command of the devotee's surviving relatives, and, as a votive offering, dedicated to Mañjushrī.

In the upper corner, above Mañjushrī's sword, is the figure of the Dhyānī Buddha Amitābha, the 'One of Boundless (or Incomprehensible) Light', of whom the Tashi Lāmas are believed to be incarnations. His colour, being red, symbolizes his likeness to the Sun, which visibly illuminates the world; but Amitābha's own enlightening influence, being invisible, is symbolized by the Sun's Secret Essence (referred to on p. 215[2]). Amitābha presides over the Western Paradise known as Devachān. He sits in the Buddha posture on a lotus-lunar throne, and holds in his hands a bowl filled with immortality-conferring *amrita*.

In the opposite upper corner is the figure of the Dhyānī Buddha Vajra-Sattva, the 'Divine Heroic-Minded Being', who presides over the Eastern Direction. He holds the *dorje* (Skt. *vajra*), the symbol of his immutability, in his right hand, and a bell, the symbol of his divine transcendent heroism, in his left hand. He, too, sits in Buddha posture on a lotus-lunar throne; and, like Amitābha and Mañjushrī, radiates an encircling rainbow-like aura and a nimbus. His colour is white, the colour associated with the Eastern Direction. (For further details concerning both Vajra-Sattva and Amitābha see *The Tibetan Book of the Dead*, pp. 108–10, 112–15.)

In this painting, the three deities represent a Divine Trinity; and, as such, symbolize the *Tri-Kāya*, or 'Three Bodies' (described on pp. 3–4, 178[1]), by which, as here, the Buddha Essence is personified, Amitābha being associated with the *Dharma-Kāya*, Vajra-Sattva with the *Sambhoga-Kāya*, and Mañjushrī with the *Nirmāṇa-Kāya*. Another aspect of the *Tri-Kāya* is shown by Illustration VII. According to *maṇḍala*, school, and degree of initiation conferred, the personifications of the *Tri-Kāya* differ; but, in essentiality, all the personifications are one.

V. THE EIGHT *GURUS*   .   .   .   . *facing p.* 100

A photographic reproduction (about one-fourth of the original size) of an old monastic painting in colour, on heavy cotton cloth, painted in Shigatse, Tibet, representing the Great *Guru* in his manifestations in eight personalities, or minds, or powers, known to the Tibetans as the *Guru-tshan-gye*, or 'The Eight Worshipful Forms of the *Guru*'.

In royal guise, as the King of Sahor, the figure of the *Guru* Padma Jungnay, 'The *Guru* Born of a Lotus', otherwise called 'He Who Leadeth all Beings of the Three Realms of Existence to Happiness',[1] occupies the central position here as in the frontispiece; and in the description of the frontispiece this manifestation of the Great *Guru* is described in detail.

[1] This appellation, and those herein given of the other Eight *Gurus*, are contained in *The Brief Precepts Composed by Padma-Sambhava of Urgyān* (*U-rgyan Pad-mas Msad-pahi Bkah-thang Bsdus-pa*), according to the translation made by Lāma Karma Sumdhon Paul, assisted by the Editor.

In the upper corner to the left of the *Guru* Padma Jungnay is shown the *Guru* Shākya Seṅg-ge, 'The *Guru* Who is the Lion of the Shākya Clan', otherwise called 'The Eight Incarnations in One Body', as a Buddha sitting on a lotus-lunar throne in the Buddha posture (Skt. *Buddhāsana*), also known as the Lotus posture (Skt. *Padmāsana*), his body bent slightly to the right as is customary among Tibetan *yogins* who are his followers, his right hand in the Earth-touching *mudrā*, his left hand holding a begging-bowl filled with food.

In the opposite corner is the representation of the *Guru* Padma-Sambhava, 'The Lotus-born *Guru*', otherwise called 'The Great King of the *Dharma*, the Patron of Religion', as a young *Bhikṣhu*, likewise posed on a lotus-lunar throne, holding in his right hand, in the attitude of bestowing benediction, a *dorje*, in his left hand a human-skull bowl of *amrita* as an offering to all deities, and in the folds of his left arm the symbolic trident staff.

Directly above the *Guru* Padma Jungnay is the figure of the *Guru* Nyima Hodzer, 'The Sunbeam *Guru*' (or 'The Sunlight One'), otherwise known as 'He Who Embraceth all Doctrines as the Sky Embraceth all Space', in the guise of a *Herukapa*, or 'Unclad One', of the Order of Great Masters of *Yoga*. His colour is that of the Sun. In his left hand he holds, by a filament of light, a sun; and in his right hand the trident-pointed staff. Being a *Heruka*, he wears human-bone ornaments, to signify his world renunciation. His head-dress of human skulls indicates his triumph over *sangsāric* existence. The tiger-skin loin-covering is a further sign of his *yogic* powers. He sits in *Bodhisattvic* posture on a lotus-sun throne. (See the description of the *Heruka* in *Tibet's Great Yogī Milarepa*, pp. xvi-xvii.)

Directly below the *Guru* Padma-Sambhava is the figure of the *Guru* Lōden Chog-se, 'The *Guru* Possessing Wisdom and Best Desires', also called 'The Transmitter of Wisdom to all Worlds',[1] in the guise of a king, sitting on a lotus-lunar throne, with his right leg extended in what is known among Tibetans as the kingly dancing pose (Tib. *Gyal-po-rolpai-tak*). In his right hand he holds a mirror, symbolical of the mirage-like or reflected (as in a mirror) nature of all *sangsāric* things; and, in his left hand, a human-skull bowl filled with the nectar of immortality, symbolical of his immunity to old age and death.

Directly below the *Guru* Shākya Seṅg-ge is the figure of the *Guru* Padma Gyalpo, 'The Lotus King *Guru*', otherwise known as 'The One Untouched by Faults, [the Representative of] the *Tri-Piṭaka* (or Three Collections of Buddhist Scriptures)', sitting on a lotus-lunar throne, with his left leg extended in the kingly dancing posture, here the same as the *Bodhisattvic* posture. In his right hand he holds aloft a double-drum (Tib. *damāru*), symbolical of his mastery of *mantric* sound; and, in his left hand, a human-skull cup filled with gems, sym-

---

[1] Cf. L. A. Waddell, *The Buddhism of Tibet* (Cambridge, 1934), p. 379.

bolical of his having discovered, by means of *yoga*, the Precious Gems of the *Dharma*.

In the lower corner to the right of the *Guru* Padma Jungnay is the figure of the *Guru* Seṅ-ge Dradog, 'The *Guru* Who Teacheth with the Voice of a Lion', otherwise known as 'The One Who Proclaimeth the *Dharma* to all the Six Classes of Beings' (enumerated on p. 205[2]), standing in the wrathful mood of a Tantric deity on a lotus-lunar throne, his right foot upon the breast of a human form, signifying the treading underfoot of all *sangsāric* existences. Being a Great *Yogī*, he wears a tiger-skin loin-covering and around his body a lion skin, the lion head of which appears above his head-dress and the claws appear on either side of him. In his right hand he holds, in an attitude menacing to evil demons who oppose the spread of the *Dharma*, a *dorje*, symbolical of his dominion over them; and in his left hand a bell, symbolical of his adeptship in *mantra yoga* and of his *yogic* power to control all classes of spiritual beings throughout the *Sangsāra*. He is enhaloed in the mystic Flames of Wisdom which consume the evils of the world. His colour is dark blue, which signifies, like that of the sky, the all-pervading and everlasting characteristic of the *Dharma*, of which he is the Guardian as well as the Disseminator. It was in this very occult manifestation that the Great *Guru*, like a supreme Saint Michael, overthrew the Forces of Darkness and enabled the Forces of the Light to prevail.

In the opposite lower corner is the figure of the *Guru* Dorje Drōlō, 'The Immutable *Guru* with Loose-hanging Stomach', otherwise called 'The One in Whose Body all Happiness Culminateth', and also known as 'The Changeless Comforter of all Beings'.[1] He, too, is shown in the wrathful mood of a Tantric deity and enhaloed in Flames of Wisdom, standing on a tigress (symbolical of the *shakti*). The treading underfoot by the tigress of a prostrate human form has the same significance as that by the *Guru* Seṅ-ge Dradog. In his right hand he holds, in the menacing attitude, a *dorje*, symbolizing almighty spiritual power, and in his left hand a magical demon-exorcising *phurbu*. His colour is red, in symbol of his power to fascinate and so discipline *sangsāric* beings. On his forehead—as on that of the *Guru* Seṅ-ge Dradog—appears the third eye of divine vision, signifying intuitive insight into Reality. It was in Bhutan, at the famous Monastery of *Pato-tak-tshang* (the 'Lion's Den of Pato'), that the Great *Guru* is said to have manifested himself as Droje Drōlō, for the purpose of disciplining the people and winning them from their practices of black magic, and to exorcise the demoniacal beings of Bhutan and establish the *Dharma* there. Similarly, each of the other Eight Manifestations was employed in accordance with need and circumstances, in order

---

[1] Cf. L. A. Waddell, op. cit., p. 379.

that to all sentient creatures there should be revealed the Path of the Great Liberation.

Directly below the *Guru* Padma Jungnay, as in the frontispiece, are shown the Five Objects of Enjoyment offered to him, the last (next to the cymbals) being the Chinese silk in two scroll-like rolls.

The *Guru* Padma Jungnay and the five *Gurus* above him, except the *Guru* Nyima Hodzer (whose bodily aura is deep blue), are enhaloed in rainbow-like radiance. The colour of the nimbi of all the six is green.

VI. EMANATION   .   .   .   .   . *facing p.* 106

A photographic reproduction (about one-eighth of the original size) of a remarkable Chinese monastic painting in colour, on a gauze-faced paper scroll, acquired by Mr. H. Sussbach, a German student, when in China in 1936, and said to date from the end of the Ming (or 'Bright') dynasty (A.D. 1368–1661). Its origin is uncertain, Mr. Sussbach having been told that it came from central China. An inscription on its back indicates that it belonged to the Yama temple of a Tantric monastery.

· At the top are the figures of two *Bodhisattvas* in super-human realms. Each is emanating from the crown of his head a light-ray (of the character described in Book I) and thereby manifesting in the world a Tantric aspect of his own *Bodhic* essence. On the light-shaft emanated from the tip of the third finger of the deity beneath the lower *Bodhisattva* is inscribed in Chinese, 'In the South-east: the *Bodhisattva* Ākāshagarbha[1] emanating the form of the Wrathful, Resplendent, Great Laughing King of Wisdom'.[2] On the similar light-shaft, emanated from the tip of the second finger of the deity below the higher *Bodhisattva*, is inscribed in Chinese, 'In the East: the *Bodhisattva* Sarvanīvaraṇa-Vishkambhin[3] emanating the form of the Wrathful, Resplendent, Exalted, Immutable King of Wisdom'.

The Ākāshagarbha emanation is three-faced, like a Brahma-Vishnu-Shiva deity, which signifies that in him the Three Divine Bodies (Skt. *Tri-Kāya*) are one. The right face is white (symbolical of purity and compassion); the middle face, like the deity himself, is blue (symbolical, like the blue sky, of the eternal nature of his *Bodhic* essence);

---

[1] The Sanskrit term *Ākāshagarbha* (Chinese: *Hsü K'ung Tsang*) is translatable as 'Essence of the Void Space (or Sky) above', and its Tibetan equivalent (*Nam-mkhahi Snying-po*) as 'Matrix of the Sky', or 'Womb of Space', or 'Receptacle of the Void'.

[2] 'King of Wisdom' is in the Chinese *Ming Wang*, corresponding to the Sanskrit *Vidyā-Rāja*.

[3] The Sanskrit term *Sarvanīvaraṇa-Vishkambhin* (Chinese: *Ch'u Kai Chang*) is translatable as 'Bar against all Impediments', and its Tibetan equivalent (*Sgrib-pa [Thams-cad] Rnam-par-sel-ba*) as 'That which clears away the Darknesses (or Delusions)'.

the left face is red (symbolical of his fascinating power). The two bells, in his first pair of hands, symbolize the Voidness of which he, as 'The Essence of the Void Space above', is the Tantric personification. The handle of the bell in his right hand is surmounted by a trident, indicating his supremacy over the Three Realms and that he has conquered the three cardinal evils, lust, ill will, and stupidity, which are the chief causes of rebirth. His next pair of hands and arms support a spear, suggestive of the spear of the Five *Ḍākinī* in the *yogic* exorcising dance of the *Chöd* Rite (described in *Tibetan Yoga and Secret Doctrines*, p. 306), and also suggestive of the Tibetan *phurbu*, both alike being symbols of dominion over demoniacal and elemental beings, one of which, of a green hue, crouches to the left of the spear's point. In three of the other four hands he holds a spiked staff (symbolical of triumph over the *Sangsāra*), a large gold ring inset with a gem, on the crown of it, and seven smaller gems (probably symbolical of the Jewels of the *Dharma*), and a golden object resembling a lotus bud. From the middle finger of the other hand he emanates the light-shaft. As he dances the *yogic* dance of supremacy over *sangsāric* existence, he treads underfoot, as do the wrathful two of the Eight *Gurus*, human beings, with parallel significance. His diadem of two human skulls indicates his triumph over death.

The Bar-against-all-Impediments (or Clearer-away-of-Delusions) Emanation appears to represent a wrathful Tantric aspect of Mañjushrī, for in his first two hands, held aloft, he holds a Book of Wisdom and the lotus blossom associated with it, and, in the second of his right hands, the Sword of Wisdom. From a gem, probably a type of the wish-granting gem (Skt. *Chintāmaṇi*) referred to in various parts of this volume, held between the thumb and middle finger of his fourth hand, he emanates three insects and a raven-like bird, signifying the sub-human kingdoms. The bird emanates, from the lower part of its mammalian-like mouth, the green demon. The lotus breast-plate and other lotus adornments, over his abdomen and shoulders and on his first pair of arms, suggest that he belongs to the Lotus Order of *Herukas*. The less prominently placed lotus adornments worn by the other Emanation signify that he, likewise, is of the same Order of Great Masters of *Yoga*. The Sarvanīvaraṇa-Vishkambhin Emanation is also three-faced, the right face being red, the left white; and the central face, being green, like his body, indicates his perennial youthfulness and the generative or creative power which he is exercising. His lotus diadem, as befits a Mañjushrī, is that of a royal prince. As he dances his *yogic* dance, he treads underfoot a demon monster with three monkey-like faces, symbolical of the power, which he confers upon his devotees, of overcoming brutish propensities, he being the *Bodhisattva* who prevents or overcomes all hindrances, or delusions.

From the head of each deity radiates a flame-like aura, apparently representing, in Chinese manner, Flames of Wisdom. After the style of a Shiva, the Supreme Patron of *yogins*, both deities wear serpents around their arms and legs, in symbol of Wisdom, they being, as Kings of Wisdom, Enlightening Deities. This is emphasized by their prominent third eye.

These two deities, Tantric personifications of the Enlightening Power of the *Dharma*, appertain to a group of Eight *Dhyānī Bodhisattvas*, known as the Eight Spiritual Sons of the Buddha, the other six being Maitreya, Avalokiteshvara, Samantabhadra, Mañjushrī, Vajra-Pāṇi, and Kshitigarbha.

In this tentative interpretation of a most unusual and very rare Chinese Tantric painting, the Editor has been guided by the symbology of Tibetan Tantricism. He gratefully acknowledges the indispensable assistance of Mr. Wang Wei-Chang, Spalding Lecturer in Chinese Philosophy and Religion in the University of Oxford, and of Mr. Yu Dawchyuan, Lecturer in the School of Oriental Studies, University of London.

VII. THE *TRI-KĀYA*, OR THREE DIVINE BODIES

facing p. 192

A photographic reproduction (about one-half of the original size) of a painting in colour, on heavy cotton cloth, painted in the Ghoom Monastery, Darjeeling, during October 1935 for the Editor, by the Tibetan artist, Lharipa Jampal Trashi (who was then painting the frescoes in the Ghoom Temple of Maitreya), to illustrate the *Tri-Kāya* of the *Bardo Thödol* Series of *yogic* treatises to which Book II appertains.

The uppermost figure is a symbolic personification of the Ādi-Buddha Samanta Bhadra (Tib. *Kun-tu Bzang-po*), the 'One of All Good', representing the *Dharma-Kāya*. His nudity signifies that the *Dharma-Kāya*, being the Unqualified, Unpredicable Thatness, is the Naked Reality. The blue colour of his body indicates that even as the blue sky is all-pervading, immutable, and eternal, so is the Primordial (Skt. *Ādi*) Buddha Essence. He sits on a lotus-lunar throne in the Buddha posture with his hands in the pose, or *mudrā*, of profound meditation.

The figure below, on the Ādi-Buddha's right, represents the four-armed form of the Great *Bodhisattva* Avalokiteshvara (Tib. *Spyan-ras-gzigs*: pron. *Chen-rä-zi*), the 'Keen-seeing Lord', who is also called the 'Great Pitier and Lord of Mercy' (Skt. *Mahākarunā*), sitting in the Buddha posture on a lotus-lunar throne. He is the spiritual son of the Dhyānī Buddha Amitābha, and incarnate in the Dalai Lāma; and the most spiritually powerful of all the *Bodhisattvas*. His dress and adornments show him to be a royal prince. His colour is white, symbolical of his immaculate nature and all-embracing mercy. His two inner hands are held palm to palm in attitude of devotion. In his right outer hand he holds a crystal rosary, symbolical of *yogic* meditation; and, in his left outer hand, a lotus, symbolical of the spiritual perfection and beauty of the *Dharma*, of which he is the Protector. He personifies the *Sambhoga-Kāya*.

The third figure represents *Guru* Rinpoch'e, the 'Precious *Guru*', one of the Tibetan appellations of Padma-Sambhava; and the description is the same as that of the Great *Guru* shown by the frontispiece. He is the personification of the *Nirmāṇa-Kāya*.

Underneath each of the three figures, written in Tibetan, is the appellation. And in the lower corner, outside the margin, below the Great *Guru*, the artist has written his own name.

VIII. BODHIDHARMA   .   .   .   . *facing p.* 194

A photographic reproduction, one-quarter reduced, of the illustration in *Truth and Tradition in Chinese Buddhism* depicting Bodhidharma, made and published by kind permission of the Rev. Dr. K. L. Reichelt, the author, and of The Commercial Press Limited, Shanghai, the publishers of the said work, which is referred to in our General Introduction. It shows Bodhidharma (of whom account is given in the Introduction to Book II) in meditation, seated on a meditation mat of leaves, three books of scripture behind him and incense burning in a bronze Chinese urn on his right.

IX. MAITREYA, THE COMING BUDDHA   . *facing p.* 240

A photographic reproduction (about one-half of the original size) of an old Tibetan painting in colour, on cotton cloth, of Maitreya (Pali: *Metteya*; Tib. *Byams-pa*: pron. *Jham-pa*), the 'Loving One', the Buddhist Messiah, who will regenerate the world by the power of divine love, and inaugurate a New Age of Universal Peace and Brotherhood. He is at present in the Tushita Heaven, whence He will descend and be born among men and become the future Buddha, to reveal anew, as did Gautama and the long Dynasty of past Buddhas, the Path leading to the Great Liberation.[1]

Maitreya sits on a lotus-lunar throne posed and robed as a Buddha. His right hand is in the *mudrā* of preaching the *Dharma*; and on its palm and on each sole of His feet appears the mystic stigmata of a double-*dorje*, like a Greek cross, formed by a golden dot inscribed by a golden circle, the symbol of the Sun, and by twelve other golden dots arranged in four groups of three each, thereby constituting, in all, the sacred number thirteen, symbolical of the thirteen degrees of enlightenment leading to the Great Liberation of *Nirvāṇa*. In His left

---

[1] In the Pāli Canon (*Digha Nikāya*, xxvi) the Buddha Shākya Muni is reported as having said: 'An Exalted One, named Metteya, will arise. . . . His followers will number thousands, whereas mine number hundreds' (cf. Warren's *Buddhism in Translation*, pp. 481–6).

hand He holds a vessel of gold, filled with the essences of purity, regeneration, and salvation for all living creatures. The dot between His eyebrows symbolizes, as does the like dot in other *Bodhic* Beings, the third eye of Divine Wisdom and Transcendent Insight and Vision. His nimbus is green; and the aura surrounding His body is dark blue, indicative of the eternal, ever-present, and all-embracing Buddha Essence. And beneath His throne are shown, as in the other Illustrations, the Five Objects of Enjoyment offered to Buddhas incarnate on Earth. They symbolize the five senses representing the physical man.

The Five Hindrances

'There are these five hindrances in the Discipline of the Noble One, which are called "veils", and are called "hindrances", and are called "obstacles", and are called "entanglements":
'The hindrance of lustful desire,
The hindrance of malice,
The hindrance of sloth and idleness,
The hindrance of pride, and self-righteousness,
The hindrance of doubt.'

The Buddha, *Tevigga Suttanta*, i. 30
(according to the translation in *The Library of Original Sources*, i, edited by Oliver J. Thatcher).

PLATE III

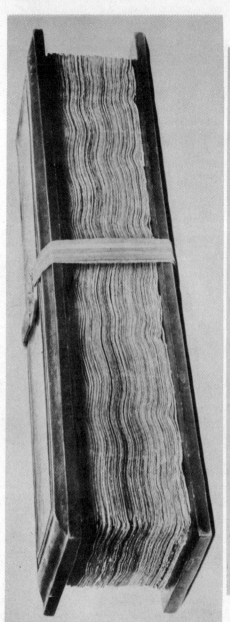

MAÑJUSHRÎ'S BOOK OF DIVINE WISDOM

Described on pages xvii–xix

THE TIBETAN BOOK OF THE GREAT LIBERATION

PSYCHOLOGICAL COMMENTARY

By C. G. JUNG

I. THE DIFFERENCE BETWEEN EASTERN AND WESTERN THINKING

DR. EVANS-WENTZ has entrusted me with the task of commenting on a text which contains an important exposition of Eastern 'psychology'. The very fact that I have to use inverted commas shows the dubious applicability of this term. It is perhaps not superfluous to mention that the East has produced nothing equivalent to what we call psychology, but rather philosophy or metaphysics. Critical philosophy, the mother of modern psychology, is as foreign to the East as to medieval Europe. Thus the word 'mind', as used in the East, has the connotation of something metaphysical. Our Western conception of mind has lost this connotation since the Middle Ages, and the word has now come to signify a 'psychic function'. Despite the fact that we neither know nor pretend to know what 'psyche' is, we can deal with the phenomenon of 'mind'. We do not assume that the mind is a metaphysical entity or that there is any connexion between an individual mind and a hypothetical Universal Mind. Our psychology is, therefore, a science of mere phenomena without any metaphysical implications. The development of Western philosophy during the last two centuries has succeeded in isolating the mind in its own sphere and in severing it from its primordial oneness with the universe. Man himself has ceased to be the microcosm and eidolon of the cosmos, and his 'anima' is no longer the consubstantial *scintilla*, or spark of the *Anima Mundi*, the World Soul.

Psychology accordingly treats all metaphysical claims and assertions as mental phenomena, and regards them as statements about the mind and its structure that derive ultimately from certain unconscious dispositions. It does not consider them to be absolutely valid or even capable of establishing a metaphysical truth. We have no intellectual means of ascertaining whether this attitude is right or wrong. We only know that there is no evidence for, and no possibility of proving, the validity of a metaphysical postulate such as 'Universal Mind'. If the mind asserts the existence of a Universal Mind, we hold that it is merely making an assertion. We do not assume that by such an assertion the existence of a Universal Mind has been established. There is no argument against this reasoning, but no evidence, either, that our conclusion is ultimately right. In other words, it is just as possible that our mind is nothing but a perceptible manifestation of a Universal Mind. Yet we do not know, and we cannot even see, how it would be possible to recognize whether this is so or not. Psychology therefore holds that the mind cannot establish or assert anything beyond itself.

If, then, we accept the restrictions imposed upon the capacity of our mind, we demonstrate our common sense. I admit it is something of a sacrifice, inasmuch as we bid farewell to that miraculous world in which mind-created things and beings move and live. This is the world of the primitive, where even inanimate objects are endowed with a living, healing, magic power, through which they participate in us and we in them. Sooner or later we had to understand that their potency was really ours, and that their significance was our projection. The theory of knowledge is only the last step out of humanity's childhood, out of a world where mind-created figures populated a metaphysical heaven and hell.

Despite this inevitable epistemological criticism, however, we have held fast to the religious belief that the organ of faith enables man to know God. The West thus developed a new disease: the conflict between science and religion. The critical philosophy of science became as it were negatively metaphysical—in other words, materialistic—on the basis of an error in judgement; matter was assumed to be a tangible and recognizable reality. Yet this is a thoroughly metaphysical concept hypostatized by uncritical minds. Matter is an hypothesis. When you say 'matter', you are really creating a symbol for something unknown, which may just as well be 'spirit' or anything else; it may even be God. Religious faith, on the other hand, refuses to give up its pre-critical *Weltanschauung*. In contradiction to the saying of Christ, the faithful try to *remain* children instead of becoming *as* children. They cling to the world of childhood. A famous modern theologian confesses in his autobiography that Jesus has been his good friend 'from childhood on'. Jesus is the perfect example of a man who preached something different from the religion of his forefathers. But the *imitatio Christi* does not appear to include the mental and spiritual sacrifice which he had to undergo at the beginning of his career and without which he would never have become a saviour.

The conflict between science and religion is in reality a misunderstanding of both. Scientific materialism has merely introduced a new hypostasis, and that is an intellectual sin. It has given another name to the supreme principle of reality and has assumed that this created a new thing and destroyed an old thing. Whether you call the principle of existence 'God', 'matter', 'energy', or anything else you like, you have created nothing; you have simply changed a symbol. The materialist is a metaphysician *malgré lui*. Faith, on the other hand, tries to retain a primitive mental condition on merely sentimental grounds. It is unwilling to give up the primitive, childlike relationship to mind-created and hypostatized figures; it wants to go on enjoying the security and confidence of a world still presided over by powerful, responsible, and kindly parents. Faith may include a *sacrificium intellectus* (provided there is an intellect to sacrifice), but certainly not a sacrifice of feeling. In this way the faithful *remain* children instead of becoming *as* children, and they do not gain their life because they have not lost it. Furthermore, faith collides with science and thus gets its deserts, for it refuses to share in the spiritual adventure of our age.

Any honest thinker has to admit the insecurity of all metaphysical positions, and in particular of all creeds. He has also to admit the unwarrantable nature of all metaphysical assertions and face the fact that there is no evidence whatever for the ability of the human mind to pull itself up by its own boot-strings, that is, to establish anything transcendental.

Materialism is a metaphysical reaction against the sudden realization that cognition is a mental faculty and, if carried beyond the human plane, a projection. The reaction was 'metaphysical' in so far as the man of average philosophical education failed to see through the implied hypostasis, not realizing that 'matter' was just another name for the supreme principle. As against this, the attitude of faith shows how reluctant people were to accept philosophical criticism. It also demonstrates how great is the fear of letting go one's hold on the securities of childhood and of dropping into a strange, unknown world ruled by forces unconcerned with man. Nothing really changes in either case; man and his surroundings remain the same. He has only to realize that he is shut up inside his mind and cannot step beyond it, even in insanity; and that the appearance of his world or of his gods very much depends upon his own mental condition.

In the first place, the structure of the mind is responsible for anything we may assert about metaphysical matters, as I have already pointed out. We have also begun to understand that the intellect is not an *ens per se*, or an independent mental faculty, but a psychic function dependent upon the conditions of the psyche as a whole. A philosophical statement is the product of a certain personality living at a certain time in a certain place, and not the outcome of a purely logical and impersonal procedure. To that extent it is chiefly subjective; whether it has an objective validity or not depends on whether there are few or many persons who argue in the same way. The isolation of man within his mind as a result of epistemological criticism has naturally led to psychological criticism. This kind of criticism is not popular with the philosophers, since they like to consider the philosophic intellect as the perfect and unconditioned instrument of philosophy. Yet this intellect of theirs is a function dependent upon an individual psyche and determined on all sides by subjective conditions, quite apart from environmental influences. Indeed, we have already become so accustomed to this point of view that 'mind' has lost its universal character altogether. It has become a more or less individualized affair, with no trace of its former cosmic aspect as the *anima rationalis*. Mind is understood nowadays as a subjective, even an arbitrary, thing. Now that the formerly hypostatized 'universal ideas' have turned out to be mental principles, it is dawning upon us to what an extent our whole experience of so-called reality is psychic; as a matter of fact, everything thought, felt, or perceived is a psychic image, and the world itself exists only so far as we are able to produce an image of it. We are so deeply impressed with the truth of our imprisonment in, and limitation by, the psyche that we are ready to admit the existence in it even of things we do *not* know: we call them 'the unconscious'.

The seemingly universal and metaphysical scope of the mind has thus been narrowed down to the small circle of individual consciousness, profoundly aware of its almost limitless subjectivity and of its infantile-archaic tendency to heedless projection and illusion. Many scientifically-minded persons have even sacrificed their religious and philosophical leanings for fear of uncontrolled subjectivism. By way of compensation for the loss of a world that pulsed with our blood and breathed with our breath, we have developed an enthusiasm for *facts*—mountains of facts, far beyond any single individual's power to survey. We have the pious hope that this incidental accumulation of facts will form a meaningful whole, but nobody is quite sure, because no human brain can possibly comprehend the gigantic sum-total of this mass-produced knowledge. The facts bury us, but whoever dares to speculate must pay for it with a bad conscience—and rightly so, for he will instantly be tripped up by the facts.

Western psychology knows the mind as the mental functioning of a psyche. It is the 'mentality' of an individual. An impersonal Universal Mind is still to be met with in the sphere of philosophy, where it seems to be a relic of the original human 'soul'. This picture of our Western outlook may seem a little drastic, but I do not think it is far from the truth. At all events, something of the kind presents itself as soon as we are confronted with the Eastern mentality. In the East, mind is a cosmic factor, the very essence of existence; while in the West we have just begun to understand that it is the essential condition of cognition, and hence of the cognitive existence of the world. There is no conflict between religion and science in the East, because no science is there based upon the passion for facts, and no religion upon mere faith; there is religious cognition and cognitive religion.[1] With us, man is incommensurably small and the grace of God is everything; but in the East man is God and he redeems himself. The gods of Tibetan Buddhism belong to the sphere of illusory separateness and mind-created projections, and yet they exist; but so far as we are concerned an illusion remains an illusion, and thus is nothing at all. It is a paradox, yet nevertheless true, that with us a thought has no proper reality; we treat it as if it were a nothingness. Even though the thought be true in itself, we hold that it exists only by virtue of certain facts which it is said to formulate. We can produce a most devastating fact like the atom bomb with the help of this ever-changing phantasmagoria of virtually non-existent thoughts, but it seems wholly absurd to us that one could ever establish the reality of thought itself.

'Psychic reality' is a controversial concept, like 'psyche' or 'mind'. By the latter terms some understand consciousness and its contents, others allow the existence of 'dark' or 'subconscious' representations. Some include instincts in the psychic realm, others exclude them. The vast majority consider the psyche to be a result of biochemical processes in the brain cells. A few conjecture that it is the psyche that makes the cortical cells function. Some identify 'life' with psyche. But only an insignificant minority regards the psychic phenomenon as a category of existence *per se* and draws the necessary conclusions. It is indeed paradoxical that *the* category of existence, the indispensable *sine qua non* of all existence, namely the psyche, should be treated as if it were only semi-existent. Psychic existence is the only category of existence of which we have *immediate* knowledge, since nothing

[1] I am purposely leaving out of account the modernized East.

can be known unless it first appears as a psychic image. Only psychic existence is immediately verifiable. To the extent that the world does not assume the form of a psychic image, it is virtually non-existent. This is a fact which, with few exceptions—as for instance in Schopenhauer's philosophy— the West has not yet fully realized. But Schopenhauer was influenced by Buddhism and by the *Upanishads*.

Even a superficial acquaintance with Eastern thought is sufficient to show that a fundamental difference divides East and West. The East bases itself upon psychic reality, that is, upon the psyche as the main and unique condition of existence. It seems as if this Eastern recognition were a psychological or temperamental fact rather than a result of philosophical reasoning. It is a typically introverted point of view, contrasted with the equally typical extraverted viewpoint of the West.[1] Introversion and extraversion are known to be temperamental or even constitutional attitudes which are never intentionally adopted in normal circumstances. In exceptional cases they may be produced at will, but only under very special conditions. Introversion is, if one may so express it, the 'style' of the East, an habitual and collective attitude, just as extraversion is the 'style' of the West. Introversion is felt here as something abnormal, morbid, or otherwise objectionable. Freud identifies it with an auto-erotic, 'narcissistic' attitude of mind. He shares his negative position with the National Socialist philosophy of modern Germany,[2] which accuses introversion of being an offence against community-feeling. In the East, however, our cherished extraversion is depreciated as illusory desirousness, as existence in the *sangsāra*, the very essence of the *nidāna*-chain which culminates in the sum of the world's sufferings.[3] Anyone with practical knowledge of the mutual depreciation of values between introvert and extravert will understand the emotional conflict between the Eastern and the Western standpoint. For those who know something of the history of

---

[1] *Psychological Types*, definitions 19 and 34, pp. 542 ff. and 567 ff.

[2] Written in the year 1939.

[3] *Saṃyutta-nikāya* 12, *Nidāna-saṃyutta*.

European philosophy the bitter wrangling about 'universals' which began with Plato will provide an instructive example. I do not wish to go into all the ramifications of this conflict between introversion and extraversion, but I must mention the religious aspects of the problem. The Christian West considers man to be wholly dependent upon the grace of God, or at least upon the Church as the exclusive and divinely sanctioned earthly instrument of man's redemption. The East, however, insists that man is the sole cause of his higher development, for it believes in 'self-liberation'.

The religious point of view always expresses and formulates the essential psychological attitude and its specific prejudices, even in the case of people who have forgotten, or who have never heard of, their own religion. In spite of everything, the West is thoroughly Christian as far as its psychology is concerned. Tertullian's *anima naturaliter christiana* holds true throughout the West—not, as he thought, in the religious sense, but in the psychological one. Grace comes from elsewhere; at all events from outside. Every other point of view is sheer heresy. Hence it is quite understandable why the human psyche is suffering from undervaluation. Anyone who dares to establish a connexion between the psyche and the idea of God is immediately accused of 'psychologism' or suspected of morbid 'mysticism'. The East, on the other hand, compassionately tolerates those 'lower' spiritual stages where man, in his blind ignorance of *karma*, still bothers about sin and tortures his imagination with a belief in absolute gods, who, if he only looked deeper, are nothing but the veil of illusion woven by his own unenlightened mind. The psyche is therefore all-important; it is the all-pervading Breath, the Buddha essence; it is the Buddha Mind, the One, the *Dharma-Kāya*. All existence emanates from it, and all separate forms dissolve back into it. This is the basic psychological prejudice that permeates Eastern man in every fibre of his being, seeping into all his thoughts, feelings, and deeds, no matter what creed he professes.

In the same way Western man is Christian, no matter to what denomination his Christianity belongs. For him man is small inside, he is next to nothing; moreover, as Kierkegaard says, 'before God man is always wrong'. By fear, repentance, promises, submission, self-abasement, good deeds, and praise he propitiates the great power, which is not himself but *totaliter aliter*, the Wholly Other, altogether perfect and 'outside', the only reality. If you shift the formula a bit and substitute for God some other power, for instance the world or money, you get a complete picture of Western man—assiduous, fearful, devout, self-abasing, enterprising, greedy, and violent in his pursuit of the goods of this world: possessions, health, knowledge, technical mastery, public welfare, political power, conquest, and so on. What are the great popular movements of our time? Attempts to grab the money or property of others and to protect our own. The mind is chiefly employed in devising suitable 'isms' to hide the real motives or to get more loot. I refrain from describing what would happen to Eastern man should he forget his ideal of Buddhahood, for I do not want to give such an unfair advantage to my Western prejudices. But I cannot help raising the question of whether it is possible, or indeed advisable, for either to imitate the other's standpoint. The difference between them is so vast that one can see no reasonable possibility of this, much less its advisability. You cannot mix fire and water. The Eastern attitude stultifies the Western, and vice versa. You cannot be a good Christian and redeem yourself, nor can you be a Buddha and worship God. It is much better to accept the conflict, for it admits only of an irrational solution, if any.

By an inevitable decree of fate the West is becoming acquainted with the peculiar facts of Eastern spirituality. It is useless either to belittle these facts, or to build false and treacherous bridges over yawning gaps. Instead of learning the spiritual techniques of the East by heart and imitating them in a thoroughly Christian way—*imitatio Christi!*—with a correspondingly forced attitude, it would be far more to the point to find out whether there exists in the unconscious an introverted tendency similar to that which has become the guiding spiritual principle of the East. We should then be in a position to build on our own ground with our own methods. If we snatch these things directly from the East, we have merely indulged our Western acquisitiveness, confirming yet again that 'everything good is outside', whence it has to be fetched and pumped into our barren souls.[1] It seems to me that we have really learned something from the East when we understand that the psyche contains riches enough without having to be primed from outside, and when we feel capable of evolving out of ourselves with or without divine grace. But we cannot embark upon this ambitious enterprise until we have learned how to deal with our spiritual pride and blasphemous self-assertiveness. The Eastern attitude violates the specifically Christian values, and it is no good blinking this fact. If our new attitude is to be genuine, i.e. grounded in our own history, it must be acquired with full consciousness of the Christian values and of the conflict between them and the introverted attitude of the East. We must get at the Eastern values from within and not from without, seeking them in ourselves, in the unconscious. We shall then discover how great is our fear of the unconscious and how formidable are our resistances. Because of these resistances we doubt the very thing that seems so obvious to the East, namely, the *self-liberating power of the introverted mind*.

This aspect of the mind is practically unknown to the West, though it forms the most important component of the unconscious. Many people flatly deny the existence of the unconscious, or else they say that it consists merely of instincts, or of repressed or forgotten contents that were once part of the conscious mind. It is safe to assume that what the East calls 'mind' has more to do with our 'unconscious' than with mind as we understand it, which is more or less identical with consciousness. To us consciousness is inconceivable without an ego; it is equated with the relation of contents to an ego. If

[1] 'Whereas who holdeth not God as such an inner possession, but with every means must fetch Him from without . . . verily such a man hath Him not, and easily something cometh to trouble him.' Meister Eckhart (*Büttner*, vol. ii, p. 185).

there is no ego there is nobody to be conscious of anything. The ego is therefore indispensable to the conscious process. The Eastern mind, however, has no difficulty in conceiving of a consciousness without an ego. Consciousness is deemed capable of transcending its ego condition; indeed, in its 'higher' forms, the ego disappears altogether. Such an ego-less mental condition can only be unconscious to us, for the simple reason that there would be nobody to witness it. I do not doubt the existence of mental states transcending consciousness. But they lose their consciousness to exactly the same degree that they transcend consciousness. I cannot imagine a conscious mental state that does not refer to a subject, that is, to an ego. The ego may be depotentiated—divested, for instance, of its awareness of the body—but so long as there is awareness of something, there must be somebody who is aware. The unconscious, however, is a mental condition of which no ego is aware. It is only mediately and by indirect means that we eventually become conscious of the existence of an unconscious. We can observe the manifestation of unconscious fragments of the personality, detached from the patient's consciousness, in insanity. But there is no evidence that the unconscious contents are related to an unconscious centre analogous to the ego; in fact there are good reasons why such a centre is not even probable.

The fact that the East can dispose so easily of the ego seems to point to a mind that is not to be identified with our 'mind'. Certainly the ego does not play the same role in Eastern thought as it does with us. It seems as if the Eastern mind were less egocentric, as if its contents were more loosely connected with the subject, and as if greater stress were laid on mental states which include a depotentiated ego. It also seems as if Hathayoga were chiefly useful as a means for extinguishing the ego by fettering its unruly impulses. There is no doubt that the higher forms of *yoga*, in so far as they strive to reach *samādhi*, seek a mental condition in which the ego is practically dissolved. Consciousness in our sense of the word is rated a definitely inferior condition, the state of *avidyā* (ignorance), whereas what we call the 'dark background of

consciousness' is understood to be a 'higher' consciousness.[1]
Thus our concept of the 'collective unconscious' would be the
European equivalent of *buddhi*, the enlightened mind.

In view of all this, the Eastern form of 'sublimation'
amounts to a withdrawal of the centre of psychic gravity from
ego-consciousness, which holds a middle position between the
body and the ideational processes of the psyche. The lower,
semi-physiological strata of the psyche are subdued by *askesis*,
i.e. exercises, and kept under control. They are not exactly
denied or suppressed by a supreme effort of the will, as is
customary in Western sublimation. Rather, the lower psychic
strata are adapted and shaped through the patient practice
of Hathayoga until they no longer interfere with the development of 'higher' consciousness. This peculiar process seems
to be aided by the fact that the ego and its desires are checked
by the greater importance which the East habitually attaches
to the 'subjective factor'.[2] By this I mean the 'dark background' of consciousness, the unconscious. The introverted
attitude is characterized in general by an emphasis on the
a priori data of apperception. As is well known, the act of
apperception consists of two phases: first the perception of
the object, second the assimilation of the perception to a pre-
existing pattern or concept by means of which the object is
'comprehended'. The psyche is not a nonentity devoid of all
quality; it is a definite system made up of definite conditions
and it reacts in a specific way. Every new representation, be
it a perception or a spontaneous thought, arouses associations
which derive from the storehouse of memory. These leap immediately into consciousness, producing the complex picture
of an 'impression', though this is already a sort of interpretation. The unconscious disposition upon which the quality of
the impression depends is what I call the 'subjective factor'.
It deserves the qualification 'subjective' because objectivity

---

[1] In so far as 'higher' and 'lower' are categorical judgements of consciousness, Western psychology does not differentiate unconscious contents in
this way. It appears that the East recognizes subhuman psychic conditions,
a real 'subconsciousness' comprising the instincts and semi-physiological
psychisms, but classed as a 'higher consciousness'.

[2] *Psychological Types*, pp. 472 ff.

is hardly ever conferred by a first impression. Usually a rather laborious process of verification, comparison, and analysis is needed to modify and adapt the immediate reactions of the subjective factor.

The prominence of the subjective factor does not imply a *personal subjectivism*, despite the readiness of the extraverted attitude to dismiss the subjective factor as 'nothing but subjective'. The psyche and its structure are real enough. They even transform material objects into psychic images, as we have said. They do not perceive waves, but sound; not wavelengths, but colours. Existence is as we see and understand it. There are innumerable things that can be seen, felt, and understood in a great variety of ways. Quite apart from merely personal prejudices, the psyche assimilates external facts in its own way, which is based ultimately upon the laws or patterns of apperception. These laws do not change, although different ages or different parts of the world call them by different names. On a primitive level people are afraid of witches; on the modern level we are apprehensively aware of microbes. There everybody believes in ghosts, here everybody believes in vitamins. Once upon a time men were possessed by devils, now they are not less obsessed by ideas, and so on.

The subjective factor is made up, in the last resort, of the eternal patterns of psychic functioning. Anyone who relies upon the subjective factor is therefore basing himself on the reality of psychic law. So he can hardly be said to be wrong. If by this means he succeeds in extending his consciousness downwards, to touch the basic laws of psychic life, he is in possession of that truth which the psyche will naturally evolve if not fatally interfered with by the non-psychic, i.e. the external, world. At any rate, his truth could be weighed against the sum of all knowledge acquired through the investigation of externals. We in the West believe that a truth is satisfactory only if it can be verified by external facts. We believe in the most exact observation and exploration of nature; our truth must coincide with the behaviour of the external world, otherwise it is merely 'subjective'. In the

same way that the East turns its gaze from the dance of
prakṛti (physis) and from the multitudinous illusory forms of
māyā, the West shuns the unconscious and its futile fantasies.
Despite its introverted attitude, however, the East knows
very well how to deal with the external world. And despite
its extraversions the West, too, has a way of dealing with the
psyche and its demands; it has an institution called the
Church, which gives expression to the unknown psyche of
man through its rites and dogmas. Nor are natural science
and modern techniques by any means the invention of the
West. Their Eastern equivalents are somewhat old-fashioned,
or even primitive. But what we have to show in the way
of spiritual insight and psychological technique must seem,
when compared with *yoga*, just as backward as Eastern
astrology and medicine when compared with Western science.
I do not deny the efficacy of the Christian Church; but, if
you compare the *Exercitia* of Ignatius Loyola with *yoga*, you
will take my meaning. There is a difference, and a big one.
To jump straight from that level into Eastern *yoga* is no
more advisable than the sudden transformation of Asian
peoples into half-baked Europeans. I have serious doubts as
to the blessings of Western civilization, and I have similar
misgivings as to the adoption of Eastern spirituality by the
West. Yet the two contradictory worlds have met. The East
is in full transformation; it is thoroughly and fatally disturbed. Even the most efficient methods of European warfare
have been successfully imitated. The trouble with us seems
to be far more psychological. Our blight is ideologies—they
are the long-expected Anti-Christ! National Socialism comes
as near to being a religious movement as any movement
since A.D. 622. Communism claims to be paradise come to
earth again. We are far better protected against failing crops,
inundations, epidemics, and invasions from the Turk than
we are against our own deplorable spiritual inferiority, which
seems to have little resistance to psychic epidemics.

In its religious attitude, too, the West is extraverted.
Nowadays it is gratuitously offensive to say that Christianity
implies hostility, or even indifference, to the world and the

flesh. On the contrary, the good Christian is a jovial citizen, an enterprising business man, an excellent soldier, the very best in every profession there is. Worldly goods are often interpreted as special rewards for Christian behaviour, and in the Lord's Prayer the adjective ἐπιούσιος, *supersubstantialis*,[1] referring to the bread, has long since been omitted, for the real bread obviously makes so very much more sense! It is only logical that extraversion, when carried to such lengths, cannot credit man with a psyche which contains anything not imported into it from outside, either by human teaching or divine grace. From this point of view it is downright blasphemy to assert that man has it in him to accomplish his own redemption. Nothing in our religion encourages the idea of the self-liberating power of the mind. Yet a very modern form of psychology—'analytical' or 'complex' psychology—envisages the possibility of there being certain processes in the unconscious which, by virtue of their symbolism, compensate the defects and anfractuosities of the conscious attitude. When these unconscious compensations are made conscious through the analytical technique, they produce such a change in the conscious attitude that we are entitled to speak of a new level of consciousness. The method cannot, however, produce the actual process of unconscious compensation; for that we depend upon the unconscious psyche or the 'grace of God'— names make no difference. But the unconscious process itself hardly ever reaches consciousness without technical aid. When brought to the surface, it reveals contents that offer a striking contrast to the general run of conscious thinking and feeling. If that were not so, they would not have a compensatory effect. The first effect, however, is usually a conflict, because the conscious attitude resists the intrusion of apparently incompatible and extraneous tendencies, thoughts, feelings, &c. Schizophrenia yields the most startling examples of such intrusions of utterly foreign and unacceptable contents. In schizophrenia it is, of course, a question of pathological distortions and exaggerations, but anybody with the slightest

[1] This is not the unacceptable translation of ἐπιούσιος by Hieronymus, but the ancient spiritual interpretation by Tertullian, Origen, and others.

knowledge of the normal material will easily recognize the
sameness of the underlying patterns. It is, as a matter of fact,
the same imagery that one finds in mythology and other
archaic thought-formations.

Under normal conditions every conflict stimulates the mind
to activity for the purpose of creating a satisfactory solution.
Usually—i.e. in the West—the conscious standpoint arbitrarily decides against the unconscious, since anything coming from inside suffers from the prejudice of being regarded as
inferior or somehow wrong. But in the cases with which we
are here concerned it is tacitly agreed that the apparently incompatible contents shall not be suppressed again, and that
the conflict shall be accepted and suffered. At first no solution
appears possible, and this fact, too, has to be borne with
patience. The suspension thus created 'constellates' the unconscious—in other words, the conscious suspense produces
a new compensatory reaction in the unconscious. This reaction (usually manifested in dreams) is brought to conscious
realization in its turn. The conscious mind is thus confronted
with a new aspect of the psyche, which arouses a different
problem or modifies an old one in an unexpected way. The
procedure is continued until the original conflict is satisfac-
torily resolved. The whole process is called the 'transcendent
function'.[1] It is a process and a method at the same time. The
production of unconscious compensations is a spontaneous
process; the conscious realization is a *method*. The function is
called 'transcendent' because it facilitates the transition
from one psychic condition to another by means of the mutual
confrontation of opposites.

This is a very sketchy description of the transcendent function, and for details I must refer the reader to the literature
mentioned in the footnotes. But I had to call attention to
these psychological observations and methods because they
indicate the way by which we may find access to the sort of
'mind' referred to in our text. This is the image-creating
mind, the matrix of all those patterns that give apperception
its peculiar character. These patterns are inherent in the un-

[1] *Psychological Types*, pp. 601 ff., s.v. Symbol, definition 51.

conscious 'mind'; they are its structural elements, and they alone can explain why certain mythological motifs are more or less ubiquitous, even where migration as a means of transmission is exceedingly improbable. Dreams, fantasies, and psychoses produce images to all appearances identical with mythological motifs of which the individuals concerned had absolutely no knowledge, not even indirect knowledge acquired through popular figures of speech or through the symbolic language of the Bible.[1] The psychopathology of schizophrenia, as well as the psychology of the unconscious, demonstrate the production of archaic material beyond a doubt. Whatever the structure of the unconscious may be, one thing is certain: it contains an indefinite number of motifs or patterns of an archaic character, in principle identical with the root ideas of mythology and similar thoughtforms.

Because the unconscious is the matrix mind, the quality of creativeness attaches to it. It is the birthplace of thoughtforms such as our text considers the Universal Mind to be. Since we cannot attribute any particular form to the unconscious, the Eastern assertion that the Universal Mind is without form, the *arūpaloka*, yet is the source of all forms, seems to be psychologically justified. In so far as the forms or patterns of the unconscious belong to no time in particular, being seemingly eternal, they convey a peculiar feeling of timelessness when consciously realized. We find similar statements in primitive psychology: for instance, the Australian word *aljira*[2] means 'dream' as well as 'ghostland' and the 'time' in which the ancestors lived and still live. It is, as they

[1] Some people find such statements incredible. But either they have no knowledge of primitive psychology, or they are ignorant of the results of psychopathological research. Specific observations occur in:

C. G. Jung, *Psychology of the Unconscious*, passim (new and revised edition in preparation under the title *Symbols of Transformation*), and *Psychology and Alchemy* (also in preparation), Part II ; J. Nelken, *Analytische Beobachtungen über Phantasien eines Schizophrenen*, Jahrbuch f. psychoanal. u. psychopath. Forschung, vol. iv. pp. 504 ff. ; S. Spielrein, *Ueber den psychol. Inhalt eines Falles von Schizophrenie*, ibid., vol. iii, pp. 329 ff. ; C. A. Meier, *Spontanmanifestationen des kollektiven Unbewussten*, Zentralblatt f. Psychotherapie, Bd. II, H. 4, 1939.

[2] L. Lévy-Bruhl, *La Mythologie primitive*, 1935, pp. xxiii ff.

say, the 'time when there was no time'. This looks like an obvious concretization and projection of the unconscious with all its characteristic qualities—its dream manifestations, its ancestral world of thought-forms, and its timelessness.

An introverted attitude, therefore, which withdraws its emphasis from the external world (the world of consciousness) and localizes it in the subjective factor (the background of consciousness) necessarily calls forth the characteristic manifestations of the unconscious, namely, archaic thought-forms imbued with 'ancestral' or 'historic' feeling, and, beyond them, the sense of indefiniteness, timelessness, oneness. The extraordinary feeling of oneness is a common experience in all forms of 'mysticism' and probably derives from the general contamination of contents, which increases as consciousness dims. The almost limitless contamination of images in dreams, and particularly in the products of insanity, testifies to their unconscious origin. In contrast to the clear distinction and differentiation of forms in consciousness, unconscious contents are incredibly vague and for this reason capable of any amount of contamination. If we tried to conceive of a state in which nothing is distinct, we should certainly feel the whole as one. Hence it is not unlikely that the peculiar experience of oneness derives from the subliminal awareness of all-contamination in the unconscious.

By means of the transcendent function we not only gain access to the 'One Mind' but also come to understand why the East believes in the possibility of self-liberation. If, through introspection and the conscious realization of unconscious compensations, it is possible to transform one's mental condition and thus arrive at a solution of painful conflicts, one would seem entitled to speak of 'self-liberation'. But, as I have already hinted, there is a hitch in this proud claim to self-liberation, for a man cannot produce these unconscious compensations at will. He has to rely upon the possibility they *may* be produced. Nor can he alter the peculiar character of the compensation: *est ut est aut non est*. It is a curious thing that Eastern philosophy seems to be almost unaware of this highly important fact. And it is precisely this fact that provides the psychological justification for the Western point of view. It seems as if the Western mind had a most penetrating intuition of man's fateful dependence upon some dark power which must co-operate if all is to be well. Indeed, whenever and wherever the unconscious fails to co-operate, man is instantly at a loss, even in his most ordinary activities. There may be a failure of memory, of co-ordinated action, or of interest and concentration; and such failure may well be the cause of serious annoyance, or of a fatal accident, a professional disaster, or a moral collapse. Formerly, men called the gods unfavourable; now we prefer to call it a neurosis, and we seek the cause in lack of vitamins, in endocrine disturbances, overwork, or sex. The co-operation of the unconscious, which is something we never think of and always take for granted, is, when it suddenly fails, a very serious matter indeed.

In comparison with other races—the Chinese for instance —the White Man's mental equilibrium, or, to put it bluntly, his brain, seems to be his tender spot. We naturally try to get as far away from our weaknesses as possible, a fact which may explain the sort of extraversion that is always seeking security by dominating its surroundings. Extraversion goes hand in hand with mistrust of the inner man, if indeed there is any consciousness of him at all. Moreover, we all tend to under-value the things we are afraid of. There must be some such reason for our absolute conviction that *nihil sit in intellectu quod non antea fuerit in sensu*, which is the motto of Western extraversion. But, as we have emphasized, this extraversion is psychologically justified by the vital fact that unconscious compensation lies beyond man's control. I know that *yoga* prides itself on being able to control even the unconscious processes, so that nothing can happen in the psyche as a whole that is not ruled by a supreme consciousness. I have not the slightest doubt that such a condition is more or less possible. But it is possible only at the price of becoming identical with the unconscious. Such an identity is the Eastern equivalent of our Western fetish of 'complete objectivity', the machine-like subservience to one goal, to one idea or cause,

xlviii BOOK OF THE GREAT LIBERATION

at the cost of losing every trace of inner life. From the Eastern point of view this complete objectivity is appalling, for it amounts to complete identity with the *sangsāra*; to the West, on the other hand, *samādhi* is nothing but a meaning-less dream-state. In the East, the inner man has always had such a firm hold on the outer man that the world had no chance of tearing him away from his inner roots; in the West, the outer man gained the ascendancy to such an extent that he was alienated from his innermost being. The One Mind, Oneness, indefiniteness, and eternity remained the preroga-tive of the One God. Man became small, futile, and essentially in the wrong.

I think it is becoming clear from my argument that the two standpoints, however contradictory, each have their psycho-logical justification. Both are one-sided in that they fail to see and take account of those factors which do not fit in with their typical attitude. The one underrates the world of con-sciousness, the other the world of the One Mind. The result is that, in their extremism, both lose one half of the universe; their life is shut off from total reality, and is apt to become artificial and inhuman. In the West, there is the mania for 'objectivity', the asceticism of the scientist or of the stock-broker, who throw away the beauty and universality of life for the sake of the ideal, or not so ideal, goal. In the East, there is the wisdom, peace, detachment, and inertia of a psyche that has returned to its dim origins, having left behind all the sorrow and joy of existence as it is and, pre-sumably, ought to be. No wonder that one-sidedness produces very similar forms of monasticism in both cases, guaranteeing to the hermit, the holy man, the monk or the scientist un-swerving singleness of purpose. I have nothing against one-sidedness as such. Man, the great experiment of nature, or his own great experiment, is evidently entitled to all such under-takings—if he can endure them. Without one-sidedness the spirit of man could not unfold in all its diversity. But I do not think there is any harm in trying to understand both sides.

The extraverted tendency of the West and the introverted

tendency of the East have one important purpose in common: both make desperate efforts to conquer the mere naturalness of life. It is the assertion of mind over matter, the *opus contra naturam*, a symptom of the youthfulness of man, still delighting in the use of the most powerful weapon ever devised by nature: the conscious mind. The afternoon of humanity, in a distant future, may yet evolve a different ideal. In time, even conquest will cease to be the dream.

II. Comments on the Text

Before embarking upon the commentary proper, I must not omit to call the reader's attention to the very marked difference between the tenor of a psychological dissertation and that of a sacred text. A scientist forgets all too easily that the impartial handling of a subject may violate its emotional values, often to an unpardonable degree. The scientific intellect is inhuman and cannot afford to be anything else; it cannot avoid being ruthless in effect, though it may be well-intentioned in motive. In dealing with a sacred text, therefore, the psychologist ought at least to be aware that his subject represents an inestimable religious and philosophical value which should not be desecrated by profane hands. I confess that I myself venture to deal with such a text only because I know and appreciate its value. In commenting upon it I have no intention whatsoever of anatomizing it with heavy-handed criticism. On the contrary, my endeavour will be to amplify its symbolic language so that it may yield itself more easily to our understanding. To this end, it is necessary to bring down its lofty metaphysical concepts to a level where it is possible to see whether any of the psychological facts known to us have parallels in, or at least border upon, the sphere of Eastern thought. I hope this will not be misunderstood as an attempt to belittle or to banalize; my aim is simply to bring ideas which are alien to our way of thinking within reach of Western psychological experience.

What follows is a series of notes and comments which should be read together with the textual sections indicated by the titles.

The Obeisance

Eastern texts usually begin with a statement which in the
West would come at the end, as the *conclusio finalis* to a long
argument. We would begin with things generally known and
accepted, and would end with the most important item of our
investigation. Hence our dissertation would conclude with
the sentence: 'Therefore the *Tri-Kāya* is the All-Enlightened
Mind itself.' In this respect, the Eastern mentality is not so
very different from the medieval. As late as the eighteenth
century our books on history or natural science began, as here,
with God's decision to create a world. The idea of a Universal
Mind is a commonplace in the East, since it aptly expresses
the introverted Eastern temperament. Put into psychological
language, the above sentence could be paraphrased thus: The
unconscious is the root of all experience of oneness (*dharma-
kāya*), the matrix of all archetypes or structural patterns
(*sambhoga-kāya*), and the *conditio sine qua non* of the phenomenal world (*nirmāṇa-kāya*).

The Foreword

The gods are archetypal thought-forms belonging to the
sambhoga-kāya.[1] Their peaceful and wrathful aspects, which
play a great role in the meditations of *The Tibetan Book of the
Dead*, symbolize the opposites. In the *nirmāṇa-kāya* these
opposites are no more than human conflicts, but in the
sambhoga-kāya they are the positive and negative principles
united in one and the same figure. This corresponds to the
psychological experience, also formulated in Lao-Tzu's *Tao
Te Ching*, that there is no position without its negation.
Where there is faith, there is doubt; where there is doubt,
there is credulity; where there is morality, there is temptation. Only saints have diabolical visions, and tyrants are the
slaves of their *valets de chambre*. If we carefully scrutinize
our own character we shall inevitably find that, as Lao-Tzu
says, 'high stands on low', which means that the opposites
condition one another, that they are really one and the same
thing. This can easily be seen in persons with an inferiority

[1] Cf. the *Shrī-Chakra-Sambhara Tantra*, in *Tantric Texts*, vol. vii.

complex: they foment a little megalomania somewhere. The fact that the opposites appear as gods comes from the simple recognition that they are exceedingly powerful. Chinese philosophy therefore declared them to be cosmic principles, and named them *yang* and *yin*. Their power increases the more one tries to separate them. 'When a tree grows up to heaven its roots reach down to hell', says Nietzsche. Yet, above as below, it is the same tree. It is characteristic of our Western mentality that we should separate the two aspects into antagonistic personifications: God and the Devil. And it is equally characteristic of the worldly optimism of Protestantism that it should have hushed up the Devil in a tactful sort of way, at any rate in recent times. *Omne bonum a Deo, omne malum ab homine* is the uncomfortable consequence.

The 'seeing of reality' clearly refers to Mind as the supreme reality. In the West, however, the unconscious is considered to be a fantastic irreality. The 'seeing of the Mind' implies self-liberation. This means, psychologically, that the more weight we attach to unconscious processes the more we detach ourselves from the world of desires and of separated opposites, and the nearer we draw to the state of unconsciousness with its qualities of oneness, indefiniteness, and timelessness. This is truly a liberation of the self from its bondage to strife and suffering. 'By this method, one's mind is understood.' Mind in this context is obviously the individual's mind, that is, his psyche. Psychology can agree in so far as the understanding of the unconscious is one of its foremost tasks.

Salutation to the One Mind

This section shows very clearly that the One Mind is the unconscious, since it is characterized as 'eternal, unknown, not visible, not recognized'. But it also displays positive features which are in keeping with Eastern experience. These are the attributes 'ever clear, ever existing, radiant and unobscured'. It is an undeniable psychological fact that the more one concentrates on one's unconscious contents the more they become charged with energy; they become vitalized, as if illuminated from within. In fact they turn into something like a substitute reality. In analytical psychology we make methodical use of this phenomenon. I have called the method 'active imagination'. Ignatius Loyola also made use of active imagination in his *Exercitia*. There is evidence that something similar was used in the meditations of alchemical philosophy.[1]

The Result of Not Knowing the One Mind

'Knowledge of that which is vulgarly called mind is widespread.' This clearly refers to the conscious mind of everybody, in contrast to the One Mind which is unknown, i.e. unconscious. These teachings 'will also be sought after by ordinary individuals who, not knowing the One Mind, do not know themselves.' Self-knowledge is here definitely identified with 'knowing the One Mind', which means that knowledge of the unconscious is essential for any understanding of one's own psychology. The desire for such knowledge is a well established fact in the West, as evidenced by the rise of psychology in our time and a growing interest in these matters. The public desire for more psychological knowledge is largely due to the suffering which results from the disuse of religion and from the lack of spiritual guidance. 'They wander hither and thither in the Three Regions . . . suffering sorrow.' As we know what a neurosis can mean in moral suffering, this statement needs no comment. This section formulates the reasons why we have such a thing as the psychology of the unconscious today.

Even if one wishes 'to know the mind as it is, one fails'. The text again stresses how hard it is to gain access to the basic mind, because it is unconscious.

The Results of Desires

Those 'fettered by desires cannot perceive the Clear Light'. The 'Clear Light' again refers to the One Mind. Desires crave for external fulfilment. They forge the chain that fetters man to the world of consciousness. In that condition he naturally cannot become aware of his unconscious contents. And indeed there is a healing power in withdrawing from the conscious world—up to a point. Beyond that point, which varies with individuals, withdrawal amounts to neglect and repression.

[1] C. G. Jung, *Psychology and Alchemy*, Part III.

Even the 'Middle Path' finally becomes 'obscured by desires'. This is a very true statement, which cannot be dinned too insistently into European ears. Patients and normal individuals, on becoming acquainted with their unconscious material, hurl themselves upon it with the same heedless desirousness and greed that before had engulfed them in their extraversion. The problem is not so much a withdrawal from the objects of desire, as a more detached attitude to desire as such, no matter what its object. We cannot compel unconscious compensation through the impetuousness of uncontrolled desire. We have to wait patiently to see whether it will come of its own accord, and put up with whatever form it takes. Hence we are forced into a sort of contemplative attitude which, in itself, not rarely has a liberating and healing effect.

The Transcendent At-one-ment

'There being really no duality, pluralism is untrue.' This is certainly one of the most fundamental truths of the East. There are no opposites—it is the same tree above and below. The *Tabula Smaragdina* says: 'Quod est inferius est sicut quod est superius. Et quod est superius est sicut quod est inferius, ad perpetranda miracula rei unius.'[1] Pluralism is even more illusory, since all separate forms originate in the indistinguishable oneness of the psychic matrix, deep down in the unconscious. The statement made by our text refers psychologically to the subjective factor, to the material immediately constellated by a stimulus, i.e. the first impression which, as we have seen, interprets every new perception in terms of previous experience. 'Previous experience' goes right back to the instincts, and thus to the inherited and inherent patterns of psychic functioning, the ancestral and 'eternal' laws of the human mind. But the statement entirely ignores the possible transcendent reality of the physical world as such, a problem not unknown to Saṇkhya philosophy, where *prakṛti* and *purusha*—so far as they are a polarization of Universal Being—form a cosmic dualism that can hardly be

[1] Cf. J. Ruska, *Tabula Smaragdina: Ein Beitrag zur Geschichte der Hermetischen Literatur*, 1926, p. 2.

circumvented. One has to close one's eyes to dualism and pluralism alike, and forget all about the existence of a world, as soon as one tries to identify oneself with the monistic origin of life. The question naturally arises: 'Why should the One appear as the Many, when ultimate reality is All-One? What is the cause of pluralism, or of the illusion of pluralism? If the One is pleased with itself, why should it mirror itself in the Many? Which after all is the more real, the one that mirrors itself, or the mirror it uses?' Probably we should not ask such questions, seeing that there is no answer to them.

It is psychologically correct to say that 'At-one-ment' is attained by withdrawal from the world of consciousness. In the stratosphere of the unconscious there are no more thunderstorms, because nothing is differentiated enough to produce tensions and conflicts. These belong to the surface of our reality.

The Mind in which the irreconcilables—*sangsāra* and *nirvāṇa*—are united is ultimately our mind. Does this statement spring from profound modesty or from overweening hybris? Does it mean that the Mind is 'nothing but' our mind? Or that our mind is the Mind? Assuredly it means the latter, and from the Eastern point of view there is no hybris in this; on the contrary, it is a perfectly acceptable truth, whereas with us it would amount to saying 'I am God'. This is an incontestable 'mystical' experience, though a highly objectionable one to the Westerner; but in the East, where it derives from a mind that has never lost touch with the instinctual matrix, it has a very different value. The collective introverted attitude of the East did not permit the world of the senses to sever the vital link with the unconscious; psychic reality was never seriously disputed, despite the existence of so-called materialistic speculations. The only known analogy to this fact is the mental condition of the primitive, who confuses dream and reality in the most bewildering way. Naturally we hesitate to call the Eastern mind primitive, for we are deeply impressed with its remarkable civilization and differentiation. Yet the primitive mind is its matrix, and this is particularly true of that aspect of it which stresses the validity of psychic phenomena, such as relate to ghosts and spirits. The West has simply cultivated the other aspect of primitivity, namely, the scrupulously accurate observation of nature at the expense of abstraction. Our natural science is the epitome of primitive man's astonishing powers of observation. We have added only a moderate amount of abstraction, for fear of being contradicted by the facts. The East, on the other hand, cultivates the psychic aspect of primitivity together with an inordinate amount of abstraction. Facts make excellent stories but not much more.

Thus, if the East speaks of the Mind as being inherent in everybody, no more hybris or modesty is involved than in the European's belief in facts, which are mostly derived from man's own observation and sometimes from rather less than his observation, to wit, his interpretation. He is, therefore, quite right to be afraid of too much abstraction.

The Great Self-Liberation

I have mentioned more than once that the shifting of the basic personality-feeling to the less conscious mental sphere has a liberating effect. I have also described, somewhat cursorily, the transcendent function which produces the transformation of personality, and I have emphasized the importance of spontaneous unconscious compensation. Further, I have pointed out the neglect of this crucial fact in *yoga*. This section tends to confirm my observations. The grasping of 'the whole essence of these teachings' seems also to be the whole essence of 'self-liberation'. The Westerner would take this to mean: 'Learn your lesson and repeat it, and then you will be self-liberated.' That, indeed, is precisely what happens with most Western practitioners of *yoga*. They are very apt to 'do' it in an extraverted fashion, oblivious of the inturning of the mind which is the essence of such teachings. In the East, the 'truths' are so much a part of the collective consciousness that they are at least intuitively grasped by the pupil. If the European could turn himself inside out and live as an Oriental, with all the social, moral, religious, intellectual, and aesthetic obligations which such a course would

BOOK OF THE GREAT LIBERATION

involve, he might be able to benefit by these teachings. But
you cannot be a good Christian, either in your faith or in
your morality or in your intellectual make-up, and practise
genuine *yoga* at the same time. I have seen too many cases
that have made me sceptical in the highest degree. The
trouble is that Western man cannot get rid of his history as
easily as his short-legged memory can. History, one might
say, is written in the blood. I would not advise anyone to
touch *yoga* without a careful analysis of his unconscious reactions. What is the use of imitating *yoga* if your dark side
remains as good a medieval Christian as ever was? If you
can afford to seat yourself on a gazelle skin under a Bo-tree
or in the cell of a *gompa* for the rest of your life without being
troubled by politics or the collapse of your securities, I will
look favourably upon your case. But *yoga* in Mayfair or Fifth
Avenue, or in any other place which is on the telephone, is a
spiritual fake.

Taking the mental equipment of Eastern man into account,
we may suppose that the teaching is effective. But unless one
is prepared to turn away from the world and to disappear
into the unconscious for good, mere teaching has no effect, or
at least not the desired one. For this the union of opposites is
necessary, and in particular the difficult task of reconciling
extraversion and introversion by means of the transcendent
function.

The Nature of Mind

This section contains a valuable piece of psychological
information. The text says: 'The mind is of intuitive ("quick-
knowing") Wisdom.' Here 'mind' is understood to be identical with immediate awareness of the 'first impression' which
conveys the whole sum of previous experience based upon
instinctual patterns. This bears out our remarks about the
essentially introverted prejudice of the East. The formula
also draws attention to the highly differentiated character of
Eastern intuition. The intuitive mind is noted for its disregard of facts in favour of possibilities.[1]

[1] Cf. *Psychological Types*, definition 36, pp. 641 ff.

The assertion that the Mind 'has no existence' obviously refers to the peculiar 'potentiality' of the unconscious. A thing seems to exist only to the degree that we are aware of it, which explains why so many people are disinclined to believe in the existence of an unconscious. When I tell a patient that he is chock full of fantasies, he is often astonished beyond all measure, having been completely unaware of the fantasy-life he was leading.

The Names given to the Mind

The various terms employed to express a 'difficult' or 'obscure' idea are a valuable source of information about the ways in which that idea can be interpreted, and at the same time an indication of its doubtful or controversial nature even in the country, religion, or philosophy to which it is indigenous. If the idea were perfectly straightforward and enjoyed general acceptance, there would be no reason to call it by a number of different names. But when something is little known, or ambiguous, it can be envisaged from different angles, and then a multiplicity of names is needed to express its peculiar nature. A classical example of this is the philosopher's stone; many of the old alchemical treatises give long lists of its names.

The statement that 'the various names given to it (the Mind) are innumerable' proves that the Mind must be something as vague and indefinite as the philosopher's stone. A substance that can be described in 'innumerable' ways must be expected to display as many qualities or facets. If these are really 'innumerable', they cannot be counted, and it follows that the substance is well-nigh indescribable and unknowable. It can never be realized completely. This is certainly true of the unconscious, and a further proof that the Mind is the Eastern equivalent of our concept of the unconscious, more particularly of the collective unconscious.

In keeping with this hypothesis, the text goes on to say that the Mind is also called the 'Mental Self'. The 'self' is an important item in analytical psychology, where much has been said that I need not repeat here. I would refer the interested

reader to the literature given below.[1] Although the symbols
of the 'self' are produced by unconscious activity and are
mostly manifested in dreams,[2] the facts which the idea covers
are not merely mental; they include aspects of physical existence as well. In this and other Eastern texts the 'Self' represents a purely spiritual idea, but in Western psychology the
'self' stands for a totality which comprises instincts, physio-
logical and semi-physiological phenomena. To us a purely
spiritual totality is inconceivable for the reasons mentioned
above.[3]

It is interesting to note that in the East, too, there are
'heretics' who identify the Self with the ego.[4] With us this
heresy is pretty widespread and is subscribed to by all those
who firmly believe that ego-consciousness is the only form of
psychic life.

The Mind as 'the means of attaining the Other Shore'
points to a connexion between the transcendent function and
the idea of the Mind or Self. Since the unknowable substance
of the Mind, i.e. of the unconscious, always represents itself
to consciousness in the form of symbols—the self being one
such symbol—the symbol functions as a 'means of attaining
the Other Shore', in other words, as a means of transformation. In my essay on *Psychic Energy* I said that the symbol
acts as a transformer of energy.[5]

My interpretation of the Mind or Self as a symbol is not
arbitrary; the text itself calls it 'The Great Symbol'.

It is also remarkable that our text recognizes the 'potentiality' of the unconscious, as formulated above, by calling
the Mind the 'Sole Seed' and the 'Potentiality of Truth'.

The matrix-character of the unconscious comes out in the
term 'All-Foundation'.

---

[1] C. G. Jung, *Two Essays on Analytical Psychology*, p. 268; *Psychological
Types*, def. 16, p. 540; *Psychology and Alchemy*, Part II; *Psychology and
Religion*, passim.
[2] One such case is described in Part II of *Psychology and Alchemy*.
[3] This is no criticism of the Eastern point of view *in toto*; for, according
to the *Amitāyus Dhyāna Sutra*, Buddha's body is included in the meditation.
[4] Cf., for instance, *Chāndogya Upanishad*, viii. 8.
[5] *Contributions to Analytical Psychology*, 1928, p. 54.

The Timelessness of Mind

I have already explained this 'timelessness' as a quality inherent in the experience of the collective unconscious. The application of the 'yoga of self-liberation' is said to reintegrate all forgotten knowledge of the past with consciousness. The motif of ἀποκατάστασις (restoration, restitution) occurs in many redemption myths and is also an important aspect of the psychology of the unconscious, which reveals an extraordinary amount of archaic material in the dreams and spontaneous fantasies of normal and insane people. In the systematic analysis of an individual the spontaneous reawakening of ancestral patterns (as a compensation) has the effect of a restoration. It is also a fact that premonitory dreams are relatively frequent, and this substantiates what the text calls 'knowledge of the future'.

The Mind's 'own time' is very difficult to interpret. From the psychological point of view we must agree with Dr. Evans-Wentz's comment here. The unconscious certainly has its 'own time' inasmuch as past, present, and future are blended together in it. Dreams of the type experienced by J. W. Dunne,[1] where he dreamed the night before what he ought logically to have dreamed the night after, are not infrequent.

Mind in its True State

This section describes the state of detached consciousness[2] which corresponds to a psychic experience very common throughout the East. Similar descriptions are to be found in Chinese literature, as, for instance, in the *Hui Ming Ch'ing*:

A luminosity surrounds the world of spirit.
We forget one another when, still and pure, we draw strength from
        the Void.
The Void is filled with the light of the Heart of Heaven ...
Consciousness dissolves in vision.[3]

[1] J. W. Dunne, *An Experiment with Time*, 1927.
[2] I have explained this in *The Secret of the Golden Flower*, pp. 21 ff.
[3] Translated from *Hui Ming Ch'ing*, Chinesische Blätter, ed. R. Wilhelm, vol. i, no. 3.

The statement 'Nor is one's own mind separable from other minds' is another way of expressing the fact of 'all-contamination'. Since all distinctions vanish in the unconscious condition, it is only logical that the distinction between separate minds should also disappear. Wherever there is a lowering of the conscious level we come across instances of unconscious identity,[1] or what Lévy-Bruhl calls 'participation mystique'.[2] The realization of the One Mind is, as our text says, the 'at-one-ment of the *Tri-Kāya*'; in fact it creates the at-one-ment. But we are unable to imagine how such a realization could ever be complete in any human individual. There must always be somebody or something left over to experience the realization, to say 'I know at-one-ment, I know there is no distinction'. The very fact of the realization proves its inevitable incompleteness. One cannot know something that is not distinct from oneself. Even when I say 'I know myself', an infinitesimal ego—the knowing 'I'—is still distinct from 'myself'. In this as it were atomic ego, which is completely ignored by the essentially non-dualist standpoint of the East, there nevertheless lies hidden the whole unabolished pluralistic universe and its unconquered reality.

The experience of 'at-one-ment' is one example of those 'quick-knowing' realizations of the East, an intuition of what it would be like if one could exist and not exist at the same time. If I were a Moslem, I should maintain that the power of the All-Compassionate is infinite, and that He alone can make a man to be and not to be at the same time. But for my part

[1] *Psychological Types*, def. 25, p. 552.
[2] Cf. L. Lévy-Bruhl, *Les Fonctions mentales dans les sociétés inférieures*. Recently this concept as well as that of the *état prélogique* have been severely criticized by ethnologists, and moreover Lévy-Bruhl himself began to doubt their validity in the last years of his life. First he cancelled the adjective 'mystique', growing afraid of the term's bad reputation in intellectual circles. It is rather to be regretted that he made such a concession to rationalistic superstition, since 'mystique' is just the right word to characterize the peculiar quality of 'unconscious identity'. There is always something numinous about it. Unconscious identity is a well-known psychological and psychopathological phenomenon (identity with persons, things, functions, roles, positions, creeds, &c.), which is only a shade more characteristic of the primitive than of the civilized mind. Lévy-Bruhl unfortunately having no psychological knowledge was not aware of this fact, and his opponents ignore it.

I cannot conceive of such a possibility. I therefore assume that, in this point, Eastern intuition has overreached itself.

Mind is Non-Created

This section emphasizes that as the Mind is without characteristics, one cannot assert that it is created. But then, it would be illogical to assert that it is non-created, for such a qualification would amount to a 'characteristic'. As a matter of fact you can make no assertion whatever about a thing that is indistinct, void of characteristics and, moreover, 'unknowable'. For precisely this reason Western psychology does not speak of the One Mind, but of the unconscious, regarding it as a thing-in-itself, a noumenon, 'a merely negative borderline concept', to quote Kant.[1] We have often been reproached for using such a negative term, but unfortunately intellectual honesty does not allow a positive one.

The Yoga of Introspection

Should there be any doubt left concerning the identity of the One Mind and the unconscious, this section certainly ought to dispel it. 'The One Mind being verily of the Voidness and without any foundation, one's mind is, likewise, as vacuous as the sky.' The One Mind and the individual mind are equally void and vacuous. Only the collective and the personal unconscious can be meant by this statement, for the conscious mind is in no circumstances 'vacuous'.

As I have said earlier, the Eastern mind insists first and foremost upon the subjective factor, and in particular upon the intuitive 'first impression', or the psychic disposition. This is borne out by the statement that 'All appearances are verily one's own concepts, self-conceived in the mind'.

The Dharma Within

Dharma, law, truth, guidance, is said to be 'nowhere save in the mind'. Thus the unconscious is credited with all those faculties which the West attributes to God. The transcendent function, however, shows how right the East is in assuming

[1] Cf. *The Critique of Pure Reason*, section i, Part I. 2, 3.

that the complex experience of *dharma* comes from 'within', i.e. from the unconscious. It also shows that the phenomenon of spontaneous compensation, being beyond the control of man, is quite in accord with the formula 'grace' or the 'will of God'.

This and the preceding section insist again and again that introspection is the only source of spiritual information and guidance. If introspection were something morbid, as certain people in the West opine, we should have to send practically the whole East, or such parts of it as are not yet infected with the blessings of the West, to the lunatic asylum.

The Wondrousness of These Teachings

This section calls the mind 'Natural Wisdom', which is very much the same expression that I used in order to designate the symbols produced by the unconscious. I called them 'natural symbols'.[1] I chose the term before I had any knowledge of this text. I mention this fact simply because it illustrates the close parallelism between the findings of Eastern and Western psychology.

The text also confirms what we said earlier about the impossibility of a 'knowing' ego. 'Although it is Total Reality, there is no perceiver of it. Wondrous is this.' Wondrous indeed, and incomprehensible; for how could such a thing ever be *realized* in the true sense of the word? 'It remains undefiled by evil' and 'it remains unallied to good'. One is remined of Nietzsche's 'six thousand feet beyond good and evil'. But the consequences of such a statement are usually ignored by the emulators of Eastern wisdom. While one is safely ensconced in one's cosy flat, secure in the favour of the Oriental gods, one is free to admire this lofty moral indifference. But does it agree with our temperament, or with our history, which is not thereby conquered but merely forgotten? I think not. Anyone who affects the higher *yoga* will be called upon to prove his professions of moral indifference, not only as the doer of evil but, even more, as its

---

[1] *Psychology and Religion*, 1938, 'Dogma and Natural Symbols', and 'A Natural Symbol'.

victim. As psychologists well know, the moral conflict is not to be settled merely by a declaration of superiority bordering on inhumanity. We are witnessing today some terrifying examples of the Superman's aloofness from moral principles.

I do not doubt that the Eastern liberation from vices, as well as from virtues, is coupled with detachment in every respect, so that the *yogī* is translated beyond this world, and quite inoffensive. But I suspect every European attempt at detachment of being mere liberation from moral considerations. Anybody who tries his hand at *yoga* ought therefore to be conscious of its far-reaching consequences, or else his so-called quest will remain a futile pastime.

The Fourfold Great Path

The text says: 'This meditation [is] devoid of mental concentration.' The usual assumption about *yoga* is that it chiefly consists in intense concentration. We think we know what concentration means, but it is very difficult to arrive at a real understanding of Eastern concentration. Our sort may well be just the opposite of the Eastern, as a study of Zen Buddhism will show.[1] However, if we take 'devoid of mental concentration' literally, it can only mean that the meditation does not centre upon anything. Not being centred, it would be rather like a dissolution of consciousness and hence a direct approach to the unconscious condition. Consciousness always implies a certain degree of concentration, without which there would be no clarity of mental content and no consciousness of anything. Meditation without concentration would be a waking but empty condition, on the verge of falling asleep. Since our text calls this 'the most excellent of meditations' we must suppose the existence of less excellent meditations which, by inference, would be characterized by more concentration. The meditation our text has in mind seems to be a sort of Royal Road to the unconscious.

The Great Light

The central mystical experience of enlightenment is aptly

[1] Cf. D. T. Suzuki, *Essays in Zen Buddhism.*

symbolized by Light in most of the numerous forms of mysticism. It is a curious paradox that the approach to a region which seems to us the way into utter darkness should yield the light of illumination as its fruit. This is, however, the usual *enantiodromia per tenebras ad lucem*. Many initiation ceremonies[1] stage a κατάβασις εἰς ἄντρον (descent into the cave), a diving down into the depths of the baptismal water, or a return to the womb of rebirth. Rebirth symbolism simply describes the union of opposites—conscious and unconscious —by means of concretistic analogies. Underlying all rebirth symbolism is the transcendent function. Since this function results in an increase of consciousness (the previous condition augmented by the addition of formerly unconscious contents), the new condition carries more insight, which is symbolized by more light.[2] It is therefore a more enlightened state compared with the relative darkness of the previous state. In many cases the Light even appears in the form of a vision.

The Yoga of the Nirvāṇic Path

This section gives one of the best formulations of the complete dissolution of consciousness, which appears to be the goal of this *yoga*: 'There being no two such things as action and performer of action, if one seeks the performer of action and no performer of action be found anywhere, thereupon the goal of all fruit-obtaining is reached and also the final consummation itself.'

With this very complete formulation of the method and its aim, I reach the end of my commentary. The text that follows, in Book II, is of great beauty and wisdom, and contains nothing that requires further comment. It can be translated into psychological language and interpreted with the help of the principles I have here set forth in Part I and illustrated in Part II.

---

[1] As in the Eleusinian mysteries and the Mithras and Attis cults.

[2] In alchemy the philosopher's stone was called, among other things, *lux moderna, lux lucis, lumen luminum*, &c.

PLATE IV

MAÑJUSHRĪ THE GOD OF DIVINE WISDOM

Described on pages xix–xxi

GENERAL INTRODUCTION

'To attain the Good, we must ascend to the highest state, and, fixing our gaze thereon, lay aside the garments we donned when descending here below; just as, in the Mysteries, those who are admitted to penetrate into the inner recesses of the sanctuary, after having purified themselves, lay aside every garment, and advance stark naked.'   Plotinus (I. vi. 6)

I. REALITY ACCORDING TO THE MAHĀYĀNA

HEREIN, in Book II, in the 'Yoga of Knowing the Mind in Its Nakedness', otherwise known as the doctrine which automatically liberates man from bondage to appearances, is set forth, in aphorisms, an epitome of the root teachings of Mahāyānic transcendentalism concerning Reality.

In common with all Schools of the Oriental Occult Sciences, the Mahāyāna postulates that the One Supra-Mundane Mind, or the Universal All-Pervading Consciousness, transcendent over appearances and over every dualistic concept born of the finite or mundane aspect of mind, alone is real. Viewed as the Voidness (known in Sanskrit as the *Shūnyatā*), it is the Unbecome, the Unborn, the Unmade, the Unformed, the predicateless Primordial Essence, the abstract Cosmic Source whence all concrete or manifested things come and into which they vanish in latency. Being without form, quality, or phenomenal existence, it is the Formless, the Qualityless, the Non-Existent. As such, it is the Imperishable, the Transcendent Fullness of the Emptiness, the Dissolver of Space and of Time and of *sangsāric* (or mundane) mind, the Brahman of the *Rishis*, the Dreamer of *Māyā*, the Weaver of the Web of Appearances, the Outbreather and the Inbreather of infinite universes throughout the endlessness of Duration.

Plotinus, the Platonic inheritor of this ancient oriental teaching, has concisely summarized it: 'The First Principle, being One, is transcendent over measure or number. . . . The Supreme Principle must be essentially unitary, and simple, while essences [derived therefrom] form a multitude.'[1] The

[1] Cf. Plotinus, Ennead V, Book V, 11; Book IX, 14. These renderings from Plotinus, and all hereinafter contained, are recensions, based upon translations contained in *Plotinos' Complete Works*, by K. S. Guthrie, as published in London in 1929, a work to which grateful acknowledgement is

Great *Guru*, Padma-Sambhava, the author of our present treatise, in Book II, page 207, sets forth the same doctrine from the Mahāyānic point of view: 'The whole *Sangsāra* [or the phenomenal Universe of appearances] and *Nirvāṇa* [the Unmanifested, or noumenal state], as an inseparable unity, are one's mind [in its natural, or unmodified primordial state of the Voidness].' In like manner, the Buddha Himself teaches that *Nirvāṇa* is a state of transcendence over 'that which is become, born, made, and formed'.[1] Accordingly, *Nirvāṇa* is the annihilation of appearances, the indrawing of the Web of the *Sangsāra*, the blowing out of the flame of bodily sensuousness, the Awakening from the Dream of *Māyā*, the unveiling of Reality.

The Buddha, and, after Him, Nāgārjuna, who compiled the *Prajñā-Pāramitā*, the chief Mahāyāna treatise on Transcendental Wisdom, aimed to avoid in their teachings the extreme of superstition on the one hand and of nihilism on the other; and so their method is that of the Middle Path, which, under Nāgārjuna, became known as the Mādhyamika. Prior to Nāgārjuna, Buddhist metaphysicians were divided into two schools of extremists, one school teaching of a real existence, the other of an illusory existence. Nāgārjuna showed that nothing can be said to exist or not to exist, for so long as the mind conceives in terms of dualism it is still under *sangsāric* bondage, and fettered by the false desire for either personal immortality or annihilation. Reality, or the Absolute, or Being *per se*, is transcendent over both existence and non-existence, and over all other dualistic concepts. According to Nāgārjuna, it is the Primordial Voidness, beyond mental conception, or definition in terms of human experience.

here made. Frequent reference is herein made to Plotinus, because he is the outstanding exponent in the West of the same *yogic* doctrines as those which form the basis of this volume. He was an eminently successful disciple of the Oriental Sages, no less than of his European *Guru* Plato; by Plotinus, these doctrines were put to the test of practice, with far-reaching results to the whole Christian world. In Plotinus, East and West cease to be twain and become one, as in reality they always have been and will be increasingly, when the Sun of the approaching New Renaissance, which shall be world-wide, rises, and waxes in brilliance and power, and dissipates the darkness of Ignorance.

[1] *Udāna*, viii. 1, 4, 3; cf. *The Tibetan Book of the Dead*, p. 68.

The Mādhyamika maintains that the World is to be renounced not as the Theravāda teaches, because of its pain and sorrow, but because it is as non-real as are dreams; it, being merely one of the many dream-states comprising the *Sangsāra*, is wholly unsatisfying. Man should strive to awaken from all the dream-states of the *Sangsāra* into the State of True Awakening, *Nirvāṇa*, beyond the range of all the glamorous illusions and hypnotic mirages of the *Sangsāra*; and thus become, as is the Buddha, a Fully-Awakened One.

This Doctrine of the Voidness is the essential doctrine of the Mahāyāna; it represents in Northern Buddhism what the *Anātmā* (or Non-Soul) Doctrine does in Southern Buddhism. Accordingly, as our treatise implies, no existing thing or being has other than an illusory existence, nor has it separate or individualized existence apart from all other beings.

As set forth in the *Avatamsaka Sūtra*, attributed to Nāgārjuna, the essentiality, or the true essence, behind all *sangsāric* things or beings is likened to a dust-free mirror, which is the basis of all phenomena, the basis itself being permanent, or non-transitory, and real, the phenomena being evanescent and unreal. And, just as the mirror reflects images, so the True Essence embraces all phenomena; and all things and beings exist in and by it. It is this True Essence which comes to fruition in the Buddhas; and is everywhere present throughout the manifested cosmos, which is born of it, and eternally present, unmanifested, throughout limitless space. There is no place throughout the Universe where the Essentiality of a Buddha is not present. Far and wide throughout the spaces of space the Buddha Essence is present and perpetually manifested.[1]

This Universal Essence manifests itself in three aspects, or modes, symbolized as the Three Divine Bodies (Skt. *Tri-Kāya*). The first aspect, the *Dharma-Kāya*, or Essential (or True) Body, is the Primordial, Unmodified, Formless, Eternally Self-Existing Essentiality of *Bodhi*, or Divine Beingness. The second aspect is the *Sambhoga-Kāya*, or Reflected *Bodhi*,

[1] Cf. S. Beal, *A Catena of Buddhist Scriptures from the Chinese* (London, 1871), pp. 124–5.

wherein, in heaven-worlds, dwell the Buddhas of Meditation (Skt. *Dhyānī-Buddhas*) and other Enlightened Ones while embodied in superhuman form. The third aspect is the *Nirmāṇa-Kāya*, or Body of Incarnation, or, from the standpoint of men, Practical *Bodhi*, in which exist Buddhas when on Earth.

In the Chinese interpretation of the *Tri-Kāya*, the *Dharma-Kāya* is the immutable Buddha Essence, the Noumenal Source of the Cosmic whole. The *Sambhoga-Kāya* is, as phenomenal appearances, the first reflex of the *Dharma-Kāya* on the heavenly planes. In the *Nirmāṇa-Kāya*, the Buddha Essence is associated with activity on the Earth plane; it incarnates among men, as suggested by the Gnostic Proem to the Gospel of St. John, which refers to the coming into the flesh of the 'Word', or 'Mind' (see herein Book II, p. 217[1]).[1]

In its totality, the Universal Essence is the One Mind, manifested through the multitudinous myriads of minds throughout all states of *sangsāric* existence. It is called 'The Essence of the Buddhas', 'The Great Symbol', 'The Sole Seed', 'The Potentiality of Truth', 'The All-Foundation'. As our text teaches, it is the Source of all bliss of *Nirvāṇa* and of all sorrow of the *Sangsāra*. Mind in its microcosmic aspect is variously described by the unenlightened, some calling it the ego, or soul.

Complete realization of the essential and undifferentiated oneness of the *Sangsāra* and *Nirvāṇa*, which, according to the Mahāyāna, are the Ultimate Duality, leads to that Deliverance of the Mind taught by the Enlightened One as being the aim and end of the *Dharma*, as it is of all systems of *yoga* and of all Schools of Buddhism and of Hinduism.[2]

II. *NIRVĀṆA*[3]

Nirvāṇa, the State Transcendent Over Sorrow, and, thus, over the *Sangsāra*, is a state of vacuity, of the Voidness of the

---

[1] For fuller interpretation of the Chinese view of the *Tri-Kāya*, the student is referred to the Rev. K. L. Reichelt's *Truth and Tradition in Chinese Buddhism* (Shanghai, 1934), pp. 357–9.

[2] See *Tibetan Yoga and Secret Doctrines*, pp. 6–7.

[3] This part of the Introduction is supplementary to the more technical exposition of *Nirvāṇa* presented in the General Introduction to *Tibetan Yoga and Secret Doctrines*, pp. 7–9, and should be read in connexion therewith.

Mahāyāna, for it is empty of all conceivable things, or qualities, which are of the *Sangsāra*, the opposite of *Nirvāṇa*. *Nirvāṇa*, as the Buddha teaches, neither is nor is not; is neither existence nor non-existence, being nor non-being, all of which are, as Nāgārjuna shows, illusory dualities. *Nirvāṇa*, being thus beyond all *sangsāric* concepts, transcends all human predication.

Nirvāṇa cannot be intellectually realized, because it is beyond intellect. Not being relative to any thing, it transcends relativity; and, being beyond conception, is of the Voidness.

All dualities depend upon the human intellect, which, in its turn, is a reflex, in the realm of appearances, of the Thatness, of the True State, of *Nirvāṇa*. The Sun gives forth light and energy, but is transcendent over both. *Nirvāṇa*, as the Voidness, is the Source of *sangsāric* existence, yet transcends it. Even as the Sun remains unchangedly the Sun, notwithstanding its emanations of light and energy, so *Nirvāṇa* remains the Quiescent, although the ultimate initiator of mundane activities. Man, mundane mind, life, energy, are illusorily individualized aspects, or manifestations, of That, which is the unique and indivisible At-one-ment of All Things; they are, as our treatise teaches, of the One Mind. Man *per se* is and has been eternally immersed in the One Mind, in the Voidness.

The True State, *Nirvāṇa*, as the Voidness, like the Sun, shines unceasingly. Man by his involution in the realm of appearances, without Right Guidance, misinterprets the world; he strives after illusion rather than reality, the evanescent rather than the permanent, the unreal rather than the Real. His mind loses its primitiveness; it becomes learned in Ignorance, puffed up with pride in its own perishable creations; from the Sea of Appearances rise up the mists and clouds of *Māyā* which hide from man the splendour of the Radiance of the Real. Through the *Māyā*, illuminated by the Radiance beyond it, man on Earth receives the feeble light of the mundane mind; he gropes in the shadows, and cannot perceive the Perfect Truth. The Buddhas are those who have penetrated Ignorance, risen above the shadows and mirages of life by the power of *yoga*, and standing, as it were, upon the summit of an exceedingly high mountain, above the clouds and mists obscuring the world of men, who prefer the valleys to the mountains, have beheld the unclouded Sun.

The process of spiritual unfoldment, to which mankind either consciously or unconsciously are parties, is a process of dissipating the *Māyā*. *Māyā* literally means 'illusion'. To a Buddha, *Māyā* is the manifestation, as the *Sangsāra*, of that creative energy inherent in the Cosmos and spoken of in the *Tantras* as the Universal Mother, or *Shakti*, through whose womb embodied beings come into existence. When this energy is latent, there is no Creation and hence no *Māyā*. Transcendence over *Māyā*, or a going out of the realm of illusion, implies transcendence over differentiation (or separateness) and transitoriness, or, in other words, a return to primordial at-one-ment, the realization, such as our text teaches, of the One Mind (or Cosmic Consciousness), the re-union of the part with the whole, emancipation from the limitations of time, space, and causation, a rising out of conditioned existence into unconditioned Being *per se*, Buddhahood. The disciple must, accordingly, view the phenomenal Universe not as something to be escaped from, but as being the very essence, in symbol, of that almighty and ineffable essence of the One Mind in eternal evolution, as do those who tread the path of the Yogāchāra. Then, indeed, does life here on this planet Earth become, as the Teachers declare, the greatest good fortune that can ever fall to the lot of sentient beings, the Supreme Opportunity. And 'Who', they ask, 'save the deluded, would prefer Ignorance to Divine Wisdom?' 'The Ten Great Joyful Realizations', as set forth in the 'Precepts of the *Gurus*' (in Volume III of this Tibetan Series), make joyous this initiation into the Mystery of *Māyā*, joyous the Pilgrimage, joyous the returning from the Other Shore, joyous the guiding of others to the Great Liberation.

The Mahāyāna maintains that not only man, but all sentient creatures throughout the *Sangsāra*, will, ultimately, thus reach the end of this evolutionary process. For the *yogin*, however, the normal process is too wearisome, too long and painful. As did Tibet's great *Yogī* Milarepa, he strives to attain the Supreme Goal in a single lifetime, that he may the sooner become a worker for world-betterment; for he is vowed, with the vow of the *Bodhisattva*, not to attain *Nirvāṇa* for himself alone, but chiefly that he may be empowered to return to the *māyā*-shrouded valleys and lead their inhabitants to the Supreme Height, to salute the Sun.

III. TIME AND SPACE

Involved in this Doctrine of Reality is the ancient Indian view of time, as set forth in the treatise, namely, that 'past', 'present', and 'future' are merely concepts of the limited *sangsāric* mind, that in the True State of the unlimited Supra-Mundane Mind there is no time, just as there is no thing. In the True State, the *yogin* realizes that even as time is, in its essentiality, beginningless and endless duration, incapable of division into past, present, and future, so space is dimensionless, and divisionless, and non-existent apart from the One Mind, or the Voidness. In other words, in the True State, Mind is the container of matter and form as of time and space.

Simultaneously with the birth of the Cosmos, time is born, and ceases with the cessation of the Cosmos. Or time is the illusory life or duration of the *Sangsāra*; and when the *Sangsāra* ceases, so does time. It is not movement that begets time; for time is merely indicated by movement, as by the movement of the hands of a clock or by that of the heavenly bodies. Time is, therefore, as Plotinus (III. vii. 11–12) also teaches, nothing more than the measure of movement.

Time, being thus a *sangsāric* concept of mind in its finite or mundane manifestation, has only a relative, not a true, existence. In like manner, 'beginning and ending of time' is merely a dualistic concept, employed by unenlightened men who are under the domination of illusion (Skt. *māyā*). There is timelessness, the unending present, eternal duration, but not past and future, for these are merely another *sangsārically* conceived duality. All things having been completely immersed in the Voidness from beginningless timelessness, are, in their essentiality, as this *yoga* shows, inseparable from it, their True State being, as the Enlightened One taught, Perfect Quiescence, transcendent over time, space, and duration. When Brahman remains quiescent in dreamless sleep there is no Universe, no multiplicity of anything, there are no minds, no consciousnesses; there is but the One Mind (or Consciousness). Time and space have vanished like the indrawn web of the spider. When Brahman passes from dreamlessness to dreaming, all things come forth in this Dream.

To Brahman the Quiescent there is only the beginninglessness and endlessness of duration which is timelessness; to Brahman the Dreamer there are past, present, and future, time, and space. In that True State of Quiescence, Mind is One, or Consciousness is One; but when Mind illusorily ceases to be the Thatness, or the One of all things, and appears to be the Many, then there arise the various states of *sangsāric* consciousness which men call states of sleeping, dreaming, waking, of being born, of living, of dying, and of after-death.

The illusory character of all these *sangsārically*-conceived concepts is clearly set forth in our ' *Yoga* of Knowing the Mind in Its Nakedness', as in the correlative *Yogas* expounded by the Doctrines of the Illusory Body, and of Dreams, in *Tibetan Yoga and Secret Doctrines*. There is, as therein taught, no fixed standard of time. The waking-state conception of time is quite different from that of the dream-state, wherein, in one night or even one moment of waking-state time, the dreamer may go through years, centuries, aeons of experiences, as 'real' in the dream-state as are experiences in the waking-state. Then, again, one dream-state may be superimposed on another dream-state, and that upon another, *ad infinitum*. These demonstrable facts of human experience are for the *yogin* incontrovertible proof of the illusoriness and unfixableness of what men call time. And he deduces therefrom, as he advances in *yoga*, that every conceivable state, of the dream-world, of the waking-world, of the after-death-world, and of the *Sangsāra* as a whole, is unreal. Then, as he wakes up from all of them, he is truly the Awakened One, transcendent over time and space.

Thus the Great Sages of India and of Tibet long ago understood the occult truths concerning time and space, of which European thinkers are only now, in the twentieth century of the Occident's as yet unbroken Dark Age, beginning to catch glimpses.

IV. THE NATURE OF MIND

Correlatively, a few of the more adventurous of those who indomitably battle against Ignorance in the occidental world are prepared to postulate as scientific another of the long-accepted axioms of their oriental brethren in scientific research, namely, that mind and matter are, in their final analysis, indistinguishable, matter being, as the 'Yoga of Knowing the Mind' also implies, merely what may be called a crystalline or illusory aspect of mind concretely manifested.[1] Of mind *per se*, concerning which the Occident has no clear, if any, conception whatsoever, our text teaches:

In its true state [of unmodified, unshaped primordialness], mind is naked, immaculate; not made of anything, being of the Voidness; clear, vacuous, without duality, transparent; timeless, uncompounded, unimpeded, colourless [or devoid of characteristic]; not realizable as a separate thing, but as the unity of all things, yet not composed of them; of one taste [i.e. of the Voidness, Thatness, or Ultimate Reality], and transcendent over differentiation.

From the standpoint of Western Science, particularly of dynamics and physics, the One Mind is the unique root of energy, the potentiality of potentialities, the sole dynamo of universal power, the initiator of vibrations, the unknown source, the womb whence there come into being the cosmic rays and matter in all its electronic aspects, as light, heat, magnetism, electricity, radio-activity, or as organic and inorganic substances in all their manifold guises, visible and invisible, throughout the realm of nature. It is thus the maker of natural law, the master and administrator of the Universe, the architect of the atom and the builder therewith of world systems, the sower of nebulae, the reaper of harvests of

[1] See *Tibetan Yoga and Secret Doctrines*, pp. 16–17.

universes, the immutable store-house of all that has been, is now, and ever shall be.

The One Mind, as Reality, is the Heart which pulsates forever, sending forth purified the blood-streams of existence, and taking them back again; the Great Breath, the Inscrutable Brahman, the Eternally Unveiled Mystery of the Mysteries of Antiquity, the Goal of all Pilgrimages, the End of all Existence.

When, as the text teaches, mind attains its True State, divested of its robes of illusion, and is naked, it is, like the Brahman, the Quiescent. Then, as temporarily in dreamless sleep or in *samādhi*, like a child that has cast aside its toys, it is transcendent over appearances, over the Cosmos as a whole. For mind in its nakedness, the world, dissolved like a dream by the Full Awakening, ceases to exist. Hence it is that when the world ceases to exist, so do time and space, they being of the same illusory nature as is the mundaneness of mind. Even as in the *Sangsāra*, time is illusorily divided into past, present, and future, or is seen severally rather than as a unity, so mind is divided into the multiplicity of finite minds. Although the Sun may shine in each of a thousand rooms of a palace, its unity is not affected; although the One Mind illuminates the innumerable myriads of finite minds, it remains inseparably a unit. Nor does the One Mind contain any thought such as men know. Although it contains all things, yet it is no thing. It comprises all existences, but has no existence.

If the One Mind partook of the essence of time, it would be subject to transitoriness and dissolution. If it partook of the essence of thought, it would not be the Quiescent. If it were a thing, it would not be the transcendent totality of things. If it were of the essence of existences, it would be subject to birth and death.

It is, therefore, the intellectually Unknowable, the Essentiality, or Thatness, of which the *Sangsāra* partakes and by virtue of which it has illusory, or relative, but not real existence.

The microcosmic mind, being the offspring of the Macrocosmic Mind, may, by process of *yoga*, attain ecstatic consciousness of its parental source and become one with it in essence. The drop may merge in the ocean. Whether the drop ceases to be a drop, whether the ocean is to be regarded as being constituted of individualized drops or as being one undifferentiated mass of water, no man can tell until the at-one-ment has come; and then, being no longer man, for him, or for that microcosmic fraction of consciousness through which he once manifested as man, the Cosmos has ceased to exist, has vanished like a dream or like a mirage.

Concerning this ultimate problem, the *Guru* Prince Shri Singha, of ancient Pegu in Burma, declared to his disciple Padma-Sambhava, 'No one yet hath discovered either the Primary Cause or the Secondary Cause. I myself have not been able to do so; and thou, likewise, thou Lotus-Born One, shalt fail in this.'[1]

How then can man, so long as he is man, solve the riddle of existence? The wisest of the *Gurus*, the Buddhas, tell us that it is only by transcending human existence, by rising above the mists of appearances into the Clear Light of Reality, and *sangsārically* ceasing to exist. Man cannot solve the problem of why he is fettered to existence until he recovers consciousness of the preceding state of freedom. If, like a prisoner long immured to a prison, he has no desire to attain freedom, he will continue in bondage indefinitely. If he no longer remembers anything of a preceding state of freedom, and, therefore, believes that there is no such state, he will continue to fix his hopes upon a worldly Utopia until suffering and disillusionment have, after long ages, performed their purpose and stirred in him that Divine Wisdom, that 'true Light, which lighteth every man that cometh into the world'. Then, like one who has lost his way in a wilderness, he will regain the Path.

Paradoxically, as every Great Teacher has taught, it is only by losing one's life that one finds life more abundantly; it is only by ceasing to exist that one transcends existence; it is only when the microcosmic becomes one with the macrocosmic that existence and the cause of existence are knowable.

---

[1] Cf. the Epitome, p. 134.

In the same metaphorical language which the late Sri Ramana Mahārshi of Tiruvannamalai employed to describe the quest of the Absolute, or Transcendent *Ātman*, of the Brāhmins, the parallel quest of the Absolute of the Mahāyāna may also be described: 'Just as a pearl-hunter, aided by heavy stones tied to his feet, dives to the bottom of the ocean and secures the precious pearl, so should man, aided by indomitable will, dive deep within himself and secure the most precious of all jewels.'[1]

Realization of the One Mind, through introspectively attaining understanding of the true nature of its macrocosmic aspect innate in man, is equivalent to the attainment of the Brāhmanical *Moksha* (or *Mukhti*), the Mahāyāna *Nirvāṇa*, the Full Awakening of Buddhahood.

V. INDIVIDUALIZED AND COLLECTIVE MIND

Unenlightened man, being far from the Full Awakening, believes himself to be possessed of an individualized mind uniquely his own ; and this illusion-based belief has given rise to the doctrine of soul. But the Tibetan Teachers declare that the One Cosmic Mind alone is unique ; that, on each of the incalculable myriads of life-bearing orbs throughout space, the One Cosmic Mind is differentiated only illusorily, by means of a reflected, or subsidiary, mind appropriate to, and common to, all living things thereon, as on the planet Earth.

Though there be but a single speaker, his voice may be broadcasted to all the millions of Earth's inhabitants and be heard by each of them individually. Though there be but a single power-house, everywhere throughout the wide confines of a metropolitan city there are electric lights. Though there be but a single sun of a planetary system, innumerable are its rays, giving light and vitality to every one of the multitudinous living things on all its planets. From one cloud fall countless drops of rain.

---

[1] See pp. 71–72, following ; also *Who Am I ?* (p. 10) there referred to. The Editor had the privilege of residing in the Mahārshi's *Āshrama* at Tiruvannamalai for a time during the early part of the year 1936 and of daily sitting at his feet then. Grateful acknowledgement is here made of the Mahārshi's kindly assistance.

Similarly, mankind are a unit of mental illusions. If men were not mentally one, there would be no collective hallucination of the world. If each microcosmic manifestation of mind in each apparently individualized being were a separate mind, it would have its own distinctive illusory world; no two men would see the world the same. It is because mankind's minds, or consciousnesses, are collectively one that all mankind see the same world of phenomenal appearances, the same mountains, the same rivers and oceans, the same clouds and rainbows, the same colours, hear the same sounds, smell the same odours, taste the same tastes, and feel the same sensations.

Thus, there is the illusory one mind, conscious and unconscious, common to all human beings, and in which all sub-human creatures of the Earth share. Upon this collectivity of mind, man's sciences are based; it gives uniformity and continuity to all human knowledge.

This illusory one mind, common to all mankind, in its conscious and unconscious aspects, directs mankind's activities and shapes all mankind's concepts. In its unconscious motivation, it controls the unitary instinct governing the life of a beehive, or of an ant colony, or flock of birds, or herd of wild animals. In its lower, or brutish, aspects, it manifests itself in the oneness of the irrational thinking and behaviour of a rioting mob.

Earth's multitude of human and sub-human creatures, each of them like a single cell, collectively constitute the body of one multicellular organism, mentally illuminated by the One Cosmic Mind. We are, as St. Paul perceived, all members of One Body; or, as the Mahāyāna likewise teaches, other and self are identical. It is because of what the Buddha designates as Ignorance, or lack of right seeing into the facts of incarnate being, that mankind fail to practise the Golden Rule. Instead of mutual helpfulness, or co-operation, we behold man's inhumanity to man, his wars amongst the members of his own body, against himself.

It is only by transcending man's collective hallucination, the hereditary and racial Ignorance which fetters man to the

illusory, the transitory and the lowly, that the Seers behold
the absolute at-one-ment not only of mankind and of every
living thing here on the planet Earth, but of the Cosmos, as a
whole. Behind all these illusory appearances, behind all personality, behind all mind and matter, man should seek the
undifferentiated Thatness, the Unborn, the Unshaped, the
Qualityless, the Non-Cognizable, the Unpredicable, beyond
what those fettered to Ignorance know as soul, or consciousness, or existence.

Nāgājuna and Ashvaghosha, the Patriarchs of the Mādhyamika School, named this beyond-Nature Reality the Voidness
(Skt. *Shūnyatā*); Asaṅga, the founder of the Yogāchāra
School, called it the Basic (or Root) Awareness (Skt. *Ālaya-
Vijñāna*), the all-transcendent consciousness of the One Cosmic Mind. To realize it is to attain *Nirvāṇa*, the omniscience
of One Fully Awakened from the Dream of Ignorance.

As our treatise on the Knowing of the One Mind teaches, it
is by knowing himself in the sense implied by the Delphic
Oracle that man *yogically* merges his microcosmic mundane
consciousness in the supra-mundane All-Consciousness; ceasing to be man, he becomes Buddha: the circumscribed becomes the uncircumscribed, the universalized, the cosmic.

So long as the dew-drop is individualized, it is subject to
many vicissitudes. It is petty, weakly, and without protection; its very existence is wholly precarious. The sunshine
may dry it up, the wind may disperse it, the soil may absorb
it, and it may cease to be. But once united with all other dewdrops, it attains the durability and mightiness of an ocean.
As the Guardians of the Great Path proclaim,

So long as the Sages have separate being, separate ideas, and
separate functions, they have but finite intelligence, and profit
only a small number of creatures; for they have not penetrated
into Buddhahood. But once entered into Buddhahood, they have
but one being, but one infinite intelligence, but one unified
function, and they render service to multitudes of creatures
forever.[1]

---

[1] Cf. *Mahāyāna Sūtralamkara*, Levi's trans., p. 92; or J. B. Pratt, *The
Pilgrimage of Buddhism* (New York, 1928), p. 258.

VI. Wisdom Versus Knowledge

Before entering the path of the higher evolution leading to Buddhahood, the disciple must learn to differentiate Wisdom from Knowledge, the real from the unreal, the transitory from the non-transitory, the *Nirvāṇic* from the *Sangsāric*; and to this end the '*Yoga* of Knowing the Mind [or Divine Wisdom] in its Unobscured Reality [or Nakedness]' is a guide. Mastery of its *yogic* precepts produces not contempt for the world of appearances, but understanding of it; not the egoism of Knowledge, whose realm is the *Sangsāra*, but the selflessness of Wisdom; not desire for self-salvation, but for the enlightenment of all sentient beings.

Accordingly, Tibetan Buddhism teaches that the lower knowledge, or worldly wisdom, is born of the bodily senses in their unenlightened *sangsāric* aspect, and that the higher knowledge, or supramundane wisdom, lies deep hidden in man, beneath its illusive reflections through mundane sensuousness, awaiting the magic touch of the wand of the *Dharma* to awaken. Thus worldly wisdom is imperfect wisdom, even as the moonlight is imperfect sunlight.

The *Kanjur* teaches that there are Eight Treasures of Learning: (1) the treasure of ever-present or innate learning, which, like its ineffable receptacle, the One Mind, cannot be lost, because indestructible; (2) the treasure of *yogic* learning, which develops the mundane mind; (3) the treasure of *yogic* reflection and meditation; (4) the treasure of learning to be retained in the mind after having been heard or understood, sometimes, as in our treatise, in the form of precepts or *yogic* formulae; (5) the treasure of fortitude in learning; (6) the treasure of secret, or initiatory, learning, or knowledge of the Doctrine; (7) the treasure of a *Bodhisattva's* saintly heart, born of indomitable faith in the *Tri-Kāya*; and (8) the treasure of spiritual perfection. The Absolute, or Divine, Wisdom (Tib. *Shes-rab*: pron. *Shey-rab*) itself is, according to the Mahāyāna, manifested or acquired in three ways: through listening to the *Dharma*, through reflecting upon the *Dharma*, and through meditating upon the *Dharma*. It is the *Dharma*, or Truth, which, transcendent over learning, teaches Wisdom, and trains the disciple to discern the true from the false, the evanescent from the everlasting, the urges of the finite human mind or intellect from the divine intuition of the supramundane consciousness, the eye-doctrine from the heart-doctrine.

Self-praise, born of pride of worldly learning, the disciple must avoid, knowing it to be one of Māra's poisoned arrows. The disciple should seek the Bread of Wisdom, of which the immortals partake; worldly learning is but the husk of the Wheat of Gold. Such knowledge as the world can give is transitory; it concerns only the external, the phenomenal. Divine Wisdom comes from the *Hridaya*, the Secret Heart; it concerns only the internal, the invisible *Sat*, the Real, the Noumenal, the Source. Knowledge is of the existent, Wisdom of the non-existent.

Wisdom dissipates the mists of illusion. Like its receptacle, the One Mind, Wisdom knows neither past nor future; it is timeless and eternal. Being of the Secret Essence of the Sun, it conquers the darkness of Ignorance. The Night flees before Wisdom, and the Day dawns. The wise reject Knowledge, but the ignorant hold it fast. Wisdom is treasured by the few, Knowledge by the multitude.

It is by the alchemy of Wisdom that the gold of life is separated from the dross. Knowledge nurtures the illusory, Wisdom the transcendent. Knowledge is treasured by those who, although alive, are dead, Wisdom by the Awakened Ones. Knowledge teaches of the Shadows and Obscurations, Wisdom of the Shadowless and the Unobscured. Knowledge appertains to the Mutable, Wisdom to the Immutable.

Those who tread the Wisdom Path transcend all the illusions of the world. To pleasure and to pain they are indifferent, knowing them to be but the two extremes of a dualism. They seek to exhaust their *karmic* attachment to Knowledge and to Ignorance of the Law. As one who was a disciple of the Tibetan *Gurus* has taught: 'Be humble if thou wouldst attain to Wisdom. Be humbler still when Wisdom thou hast mastered.'

Those who have possessed Wisdom have been the Teachers

of Men and the Directors of Culture. Those who have possessed only Knowledge have been the war-lords of nations and the creators of Dark Ages.

The aspirant for Wisdom must not become fettered by the false learning of men. The senses, the source of all the sorrow of the *Sangsāra*, must be *yogically* disciplined, and all misleading mental concepts be dominated. Personality must be impersonalized. Neither praise nor blame, success nor failure, good nor evil, are to be allowed to turn one from the course of those right actions constituting the Noble Eightfold Path. As the treatise itself teaches, the treader of the Path must pass beyond illusion's realm and reach that true state of immutableness personified by the Dhyāni Buddha Vajra-Sattva.

Apart from their all-embracing categories of Reality, wherein Knowledge and Wisdom were a unity, the Oriental Sages of old possessed no such classification of phenomenal appearances as that of modern Occidental Science. But today, understanding of the external world, with which our scientists are chiefly concerned, has come to be called Knowledge in contradistinction to that understanding called Wisdom with which the masters of *yoga* are concerned.

Knowledge is differentiable; Wisdom, transcendentally conceived, as partaking of the One Mind, is a homogeneous whole, incapable of differentiation. Knowledge is essentially utilitarian and mundane; Wisdom transcends utilitarianism and the concrete. Knowledge may be racial, or national, and is ever limited; Wisdom is universal, or catholic. Knowledge, being wholly dependent upon transitory phenomena, is fallible and illusory; it is the offspring of the Great Mother *Māyā*; it deludes man, and veils from him Reality. Its characteristics are, therefore, dependence and incompleteness; whereas those of Wisdom are independence and completeness; for Wisdom is the unique root and the at-one-ment of all understanding. It is Wisdom which enables the Sages to apply Knowledge wisely.

Knowledge, like human life itself, if employed aright, becomes, for occidental man, a pathway to the all-complete Wisdom; for him it serves as a light on the quest for self-realization. But for the oriental *yogin*, the Pathway of Knowledge is too full of pitfalls, too wearisome and long; by what the Tibetan *Gurus* call the 'Short Path', he attains to Wisdom first, and then, as from the heights of a great mountain, surveys the Kingdom of *Māyā*, which is the Kingdom of Knowledge. Comprehension of noumena automatically produces knowledge of phenomena. 'Who', the Tibetan Sages ask, 'would be so foolish as to prefer a pellet of goat's dung to the Wish-Granting Gem?'

As set forth above, it has ever been necessary for the aspirant after Wisdom to renounce Knowledge, to cleanse his mind of all intellectualism preparatory to the incoming tide of that knowing which, as Plotinus teaches, is above intellect. Unguided by Wisdom, Knowledge ever leads to bitter disillusionment, even as life leads to death.

Knowledge, being the product of utilitarianism, is the foundation of the world's educational systems, designed chiefly to prepare mankind for the parasitic exploitation of the riches of nature and thus to enhance their own *sangsāric* sensuousness. But Wisdom, as the Buddhas and Wise Ones have taught, being born of world renunciation, of selflessness, leads not to worldliness, but to *Bodhisattvic* Altruism.

Fettered to the Wheel of Knowledge, the race of men pass from disillusionment to disillusionment unceasingly. Misled by the will-o'-the-wisps of *sangsāric* sensuousness, few there are among the millions of incarnate beings who escape the quagmires and the mirages of worldly existence. Steeped in Knowledge, unguided by Wisdom, they are overwhelmed by pride; and not until myriads of lifetimes have been frittered away in the worthless doings of *Māyā's* Kingdoms do they become humbled and seek for freedom. Then there enter into the darkness of their animal nature the first rays of the New-born Sun.

It is for those who have been aroused by the Light of Dawn, who now hunger after Wisdom, and are prepared to put Knowledge aside as being of no further use on the Pilgrimage, that this book has been written.

Abuse of worldly learning leads to that destructiveness and

retrogression of which we who live in this century are the witnesses. Many of the forces discovered by Western Science have been harnessed more to the degradation than to the upliftment of man. Until Knowledge shall be transmuted into Wisdom by the alchemy of spiritual understanding, which sees that all things are one and that the outer laws of Nature are no more than emanations or reflexes of inner laws, man will remain, as he is now, in bondage to *Māyā* and Ignorance. The chief purpose of Science should not be to exploit for purely selfish and uninspiring utilitarian ends the forces of the phenomenal universe, but to investigate and so come to know and apply for social betterment the far mightier forces of the Atom of Atoms, present in man himself.

It is in Wisdom, not in Knowledge, that in future time man will, at last, discover Right Law, Right Society, Right Government. When his age-long quest for happiness in Knowledge shall have been abandoned as futile, he will find transcendence over sorrow in Wisdom. He will then have realized that in Wisdom alone is there true power; that Wisdom is the sole source of true progress; that Knowledge is the creator of Iron Ages and Wisdom the creator of Golden Ages.

The problem herein presented is a problem not for Europe and America alone; it must be faced by every Oriental who has grown intoxicated with the wine of westernization, by commercialized and Knowledge-loving oriental nations, as by all in Hindustan who have allowed the world-obsessing demons of politics and hankerings after the perishable comforts and pleasures afforded by Western Science to become their tutelary deities. In the Acquarian Age, as in this New Age now being entered upon, India, if she remains faithful to those Great Masters of Wisdom who have preserved her since prehistoric times, who have enabled her to witness the passing of Egypt and Babylon, of Greece and Rome and Spain, shall once more, phœnix-like, arise from the ashes of the present and, strengthened by realization of the failure of Knowledge, retain the spiritual leadership of the world. If she chooses Knowledge and ceases to cherish Wisdom, then shall history record her temptation and her fall. Then shall the whole

Earth, as never before in the annals of time, be conquered by Ignorance and Darkness. The progress of humanity will be retarded for centuries, perhaps for millenniums. Its great cities, the strongholds of Knowledge, will become the grave-yards of their builders. Barbarism will have conquered not a race, a continent, or an empire, but the whole man-bearing Planet. And not until those who seek to guide, but who cannot guide when guidance is refused, send a new Messenger, a new Culture Hero, shall the Sacred Fire be rekindled in the hearts of men.

VII. ILLITERACY AND UTILITARIANISM

The subject-matter of the ' *Yoga* of Knowing the Mind in Its Nakedness' ends with the statement, 'Even a cowherd [or an illiterate person] may by realization attain Liberation'. The Great *Guru* himself, like the Buddha, having exhausted literacy, and ascertained, as have all Sages, its non-essentiality, did not insist upon it in his disciples. One of the most successful of these was the illiterate cowherd Hūm-Kāra, of whom our Epitome tells. Nor have all Prophets and Teachers been scholars. Eminent Moslem authorities believe that Mohammed was unable to read and write, and that he dictated the *Koran* under angelic inspiration. In his youth, he, too, had been a shepherd boy, tending his flocks in the wild mountains of Arabia, where he meditated and practised *yoga*, and so attained divine insight. Although the boy Jesus taught in the synagogue and confounded the learned, his training was that of a carpenter; and there is no evidence that He was literate apart from the uncertain passage in the Gospel of St. John (viii. 8), wherein it is said that with His finger He 'wrote on the ground'—whether in symbols, letters, or meaninglessly is unknown.

Milarepa, Tibet's Great *Yogī*, when confronted by a proud *pandit*, representative of the worldly arrogance of the intellectually learned, addressed him thus:

Accustomed long to meditating on the Whispered Chosen Truths,
I have forgot all that is said in written and in printed books.

Accustomed, as I've been, to study of the Common Science,
Knowledge of erring Ignorance I've lost.

.   .   .   .   .   .

Accustomed long to keep my mind in the Uncreated State of
    Freedom,
I have forgot conventional and artificial usages.

.   .   .   .   .   .

Accustomed long to know the meaning of the Wordless,
I have forgot the way to trace the roots of verbs and source of
    words and phrases;
May thou, O learned one, trace out these things in standard
    books.[1]

To most Occidentals, illiteracy is regarded as a most fright-
ful evil. This is due, in large measure, to their bondage to
appearances, their educational systems being almost wholly
utilitarian and directed to the production of material things
—many of which are quite unnecessary for true progress
—and to the exploitation of the Earth's natural resources
rather than to the knowing of man *per se*. Oriental thinkers,
who long ago realized the short-comings of literacy un-
directed by spiritual insight, have always maintained that
one need not be able to read and write or hold academic
degrees in order to attain the truly Higher Education. The
Editor, in his own world-wide study of humanity, has found
many of the noblest and wisest men and women wholly illiterate. He has intimately known illiterate peasants in remote
parts of Eire, in the western Hebrides, on the Continent of
Europe, in Egypt, Ceylon, India, Tibet, and China who were
better thinkers and more cultured than most graduates of
colleges and universities. The two French peasant girls, Joan
of Arc, and Bernadette Soubirous to whom the Lady of Lourdes
appeared, are illustrations, out of many in all ages and faiths,
of how spiritual power is transcendent over what men proudly
call 'education' and 'culture'. St. Catherine of Siena, too,
was an illiterate daughter of the people, who attained spiritual
illumination after three years of *yogic* retreat and meditation

---

[1] For the full narrative, see *Tibet's Great Yogī Milarepa* (pp. 244 ff.),
which illustrates, as a whole, the remarkable results of the practical application of the teachings set forth in our present volume.

and then returned to the world and dominated the political life of Italy.

The Occident is as misdirected educationally as it is socially and economically. The chief purpose of occidental education and government appears to be to foster economic prosperity by continually increasing unnecessarily the wants of the people, and thus to keep factories occupied. Naturalness, and that dignified simplicity of the Simple Way of Lao-tze, which Thoreau, Lao-tze's American disciple, taught, without any apparent effect other than academic upon Americans, survive only in inaccessible regions of 'lost horizons', and largely among such as are illiterate cowherds and peasants.

Education, as conceived in the Occident, results in not much more than an increase of international economic competitiveness, more and more utilitarianly applied science, largely directed to destructiveness and war, and mechanical devices intended to increase animal comfort. And occidental progress implies ever new creation of fresh fetterings to appearances, to *māyā*, to unreality.

Occidental 'education', whether called 'higher' or 'lower', is, in fact, as the *Gurus* maintain, merely training for the purpose of gaining a living, and, as such, should be regarded as the lowest; the truly Higher Education is directed to the one end of transcending appearances, to attaining a more satisfactory state than the human state of being. But until Occidentals believe that such a superior state is attainable, they will continue to exploit one another, and to strive after purely materialistic standards of 'education' and 'living' called 'higher'.

Unless Science, like Philosophy, is directed chiefly to human betterment, to raising the spiritual, along with the material, standard of life on Earth, it is not, in the oriental view, worthy the name Science. Thus, the true concern of chemistry should be, as it was when it was known as alchemy, the quest for the elixir of life in the occult sense, for the philosopher's stone which transmutes the human into the divine, and not for purely utilitarian ends, fostering selfishness rather than altruism. An astronomy concerned merely with the physics

and mechanics of the Universe or with the calculation of
celestial distances and the cataloguing of stars, and wholly
neglectful of the application of astronomical knowledge to the
end that man may be better understood in his relation to the
heavenly bodies, as in astrology, is equally utilitarian and
spiritually fruitless.

When, on the contrary, the Great *Guru* studied the science
of the stars in its original form of astrology, he applied it to
understanding man. Similarly, instead of undertaking any
such intellectual pursuit as that which is entailed by the study
of dogmatic theology, he practised the applied psychological
science of *yoga*. He applied himself to arts and crafts not in
order to win worldly wealth, but to acquire a better understanding of the worldly activities of men. His study of
linguistics was not directed to philology, but to the comprehension of human mentalities, and to the reading of the riddle
of existence by confabulating with gods and demons and
other sentient creatures throughout the *Sangsāra*. He did not
study systems of philosophy and *yoga* in order to become a
pandit, but to master life. And, like Milarepa's, Padma-
Sambhava's goal, in all that he studied under his many *gurus*
on Earth and in non-human worlds, was not simply knowledge
of the mundane, but, more especially, of the Divine Wisdom
of the Supra-mundane. The Great *Guru* sought not intellectual power, but insight into Reality, beyond the *Sangsāra*, in
the True State, in the vacuity of the Voidness.

Here again the late Mahārshi of Tiruvannamalai contributed independent confirmatory testimony: 'There may come
a time when one shall have to forget all that one has learnt.
Rubbish that is swept together and heaped up is to be thrown
away. No need is there to make any analysis of it.'[1]

On behalf of Europe, Plotinus likewise testifies to the same
truth, which, being realizable, and thus capable of proof, has
been expounded by Seers during all epochs, in all nations,
races, and faiths, in parallel manner:

Our comprehension of the One cometh to us neither by scientific
knowledge, nor by thought, as doth the knowledge of other

[1] This recension is based upon *Who Am I?* (cf. p. 14).

intelligible things, but by a presence which is superior to science. When the knowing-principle in man acquireth scientific knowledge of something, it withdraweth from unity and ceaseth to be entirely one; for science implieth discursive reason and discursive reason implieth manifoldness. We must, therefore, transcend science, and never withdraw from what is essentially One; we must renounce science, the objects of science, and every other intellectual pursuit. Even Beauty must be put aside, for beauty is posterior to unity, being derived therefrom, as is the light of the day from the Sun. Accordingly, Plato saith that Unity is unspeakable and indescribable. Nevertheless, we speak and write of it only to stir our higher natures thereby, and so direct them towards this Divine Vision, just as we might point out the road to someone who desireth to traverse it. The teaching itself goeth only so far as is requisite to point out the Path and to guide one thereon; the attaining of the Vision is the task of each one alone who seeketh it.[1]

Plotinus thus demonstrates that Beauty, or Art (conceived as an emanation of the One Mind), is not of a primary nature, as is sometimes assumed in aesthetics, but of secondary nature and importance. This accords with the *yogic* view, as set forth herein in Section IX, entitled 'Good and Evil'.

It is not commonly recognized among Occidentals that there are methods of imparting culture other than through literacy, which, according to the *Gurus*, is the least efficient of all. Four methods are employed in the Orient: (1) through telepathy, or psychic osmosis; (2) through abstract symbols, such as *mudrās* made by the various members of the body, and *maṇḍalas* inscribed on the earth or painted on paper, cloth or wood; and also through concrete symbols, which may be geometrical forms, images, living animals and their effigies, the celestial bodies, and magically produced forms; (3) through sound, as in music or audibly expressed *mantras*, or spoken words, which are often whispered into the ear of the neophyte in initiations; (4) through written words, setting forth the secret doctrines, usually in symbolical and very abstruse technical and metaphorical style. The first method is the highest, the fourth is the lowest method of imparting the Higher Learning.

[1] Cf. Plotinus, VI. ix. 4.

VIII. THE GREAT *GURU*

In the following presentation of Padma-Sambhava, the Great *Guru* and Culture Hero, there is no need to consider, save in passing, sectarian criticism of him. Although some who are of the Gelugpa, or Reformed School, which grew out of the Nyingmapa School founded by Padma-Sambhava, may be his critics, he is, nevertheless, reverenced by all sects of Tibetan Buddhism; and on Yellow-Cap altars, both in temples and private homes, as on those of the Red Caps, and in all the chief Gelugpa monasteries such as Sera, Drepung, and Ganden, his image occupies a place of prominence, sometimes alongside that of the Buddha. In the Yellow Cap, or Gelugpa, Monastery at Ghoom, in Darjeeling, for instance, while the Editor was living just outside it, the Gelugpa artist, then painting frescoes of various members of the Buddhist pantheon, took quite as much delight in painting the figure of Padma-Sambhava on one wall as of Tsong-Khapa, the founder of the Gelugpa School, in a corresponding position of prominence on the opposite wall. The criticism vulgarly directed against the character of the Great *Guru* is considered at some length in the Section entitled 'Good and Evil' which immediately follows, and that relating to his Tantricism receives consideration in the next Section entitled 'Tantric Buddhism'.

The historic fact, that during the latter part of the eighth century A.D. Padma-Sambhava was recommended to the King of Tibet by some of India's most famous scholars as being the greatest master of the occult sciences then known, is sufficient attestation of the high esteem in which the Great *Guru* was held by his contemporaries.

The King, Thī-Srong-Detsan, who reigned from A.D. 740 to 786, having accepted the recommendations, invited Padma-Sambhava to Tibet to help in the re-establishment of Buddhism. The Biography tells of the *Guru's* acceptance of the royal invitation and of his departure from Bōdh-Gayā in December of the year 746, and of his arrival in Tibet early in the spring of the following year. The *Guru* spent a number of years in Tibet; the Biography, typically oriental in its exaggeration of numbers, states that he passed III years there. At all events, he supervised the building of the first Buddhist monastery in Tibet, that at Sāmyé, overthrew the ancient ascendency of Tibet's shamanistic pre-Buddhist religion known as the Bön (or Bön-pa), and firmly established the Tantric or deeply esoteric form of Tibetan Buddhism. As a direct result of Padma-Sambhava's efforts, the people of Tibet were elevated from a state of barbarism to a state of unsurpassed spiritual culture. He is, therefore, truly one of the greatest of the world's Culture Heroes.

His less critical devotees generally regard the strange stories told of him in the Biography as being literally and historically true; the more learned interpret them symbolically. And the anthropologist observes that the historic Padma-Sambhava, like the historic King Arthur, is barely discernible amidst the glamour of legend and myth. As a master of miracles, Padma-Sambhava resembles the famous Pythagorean, Apollonius of Tyana (who died about A.D. 96); and there appears to be no good reason for doubting the adeptship in magic of either hero. Precisely like Apollonius, Padma is credited with having understood the languages of men and of beasts, and with ability to read their most secret thoughts. Both heroes alike dominated demons, resuscitated the dead, and, in all their supernormal deeds, strove to deliver the unenlightened from Ignorance. Having been white magicians, their aim was always altruistic and productive of good. There is probably no miracle attributed to Jesus or the Apostles which Apollonius, like Padma, could not perform.[1] Greek and Roman

[1] As the late Lāma Kazi Dawa-Samdup contended, Christian theology is open to criticism for its insistence upon the paramount importance of miracles in the life of Jesus, whom the Lāma regarded as being a Great Yogī and Bodhisattva. Partly because of this insistence, modern sages of the Orient say that Christianity, as interpreted by Church Councils, is representative of a purely exoteric religion. In this connexion they refer to its animistic teachings concerning the soul, its range of vision limited to the Sangsāra (i.e. to Earth, Heaven, and Hell), and its lack of any doctrine (such as Gnostic Christianity, which it has decreed to be heretical, did hold) concerning transcendence over this purely sangsāric eschatology comparable with the Brāhmanical Moksha or the Buddhist Nirvāṇa. And in their view, the performance of miracles—as Jesus Himself implied by saying that His followers would do greater things than He had done—is no proof, as it is

accounts of moving and speaking images find parallels in the Biography.[1] Even the striking of a rock with a staff, resulting in the immediate issuance of water, quite after the manner of the water-miracle performed by Moses, is credited to Padma. According to trustworthy tradition and accounts of modern travellers who have visited the place, the water continued flowing and still issues from the rock to this very day.

The date of the Great *Guru's* appearance, as a babe in the midst of the lotus on the Dhanakosha Lake, cannot be stated with historical accuracy. One of the prophecies, mentioned in our Epitome of the Biography, would make the date to be twelve years after the Buddha's passing, while other prophecies recorded in the Biography name various irreconcilable dates. On folio 333 of our text of the Biography, Padma himself is quoted as having said it was eight years after the passing. The Biography takes for granted the belief that Padma, having been immune to illness, old age, and death, is still alive and preaching the *Dharma* to non-human beings, that he flourished in the human world from the unrecorded time of his supernormal birth, presumably soon after the death of the Buddha, in the fifth century B.C., to the time of his departure for the land of the *Rākṣhasas*, 111 years after the date of his arrival in Tibet, or in A.D. 858.[2] The Biography attributes to Padma the statement that he had been alive for three thousand years; and in *The Prophecies of Guru Pema Jungnay* he is reported as having said, 'I uncovered the Chosen Truths, and, turning the sacred wheel of the

vulgarly assumed to be, of spiritual greatness; it is merely the *sangsāric* exercise of powers of magic, which is quite as capable of evil as of good. It was this miraculous aspect of Christianity which converted St. Augustine and proved to be the chief attraction for the emotional and irrational slave converts throughout the spiritually decadent Roman Empire.

[1] An adept in *yoga* can accumulate energy in his own body and, by a sort of wireless radiation, infuse it into an inanimate object, causing that object to move as he wills, just as an electric current, either with or without a connecting wire from an electric accumulator, can be conveyed to a machine and set it in motion. It is in like manner that a far distant *guru* transmits a current of psychic energy to encourage and aid a disciple.

[2] According to Tibetan chronicles, Padma-Sambhava resided in Tibet for about fifty years, and announced his approaching departure in A.D. 802. Cf. L. A. Waddell, *The Buddhism of Tibet* (Cambridge, 1934), p. 32[1].

Dharma, I made India happy; and there I lived for 3,600 years'.[1]

Learned *lāmas*, both of the Reformed and Unreformed Sects, believe that when the Buddha was dying He said, 'I will take rebirth as Padma-Sambhava for the special purpose of preaching the Esoteric *Dharma*'. This belief appears to be based upon a passage in the *Kanjur*, or the Tibetan Canon, to the effect that the Buddha when about to pass away was asked why He had not taught the Tantric Mysteries, and made reply that, having been born of a human womb, He was unfitted to do so, that He needed to attain superhuman birth in order to enjoy the pure body through which alone the Secret Doctrine of the *Tantras* can be revealed. He added, 'In the Heaven-Worlds I will convoke a vast assembly of the Great Ones, from the Ten Directions, and decision shall be taken as to whether or not the Tantric Mysteries are to be taught'. Accordingly, when the Buddha had passed on, the divine convocation was called together by Him; and the Buddhas of past aeons and many Great *Bodhisattvas* assembled and reached a favourable decision. And thus, as Tibetan Buddhists believe, the Buddha Gautama once more took birth on Earth, as Padma-Sambhava; and the tenth day of the fifth month of the Tibetan calendar is sacred to this coming into incarnation of the Great *Guru*.[2]

The supernormal birth of Padma-Sambhava from a lotus blossom signifies immaculate birth, that is, birth unsullied by a human womb. Such birth, so the *Kanjur* account implies, is essential to a Tantric incarnation or emanation of the Buddha Essence. Lotus birth is normal among *devas* in the

---

[1] This excerpt comes from fragmentary translations of the said work by the late Lāma Kazi Dawa-Samdup which the Editor recently discovered in the Lāma's notebooks.

[2] Although the Great *Guru's* day of birth is held to be the tenth of the fifth month of the Tibetan calendar, the birthday celebration has been shifted to the fifteenth day, because that is the full-moon day. This day, the fifteenth, is called by the Great *Guru's* devotees '*Jamling Chisang*', or 'The Blessed Day for the World'. Also the tenth day of the fifth month, the true birthday, and, correlatively, the tenth day of every month of the Tibetan calendar, are observed as the Great *Guru's* Day, and the Tibetans call it '*Tse-chu*', which means 'The Tenth'.—Lāma Karma Sumdhon Paul.

various *deva* worlds; and, although Padma-Sambhava is not
the only one of humankind said to have been born of a lotus
blossom, his devotees believe him to be the only Buddha so
far born in that manner. Another marked characteristic of
the Great *Guru*, as suggested by Illustration V, was his exercise of the *yogic* power, said to be still practised in Tibet,
of shape-shifting, multiplication and invisibility of bodily
form.[1] The description of the Illustration tells of the Eight

[1] The Tibetan belief concerning this *yoga* of dominion over bodily form
may be summarized as follows:

Through transcendental direction of that subtle mental faculty, or psychic power, whereby all forms, animate and inanimate, including man's own
form, are created, the human body can either be dissolved, and thereby be
made invisible, by *yogically* inhibiting the faculty, or be made mentally
imperceptible to others, and thus equally invisible to them, by changing the
body's rate of vibration. When the mind inhibits emanation of its radio-
activity, it ceases to be the source of mental stimuli to others, so that they
become unconscious of the presence of an adept of the art, just as they are
unconscious of invisible beings living in a rate of vibration unlike their own.
Inasmuch as the mind creates the world of appearances, it can create any
particular object desired. The process consists of giving palpable being to a
visualization, in very much the same manner as an architect gives concrete
expression in three dimensions to his abstract concepts after first having
given them expression in the two dimensions of his blue-print. The Tibetans
call the One Mind's concretized visualization the *Khorva* (*Hkhorva*), equivalent to the Sanskrit *Sangsāra*; that of an incarnate deity, like the Dalai
or Tashi Lāma, they call a *Tul-ku* (*Sprul-sku*), and that of a magician a
Tul-pa (*Sprul-pa*), meaning a magically produced illusion or creation. A
master of *yoga* can dissolve a *Tul-pa* as readily as he can create it; and his
own illusory human body, or *Tul-ku*, he can likewise dissolve, and thus out-
wit Death. Sometimes, by means of this magic, one human form can be
amalgamated with another, as in the instance of the wife of Marpa, *guru* of
Milarepa, who ended her life by incorporating herself in the body of Marpa.

Madame Alexandra David-Neel, who investigated these magical matters
among the Tibetans, states that 'a phantom horse trots and neighs. The
phantom rider who rides it can get off his beast, speak with travellers on
the road, and behave in every way like a real person. A phantom house
will shelter real travellers, and so on.' See *With Mystics and Magicians in
Tibet* (London, 1931, p. 316, and throughout chapter viii), a work to which
the Editor gratefully acknowledges assistance. Similarly, a master magician,
such as the Great *Guru* was, can multiply his own or any other illusory form.
Madame David-Neel herself, after some months' practice, succeeded in
creating the form of a monk which followed her about and was seen by
others. She lost control of it, whereupon it grew inimical; and only after six
months of difficult psychic struggle in concentration was she able to dissi-
pate it (cf. ibid., pp. 314–15). In like manner, 'mediums' in the Occident
can, while entranced, automatically and unconsciously create materializa-
tions which are much less palpable than the consciously produced *Tul-pas*,
by exuding 'ectoplasm' from their own bodies. Similarly, as is suggested by

Bodily Manifestations which were employed by him, according to need, to make most fitting appeal when preaching the *Dharma* to various types of men, gods, and demons. In the *Great Crown Sutra*, according to a version prepared by the late Mr. Dwight Goddard, the Buddha urges all Great *Bodhisattvas* and *Arhants* to choose to be reborn in the last *kalpa* (or creation period), and to employ all manner of bodily transformations for the sake of emancipating sentient beings. In the Biography itself the Great *Guru* is represented as being able to assume every conceivable shape, animate and inanimate. Our frontispiece, in colour, represents the Great *Guru* in his more ordinary form, as the royal Prince or King of Sahor. In *The Scripture Concerning Ti-ts'ang's Fundamental Promises* (Chinese: *Ti-ts'ang Pen-yüan Ching*) the Buddha says, as He blesses the multitudinous forms in which the *Bodhisattva* Ti-ts'ang, for the sake of saving others, has incarnated during many *kalpas*:

I constantly take various forms and make use of countless different methods to save the unfortunate. I change myself into a heavenly god like Brahma, into a god of transformations, into a king, a minister, or a relative of a minister. I manifest myself as a nun, as a man who devotes himself to Buddhism in the quiet of his own house, as a woman who gives herself to meditation in the stillness of home. I do not hold obstinately to my Buddha body. I take upon myself all the above-mentioned bodily forms in order to be able to rescue all [beings].[1]

As will be seen in the Epitome of the Biography, Padma-Sambhava was ever active, even as a child. His early life as a royal prince and his renunciation resemble those of the Buddha. In the beginning of his religious career he is the pupil rather than the teacher; he exhausts the learning of every type of human and non-human *guru*, and receives numerous initiations and initiatory names. Afterwards, in company with his *shakti* and chief disciple, Mandāravā, he is

instances of phantasms of the living reported by psychic research, a thought-form may be made to emanate from one human mind and be hallucinatorily perceived by another, although possessed of little or no palpableness.

[1] Cf. K. L. Reichelt, op. cit., p. 109.

shown practising *yoga*. More often he is represented preaching the *Dharma*. His mission in the human world takes him to all parts of India, to Persia, China, Nepal, Bhutan, Sikkim, and Tibet. At other times he is in non-human worlds, either being taught by Buddhas or teaching gods, demons, unhappy ghosts, and inhabitants of the hells.

In short, as stated in other words in the Introduction to the Epitome, around Padma-Sambhava are centred, like systems of worlds around a Central Sun, legends, mythologies, doctrinal systems, hierarchies of deities, and the root teachings of Mahāyāna Buddhism, aureoled by all the gorgeous glamour of oriental imagery. His field of action is the Cosmos; his religious mission embraces every sentient creature, in all worlds, paradises, and hells. Master of all human arts and crafts and systems of philosophy, an initiate of all schools of the occult sciences, perfect in *yoga*, transcendent over good and evil, immune to illness, old age and death, and not subject to birth, and thus greater than the Buddha Gautama, he is the idealized exponent of the Divine Wisdom practically applied.

So viewed, Padma-Sambhava is the world's supreme Culture Hero. Osiris, Mithras, Odin, Odysseus, Arthur, Quetzalcoatl, and the others equal him in some things, but not in all.

Much of the Biography is written in symbolical language, which, to interpret fully, would require one who has had complete initiation in all schools, exoteric and esoteric, of Tantric Buddhism, such as no known Occidental has had. The section entitled 'Tantric Buddhism' will illustrate this in more detail.

Consideration of the general and by far the most serious criticism directed against the Great *Guru* by those who disapprove of his Tantric doctrines, namely, that he advocates disregard for all commonly recognized standards of right and wrong, is reserved for the special Section entitled 'Good and Evil', where this charge is met at the necessary length. Consideration may here be given to the related and equally serious charge that the Great *Guru* was a slave to strong drink and that he advocated the use of wine among his followers.

Devotees of the Great *Guru* with whom the Editor discussed this charge, have replied:

Yes; it is true that the Precious *Guru* did drink to the point of
intoxication, and taught his disciples to do likewise. But the
liquor was the ambrosia of the gods, the elixir of life, the nectar of
immortality. They who quaff deeply of it become so intoxicated
that they lose all consciousness of the world of appearances.

In most images and paintings of Padma-Sambhava, as in
the frontispiece of this volume, he is shown holding in his left
hand a cup made of a human skull, symbolical of renunciation
of the *Sangsāra*, filled with this divine liquor, which he offers
to all who choose him as their *Guru*, bidding them drink of it
and so attain the Great Liberation. In Sūfism, as illustrated
by the symbolical poem of Omar Khayyām, wine-drinking
and intoxication have the same esoteric significance.

Parallel criticism is directed against modern Hindu Tantrics of Bengal. There are those of them who are of the Inner
Circle and those who are of the Outer Circle. To the former,
the latter are the uninitiated, the immature, awaiting enlightenment. Those who are of the Outer Circle, the exotericists, drink real wine, eat real flesh, and have real *shakta* and
shakti sexual union. But to those who are fully initiated, all
these things are done symbolically; for to them it is given to
know the Mysteries, but to them that are without it is not
given.[1] When the Great *Guru* was accused of conjugal irreg-

---

[1] Cf. Arthur Avalon (Sir John Woodroffe) *Tantra of the Great Liberation*
(London, 1913), pp. cxv–cxix. The aim of Tantric worship is union with the
Brahman; and, men's propensities being such as they are, this is dependent
upon the special treatment prescribed by the *Tantras*. Woman must be
recognized as the image of the Supreme Shakti, the Great Mother, and worshipped with the symbolic elements, by use of which the Universe itself is
employed as the article of worship. Wine signifies the power (*shakti*) which
produces all fiery elements; meat and fish symbolize all terrestrial and
aquatic creatures; *mudrā* (in this symbolism, parched grain) symbolizes all
vegetable life, and *maithuna* (sexual union) symbolizes the will (*ichchha*),
action (*kriyā*), and knowledge (*jñāna*), in relation to the Shakti of the
Supreme Prakriti (or matrix of Nature), whence arises that keen pleasure
which accompanies the process of creation. Thus there is offered to the
Great Mother the restless life of Her Universe.

'Wine' is said to be 'that intoxicating knowledge acquired by *yoga* of the
Parabrahman, which renders the worshipper senseless as regards the

ularities (as set forth on page 161, following) he forgave his
critic, and thought to himself, 'Inasmuch as this fellow is
ignorant of the inner significance of the Mahāyāna and of the
yogic practices appertaining to the three chief psychic nerves,
I should pardon him.'

Thus the age-old conflict between esotericism and exotericism still disturbs Buddhism and Hinduism. Islam, too, with
its 'heretical' Sūfis, the esotericists, and its orthodox exotericists, is disturbed by it. In Christianity it completely dis-
rupted the primitive church. The Christian exotericists,
derived largely from uncultured slave populations, inaugur-
ated a religious revolution against the Christian esotericists,
the cultured and well-born followers of the Gnosis; and, the
revolt being successful, the exotericists used the church councils to anathematize the esotericists as a whole. Thus that
form of Christianity which was shaped by the church councils
of the triumphant revolutionaries, and which today dominates

---

external world'. Meat (*māngsa*) is not any fleshly thing, but the act whereby
the *sādhaka* [or devotee] consigns all his acts to Me (*Mām*). *Matsya* (fish) is
that *sattvika* [or pure] knowledge by which, through the sense of 'mineness',
the worshipper sympathizes with the pleasure and pain of all beings. *Mudrā*
is the act of relinquishing all association with evil which results in bondage;
and *maithuna* is the union of the Shakti Kuṇḍalinī with Shiva in the body of
the worshipper. This, the *Yogint Tantra* says, is the best of all unions for
those who have already controlled their passions (*yati*). According to the
Agamasāra, wine is the *somadhārā*, or lunar ambrosia, which drops from the
brāhmarandra. *Māngsa* (meat) is the tongue (*mā*), of which its parts (*angsha*)
are speech; the *sādhaka*, by 'eating' it, controls his speech. *Matsya* (fish) are
those which are constantly moving in the two rivers of *Idā* and *Pingalā*. He
who controls his breath by *prānāyāma*, 'eats' them by *kumbhaka* [retention
of breath in *prānāyāma*]. *Mudrā* is the awakening of knowledge in the peri-
carp of the Great *Sahasrāra* Lotus, where the *Ātmā*, like mercury, resplendent as ten thousand suns, and deliciously cool as ten million moons, is
united with the Devi Kuṇḍalinī. The esoteric meaning of *Maithuna* is thus
stated by the *Āgama* to be 'the union on the purely *sāttvika* plane, which
corresponds on the *rājasika* plane to the union of Shiva and Shakti in the
person of their worshipper'. This union of Shiva and Shakti is a true *yoga*,
from which, as the *Yāmala* says, arises that joy known as the Supreme Bliss
(ibid., pp. cxv–cxix).

Thus the use of all these elements is sacramental, and their abuse is
sacrilege. It is easy to see how they can be misused and result in orgies, as
with those hypocrites who follow the 'left-hand path', in Bengal and elsewhere. But there are also those, less in evidence, who follow the 'right-hand
path', for whom the Tantric method is a support to a life of virtual absti-
nence and, indeed, of asceticism.

Christendom, represents chiefly the popular or exoteric tradition.[1]

Modern Christians, both within and without the Churches, who favour or follow the Gnostic tradition, are inclined to view much of the New Testament esoterically, the Gospel of St. John being for them evidence of the esotericism originally underlying Christianity as a whole.[2] Accordingly, holding to the symbology of the Mysteries of Antiquity, which was also that of the Gnostics, they interpret the wine-drinking of the

---

[1] Cf. G. R. S. Mead, *Fragments of a Faith Forgotten* (London, 1931), passim. The Editor is well aware of the contention of the Christian exotericists that Gnosticism is derived from pre-Christian sources and that its Christianized forms are essentially non-Christian. The same argumentation can be employed against exoteric Christianity itself, as St. Augustine has suggested; for there is no fundamental doctrine of the Christian Faith which is uniquely Christian, or without pagan parallel. Some of the outstanding elements or practices associated with the teachings of the Gnostics (or 'Knowing Ones'), suggestive of the esotericism which distinguishes 'heretical' Christianity from 'orthodox' Christianity, may be briefly outlined as follows:

(1) The view that the *Christos*, made manifest in the flesh in Jesus, is the mystical archetype of the Primal Man, the *Ā-dām*; that the *Christos* is innately present in all men and capable of being realized by them. In the '*Yoga* of Knowing the Mind', the Buddha, too, is said to be similarly innate and realizable.

(2) The doctrines of unerring cause and sequence in regard to thought, word, and deed (*karma*), and rebirth based upon these.

(3) A doctrine concerning divine hierarchies that constitute an unbreakable chain of being, of which man is a link; and the corollary teaching that ultimately all living creatures, members of One Body, will attain Deliverance by virtue of knowing the Mysteries of the *Gnosis*.

(4) A doctrine of emanations, or of the descent of the divine into generation, comparable to that of the Mahāyāna; and thus a doctrine of pre-existence, such as the learned Origen of Alexandria held to be Christian and for belief in which he was anathematized.

(5) A highly evolved mystical symbology.

(6) The use of *mantras*, or words of power.

(7) And particularly an eschatology (elsewhere referred to herein in another context) which, unlike that of exoteric Christianity, is supra-*sangsāric*; the exoteric Christian eschatology being entirely *sangsāric* because of the exoteric teachings that the human principle of consciousness does not pre-exist before man's birth, that man lives but one life on Earth, that after death man is destined to pass an endless eternity either of blissfulness in Heaven or of suffering in Hell.

[2] Cf. G. R. S. Mead, *The Gnostic John the Baptizer* (London, 1924), pp. 123–6, excerpts from which are incorporated in the annotations to Book II (p. 217[1]).

Lord's Supper in much the same manner as would Sūfis and the Tantric devotees of Padma-Sambhava. Many, if not all, of the miracles attributed to Jesus they also interpret Gnostically, including the wine-making miracle, which nowadays is often cited, when viewed exoterically, to justify the traffic in alcoholic beverages throughout Christendom, and the manufacture and sale for ecclesiastical revenue of rare liquors and fine wines by Christian monks.

It is, therefore, essential to a right understanding of the Great *Guru* that he be judged not from the viewpoint of his critics, whether these be of the Outer Circle or complete exotericists, but from his own viewpoint, which, as we are well aware, the overwhelming majority of those occidentally-minded will be prompted by their own peculiar social and religious psychology to question, if not reject outright.

In concluding this Section, the Editor quotes from matter dictated to him by one of his *gurus*:

It is unnecessary to give overmuch consideration to the opinions of the vulgar concerning the Precious *Guru*. The self-evident fact is that no one save a Great Master of *Yoga* could have written the ' *Yoga* of Knowing the Mind in Its Nakedness ', the authorship of which is accepted as being his. No man of uncontrolled appetites and passions could have conceived such a supreme teaching. When, too, there is taken into account the historic fact that Padma-Sambhava, as the specially invited guest of King Thi-Srong-Detsan, was the first great teacher of the Doctrine of the Enlightened One to the people of Tibet, that he lifted them socially from crude barbarism to unsurpassed religious insight, that all sects of Tibetan Buddhists revere him, the Precious *Guru* cannot but be regarded as being one of the chief Culture Heroes and Enlighteners of our common humanity.

IX. GOOD AND EVIL

Padma-Sambhava, like all other Culture Heroes, Prophets and Teachers, has not been immune to the criticism, and, even in our own times, to condemnation by the unenlightened, as has been mentioned above. This has been due almost entirely to his utter disregard of social, moral, and dogmatic religious conventionalities or established codes of conduct based upon mankind's limited conceptions of good and evil, instances of which are very common throughout the Biography and our epitome of it. In order, therefore, that the Great *Guru* may be understood by his own standards of right and wrong, adequate consideration should herein be given to the Vedāntic, and, more particularly, the Tantric, view of Good and Evil.

As Krishna teaches in the *Bhagavad-Gītā*, life is a conflict between two opposing forces, good and evil; or, as the *Mahā-bhārata* esoterically implies, between light and darkness, between Kuruvas and Pāndavas. The *Rāmāyana*, the other of India's two great epics, also tells of the same aeon-old struggle, between *Dharma* (or Righteousness), personified in the *Avatāra* Rāma, and *Adharma* (or Unrighteousness), personified in the demon-king Rāvana. In ancient Egypt the same teaching was set forth in the symbolical story of the slaying of the divine Osiris by his demon brother Set. The Great Mother Isis, viewing this mysterious tragedy inherent in the Cosmos itself, made dire lamentation. A parallel account of this conflict, in which all living things are *karmically* engaged, was dramatically represented in the Orphic Mysteries by the slaying of Dionysus Zagreus, symbol of life and regeneration, by his Titan brethren, symbol of death and destruction.

Or life is like a shuttle moving from right to left and from left to right unceasingly, carrying the thread of being with which is woven on the warp and woof of sensuousness, by each microcosmic consciousness, the *karmic* pattern. The Buddha, too, saw this continuous oscillation, this heart-throb of Nature, this Dance of Shiva, the Destroyer and Regenerator, and of Vishnu, the Restorer and Sustainer, and the state beyond both, personified by Brahma. The Supreme State, the state of at-one-ment, is the supra-mundane state of transcendent equilibrium, wherein negative and positive become undifferentiated, wherein the two opposing charges constituting the atom merge in primordial unity, wherein neither good nor evil exists.

The Buddhist Tantricism of Padma-Sambhava, like Hindu Tantricism, postulates, in harmony with these more ancient teachings underlying all Tantric Schools, that good and evil are inseparably one; that good cannot be conceived apart from evil; that there is neither good *per se* nor evil *per se*. This doctrine is expounded in the '*Yoga* of Knowing the Mind in Its Nakedness', particularly in the section entitled 'The *Yogic* Science of Mental Concepts'. Therein it is said that 'the various views concerning things are due merely to different mental concepts. . . . The unenlightened externally see the externally-transitory dually. . . . As a thing is viewed, so it appears.'

Hence, as the Great *Guru* himself teaches in the treatise, life, being a fabric of correlative, interdependent, interacting dualities, cannot be understood without knowing both aspects of the dualities; and the Great Liberation is consequent upon attaining that state of transcendence wherein all dualities become undifferentiated Wisdom. Impartial judgement cannot be reached without knowing both sides of a question; and evil must be philosophically understood and tested along with good if man is to see life steadily and see it whole. No chemist or physicist would fail to test every possibility of a chemical compound or substance or of an energy. Much has been argued, often unwisely, about white magic and black magic; and yet all magic is alike; it is merely the way in which magical power is employed that makes its usage good or bad. The supreme law of the inseparableness, as set forth in this volume, of good and evil, of white and black, of negative and positive, is too often forgotten or else not recognized; and its non-recognition constitutes Ignorance (in Sanskrit, *Avidyā*).

Tantricism, in its higher esoteric reaches, of which Europeans have but little knowledge, propounds, as do all philosophies, ancient and modern, based upon the occult sciences, that the ultimate truth (at least from the viewpoint of man) is neither this nor that, neither the *Sangsāra* nor *Nirvāṇa*, but at-one-ment, wherein there is transcendence over all opposites, over both good and evil. From the One proceed all dualities, and in the One they dissolve in undifferentiation;

and thus, ceasing to exist as dualities, they are realized by the *yogin* to be phantasmagoria, will-o'-the-wisps of the mind, children of *Māyā*.

It is perhaps not generally recognized that all Enlightened Seers, throughout the ages, teach essentially the same *yogic* doctrine as that of our present treatise. As Sri Ramana Mahārshi, the recently deceased sage of Tiruvannamalai, south India, taught, 'All scriptures, with one voice, declare that control of the mind is absolutely necessary for the attainment of salvation. Hence, control of the mind is the goal to be aimed at.'[1] And the Mahārshi summarized the *yogic* doctrine of good and evil thus:

There are no two such things as a good mind and an evil mind. It is one and the same mind. *Vāsanās* (tendencies) cause desires and attractions which may be at times good and at other times bad. The mind when influenced by good *vāsanās* is, for the time being, considered good, and, when under the influence of evil *vāsanās*, bad. However bad some may seem to be at times, they ought not to be disliked, nor should we conceive prejudice in favour of those that seem for the time being friendly and beneficent to us. Shun both likes and dislikes.[2]

Here, then, is a master of *yoga*, living until quite recently in south India, who had no knowledge whatsoever of our treatise, setting forth, as a direct result of his own life-long *yogic* research and ultimate realization, precisely the same paramount conclusions as those reached by Padma-Sambhava nearly twelve centuries ago in north India.

Plotinus, too, teaches that evil is quite as necessary as good. 'Even evil', he says, 'is useful in certain ways, and can produce many beautiful things; for instance, it leadeth to useful inventions, it forceth men to prudence, and preventeth them from falling asleep in an indolent security.'[3]

So long as men are held in the bondage of appearances, so long will they use such terms as moral and immoral, right and wrong, good and evil, and enact laws to preserve virtue and

---

[1] Cf. *Who Am I?* (p. 13), a booklet summarizing the Mahārshi's teachings, published by his *Āshrama* in Tiruvannamalai, in 1932.
[2] Cf. ibid., p. 15.
[3] Cf. Plotinus, II. iii. 18.

to destroy vice; not knowing that all sentient beings are members of one body, even as the Christian seer St. Paul perceived; and that, therefore, whatever punishment be meted out to the one part cannot but affect all parts of the social organism. In this connexion the writer recalls how, when a student under the late Professor William James, he was taught that if even the most inconspicuous Eskimo within the Arctic Circle were to suffer pain or misfortune, it would inevitably affect, although unconsciously, every other human being on the planet. And the eminent psychologist illustrated his teaching by pointing out that if the tiniest pebble were picked up and placed elsewhere, even at a very short distance from its original resting place, the whole centre of gravity of the Earth would be shifted.

For these reasons, none of the Fully Enlightened Teachers have advocated, as do the unenlightened multitude, the infliction of suffering and death upon others. Throughout uncounted millenniums, even as now, the unenlightened, the world-fettered, have maintained that this doctrine of the Enlightened Ones is impracticable, that if society is to be held together there must be the jungle law of eye for eye, tooth for tooth. Because of man's failure to rewrite his legal codes in the light of Divine Wisdom, the world today is probably more given to serious crime, particularly in the legalized form of war, than at any epoch in known history. And, notwithstanding that humanly instituted laws have failed to make man good or brotherly or wise after all these millenniums, Ignorance remains unshaken. Inevitably, as the Great *Gurus* teach, what men sow in law-courts or on battle-fields produces ever new harvests; and the sowing will continue until they recognize, individually and collectively, the Higher Law of the Divine At-one-ment of mankind, irrespective of nationality, race, religion, or social status, and, equally, of everything that lives.

It was in order to show to mankind the method of overcoming their bondage to appearances, to mentally-fettering concepts of dualism, that the Buddha expounded the *Dharma*. He has been called the Fully Awakened One, because, as He

sat under the Bodhi-Tree at Bōdh-Gayā, His spiritual insight
was awakened from latency and He saw life as a fabric of
dream illusions upon which men fix their gaze and become
fascinated as though in a hypnotic trance. Among His disciples were those who had been murderers, bandits, harlots;
and to none, no matter what their past deeds may have been,
did He refuse guidance.[1]

When a certain youthful disciple was unable to attain
mental concentration because of the haunting features of a
beautiful maiden, regarded by him as the most beautiful of all
maidens in the world of men, the Buddha, soundly scientific
in His applied psychology, had the disconsolate disciple
brought face to face with the still more beautiful maidens of
the *deva* worlds; and, in the end, the disciple, guided by *yoga*,
became thoroughly disillusioned, and recognized, as should
all human beings, male and female alike, the folly of being
mentally perturbed by illusory appearances.

Similarly, a modern *guru*, in India, had a disciple distracted
by longing for a courtesan, who, being much sought after by
the influential and wealthy, was quite beyond the disciple's
reach. The *guru* prepared a special *mantra* containing the
courtesan's name, and, going to the love-sick disciple, said,
'My son, I advise thee to enter into solitary retreat; and then,
fixing thy mind upon the courtesan to the exclusion of all
else, to repeat this *mantra* incessantly by day and by night.'
After some days the *guru* went to see how the disciple was
progressing, and found him to be completely cured; the disciple had attained the ecstatic vision of the at-one-ment of all
living things and realized that he and the courtesan were, in
fact, one and inseparable, beyond name and form.

Thus, by understanding, and sublimation if needs be, not
by suppression uncontrolled by philosophy, the *yogin* is to

---

[1] The late Mahārshi of Tiruvannamalai, also unattached to good and evil,
taught, 'Let a man's sins be great and many; yet he should not weep and
wail saying "I am a sinner, and how can a sinner attain salvation?" Let him
cast away all thoughts of being a sinner, and take to *Swarūpa-dhyāna* [a
yogic practice of introspection like that set forth in our treatise and in the
"*Yoga* of the Great Symbol"] with zeal; he will soon be perfect.' (Cf. *Who
Am I?*, p. 10.)

attain indomitable control of mind. As the *Guru* Phadampa
Sangay concisely teaches,

Draw strength from the Unobstructed; let the Stream flow
naturally;
No suppression, no indifference should there be.[1]

The opposite and wrong method, as modern psycho-analysts
have lately discovered, leads to mental, physical, and psychic
disorders.

It is only by philosophically tasting life in its many aspects,
good and bad alike, that the wise man attains, through experience, the power, born of understanding and consequent
disillusionment, to transcend life. No *yogin*, Tantricism
teaches, should ever experiment with life unless guided by
Divine Wisdom.

A libertine is one who has neither any such guidance nor
any consciousness of the true purpose of human existence;
like a ship at sea without compass and rudder he fails to
reach the Other Shore. And, being a prey to the whims of
animal passion, he retards his super-animal, or spiritual, unfoldment and increases his bondage. If, on the contrary, he
were guided in all his acts, good and bad, by philosophy, he
would extract from life's experiences the Nectar of Immortality; and, at last, when the complete disillusionment and
awakening came, he would claim his freedom.

Discipline and self-control of mind and body must never
be abandoned. The *yogin's* aim should be to increase, day by
day, life by life, their efficiency, until all dualities disappear
from his mental vision of the world. Neither should he prefer
unrighteousness to righteousness; for, as the Noble Eightfold
Path suggests, it is easier for man, while striving after that
Nirvāṇic state wherein both good and evil are recognized as
nothing more than mental concepts, products of *māyā*, to
overcome the wrong by adhering to the right. But if, through
lack of right guidance, man has strayed into evil, he is neither
to be made an outcast nor put to death on that account; for,
no matter what his human character may be, he is inseparably
a part of the whole, and until all parts attain Enlightenment

[1] See the annotation to this aphorism on p. 247 following.

there can be no Perfect, or Complete, Enlightenment for any. The inseparableness of all living things is as natural as it is inescapable. When the devotee has realized this law of being, all striving for self-interest, even for self-salvation, is abandoned; and, in the Great Awakening, he automatically becomes one of the Order of Infinite Compassion, vowed to the sole purpose of helping to overcome Ignorance.

Viewing life on Earth in this wise, as a state wherein to know and so transcend both good and evil, and all opposites, the neophyte must neither be elated by success nor dejected by failure, for these, too, are merely another duality. Seeking nothing for himself alone, but striving for the upliftment of all creatures, he must follow the Middle Path, without attachment either to good or to evil, knowing them to be of the two extremes. As our text teaches, he must attain this transcendent state of at-one-ment wherein there is neither defilement by evil nor alliance with good.

Error will be inevitable, for he is still in the imperfect human state, far below the status of Buddhahood; and yet, having attained the human state, which is much in advance of the sub-human states, he must not live the brutish life but the life of the aspirant for Enlightenment. Deliberate choice of the life of animal sensuousness leads not merely to a stoppage of progress on the Path, but to retrogression which may require many lifetimes of *karmically* imposed suffering to overcome, if degenerative disintegration of the human personality is to be avoided. But should it be the neophyte's *karmic* lot to taste of evil that he may transcend it by knowing its illusory and, therefore, wholly unsatisfactory character, he must not become attached to it. Attachment to evil for its own sake results in criminality; and criminality is one of the most terrible of all impediments on the Path. Likewise, attachment to good because of fear of the fruits of evil-doing is also an impediment.

The Middle Path goes to neither extreme. The Buddha accepted the hospitality of a courtesan as graciously as He did that of a virtuous king; and He awakened both from their Ignorance. He knew that it is not external appearances, not

Ignorance-born attachment to evil or to good, not a state of sensuality or a state of virtue which really matter, the Goal to which He directs being the Deliverance of the Mind.

Not only actions, but thoughts, too, as emphasized in the *Bardo Thödol*, must be dominated. By keeping to the Middle Path of non-attachment, no thought appertaining to either extreme can take root and grow. On any other Path, thoughts, becoming fixed on evil, turn into an army of demons who make the pilgrim a captive slave, and for ages all spiritual progress may cease.

Although the pilgrim is already fettered to sensuousness, he should face it fearlessly, then understand it and dominate it, and transmute it. With all thoughts concentrated on the Pilgrimage and the Goal, every impediment can be surmounted. If habits born of ignorance-directed actions of the past, whether moral or immoral, exist, they will continue to be fetters until killed out. Vice cannot be conquered by acquiescing in it or weakly giving way to it, but by realizing its unsatisfactoriness, its purely *sangsāric* nature, its power to impede one's progress towards supra-mundaneness. Once recognized to be a barrier on the Path, vice becomes an incentive to the removal of the barrier and thereby a stepping-stone to a higher than human consciousness. Accordingly, vice dominated by Wisdom is equivalent to good giving insight into evil.

As suggestively set forth in the ' *Yoga* of Knowing the Mind in Its Nakedness', unless all ignorance-created barriers, whether regarded as resulting from good or from evil actions or thoughts, are removed through the exercise of Divine Wisdom, the pilgrim, unable to pass on, grows confused, and another incarnation ends in failure. Once again the icy winds of Ignorance have blighted the promise of the Springtime ; and a new Springtime must be awaited beyond the Winter of death before new efforts can be put forth.

The external Universe, as a whole, with its hypnotic glamour, its sensuous enticements of sights and sounds, odours and other *sangsāric* stimuli, which result in what mankind call good and evil sensations, thoughts and actions, must be transcended; and the pilgrim must live in the inner silence of neutrality.

Even art, called a good by the multitude, whether pictorial, sculptural, musical, or dramatic, becomes an impediment if allowed to create sensuous attachment to the world. For this reason, the Prophet of Arabia, more completely than any other Teacher, prohibited all images or representations of the Supreme. Men, being spiritually unenlightened, degrade the supra-*sangsāric* by visualizing and depicting it in unreal *sangsāric* form; and thus, in the view of Mohammed, men by venerating or worshipping or even aesthetically enjoying the creations of their own unenlightened minds tighten not only their own fetters to the *Sangsāra*, but the fetters of the vulgar multitude who see the untruthful and misleading images and presentations. The Buddha similarly taught that it is not productive of enlightenment, but fettering, for mankind to take part in or witness worldly shows or spectacles or to be enamoured of music and dancing; and to the *Sangha*, in particular, He prohibited all such sensuous pleasures.

In this relationship, as in that of good and evil and of all dualism as a whole, the popular or accepted consensus of opinion is not to be followed by the neophyte. He is bidden to ponder such teachings as are set forth in 'The Precepts of the *Gurus*', and to realize that the Great Man differs in every thought and action from the multitude.[1]

The conception of death as an evil and the conception of life as a good, illustrate better than most other dualities the illusoriness of all mental concepts and of all dualism; for there is for the enlightened neither death *per se* nor life *per se*. The illusory phenomena of what the unenlightened call death and life are only moods or aspects of something which is *sangsārically* indescribable, that indestructible essence, microcosmically innate in man, capable of transcending both death and life and attaining what has been called *Nirvāṇa*. In other

[1] See *Tibetan Yoga and Secret Doctrines*, Book I. In this connexion, the Editor directs attention to Dr. Jung's sound and timely warning (set forth above, on p. lxii) concerning those who, ignorantly practising *yoga* in the Occident, fail, like the worldly, to attain that supreme moral indifference implied in *yogic* undefilement by evil and non-alliance with good.

words, death and life are, as concepts, modifications of consciousness in its finite or mundane manifestation, and in the state of the supra-mundane consciousness, or *Nirvāṇa*, they, like good and evil and all other *sangsārically*-conceived dualities, have no existence. It is, therefore, only mind in its limited finiteness that conceives of death as being an evil and of life as being a good.

Man dies daily when he sleeps, and yet he is not dead; and that death which comes at the end of every lifetime is merely a longer sleep than that which comes at the end of every day. The content of the nightly dream-state is, in large measure, and commonly, the product of the day-time waking-state; the content of the dream-state of death is, in similar degree, the product of the waking-state of life. And neither death nor life are either good or evil save as their percipient conceives and makes them to be so. Both equally are dream-states of the same *sangsāric* character and content, wholly illusory and unsatisfying. Whether alive or dead, unenlightened man is continually enwrapped in the Sleep of Ignorance; and it is the sole purpose of the Great *Guru*, transcendent over all dualities, as shown in his teachings in the ' *Yoga* of Knowing the Mind in Its Nakedness', to cause man to awaken.

No master of *yoga*, such as the Great *Guru* was, does anything merely to accord with the conventional standards of good and evil; for he knows that it is not the external aspect of an act, but the internal intention initiating it, which makes an act right or wrong. For illustration, an officer appointed to enforce law may be obliged to commit the same acts as those for which the common citizen is punished; in order to punish theft, society steals from the thief his personal liberty; in order to punish the practice of slavery, the state itself makes the practitioner a slave, condemning him to penal servitude without other wage than his bare maintenance, precisely as in illegal slavery; in order to punish murder, the state itself commits murder. In some instances, as in the employment of 'stool-pigeons' in the United States, agents of the state decoy suspects to commit punishable offences in order to arrest and convict them; or the 'third degree' method may be employed to extort confession, with excessive cruelty to the person, comparable to that of the Spanish Inquisition in its enforcement of ecclesiastical law. Thus, the acts of those who wilfully break the law are regarded as evil, and the same acts when performed by law-enforcement officers are regarded as good, the incentive behind the several acts being the determinant.

Speaking from the viewpoint of social psychology and anthropology, there is no socially, religiously, or traditionally fixed standard of morality historically known. What one age or religion or society has deemed right in morals another has decreed to be wrong. The history of European morals since the days of Plato (427–345 B.C.) records very violent oscillations from one extreme to another. And, seeing that man's progressive evolution from the animal status to that of the super-animal is far from completion, no moral standard among those so far tried by one society or another appears to be fixable. In illustrative substantiation of this, the instances which follow are applicable.

King Solomon, regarded by his contemporaries as the very incarnation of wisdom and justice, 'had seven hundred wives, princesses, and three hundred concubines'.[1] Polygamy was thus legal in his time among the Jews; and although, as the same text adds, 'his wives turned away his heart' [from the Lord], there is no account of Jehovah's having denounced the institution of polygamy itself. It is still legal among the Moslems, whose faith is based upon and evolved out of that of the Jewish people. Today, in most occidental countries, polygamy, or bigamy, is punishable by long years of imprisonment. When, in the deserts of Utah, the Church of Mormon of Latter Day Saints arose and began to practise polygamy after the fashion of the great men of the Old Testament, their fellow countrymen, who worshipped the same God, speedily enacted a constitutional amendment outlawing polygamy;

---

[1] i Kings xi. 3. There is, too, the esoteric interpretation which makes the 700 wives and 300 concubines to be personifications of human attributes such as feelings, passions, and occult powers, the Kabalistic numbers seven and three being taken to be the keys. 'Solomon, himself, moreover, being simply the emblem of Sol'.—H. P. Blavatsky, in *Lucifer* (London, Nov. 1888).

and now no immigrant is allowed entry into the United States of America if he favours or advocates a plurality of wives. In Buddhist Tibet, a plurality of husbands is legally allowable; in Christian England, a woman who claims more than one husband is chargeable with crime. Throughout Europe and the two Americas, adultery, though frequently sworn to in divorce courts and found very useful, goes unpunished; in Arabia it receives capital punishment.

In ancient Greece, by far the most cultured society yet evolved in the Occident, pæderasty was not only tolerated and legalized, as in Athens where contracts based upon it were recognized in courts of law, but it was regarded as having spiritual value, and attempts were made to apply it to social good. In the Dorian States and among the Spartans it was established as a martial institution. Throughout the Greek Empire it acquired religious sanction, as suggested by the symbolical sun-myth of Ganymede and Zeus and similar myths. It was widely sung by poets, and the great dramatists, Aeschylus and Sophocles, made it a subject of drama.[1] Then, about seven centuries later, Europe began to experiment with another theory of good and evil; and under Constantine (A.D. 288?–337) pæderasty became punishable with death. In A.D. 538, Justinian, believing that pæderasty was the direct cause of plagues, famines, and earthquakes, accepted Constantine's precedent as being thoroughly Biblical and Christian, and also decreed pæderasty to be a capital offence.[2] It remained so in most states of Europe until the time of Napoleon (1769–1821) who crystallized in the Napoleonic Code a revulsion of feeling against the inhumane codes of the Christian Emperors; and again there was change of moral standard. In the year 1889 Italy, too, adopted that part of the Napoleonic law relating to pæderasty, which, in England

---

[1] Cf. J. A. Symonds, *A Problem in Greek Ethics* (London, 1901), passim.
[2] Cf. J. A. Symonds, *A Problem in Modern Ethics* (London, 1896), p. 131, and passim. Justinian in the preamble to his *Novella* (77) states: 'It is on account of such crimes that famines and earthquakes take place, and also pestilence.' This serves as one, out of many interesting instances, of the unscientific influences which have shaped so much of modern European criminal procedure.

and the United States and a few other countries still under
the influence of the older scientifically unsound codes, remains a felony punishable by long years of imprisonment or
even penal servitude for life.

Thus, concomitant with change of religious, and, sometimes,
social or political, outlook, standards of morality, or at least
certain categories of them, also change. Given time enough,
the change may be as much from left to right or from right to
left as in parliamentary governments; and whether the change
be designated as being towards right or towards left depends,
as in politics or religion, upon party or church affiliation.
Changes of this nature, as illustrated in our own generation by
Soviet Russia, may be dependent, when religious and ordinary
political influences are inoperative, upon personal opinions of
governing factions, who arbitrarily, like ecclesiastical factions
when in power, impose their opinions upon the governed. For
instance, in the first enthusiasm for social reform immediately
after the Revolution, the old ecclesiastically formulated laws
governing sex relationships were abolished, even those penal-
izing homosexuality. Then, quite recently, there was a regres-
sion, parallel to that after the French Revolution; and what
at first was regarded as right and legal became wrong and
illegal.

Not only is there no one world-wide standard of right and
wrong under which mankind live, but much the greater part
of mankind are subject to two standards of right and wrong,
that of their religion or church and that of their nation; and
between the ecclesiastical and the civil codes of law there exist
irreconcilable and far-reaching differences. Then, again, as
between one canon law and another, such as that of Islam, of
Hinduism, and of Christendom, there are far greater conflicts.
Even within a single religious jurisdiction, where if nowhere
else uniformity might be expected, there are numerous serious
divergences, as, for example, between the canon law of the
Church of Rome and that of the various non-Roman Churches
of Christendom. This condition also prevails among antagonistic Islamic sects; and, to a certain extent, in Hinduism, as
between one caste or religious school and another.

Thus, according to the moral standard of the Church of Rome, and also of that of the Established Church of Holland, marriage performed outside the pale of the Church is invalid, and the issue therefrom illegitimate. When the Dutch held Ceylon, their Church socially ostracized all Singhalese who were not communicants and declared them ineligible for public office and their children without legal status. In Spain, when the standard of good and evil of the Church of Rome was practically applied, with the Holy Inquisition as the enforcement agency, the effect on society was even more marked, for those who persisted in adhering to any other moral standard were legally liable to torture, mutilation, and death. Should the same standard of good and evil be applied today, in like manner, in any Protestant country, such as England or the United States of America, there would result a most disastrous moral-standard warfare.

Throughout Christendom itself there are three standards of morality, that of the secular state, that of the churches, and that of the Sermon on the Mount and the Golden Rule of the New Testament. The first, being based upon the law codes of the Roman Empire, is pagan; the second, being based upon worldly expediency and rulings of church councils and synods, is ecclesiastical; the third, being based upon the teachings of the Founder of Christianity, is Christian. Any one of these three standards of morality is incapable of being reconciled with another. In India, for instance, there is even greater disagreement as to what is right and wrong; for there are not only the three quite irreconcilable standards of the Christian community, but similarly conflicting standards of other religions, such as those of Hinduism, Islam, Buddhism, Parseeism, Judaism, and primitive Animism.

A still more striking illustration of the remarkable inconsistency between the theory and practice of what men call right and wrong, presents itself in the social phenomenon of war. In times of peace, the state penalizes forgery, perjury, theft, arson, destruction of another's property, assault and battery, and murder, and even threats to commit any of these acts; but in times of war it compels each of its militarily trained citizens, under penalty of death, to commit, wherever necessary for victory, any or all of them. It trains its cleverest young men and women to practise every act of deceit and dishonesty which may be required to obtain military secrets from neighbouring states, employing, when needed, any of the variants of eroticism and prostitution, including homosexuality;[1] but if it apprehends similarly trained foreign citizens within its own territory, it either imprisons or shoots them. There appears to be no crime known to the underworld which a nation's secret service will not sanction, especially in time of war, for the purpose of outwitting an enemy nation. War, being an abrogation of ethical and cultural systems, recognizes no standard of good and evil.

If, as the *Gurus* teach, men would seriously consider these things, the illogical and impracticable nature of the moral standards of the unenlightened multitude would be self-evident, and human society would speedily advance beyond the mental status of brute creatures and transcend the law of the jungle.

Plato, the greatest of Greek Sages, spent many years in an attempt to define Justice, or what the Hindu Sages call *Dharma*. He recognized the evils of democratic governments, wherein it is not the right, or justice, which always prevails, but the will of the philosophically untrained vulgar majority; and that it is fallacious to assume that the minority are always wrong. It is with these conditions in view that the *Gurus* teach that the great man is he who differs in every thought and action from the multitude. Accordingly, it has ever been the lone pioneers of thought, the sowers of the seed of new ages, the Princes of Peace, rather than the Lords of War, and the minorities (who may be the disciples of the Sages), that have suffered martyrdom and social ostracism at the hands of the majority, who impose their standards of good and evil upon the helpless minority.

It is, therefore, very unwise to accept without question, as is nowadays customary in many modern states where un-

---

[1] Cf. Dr. Magnus Hirschfeld, *The Sexual History of the World War* (New York, 1941), pp. 125, 239, 252, 258–64.

sound moral standards prevail, the verdict of the people, whether expressed by a jury in a court of law or through the ballot box, as to what is justice, right or wrong, good or evil. So long as mankind are more selfish than altruistic, the majority are unfit to dominate the minority, who may be much the better citizens. As both Plato and the Wise Men of the East teach, the democratic-majority standard of judgement as to what is moral and immoral conduct is unreliable.[1]

As the word *morals*, in the sense of *custom*, indicates, moral conduct, or morality, is that which any particular society has grown used to and so accepted as being customary. Accordingly, for certain societies infanticide, or head-hunting, or killing of the physically unfit and aged are a good, and for other societies an evil; and until all peoples agree upon uniform customs there can be no one moral standard. Without taking into account the motive initiating an act and the social environment in which the act is done, no right judgement can be reached as to whether any act is good or bad.

Mankind's various standards of aesthetics (which in many respects are inseparable from the standards of morality), in art as in everyday life, are as chaotic as those of good and evil. For instance, in classical Greece the consensus of philosophical opinion declared the human male form the most beautiful of all forms in nature; and now, in the Occident, it is, according to vulgar opinion, the female form which is held to be the most beautiful. Throughout India, naked holy men wander about in public, as the Great *Guru* did when so inclined, and are venerated; in Canada, when the devout Russian Doukhobors (or 'Spirit-Wrestlers') publicly appear in their natural state, they are forcibly clothed and hurried off out of sight to prisons. Images of Osiris in his phallic aspect, as Lord of Fertility, still stand in their original shrines

[1] It is not, however, suggested that the alternative is the modern dictatorial state, but rather a social order inspired and directly guided by altruistically minded leaders of divine insight and training in the science of right government, somewhat after the type of the Governors of Plato's *Republic*, transcendent over racial, national, religious, and traditional limitations, and ever striving for the federation rather than the dismemberment of the world.

along the Nile; the *lingam* (or imaged generative organ) of
Shiva is worshipped by Hindus today; and their temples
depict in sculptured stone what the *Kama Shastra* (or 'Treatise on Sensual Love') describes in words; and in the various
countries where Tantricism prevails, including Tibet, imaged
or painted representations of the *Shakta* and *Shakti* in *yab-
yum* posture (or father–mother embrace) are sacred. But were
any such products of oriental art to be permitted entry into
occidental countries, they would be kept under lock and key
and capable of being seen only *in camera*, and books describing them in language of the multitude would be labelled porno-
graphic, and not be available without apologetic request or
perhaps written permission from some superior person.
Marbles in the nude, from the classical age of Greece, which
adorn the Vatican Library and Art Gallery, at present wear
Italian-made plaster-of-Paris fig-leaves.

  Those who pride themselves on their own peculiar racial or
religious standards of virtue and vice, right and wrong, good
and evil, thinking them alone infallible, resemble certain
members of the Younghusband military expedition to Lhāsa,
who wrote down in their diaries, and possibly still believe,
that the people of Lhāsa welcomed them with hand-clapping.
The people did clap their hands as the foreign invaders entered
the Holy City, but not to welcome them. Unknown to most
Europeans, handclapping is never by custom employed in
Tibet to signify appreciation; it is only so employed magically
to exorcize evil spirits and demons.

  A very large part of the world's troubles is due to these conflicting standards of aesthetics and of morals. The soundest
standard of judgement of human conduct appears to be the
Great *Guru's*, based upon the intention of thought and action.

  The theory that a good end justifies evil means is, as all the
Gurus hold, fallacious, because it assumes that good alone is
desirable, whereas that which is really desirable is neither
good nor evil, but transcendence, in the *yogic* sense, over both.
In the realm of nature, the negative is quite as necessary as the
positive. No universe could be constituted of absolute positive-
ness; if the atom lost its negativeness, it would not be an

atom. And thus, as Plotinus says, 'without the evils in the Universe, the Universe would be imperfect'.[1]

It ought now to be clear that, instead of there being, as is sometimes carelessly assumed, a fixed standard of morality or of aesthetics, even in any one nation or religious jurisdiction, there is universally a condition of chaotic confusion as to what mankind should or should not do or believe to be proper and right. Accordingly, it is incumbent upon the critics of the Great *Guru*, firstly to state from the standpoint of what moral standard they judge him, and, secondly, to show wherein that standard is preferable to each of the many other moral standards which govern human society at the present time or have governed it in past ages.

Criticism may very fairly be directed against Padma-Sambhava, as it is, by Buddhists who are not of his School, on the ground that a number of the strange deeds attributed to him in the Biography, or by tradition, are at variance with the Noble Eightfold Path and the Ten Precepts. His more learned devotees reply that the stories therein representing him in such light being wholly legendary and symbolical, as some if not all of them clearly are, really emphasize rather than oppose the teachings of the Buddha, as shown, for instance, by the humorous account of the slaying of the butchers, and that of the wine-drinking *Heruka* (on pages 138, 162, following).

It is, of course, not germane to this discussion of good and evil to consider the contention of the Southern Buddhists that their Pāli Canon is the only true canon, and that, therefore, the Tibetan Canon and all Buddhist *Tantras* are largely heretical. In the same way, it is not necessary to consider the similar charge of the modern Christian Churches that the Canon of Gnosticism is heretical, as they have decreed it to be. The devotees of the Great *Guru* do maintain, however, as the *Kanjur* account of the prophesied incarnation of the Lotus-Born One suggests, that he, being a Tantric manifestation of the Buddha Essence, teaches a more transcendental doctrine than did the Buddha Gautama; and that the

[1] Cf. Plotinus, II. iii. 18.

Pāli Canon expounds a purely exoteric Buddhism, intended for the multitude, whereas the Tibetan Canon, which is largely Tantric, expounds, in addition, a purely esoteric Buddhism, intended for higher initiates. Hence, the moral standard of the Great *Guru* is also transcendental, although in strict accord with the *Dharma*, when viewed both exoterically and esoterically.

Evil, otherwise viewed, is that which impedes self-realization; it is that which inhibits man from transcending Ignorance and attaining the full enlightenment of Buddhahood. Accordingly, Evil has been personified as the Devil, as Māra, as the Tempter who makes the illusory so enticingly glamorous that, by a sort of hypnosis, he who beholds the deceptive glamorousness loses self-control, and is, as long as the spell remains unbroken by Wisdom, fettered to appearances, and incapable of extricating himself from the meshes of the *sangsāric* Web of *Māyā*.

The natural, or uncreated and primordial state, the *Nirvānic* state, being a state of at-one-ment with all that is, whatever prevents its realization is Evil and whatever fosters its realization is Good. But neither Evil nor Good being absolute, or real in itself, each is no more than a state of consciousness, the one making for attachment to the transitory, the other making for freedom from the transitory. When this freedom has been attained, both Good and Evil have lost their purpose and become inoperative; they are transcended, and the freed one has attained the state beyond Good and Evil, beyond all opposites, which exist and operate only in the *Sangsāra*.

Because Evil is an impediment and Good an assistance to the attainment of the Full Awakening, all Great Teachers have taught of the need for virtuous conduct, not as an end in itself, any more than the mere physical training of an athlete is an end in itself, but only as a means to an end far greater than itself. And just as chastity is essential to the gaining of spiritual insight into reality, although, likewise, only a means to that end, it, too, is inculcated for all disciples who would tread the path to freedom from *sangsāric* existence, from the lowly condition of attachment to the world and animal sensuousness; and is, in this aspect, Good, while licentiousness is, for the opposite reasons, Evil.

The Noble Eightfold Path, or the Sermon on the Mount, or any other system of right conduct, is not merely a category of so many apparently restrictive rules, but an efficient and long-tested method for evolving beyond the human state and attaining the *Nirvāṇic* state. A boat is necessary only so long as there is a body of water to be traversed, and spiritual disciplines are necessary only so long as there is Enslavement; when Emancipation has been attained, there is no longer any path to be trodden nor any commandments to be kept: one more pilgrim has reached the Other Shore.

If he who dwells in the Valley of Ignorance should aspire to climb to the summit of the Mountain of Enlightenment, he must begin at the mountain's base, and, laboriously, step by step, enduring fatigue and perhaps despondency, advance to the goal. And once he stands on the summit, the compass, which guided him through the mists and clouds, and the Alpine staff, which supported his footsteps and gave to him assurance against dangers, may be cast aside; these were, at the outset, necessary, now they have become unnecessary. When the end has been attained, the means may be discarded. So it is with Good, or Virtue, or rules of right conduct when the Great Consummation of incarnate existence on Earth has been realized.

Good and Evil are the two-forked trunk of the Tree of Life, sprung from a single Seed. Each fork alike has its support in the root-system of the One Tree. The same sap flows to and nourishes both forks equally.

Or Good and Evil may be viewed as being like twins, off-spring of one Father–Mother. They are compensatory, the one to the other, like the right and left ventricles of the heart. They are the two hands doing the work of the Cosmic Body, the two feet by which humanity traverses the Highway of Life leading to the City of *Nirvāṇa*. If either be amputated, there is crippling. Virtue of itself leads to good results, vice to evil results. The Sage who knows both Good and Evil to be one and inseparable is transcendent over both. It is only in the *Sangsāra* that opposition is operative. In the Beyond-Nature, in the Voidness, there is but the Unmodified, the Primordial, the Unformed, the Unmade, the Unborn, the All-Embracing Womb whence comes forth into being the manifested Universe. The *Dharma*, or the Supra-mundane Law of the Cosmos, enthroned upon the Immutable Throne of *Karma*, crowned with the Double Crown of the Two Opposites, holding the Sceptre of At-one-ment, robed in the gold and purple robes of Justice, guides all sentient creatures to Understanding and Wisdom by means of Good and Evil.

This Section, which is necessarily the longest and in some respects the most important part of this Introduction, will be fittingly concluded by summarizing in a tenfold category the essentialities of the moral standard of the Oriental Sages, by which alone the Great *Guru* should be judged:

(1) Good and Evil, when viewed exoterically, are a duality, neither member of which is conceivable or capable of mentally existing independently of the other. Being thus inseparable, Good and Evil, when viewed esoterically, are intrinsically a unity.

(2) A thing is considered to be either good or evil in accordance with the mental state in which it is viewed, the state itself being determined by racial, social, or religious environment and heredity. Otherwise stated, as by Shakespeare, 'there is nothing either good or bad, but thinking makes it so'.[1]

(3) There being nothing which has other than an illusory existence in the mundane mind, nothing can be said to be either good or evil *per se*.

(4) Inasmuch as it is the motive and intent initiating an act which determines its character, no act, in itself, can be either good or evil; for the same act when performed independently by two persons, one with altruistic the other with selfish motive and intent, becomes both good and evil.

---

[1] Cf. *Hamlet*, ii. ii. 245.

(5) There being nothing which is good *per se* or evil *per se*, Good and Evil, like all dualities, are hallucinatory concepts of the *sangsārically* constituted mind of their percipient. As such, like the world of appearances (which is merely a conglomerate of *sangsāric* concepts), they have only a relative, not an absolute, or true, existence.

(6) Hence, doctrines concerning a state of absolute evil called Hell and a state of absolute good called Heaven, being based entirely upon *sangsārically*-born concepts, are also entirely relative and illusory; *Nirvāṇa* is beyond good and evil.[1]

(7) Accordingly, all standards of morality founded upon any such doctrines are unstable; and, like the *Sangsāra* itself, by which they are circumscribed, from which they arise, and upon which they are dependent for their illusoriness, they are ever-changing and transitory, like the mundane mind of their creators and advocates, and, therefore, unsatisfactory and unfixable.

(8) Not until mankind shall transcend dualism and phenomenal appearances, and realize the natural at-one-ment of all living creatures, will they be able to formulate a sound standard of morality.

(9) Such a standard will be based entirely, not partially, as are prevailing standards of morality, upon worldwide *Bodhisattvic* altruism.

(10) Its Golden Rule may be stated thus: 'Do unto others and to yourself only that which fosters Divine Wisdom and will guide every sentient being to the *Bodhi* Path of transcendence over the *Sangsāra* and to the Final Goal of Deliverance from Ignorance.'[2]

---

[1] This is suggested also by Dr. Jung's Commentary, pp. l–li, above.

[2] The teaching, that men should do unto others what they would that others should do unto them, is capable of misconstruction, or misapplication, notwithstanding that its intent is obviously right. For so long as men are fettered to the *Sangsāra* and misled by its delusive glamorous mirages, and thus in bondage to Ignorance, they are quite incapable of knowing in what right action, either to themselves or to others, consists.

X. TANTRIC BUDDHISM

Padma-Sambhava, having come to be regarded by his many devotees throughout Tibet, Mongolia, China, Nepal, Kashmir, Bhutan, and Sikkim as being peculiarly a Tantric emanation or reincarnation of the Buddha Gautama, exercised a very profound influence on the shaping of Mahāyāna Buddhism; and this influence, in its own sphere of Tantricism, was probably as far-reaching as was that of Nāgārjuna in the shaping of the Doctrine of the Voidness, as set forth in the canonical *Prajñā-Pāramitā*.

Tantricism itself, in its two aspects, Hindu and Buddhist, is as yet too little investigated to make possible, at this time, incontrovertible or exhaustive statements concerning its origin, which, however, seems to have been exceedingly complex. According to some scholars who have looked into the problem more or less superficially, the Yogāchāra School, which originated under Asaṅga, a Buddhist monk of Gandārā (now Peshawar), in north-west India, presumably about A.D. 500, appears to have leavened the Mahāyāna as a whole. In other words, the method of attaining ecstatic union with the One Mind (or Absolute Consciousness), known as *yoga* (which Patanjali in his *Yoga Sutras* first systematized about the year 150 B.C.), being the basis of the Yogāchāra, *yoga* is, undoubtedly, one of the chief roots of Tantricism. From this point of view, we should, perhaps, be justified in defining Tantricism as being a school of eclectic esotericism based fundamentally upon *yoga* practically applied, both to esoteric Brāhmanism and to esoteric (or Mahāyāna) Buddhism.

Another of the peculiarities of Tantricism, which distinguishes it from all other living cults, is its personification of the dual aspects of the procreative forces in nature, the *shakta* representing the male (or positive) aspect and the *shakti* representing the female (or negative) aspect. As a direct outcome of this, there appear to have developed, within the Mahāyāna, the Vajrayāna and Mantrayāna Schools, which represent a blending with the earlier Yogāchāra School. By the middle of the seventh century A.D., when Tantricism was well established in India, both in its Shaivaic (or Hindu) and its Buddhistic form, the many Buddhas and *Bodhisattvas*, and corresponding Hindu deities and saints, were already being imaged there, each with an appropriate female energy or *shakti*; and that peculiar esotericism which is inseparable from Tantricism was already highly evolved. It was this form of Tantric Buddhism which Padma-Sambhava introduced into Tibet during the second half of the eighth century.

Then, as is believed, early in the second half of the tenth century, the Kālachakra form of Tantricism was more or less developed in northern India, Kashmir, and Nepal. The Kālachakra doctrine is said to have originated in the mysterious secret land of Shambhala.[1] According to the late Sarat Chandra Dās, Shambhala was 'a city said to have been located near the river Oxus in Central Asia'; and the Kālachakra had become a distinctly Buddhistic system by the eleventh century, and introduced the cult of the Ādi (or Primordial)-Buddha. In India, varieties of the cult assigned to Shiva or to Gaṇesha (as the Hindu God of Wisdom) the position of Ādi-Buddha.[2]

Possibly, as we venture to suggest, one source, if not the most primitive source, of the Kālachakra system may yet be discovered to have been in the ancient pre-Buddhistic Bön religion of Tibet. If so, the seed of the system already lay in the Tibetan mind and found in Padma-Sambhava's form of Tantricism a favourable environment, long before the time when the Kālachakra, as a distinct School of Buddhism, is believed to have arisen in countries adjacent to Tibet. The association of the Kālachakra system with Shambhala, which

---

[1] Cf. L. A. Waddell, *The Buddhism of Tibet* (Cambridge, 1934), pp. 13–17, a work to which the Editor is much indebted, although he cannot agree with its author's opinion that Tantric Buddhism's 'mysticism became a silly mummery of unmeaning jargon'. Although this may be a common opinion among non-initiated Europeans, it is, as the late Sir John Woodroffe once remarked to the Editor, no more than their opinion. Sir John was himself a Tantric initiate, and the foremost occidental authority on Tantricism of our epoch. To his works, mostly published under the pseudonym 'Arthur Avalon', students are referred for right understanding of Tantricism. In *The Tibetan Book of the Dead* (pp. 213–20) there is a brief exposition of Tantricism, based chiefly upon Sir John's works, which will serve as a supplement to our present more historical exposition.

[2] Cf. S. C. Dās, *Tibetan-English Dictionary* (Calcutta, 1902), p. 632.

many *lāmas* say is somewhere unknown in Tibet or to the
north of Tibet, is significant in this connexion. Furthermore,
and of greater importance, is the documentary evidence from
original Tibetan sources, as set forth in the *Bardo Thödol*, and
in the text of the *Chöd* Rite (presented in Book V of *Tibetan
Yoga and Secret Doctrines*) that, long before the rise of Tibetan Tantric Buddhism, the ancient Bön faith of Tibet pro-
pounded a highly developed cult of wrathful demons, of
which the *To-wo* and *Drag-po* (corresponding to the *Bhairava*
and *Heruka* of Hindu Tantricism) are outstanding representa-
tives. And within the very elaborate demonology of the Bön
faith probably lie the prototypes not only of the Wrathful but
also of the Peaceful Deities of Tibetan Tantricism.

In the Kālachakra system, the inscrutable powers which
work through nature, bringing into manifestation universes
and then absorbing them, and causing men to live and to die,
are personified not only in their dual aspect by the *Shakta* and
Shakti as in the older Tantricism, but also in their dual functions of preservation (represented in Hinduism by Vishnu)
and destruction (represented in Hinduism by Shiva). Thus
there came into Tantricism two new groupings of deified personifications, one being the order of Peaceful Deities, personifying the powers making for preservation, the other being
that of the Wrathful Deities, personifying the powers making
for destruction. And, as will be observed throughout the Epitome of the Biography, in Tibetan Buddhism, all Buddhas,
Bodhisattvas, gods and goddesses and lesser deities are visualized or represented in both the peaceful and wrathful aspect.
Today, the form of Tantricism most prominent in Tibet is the
Vajrayāna, or 'Path of the Indomitable Thunderbolt of the
Gods'.

If the compilation of the Biography be really that of
Padma's disciple, the Tibetan lady Yeshey Tshogyal, who was
contemporaneous with him, then, as the Biography's internal
evidence indicates, the Vajrayāna form of Tantricism was
already highly developed by the latter half of the eighth
century and also the Kālachakra system, into which the
Mantrayāna and Vajrayāna practices were eventually incor-

porated. If, on the other hand, the Biography is of later date than the colophon assigns to it, and the presumption that the Kālachakra system was unknown to Tantricism prior to the tenth century is sound, the Tantricism of the Biography must, therefore, be taken to be of a form more highly developed than that introduced into Tibet by Padma-Sambhava himself. The true date of the Biography will, no doubt, eventually be established; and then, when the Biography and similar biographical records of the Great *Guru* have been critically examined, much new evidence will be adduced to clarify our present uncertainties concerning Tantricism's origin.

Whatever be the origin or age of Tantricism, it has unquestionably been an influence of the first importance throughout the whole empire of Mahāyāna Buddhism. Our Illustration of the Chinese Tantric representation of Mañjushrī in wrathful aspect is significant of this influence in China, and that of Mañjushrī in peaceful aspect is significant of this influence in India, Tibet, Nepal, and other of the Himalayan regions culturally related thereto.

Philosophically viewed, Tantricism, Hindu as well as Buddhist, aims to interpret human nature pragmatically. For this reason, the *Tantra Shāstra*, historically the latest of the *Shāstras*, is held to be the *Shāstra* best fitted for the *Kali-Yuga*, the present age.

Unlike most other faiths, Tantricism teaches understanding and sublimation of the chief force active in humanity, namely, the reproductive force, and opposes the more prevalent and scientifically unsound teaching concerning the forcible suppression of it. By that all-important force in nature, birth is balanced with death; the current of the *Prāṇic* River of Life, whereby all worlds and suns are sustained, is kept flowing, and the growth from higher to lower states of consciousness, even to the Final Emancipation of Buddhahood, is made possible. Thus it is that Tantricism propounds a science of sex, such as the late Sir John Woodroffe (pseudonym, Arthur Avalon) suggested in *The Tantra of the Great Liberation*, in *The Serpent Power*, and in *Shakti and Shakta*.

Even our own Occidental Science has now discovered, as the scientists of the Orient discovered long ago, that there is direct relationship between the highest mental and psychic powers in mankind and the secretions of the sex glands, and that physical youthfulness and efficiency are dependent upon conservation of the reproductive essences. All religions likewise, even the most primitive, have recognized that there is inseparableness between the sex-energy and spiritual growth. In the early Christian church, the ruling that a sexually incomplete man could not fittingly serve the church as a priest was made a basis for deposing the learned and saintly Origen of Alexandria from presbyterial status. Having applied literally rather than esoterically the New Testament command referring to the cutting off of an offending member of the physical body, Origen, at the age of 21, had made himself a eunuch physically rather than spiritually. Similarly, Indian *gurus* now teach that to attain the bliss of *samādhi* the sexual power must be complete and active, yet sublimated, and under as complete control as an aeroplane is by its pilot. In the Occident, the Society of Jesus, equally, insists that candidates for its priesthood must have attained dominion over their sexuality. But, for the oriental *yogin*, mastery of the 'serpent power' does not imply celibacy in the Christian monastic sense, for many of the Great *Rishis* of India had offspring. And today, as in the time of Padma-Sambhava, Tantric priests or *lāmas* may or may not marry, celibacy for them being optional; but it is only the Ngag-pas (Skt. *Mandar*) among the Nyingmapa *lāmas* of Padma-Sambhava's School who commonly marry.[1] Marpa, the *guru* of Milarepa, for example, was married and had a son. The *Bodhisattva* Gautama, too, before he became the Buddha, was married and had a son; and both the son and the wife became faithful disciples of the Enlightened One.

It is because sex plays so large a part in the various accounts of Padma-Sambhava which have been handed down that he

---

[1] Ngag-pa *lāmas*, being reputed to be expert magicians, are employed by Tibetans of all sects to bring about rain in times of drought or to protect growing crops from destructive hail.

is looked upon, by many who misunderstand Tantricism, as the very antithesis of what a holy man should be. The standards by which such critics judge the Great *Guru* are those of the unenlightened, and usually those of the Occident. In his own time such critics were not lacking, as the episode (recorded on page 161, following) concerning the suspicions of one who had professed to be his friend shows. Therefore, without at least some general comprehension of Padma-Sambhava's Tantricism, such as the present Section affords, this volume as a whole is apt to be misinterpreted.

XI. Astrology

The Biography makes it clear that astrology was quite as influential in the life of Padma-Sambhava as it is known to have been in the lives of many other, if not all, of the Sages of the Mahāyāna, and as it still is in the life of every Oriental who has remained true to his or her wisdom-born ancestral heritage.

Learned Indian astrologers maintain that astrology *per se* is of all sciences the most important, because there can be no true art of living apart from it. In so viewing astrology, they exclude, as being unworthy the name astrology, almost all of that which passes for astrology in the Occident and the greater part of that which is popularly called astrology in the Orient.

Astrology regards man as being not only a microcosm of the macrocosm, but as being, like all *sangsāric* things, a product of multitudinous astral and cosmic influences; for in him they find focus, and shape his physical, mental, and psychic environment. Astrology does not, however, imply fatalism; for the master of *yoga* is also the master of astrological influences, and, by knowing them, is enabled scientifically to chart the course of his Vessel of Salvation across the Sea of Existence in such manner as to avoid hidden reefs and shallows, and be prepared for tempests and contrary currents and, at last, attain the safety of the Other Shore. Notwithstanding that his body and mental tendencies and environment are shaped by astrological influences, the Sage thus remains the master of his own fate despite them. Similarly, a ship on the high seas is the product of man's labour and inventive skill, and no matter what inherent weaknesses or imperfections it may possess, or whether it be of one shape or another, great or small, the captain has free will to direct its course in any direction, and bring it through all dangers to the port desired.

Each moment in time is as much different from another as one leaf on a tree is different from all the other leaves, because the effects of these innumerable astrological influences are never for two consecutive moments exactly the same. Owing to the incessant movements of the heavenly bodies and of the Earth, the angle of the focus, and correlatively the character of the influences, unceasingly change. It is upon this premise that astrology is founded.

Accordingly, all visible and invisible things, organic and inorganic, man, beast, plant, crystal, and every material, aqueous or gaseous substance, being responsive to these influences, are branded by them in terms of *sangsāric* time. This is very curiously illustrated by the practice of wine-tasting, and also, in lesser degree, by that of tea-tasting. A master wine-taster, although totally ignorant of the source and age of a certain vintage, can, by tasting it, determine with mathematical exactitude where the grapes were grown, their quality and species, and when they were pressed.[1] Ultimately, when fully developed, the practice of tea-tasting should result in the taster being able to determine not only the quality, but also the exact origin of the tea and the date of its production and curing.

As taste is a very subtle thing, totally invisible and knowable only by experience, it is, in this sense, comparable to something psychic; we might even call it the essential psychic quality or flavour of a living organism. It is precisely in this way, astrology maintains, that every organic and inorganic substance has its own peculiar astrological characteristic or taste; and an astrologer is a taster or calculator of the astro-

---

[1] For this very suggestive reference to wine-tasting, the Editor is personally indebted to Dr. Jung, who contributed it to a discussion which touched upon astrology at a luncheon in Balliol College, during the time of the Tenth International Congress for Psychotherapy held in Oxford in the summer of 1938.

logical quality of a given moment in the transitory cycle of time. By knowing the astrological influences operative at any given moment of nativity, it is thus possible to ascertain the physical, mental, and psychic characteristic or taste of a human being; and, also, how another and unlike combination of influences, radionic, magnetic, psychic, and physical, emanating from Moon and Sun, Stars and Cosmic Spaces, will affect those already stamped upon the individual at the moment of birth.

Sufficient scientific data are available to suggest that the study of these astrological influences would be of fundamental importance also to botanists and zoologists. The Editor recalls how an old Yankee schoolmaster used to demonstrate to him, in schoolboy days, proofs, derived from experiments, that each phase of the moon has a definite effect not only, as is popularly believed, upon the growth of vegetation and the maturing of seeds, but also upon the fertility of domestic animals. Similarly, in Ceylon, horary astrology is so highly evolved that astrologers there have assured me that if the seed of a mango be planted at the exact moment when there is a certain rare combination of astrological influences, the seed will speedily sprout and fruit be produced as soon as three or four leaves have appeared on the young tree.

Likewise, some of the most fascinating phenomena elicited by biological research appear to merit astrological explanation. For illustration, the Great Barrier Reef Expedition of 1928–9 found that the pearl oyster has annually two breeding seasons, six months apart, 'at the full-moon in May and in November'.[1] The coral *Pocillopora bulbosa*, in the shallow pools on Low Isles, Australia, was found to have three reproductive periods, the first period occurring at about the time of new moon during the months of December to April, the second period at about the time of the full moon in July and August, and the third in May and June, when there is a transitional period from new moon to full moon.[2] The marine Palolo worms (*Palolo viridis*), used as food by the natives of Samoa

[1] Cf. T. A. Stephenson, in *Nature* (London, 6 May 1933), p. 665.
[2] Ibid. (London, 29 Apr. 1933), p. 622.

and Fiji, leave their homes in the fissures of the coral reefs and swarm to the shores of these islands in countless myriads at two fixed periods annually, in October and in November, on two successive days, which are, 'at dawn on the day on which the moon is in her last quarter and at dawn on the day before'.[1] Thirteen lunations occur between the appearances of the Palolo every third year, or, in other words, the Palolo adjusts itself, in the long run, to solar time. Mr. S. J. Whitmee, who made this suggestive discovery, says, 'A most remarkable compensation for the difference between *lunar* and *solar* time is made by some natural process in the development of this little annelid. I am not at present prepared to give an opinion as to how this can be effected'.[2]

There might also be cited parallel biological phenomena showing a definite connexion between the phases of the moon and periodicity in the life-cycles of other marine creatures, as, for illustration, the spawning time of fish, when the fish pass from the depths of the oceans to the shallows of the shores or to the fresh waters of estuaries and rivers, or, again, the run of herring on the coasts of Britain or of cod on the Grand Banks of Newfoundland. The season of rut in wild animals, and of the monogamous mating followed by the communal migration of birds and butterflies, are also suggestive of astrological influences. Thus, each year, on the nineteenth day of March the famous swallows (*Hirundo erythrogaster*) of the San Juan Capistrano Mission in California return to their nests after their winter outing in the lands to the south; and they take their departure from the Mission, quite as regularly, on the twenty-third day of October. Records of their annual arrival and departure have been kept by the Mission fathers for many years, and never yet have the swallows failed to arrive and depart at these fixed dates, even in leap years;[3]

---

[1] Cf. A. Sedgwick, *A Student's Text-Book of Zoology* (London, 1898), p. 481; *The Cambridge Natural History*, vol. ii (London, 1910), p. 297.

[2] Cf. S. J. Whitmee, *Proceedings of the Zoological Society of London*, 1875, pp. 496–502.

[3] The Editor is indebted to the late Rev. A. J. Hutchinson, Custodian of the Mission, for this information, contained in a letter dated 19 September 1938.

for, like the Palolo worms, they adjust their cyclic movements to solar rather than terrestrial time.

Here, of course, we approach the problem of instinct, which also, in the last analysis, is claimed by astrologers to be the evolutionary outcome of astrological fixation, or what otherwise may be termed astrological periodicity, as shown in breeding seasons. In the view of some learned astrologers, even the origin and mutation of species, and the law of biological evolution as a whole, are best explained astrologically.

Although there are the ordinary external stimuli which are obviously and generally effective in the determination of breeding seasons, such as temperature, latitude, light, and rainfall, not all birds and animals are invariably responsive to them, as Dr. John R. Baker, of the University of Oxford, demonstrates in his essay, 'The Evolution of Breeding Seasons'.[1] Other influences must be considered. Also, 'Internal rhythm can never account wholly for the timing of breeding seasons, for it would get out of step with the sun in the course of ages, but it is likely that it plays its part in making many species quick to respond to the external factors.'[2] Some interesting instances are cited by Dr. Baker of the lack of response to the terrestrial environmental stimuli.

'Some species of birds have quite different breeding seasons on the two sides of Ceylon, and it is thus certain that length of day does not control them. It is possible that intensity of visible or ultra-violet illumination is the cause.'[3] Despite severe cold, the *Nestor notabilis* parrot of the Nelson Province of New Zealand breeds in mid-winter.[4] Even where there is a constant temperature, as in the tropics, it is usual for birds to have breeding seasons, as the Oxford University Expedition to the New Hebrides discovered. 'The climax was presented by the insectivorous bat, *Miniopterus australis*, the adult females of which all become pregnant once a year about the beginning of September, despite the constancy of climate and the fact that they hang all day in a dark and almost ther-

[1] A Reprint from *Evolution Essays* presented to E. S. Goodrich, ed. by G. R. De Beer (Clarendon Press, Oxford, 1938).
[2] J. R. Baker, ibid., p. 166.   [3] Ibid., p. 168.   [4] Ibid., p. 169.

mostatic cave.'[1] Thus temperature, too, does not appear to be the determining influence. Some birds seem almost insensitive to latitude as well.[2] Rainfall (which is itself the direct result of astrological influences, according to astrologers), although a far more important factor, is not always the determining cause of the breeding seasons of certain animals.[3]

Man and domesticated animals appear to be less susceptible than animals in the state of nature to all such obvious external stimuli, and, as the astrologers maintain, to invisible astrological stimuli also. The lower the organism and more primitive the environment—as in the instances of the pearl oyster, coral and marine worms—the more direct is the response. In inorganic substances, as research in radio-activity may some day discover, the response is said to be entirely automatic.

Astronomical data, too, have already been accumulated pointing to the reasonableness of at least some of the postulates of astrology. And more and more, as astronomers advance in their quest, very recently begun, for the source of cosmic rays, and physicists in their related quest concerning radio-activity, both alike will enter the realm claimed by astrology. Then, as they begin to study the effects of these radiations upon the Earth and upon living things, there will be laid foundations for an occidental science of astrology.

No person of intelligence nowadays doubts the effect of sunspots on the Earth's magnetic and climatic conditions, nor that the Moon, aided by gravitational forces, causes tides in oceans and in the apparently immovable land surfaces of continents. It is only in the Occident that the far more important effect of all such astrological influences on man himself is either denied or arrogantly ignored or left to the exploitation of ignorant charlatans who make scientists averse to inquiry. The well-established law of gravitation alone contributes additional scientific evidence tending to give validity to certain of the claims of oriental astrology. Until quite recently, Western Science has been far more concerned with the external visible Universe than with the internal invisible

---

[1] J. R. Baker, *Evolution Essays*, ed. G. R. De Beer (Clarendon Press, Oxford, 1938), p. 163.   [2] Ibid., p. 164.   [3] Ibid., p. 172.

universe in man; but, fortunately for man, Western Science appears to be destined to become more and more anthropocentric.

Quite unlike scientists, many eminent occidental philosophers and poets, among whom were Roger Bacon and Shakespeare, have been keenly interested in astrology. Nor has Christianity itself escaped its influence, as the Christianized story of the coming of the Wise Men from the East guided by the star over Bethlehem shows. In an earlier and historic version of this astrological story, concerning the birth of the *Bodhisattva* Gautama, the Wise Men were astrologers, who came and cast the horoscope of the royal babe and thus foretold how he was destined to become either a universal emperor or a Buddha. And on the babe's body they saw the thirty-two signs of his coming greatness, as astrological time-markings, cumulatively inherited from many previous incarnations.

Astrology is, of course, historically and scientifically, a subject far too vast to consider at further length here. The Biography itself will contribute much to the present discussion. Our sole purpose in discussing astrology, even in this rather superficial manner, is to suggest that it may yet prove to be, for occidental scientists, the source of a new science—apart from astronomy, which has sprung from it—even as alchemy was the source of chemistry and modern psychology. Then, eventually, if occidental civilization endures sufficiently long, an age may come when the universities of Europe and of the two Americas will see fit to follow the illustrious tradition of the far-famed Buddhist and other universities of the Orient, such as Nālanda, the Oxford of ancient India, and institute chairs and departments of astrology. Even today, in all the chief monastic schools of Tibet, astrology is inferior in importance only to religion and metaphysics; and in modern India there still survive colleges of astrology. In our view, it is unreasonable to assume that a people so practical as the Chinese or so scientifically religious as the Hindus and Tibetans have been foolishly deluded in their age-long faithfulness to astrology.[1]

[1] The interested student is directed to the discussion of astrology

XII. THE *YOGA*

The '*Yoga* of Knowing the Mind in Its Nakedness' is *Jñāna Yoga* in purest form. Thus, quite unlike the many complex and often dangerous *yogas* dependent upon breathings and ordinary meditations, it can be safely practised without a *guru*, providing the practitioner leads a normal and well-regulated life. A living *guru* is, nevertheless, desirable, not only in solving the many *yogic* problems which are certain to arise, but chiefly to safeguard one from error and to supervise one's progress personally. Still, if a trustworthy *guru* is not available, the *yogin* need not hesitate to proceed alone, remembering always the aphorism, 'When the disciple is ready, the master will appear'. Those best fitted to profit by this *yoga* are, consequently, *yogins* who have gone beyond, either in this or some previous life, preliminary *yogic* practices.

The author of our treatise, whether Padma-Sambhava, as stated in the Colophon, or some person unknown, was, as internal evidence suggests, an adept in *yoga* with most unusual insight into Reality. There is, however, no sound evidence at present available which would tend to discredit the Colophon's assertion that the Great *Guru* himself wrote it as a direct outcome of his own realization.

Its concise perceptual teachings must be meditated upon one by one, with unlimited patience, and exhaustively. Otherwise, the only result will be an intellectual comprehension of them. This *yoga* is, therefore, apt to make little or no appeal to those of whom it has been said, 'It is as easy to teach them philosophy as to eat custard with a spoon'. Nor is it likely to attract the attention of those who are striving for worldly riches, comfort, and fame rather than for Freedom. A treatise such as this purports to be, the very quintessence of the Mahāyāna expounded in few words, cannot but be addressed to those already in possession of that profound insight which is the fruit of disciplined mind.

The goal of this *yoga* is the attainment of *Nirvāṇa*, or of

contained in *Tibetan Yoga and Secret Doctrines* (pp. 286–7), to which this present discussion is complementary.

complete awakening from the *Sangsāra*, simultaneously with which comes the Supreme Realization that both *Nirvāna* and the *Sangsāra* are eternally indistinguishably one. And this constitutes the Great Liberation.

Nirvāna being eternally at the basis of all existence, its attainment is dependent upon the *yogic* process of transmuting the mundane mind into the Supra-mundane Mind, success in which is equivalent to winning the philosopher's stone of the medieval alchemists, or to mastering their occult teaching concerning the transmutation of base metal into gold. The process is normally threefold. Firstly, through study and research, comes intellectual comprehension of Divine Wisdom. Secondly, the aspirant advances to intuitional insight. Thirdly, he stands face to face with the Nakedness.

It will assist and encourage the practitioner to have placed before him or her, for comparative study here, a brief outline of this same system of *Jñāna Yoga* from the Brāhmanical viewpoint, as expounded by a recently living Master of it, the late Mahārshi of Tiruvannamalai:

Right inquiry (Skt. *vichāra*) is the only efficacious method of tranquillizing the mind. Although the mind may be brought and kept under control by other means, such, for example, as breath regulation (Skt. *prānāyāma*), it invariably rebounds again and again. So long as the breath is restrained, the mind remains tranquil, but the moment the restraint is relaxed, the mind bounds up, and is tossed about by its inherent tendencies (Skt. *vāsanās*) resulting from past deeds (Skt. *karma*).

Both the mind and the vital force (Skt. *prāna*) have a common source. Thoughts are the manifestations of the mind. The thought 'I' is the root-thought which first springs from the mind, and this is egoism (Skt. *aham-kāra*). *Prāna* also arises from the same source as egoism. Therefore, when *prāna* is controlled, the mind, too, is controlled; and when the mind is controlled the breathing is brought under control. Breath (or *prāna*) is considered to be the gross expression or index (Skt. *sthūla*) of the mind. During one's lifetime the mind keeps the *prāna* within the body, and at the moment of death the mind and *prāna* depart from the body simultaneously.

Prānāyāma may help to bring under control, but not to

annihilate, the thought-process. Similarly, meditation upon a form (Skt. *mūrti-dhyānam*), repetition of a formula (Skt. *mantra-japam*), accompanied by food-discrimination, are no more than intermediate steps towards mind-control. The mind becomes fixed on a single object by *mūrti-dhyānam* or *mantra-japam*, just as the restless trunk of an elephant when given a chain to hold remains steady and makes no attempt to catch hold of any other object.

Each thought by itself is extremely weak, because the mind is distracted by countless and ever varying thoughts. The more the thoughts are restrained the more the mind concentrates and, consequently, gains strength and power. Success is assured if the mind is trained in *ātmā-vichāra* [or right inquiry into Reality].

Of all disciplines, food-discrimination, i.e. partaking of only *sāttvic* [or pure, vegetarian food], and in moderate quantities, is the most important. By means of this, the mind is rendered more and more *sāttvic* [or pure], and *ātmā-vichāra* more and more effective.

Countless *vāsanās*, or tendencies caused by past *karma*, reside in the mind. These have accumulated, from time immemorial, during untold past lives. Like waves upon the ocean, they rise on the mind, one after another.

As progress is made in *swarūpa-dhyāna* [or meditation on Truth, or the Real], these *vāsanās* are suppressed and vanish, no matter how old and deep they are. One should become firm and steady in *swarūpa-dhyāna* and allow no room for any doubt whether all the accumulated *vāsanās* can ever be extinguished and the mind can ever be transmuted into *Ātmā-Swarūpam* [or the Ultimate Truth, or Thatness]. . . .

So long as *vāsanās* adhere to the mind, one should pursue the quest of 'Who am I?' Continuing on this quest, one should suppress each thought as soon as it arises in the mind. Freedom from all attraction of every extraneous thing is called *Vairāgyam*, or desirelessness; and clinging to *Ātmā-Swarūpam* unswerved is *Jñānam*, or Wisdom, i.e. true understanding. Both *Vairāgyam* and *Jñānam* ultimately lead to the same goal.[1]

The *yogin* is to recognize that there are aspects of mind as innumerable as are the various modes of its manifestation, not only in human and sub-human creatures on Earth, but in

---

[1] This matter as quoted is the Editor's recension of matter contained in *Who Am I?* (pp. 7–10).

all other sentient beings throughout the *Sangsāra*. He is not to regard the Universe, in the manner of Christian theology, as being centred in man, but in mind. The *Abhidharma* makes four general classifications of mind: (1) mind manifested through animal sensuousness (Skt. *kāma-vicāra*); (2) mind manifested through living organisms or forms (*rūpa-vicāra*); (3) mind manifested independently of form (*arūpa-vicāra*); and (4) mind in its primordial, unmodified condition of nakedness (*lokottara-vicāra*). Mind is further divisible in accordance with its *sangsāric* manifestations. Or we may say that there are two chief aspects of mind, *sangsāric* and *nirvānic*; mind *per se*, or unmodified consciousness (*chit*), transcends both.

So long as there is mind *sangsārically* manifested, there is suffering, for suffering is inherent in transitoriness, in illusion, in Ignorance (*Avidyā*). Not until *sangsāric* mind is transcended can there be an end of suffering.

All things, bodily forms, sensations, perceptions, concepts, subjective differentiation, mind, or consciousness, in their *sangsāric* aspects are unreal in the sense that they are merely illusive reflections of Reality, as the One in the Many. The moonlight is not truly moonlight, it is only a reflex of sunlight; it illusorily appears to be what it is not, and is in that way unreal. Similarly, all *sangsāric* things appear to be real, like images seen reflected on the calm surface of a pool. If one is to know the Real, and not its pale illusory reflections, one must attain the Real; if one seeks the source of the light of the Sun itself, it is not to be found in the Moon. Likewise, the One Mind, or the Ultimate Consciousness in its primordiality, can be known only by itself alone, not by its *sangsāric* manifestations. In the words of Plotinus, 'Seek not to see this Principle by the aid of external things; otherwise, instead of seeing It itself, thou shalt see no more than its image'.[1]

Thus the essential objective of the *yogin* is *yogic* understanding of his own microcosmic aspect of mind, in order that mind may be realized in its true state. In speaking of this process, Professor D. T. Suzuki, the eminent authority on Zen Buddhism, with which our present '*Yoga* of Knowing the

[1] Cf. Plotinus, v. v. 10.

Mind in Its Nakedness' has much in common, describes it as the seeing the [One] Mind within the inner nature of one's own being, in accordance with the teachings of Bodhidharma, the Founder of Zen Buddhism, known in Japan as Daruma.[1] As our text emphasizes, the Microcosmic Mind is inseparable from the Macrocosmic Mind, both alike being of the One Essence of the Supra-mundane Mind. 'Nor is one's own mind separable from other minds.' The *yogin's* whole aim is to yoke the microcosmic aspect of mind, innately shining, yet hidden beneath the dense mists of Ignorance, with its parental source, the macrocosmic mind, and so attain transcendency over all dualities and all illusory appearances, the constituents of the *Sangsāra*.

Plotinus describes the process thus:

We must, therefore, meditate upon the mind in its divinest aspect in order to discover the nature of intellect. This is how we may proceed: from man, that is from thyself, strip off the body; then lay aside that subtle power which fashioneth the body; then separate thyself from sensuousness, hankering, and anger, and each of the lower passions that incline thee towards worldly things. What remaineth afterwards in the consciousness is what we call the 'image of intelligence', which emanateth from the mind, as from the mighty orb of the Sun emanateth the surrounding sphere of luminosity. Above intellect, we shall meet That which is called the 'nature of the Good'. The Good, which is transcendent over the Beautiful, is the source and essentiality of the Beautiful. Man must amalgamate himself with the Principle that he possesseth innately. Then, from the manyness that he was, he will have become one.[2]

Accordingly, it is by deep introspective meditation, and not by purely intellectual means, that this *yoga*, like Buddhism itself, can be comprehended. In the words of the Buddha, 'Without knowledge there is no meditation; without meditation there is no knowledge. He who hath both knowledge and meditation is near unto *Nirvāṇa*.'[3]

[1] Cf. D. T. Suzuki, *The Message of Bodhidharma*, in 'The Aryan Path' (Bombay, Jan. 1936).

[2] Cf. Plotinus, v. iii. 9; I. vi. 9; VI. ix. 3.

[3] *The Dhammapāda*, aphorism 372, as translated by Irving Babbitt (Oxford University Press, New York and London, 1936).

XIII. The Problem of Self (or Soul)

In the process of introspectively meditating upon the aphoristic teachings concerning the One Mind, the disciple will inevitably come face to face with the age-old problem of what man is. He will intuitively ask himself, Why am I? What am I? Am I a something, a self, a soul, eternally separate and different from each of the countless myriads of similarly constituted beings I see round about me in various states of existence? Is the glamorous world of appearances real? Are all these inanimate objects and all these living, breathing creatures, in the midst of which I find myself, real? Or are they, as the Buddhas declare, no more than the content of a *karmic* mirage, the stuff composing the dream of life?

When the truth begins to come from within, very feebly at first, like the consciousness of a man awakening from the torpor of a drugged sleep, or like the first traces of dawn coming forth in an eastern sky, the disciple will realize gradually that only by transcending the realm of separateness and attaining super-consciousness of the immutable at-one-ment of all things, organic and inorganic, can the age-old problem be solved. The more the disciple meditates upon what the self has in common with other selves, the more he will discover the impersonal self common to all selves. Thence he will reach the conclusion 'that if one and the same factor is the core of each individual's selfhood, no individual in its true essence has individuality. There would be nothing like *my* self; there would be only the Self.'[1]

As the Sages have repeatedly emphasized by means of paradoxical aphorisms, it is only by losing oneself that one finds oneself, it is only by self-surrender that one attains self-victory, it is only by dying on the Cross of the *Sangsāra* that one attains life more abundantly, and becomes a Light in the Darkness. It is by impersonalizing the personality, by self-extinction, by realizing the voidness of every objective ap-

---

[1] The Editor here acknowledges indebtedness to the clear and concise thinking set forth by Dr. Edward Conzé in his booklet entitled *Contradiction and Reality* (London, 1939), pp. 13-14.

pearance throughout the Universe, that the disciple reaches that understanding of self to which the text directs him.

To tread this path successfully, the *karmically*-inherited tendency to emphasize the self through attachment to the results of worldly activities must be neutralized; self-aggrandizement, self-glorification, must give place to self-diminution and complete passivity.[1] Then all opposition between the self and the world of appearances will subside, even as the waves on a sea subside when the wind has ceased. It is in this state that

the self loses itself and all measure, sinks into a measureless being that is without limitations, foundations, and determinations. It is devoured by being, in which no more one thing is opposed to another. In consequence, there is nothing to which the person opposes himself. This is achieved by identification with all things and events as they come along, and as they are. The self relaxes and becomes empty. The entrance of reality is no longer barred by predilections of one's own which, being peculiar to the individual, could act as a distorting medium. Things are experienced as they are, as one sees the bottom of a lake through clear and quiet water.[2]

Expositions of the Buddhist doctrine of non-self, or non-soul, frequently exhibit looseness of thinking and misleading argumentation, sometimes by Buddhists themselves. The Buddha did not teach that there is no self, or soul; He taught that there is no self, or soul, that is real, non-transitory, or possessed of unique and eternally separate existence. In Buddhism, salvation is not of a self, or soul; it is entirely dependent upon what the Buddha declared to be the deliverance of the mind from the *sangsāric* bondage imposed by Ignorance (Skt. *Avidyā*), from the erroneous belief that appearances are real and that there are individualized immortal selves, or souls.

When there is no longer a clinging to selfhood, when all the

___

[1] This teaching of the Clear-Seeing Ones, the Conquerors of Self, the supra-*sangsāric* Supermen, who are humanity's true guides, is quite the antithesis of that of men who are fettered to the *Sangsāra* and enamoured of the tyrannizing passions and the warfare of the animal-man.

[2] Cf. Edward Conzé, op. cit., pp. 16–17.

external play of *sangsāric* energies is allowed to subside, because there is no longer attachment to any of them, then there is that state of absolute quiescence of mental activities which our text refers to as the natural state of the mind. When the human consciousness of illusory appearances has been swallowed up in the supra-mundane consciousness of the *Arhant*, then the Path leading to Limitless Understanding and Divine Wisdom, to transcendence over the limitations *karmically* imposed by existence in the *Sangsāra*, has, indeed, been entered upon. On that Path, the aspirant advances to the state beyond self; he loses himself; the purified drop reunites with the Cosmic Ocean of Being. The illusory micro-cosmic mind dissolves; there is only the One Mind; there is Final Emancipation, Perfect Buddhahood.

Only when Ignorance has been done away with, only when the limited self, or soul, has been alchemically resolved into its *karmic* constituents, and the littleness of the man has become the greatness of a Buddha, is the Goal reached.

Among all the Buddha's teachings, that of non-soul (Skt. *anātma*: Pāli *anattā*) is of supreme importance,

for therein, having discarded personality and permanent substance, He preached a moral law, without anyone or anything on which the law would be binding, and proclaimed a salvation to be attained by a great endeavour, which apart altogether from the existence of somebody entitled to reach the goal, consisted not in a blissful, eternal survival in a heaven or some such abode of joy, but merely in a quiescence from the things that men generally value in life.[1]

Thus, by successful practice of the *Yoga* of the One Mind, the aspirant realizes that the illusory separateness of things camouflages reality, that Ignorance is the price paid for illusorily enjoying distinctness and the sense of selfhood. This supreme realization will receive further exposition, from the viewpoints of Psychology and Therapy, in the Section which immediately follows.

[1] Cf. *The Buddhist Doctrine of Anattā* by Dr. G. P. Malalasekara, in the Vaisaka Number of *The Mahā-Bodhi* (Calcutta, May and June 1940), pp. 222-3.

XIV. The Psychology and the Therapy

Psychologically considered, the ' *Yoga* of Knowing the Mind in Its Nakedness' is a system of practically applied transcendental sublimation of life, in keeping with that of the Noble Eightfold Path, which is itself entirely a process of greater and greater sublimation. As study of the mind of children shows, there is a natural inborn tendency in man to transcend the external world of non-homogeneity and to seek a state of homogeneity, such as that of the supra-mundane at-one-ment which results from the *yogic* knowing of mind in its unobscured naturalness. It is out of a realm of nothingness, metaphorically akin to the philosophical Voidness of the Mahāyāna, that the child creates its own world of fantasy, which, like the state of *Nirvāṇa*, being a state of homogeneity, is harmonious and blissful.

The quest for homogeneity is common not only to children, but to mature humanity of all races and times. In the more primitive societies, it manifests itself in myths and wonder-tales of faerie, where everything normally impossible becomes realizable in a homogeneous state of all-embracing transcendent magic. In the most culturally advanced societies it manifests itself in dreams of an ideal commonwealth like that of Plato's or a world utopia such as that conceived by a Sir Thomas More or a Karl Marx, or the Heaven on Earth of the Christians, or the Paradise of Islam.[1]

Likewise, there appears to be deep-hidden in the unconscious, awaiting favourable opportunity to come forth into the conscious, a transcendent geometrical symmetry, like that referred to by the Greek philosophers in such aphorisms as 'God geometrizes', or 'The Universe is founded on number'; and, also, a divine beauty and perfect harmony. Here, too, there lie in embryo, awaiting to be born into the lives of men,

[1] We gratefully acknowledge in this connexion the help of the very fruitfully suggestive paper by Dr. A. Groeneveld, of Holland, entitled 'Early Childhood and its Mechanisms: Isotropism (Homotropism) and Canontropism', and that by Dr. F. Künkel, of Germany, entitled 'Das "Wir" als Faktor in der Heilpaedogogik', which were read on 30 July 1938 in Oxford, before the Tenth International Medical Congress for Psychotherapy.

unwavering constancy, indomitable will, and power to transform the world.

Dr. C. G. Jung, the eminent psychologist, in his presidential address concluding the proceedings of the Tenth International Medical Congress of Psychotherapy, held in Oxford from 29 July to 2 August 1938, emphasized the importance of a philosophical preparation for understanding primitive thought. The soundness of this contention cannot be questioned. As a direct result of our own researches, we found that the more primitive, or more unfettered by civilization's inhibitions, a society is, the more natural it is. Accordingly, then, the mind of primordial man must have been the freest from illusion (Skt. *māyā*), and the mind of twentieth-century man in London, New York, Paris, or Berlin, the most fettered to illusion. What is today known as social progress is essentially movement away from primitive naturalness. As has been suggested in Section VII above, it is in the study of unsophisticated or so-called primitive societies that the psychologist, equally with the anthropologist, will make the nearest external approach to that state referred to in our treatise as the seeing of mind in its nakedness. In other words, the 'uncivilized' man is a clearer percipient and thus a sounder interpreter of life than the 'civilized' man. This I discovered during my four years of research among the Celtic peasantry of Ireland, Scotland, Isle of Man, Wales, Cornwall, and Brittany, and set forth in *The Fairy-Faith in Celtic Countries*.[1]

The more 'civilized' and utilitarianly educated the man, the less fitted he is to understand himself in the sense of the well-known Greek aphorism, Γνῶθι Σεαυτόν, 'Know Thyself'. The child, like the primitive man and the illiterate peasant, is much nearer the True Vision. There have been no more profound psychologists than the Great Teachers, who, with unanimity, have proclaimed that the neophyte must become as a little child before he can enter into the Realm of Truth.

[1] This, the Editor's first important work, has long been out of print. The new edition of it, now being prepared, should appeal to readers of our Tibetan Series, wherein the *ḍākinī* and various other orders of fairy-like beings receive, as they do in this volume of the Tibetan Series, much attention.

Here, then, is the psychological reason why the *Gurus* teach renunciation of the world, the putting aside of the intellectualisms of men, the need of being born again to a higher perception; and why the wisdom of babes is greater than that of scholars.

Animal instincts, whereby the multitude are chiefly guided and through which they are controlled by the state, must be transcended. The transcendent sublimation through knowing the mind in its nakedness cannot be brought about by exercise of lowly brutish propensities, which also are inherent in man's nature, but by virtue of the ascendency of the higher propensities latent in the unconscious, even of the unborn child. Self-control and indomitable will are preliminary prerequisites for one who would master the divine alchemical science of mind. Apart from self-control, there can be no dominion over the animal in man; apart from indomitable will, there can be no sublimation of life.

Although psychology, as we know it, is peculiarly occidental, particularly in its terminology and methods, there is a psychology which by contrast is essentially transcendental, far older and more mature, known to Orientals as *yoga*. In order, therefore, to understand the psychology of the teachings set forth in this volume there must be adequate understanding of *yoga* itself; and the student is directed to the three previous volumes of this Tibetan Series, wherein *yoga* in its various aspects has been expounded. The two preceding Sections of this Introduction are complementary thereto.

As will be observed, the *yogic* doctrine of concepts set forth in our present treatise parallels that of the *Bardo Thödol* concerning the mental content of the percipient of the after-death state. During countless ages, mind, in its mundane reflex, has been experiencing *sangsāric* sensuousness. Like blotting-paper incorporating ink, it has absorbed concepts. In its primordial condition it was as colourless and clear as pure water. Like drops of various coloured fluids, some almost transparent and colourless, others black as soot, so many varying concepts have been received by it that its natural transparency and colourlessness have been lost. It is this condition of cloudiness or obscuration, called Ignorance, which now prevails in the mind, that *yoga* is intended to eliminate.

The first step in the process of removing the ink from the blotting-paper and the foreign substances from the water is dependent upon recognition of the illusory and non-real character of concepts. The *yogin* must come to realize that the world of human concepts is merely a product of the microcosmic mind even as the Cosmos is the product of the macrocosmic mind. He must be able to control the mechanism of his mind as completely as a master engineer does that of an engine; he must be able at will to bring the thought-process to a dead stop.

When Mind is the Quiescent, and there is no thought-process, it is the One; when it emanates intelligence, intelligence thinks beings, and causes them to exist, and is the beings. According to Plotinus, 'Considered in its universality, Intelligence containeth all entities as the genus containeth all species, as the whole containeth all parts. Intelligence resideth within itself, and by possessing itself quiescently, is the eternal fullness of all things.' But thought does not itself think:

It is the cause which maketh some other being to think. The cause, however, cannot be identified with that which is caused. So much more reason is there then to say that the cause of all these existing things cannot be any of them. Accordingly, this Cause must not be conceived as being the good it emanateth, but as the good in a higher sense, that Good which transcendeth all other goods. Inasmuch as the One containeth no difference, It is eternally present; and we are eternally present in the One, as soon as we contain no more difference.

He who would attain to this state of non-differentiation, must practise psychic analysis of himself: 'Withdraw within thyself, and analyze thyself.'[1]

The writer is frequently asked, 'What purpose is served by concentrating the mind upon some external object or by attaining mental one-pointedness?' The answer is that the *yogin* thereby gains control of his thinking-process, very much after the manner of a man attaining control of an engine by

[1] Cf. Plotinus, v. ix. 6, 8; vi. ix. 6, 8; i. vi. 9.

studying its mechanism. The finite aspect of mind, undomin-
ated by *yoga*, is as unruly as a wild horse. It must be caught,
as Milarepa teaches, and tied up. Not until it is tied up with
the rope of one-pointedness can it be tamed and put in a
corral for close observation.

The whole aim of the *yogin*, in this particularly psychological *yoga*, is research into the origin, nature, and powers of the
dynamo, the mind, the energy of which runs his body. When,
eventually, he becomes able *yogically* to dissect or take it to
pieces, then only will he know it, and by knowing it know
himself.

One of the most remarkable aphorisms of oriental psychology is, 'To whatever the mind goeth (or is attached), that
it becometh.'[1] For illustration, it is by fixing the mind upon
agriculture that a man becomes an agriculturist, or upon
chemistry a chemist, or upon evil a criminal, or upon good a
saint. The agriculturist is merely the outcome of his accumulating, by will power, mental concepts called agriculture, and
so on for the chemist, the criminal, and the saint; each has
become that to which his or her mind has gone. As the *Maitri
Upanishad* (vi. 34) teaches,

> The *Sangsāra* is no more than one's own thought.
> With effort one should therefore cleanse the thought.
> What one thinketh, that doth one become.
> This is the eternal mystery.[1]

This psychology is clearly brought out in the *Bardo Thödol*.
The character of the after-death existence, as it teaches, is
dependent upon the character of the mental content of the
deceased, precisely as the character of human existence is
determined by the mental content of its experiencer. There is,
however, this difference: the after-death state is passive, that
is, digestive of the experiences of the human state; the human
state is a state of activity, of the storing up of concepts as
mental content. Immediately mind in its *sangsāric* aspect is
divested of its grosser physical integument, which enabled it
to accumulate concepts, it automatically relaxes, the mental

---

[1] According to a translation privately made by Mr. E. T. Sturdy.

tension born of the activities of life on Earth having been removed by death. Like a clock which has been wound up, it then begins to run mechanically, impelled by *karma*, and it runs so until it is run down, whereupon there is rebirth to store up fresh energy. The winding up results from the activities of the human existence just ended, the running results from the burning up in the after-death state of passivity of the stored-up energy derived from those activities, and the consequent release of their *karmic* potentialities. Similarly, vegetative activities result in coal, and the burning of the coal releases, in the form of heat, light, and gases, the stored-up energy derived from the vegetative activities.

As the teachings set forth in our treatise imply, the ultimate aim of the *yogin* is to put an end to this perpetual and monotonous oscillation of mind between the latency of the after-death state and the activeness of the human state. But he cannot do so until he stops the dynamo of mind from accumulating ever fresh energy with which to keep running its bodily machine. At the outset of his efforts to accomplish this supreme task, he must apply the *yoga* expounded by the precepts in a thorough psychological self-analysis.

There then ensue very definite and classifiable mental states, which may be enumerated as follows: (1) the initial comprehension that the finiteness of mind is due to aeons of misdirected concept-forming; (2) after the necessary halting of the thought-process has been accomplished, the *yogic* psychic analysis of the mental content; (3) the discovery of the purely illusory character of the concepts forming the mental content; (4) the inevitable disillusionment concerning the world of apparent reality; (5) the resultant birth of an indomitable resolve to purge the mind of its Ignorance, and thereby restore it to its primordial naturalness; (6) the realization of the psychic inseparableness and at-one-ment of all things and minds, equivalent to the realization of that native homogeneity innate in man and postulated by occidental psychologists as being more clearly discernable in the mind of the child; (7) the Ineffable Union with the One Mind, which is the transcendent fruit of *Yoga*, or divine yoking of the microcosmic with the macrocosmic, the complete Sublimation of Life, the Transmutation of Ignorance into Wisdom.

In this psychological *yoga* lie the fundamentals of true therapy, to which a few of the pioneer scientists of the Occident are now, rather belatedly, beginning to give serious attention. There cannot be Health so long as Ignorance remains uncured; there cannot be Sanity so long as there is belief that the world of appearances is real or that there exists the eternal separateness and pluralism implied by the doctrine of soul.

The technique of this Higher Medicine—as suggested by Dr. Jung's Foreword-Commentary—rather than being dependent upon knowledge merely of mental phenomena, as these are understood by occidental psychology, with its concentration upon fact-collecting, is more akin to that of the analytical psychologist. The Buddha, like the Christ, has been very rightly called the Great Physician. But His method of treatment is not imposed from without; it is applicable only by the patient himself, through *yogic* introspection, as has been more fully explained herein elsewhere.

The Cure is dependent upon the elimination from the conscious mind of all seeds, both active and latent, of desire, of all elements of Ignorance. Until this elimination is accomplished, man cannot enjoy mental health; he cannot see things as they are, for his eyes are *sangsārically* jaundiced; he remains obsessed with innumerable fantasies, mere will-o'-the-wisps of the mind; he is, in the Buddhistic sense, irrational, even to the point of insanity, as regards Reality. Like a mad man, he goes from birth to birth repeatedly; and, becoming a menace to every sentient creature, wherever he wanders he incessantly sows warfare and selfishness. Only when the mind attains what our text calls the Natural State is there Deliverance from Delusion and from Insanity.

This, then, is Right Psychology and Right Therapy, the knowing of and the transcendence over the conscious psyche, the ego of illusoriness. It is the 'Yoga of Knowing the Mind in Its Nakedness', the Clear Seeing of Reality. It is that Deliverance of the mind which the Enlightened One proclaims to be the Goal of the *Dharma*. It is the Great Liberation.

XV. Origin of the Text

The original Tibetan text of the 'Yoga of Knowing the Mind in Its Nakedness', which constitutes the Great Liberation, belongs to the *Bardo Thödol* series of *yogic* treatises concerning various methods of attaining transcendence over Ignorance. This will be obvious upon making comparison of its transliterated title with that of the *Bardo Thödol* itself in *The Tibetan Book of the Dead*. The whole series appertains to the Tantric School of the Mahāyāna, and is believed to have been first committed to writing during the eighth century A.D. The authorship of our present treatise is attributed to Padma-Sambhava himself. The text is said to have been hidden and subsequently recovered by the *tertön* (or taker-out of hidden treasures of sacred writings) Rigzin Karma Ling-pa.[1]

The Block-Print employed contains sixteen such treatises, corresponding to the first sixteen of the cycle of seventeen enumerated in *The Tibetan Book of the Dead* (pp. 71–72) ; and the 'Yoga of Knowing the Mind in Its Nakedness' is the tenth of the series. The last sentence of the Block-Print reads: 'The block-types [of this Block-Print] belong to the Tan-gye-ling Monastery'. This monastery is situated in the northern quarter and within the walls of the city of Lhāsa; and its abbot, one of the four *lāma-tulkus*, or grand *lāmas* who successively reincarnate, bears the title Demo Rinpoch'e, the 'One of Precious Peace.' He is said to be the incarnation of the illustrious Tibetan King Srong-Tsan-Gampo's minister of state, Lon-po Gar.[2]

[1] See *The Tibetan Book of the Dead*, pp. 73–77.

[2] Each of the other three *lāma-tulkus*, upon reincarnating, becomes the abbot of one of the three other of the four chief monasteries of Lhāsa, which are, Kundeling, Ts'omoling, and Ts'ech'ogling. The Government of Tibet being controlled by these four monasteries, called 'The Four *Lings* (or Places)', the Regent, when the Dalai Lāma is dead or until he attains his majority at the age of 18, is always the eldest of these four *lāma-tulkus*, who then rules as the King of Tibet. (Cf. L. A. Waddell, op. cit., pp. 253–4.) The reincarnations of all four of these abbots are discovered and chosen in much the same manner as is the reincarnation of the Dalai Lāma. Lāma Karma Sumdhon Paul, the chief of the two translators of our text, described to me the installation of the present Demo Rinpoch'e, which he witnessed in Lhāsa on 13 Oct. 1909, at the Tangyeling Monastery. The 'One of Precious Peace' was then a bright-faced boy of about 13 or 14 years of age. All the high

The history of the Block-Print text of the Biography of Padma-Sambhava is given at the end of our Epitome of it; and that of the manuscript text of *Guru* Phadampa Sangay's Teachings on the title-page of Book III, herein.

XVI. THE TRANSLATORS

The translator of the excerpts upon which our 'Epitome of the Life and Teachings of Tibet's Great *Guru* Padma-Sambhava' is based, the late Sardar Bahādur S. W. Laden La, C.B.E., F.R.G.S., A.D.C., I.P., passed away in Kalimpong on 26 December 1936, less than a year after the time of the completion of the translation. Of ancient Tibetan ancestry, he was born on 16 June 1876 in Darjeeling, and there received his education. In 1898 he joined the corps of the Darjeeling Police, and soon attained official rank. In 1903–4 he was deputed to the Staff of the Tibetan Mission of Colonel Younghusband. After this he was an assistant to Colonel O'Connor in connexion with His Holiness the Tashi Lāma's tour throughout India. In 1906 he assisted the British Government when the question of an important treaty with Tibet and of indemnity had to be discussed with the Tibetan Minister. In 1907 he founded the General Buddhist Association, of the Darjeeling District, and was its first President. In 1909 he became the Founder-President of the Himalayan Children's Advancement Association which has already educated and placed over 600 orphans and poor boys. It is said that he spent out of his own pocket over Rs.25,000 in this noble work. In 1910 his

dignatories of the Lhāsa Government attended the installation, which is a very important affair of state; and for a number of days the Holy City abandoned itself to religious festivities. Differences having arisen between the late Dalai Lāma and the previous Demo Rinpoch'e, the late Dalai Lāma took over the administration of the wealth and income of Tangyeling and decreed that no more of the incarnations of the Demo Rinpoch'e would be recognized. The Demo Rinpoch'e made reply, saying that he would next incarnate in the Dalai Lāma's own family and compel the Dalai Lāma to recognize him. Accordingly, soon after the Demo Rinpoch'e's decease, a son was born to the Dalai Lāma's sister with every physical and mental characteristic of the late Demo Rinpoch'e; and the Dalai Lāma, being obliged to admit that the boy really was the reincarnated Demo Rinpoch'e, permitted his installation as the head of Tangyeling and cancelled the decree against him.

services were requisitioned by the Political Department of the Indian Government in connexion with the journey of His Holiness the Dalai Lāma to visit the Viceroy and make pilgrimage to the Buddhist Holy Places of India. Later, he was deputed to Tibet to settle terms between the Chinese and Tibetans as a representative of the British Government; and part of his duty consisted in helping to lead the Chinese Amban, Lien-Yu, and General Chung and the Chinese troops out of Tibet, whilst Colonel Willoughby held the Indian frontier.

It was said that the Tibetans were then much incensed against the Sardar Bahādur because of his services with the Younghusband Mission. According to rumour, at the time of the Mission, in 1904, the Tibetan Government had offered a reward of Rs.10,000 for his head and hands. But, after some years, all this was overlooked, and he was appointed by the Tibetan Government to accompany to England four carefully chosen Tibetan boys of good family, who were sent there at their Government's expense to acquire a modern technical and scientific education and return to Tibet to train their fellow countrymen. And he went to England also entrusted with credentials as envoy of His Holiness the Dalai Lāma, and, as such, carried letters and presents to Their Majesties in Buckingham Palace. In 1914, after his return, he attended the Tibetan–Chinese Conference at Simla, and thence accompanied the Prime Minister of Tibet to Sikkim.

During the First World War the Sardar Bahādur assisted in raising war loans and in recruiting the hill tribes. He was mentioned in dispatches, and in 1917 received the military title of Sardar Bahādur. Then, in 1921, when Sir Charles Bell went to Lhāsa with the object of cementing the friendly relationship with the Tibetan Government, the Sardar Bahādur was appointed his personal assistant.

In 1923 the Tibetan Government again enjoyed the Sardar Bahādur's services, for which they had been asking the Government of India for two years. This time, he organized a Police Force in Lhāsa and, also, the Tibetan Army. During the following year, in recognition, the Dalai Lāma conferred upon him the highest distinction in Tibet by raising him to the rank of a *Dzasa* or Tibetan Peer. Previously, in 1912, when some misunderstanding existed between His Holiness the Dalai Lāma and His Holiness the Tashi Lāma, the Sardar Bahādur succeeded in bringing about a friendly agreement between them. For this good service, His Holiness the Dalai Lāma conferred upon the Sardar Bahādur the title of *De-Pon* (or General) and a Premier Class Gold Medal of the Order of the Golden Lion, the first of its kind struck in Tibet, which is a massive gold nugget bearing the name of the Dalai Lāma. His Holiness the Tashi Lāma presented to the Sardar Bahādur a gold medal and conferred upon him the title of *Deo-nyer-chhem-Po* or Lord Chamberlain of the Court of Tashi Lhunpo.

The Sardar Bahādur, who was the most active of Tibetan Buddhist laymen in the maintenance and support of the *Dharma* among his Himalayan peoples along the Indian–Tibetan frontier, was the President and Patron of ten Buddhist monasteries, among which are those at Ghoom, Kurseong, Darjeeling, and Lopchu. Owing almost wholly to his financial assistance, the Ghoom Monastery was reconstructed, and then, after the disastrous earthquake of 1934, repaired, and its Mahāyāna Chapel built.

In 1927 he was made a Chevalier of the Order of Leopold II by the King and Queen of Belgium. In the midst of winter, in January 1930, he was sent to Lhāsa by the Indian Government in connexion with a very serious disagreement between Tibet and Nepal; and by his tactful and diplomatic intervention prevented war between the two countries. For this outstanding service he was made a Commander of the British Empire. Later on in the same year, 1930, he made his last visit to Lhāsa. This was for the purpose of personally presenting Colonel Weir, the Political Officer of Sikkim, and Mrs. Weir to the Dalai Lāma, Mrs. Weir thereby becoming the first English lady to be honoured by an introduction at the Court of His Holiness the Dalai Lāma at Lhāsa.

In June 1931 the Sardar Bahādur, after thirty-three years of public life, retired from Government Service; but to the day of his death he gave himself, in the true *Bodhisattvic* spirit, to the good of others. Thus, in the same year, he accepted the Presidency of the Hillmen's Association; he was active in the Boy Scouts' Clubs; in 1923 he was elected Vice-Chairman of the Darjeeling Municipality, and became vested with the full authority of a Chairman; and for his many educational, religious, and philanthropic activities he was probably the most beloved citizen of Darjeeling, as indicated by his mile-long funeral procession to the Ghoom Monastery, where his body was cremated. He was an Honorary Aide-de-camp to His Excellency the Governor of Bengal; and it was in grateful recognition of the voluntary services which the Sardar Bahādur rendered in connexion with the three Mount Everest Expeditions that he was elected a Fellow of the Royal Geographical Society.[1] The Sardar Bahādur was one of the really true Buddhists of our generation, who not only fostered but also practically applied the Precepts of the Enlightened One. Of the Great *Guru* Padma-Sambhava he was a fervent devotee. He had scholarly command of ten languages, English, Tibetan, Hindustani, Kyathi, Bengali, Nepalese, Lepcha, and other Himalayan tongues. Save for his assistance, Book I of this volume would never have been written. As to a *Guru*, and a *Bodhisattva* far advanced on the Great Path, the Mahāyāna, the Editor here acknowledges with profound gratitude his own personal indebtedness to the Sardar Bahādur. And all who read this book are, in like manner, the Sardar Bahādur's debtors.

There now follows a brief biographical account of the two translators of Book II.

Lāma Karma Sumdhon Paul was born in Ghoom on 4 September 1891 of Tibetan ancestry. As a boy, his education commenced, and continued for three years, under the learned Mongolian Lāma Sherab Gyatsho, of the Ghoom Monastery. Later, he entered the Darjeeling High School with a government scholarship and there completed his studies at the age

---

[1] For a large part of this biographical matter the Editor is indebted to *The Darjeeling Times* of 2 Jan. 1937 wherein there appears a special article concerning the death of the Sardar Bahādur, entitled 'The passing of a Truly Great Man', covering four pages.

of sixteen. His first post was as a government employee in the Deputy Commissioner's Office, Darjeeling.

During 1905–6 he was attached to the staff of the Tashi Lāma as an interpreter and accompanied His Holiness on a tour of India and afterwards to the Monastery of Tashi Lhunpo ('Heap of Blessings'). For about seven months he resided in this monastery of the Tashi Lāma, in intimate personal contact with His Holiness. 'My own impression', he said in reply to the Editor's query, 'is that His Holiness the Tashi Lāma really regarded himself as being an incarnation of the Buddha Amitābha. His officials told me that His Holiness possessed many unusual psychic powers, and the Tibetan Priesthood, as a whole, recognized in him the Supreme Head of the Esoteric Doctrines.'

Of the daily activities of His Holiness, the Lāma added:

He arose before dawn, prayed, and performed his personal religious duties. At about 5.30 a.m. he partook of tea and light refreshments. The early morning was taken up chiefly with receiving visiting officials of the Church. At about 10 a.m. he took a regular meal. Afterwards, he would attend the temples, bless pilgrims, and see visitors. I always left his presence soon after sunset, and went to my own apartments; but I was told that His Holiness retired late, after a very long day's work.

In India, at Bōdh-Gayā, Benares, and Taxila, His Holiness gave many religious discourses and blessed the people by touching their head. In public blessings he generally held an arrow to which were attached various coloured Tibetan scarfs, and with these he touched the head of those he blessed. In bestowing blessings privately he used his hands alone. He taught us especially concerning the coming Buddha, Maitreya, and read texts referring to Him and made prayers to Him.

In 1908 the Lāma Karma Sumdhon Paul went to Lhāsa and remained there for almost one year, visiting temples and monasteries and making pilgrimages. At that epoch the Dalai Lāma was absent in China. After returning to Darjeeling the Lāma became the headmaster of the Ghoom Middle English School. In 1924 he became the first successor to the late Lāma Kazi Dawa-Samdup in the Department of Tibetan Studies of the University of Calcutta. Very successfully he occupied that post for about ten years, retiring in 1933, whereupon he was appointed Head Lāma of the Government High School, Darjeeling, as he is, in 1935. There appeared in 1934 his translation into English of the *Dri-med-Kun-lDen's Namthar*, or *Birth-Story of Sarva-Vimala, King of Religion*, published by the Calcutta University.

Lāma Lobzang Mingyur Dorje, too, was born in Ghoom of Tibetan parentage, in the year 1875, and also had as his *guru* the same venerable abbot Lāma Sherab Gyatsho, who had come from Mongolia some years previously and founded the Ghoom Monastery. His discipleship under this learned Lāma began at the age of 10 and continued for fifteen years, and then, at the age of 25, he left the Monastery and, as his first scholarly work, aided the late Rai Bahādur Sarat Chandra Dās to compile his *Tibetan–English Dictionary* (Calcutta, 1902), now the standard treatise of its kind. At this task of compilation, Lāma Lobzang Mingyur Dorje worked for almost five years; and, although it was due to him, assisted by his *guru* in the Ghoom Monastery, more than to the Rai Bahādur that the Dictionary was accurately arranged, unfortunately no credit was given to him or to his *guru* in its preface.

Soon after the Dictionary was completed, the Lāma was appointed Head Lāma of the Government High School, Darjeeling. He held this post with great honour for thirty years, and then, as is customary, retired on a pension. But he was still a vigorous man; and, being a true scholar, he made this retirement an opportunity for yet wider social service. First we see him at the Urusvati Himalayan Roerich Research Institution, where he worked for four years on another Tibetan–English Dictionary and in experimenting with Tibetan methods of treating cancer and other diseases, with valuable results. Then, on 1 August 1935 he was appointed to the Tibetan Instructorship for Research in Tibetan in the University of Calcutta, becoming the late Lāma Kazi Dawa-Samdup's second successor.

These two Lāmas, the translators of Book II, did much to raise the standard of Tibetan studies not only in the Darjeeling High School but in the University of Calcutta as well, and both were intimately acquainted with the late Lāma Kazi Dawa-Samdup.

Of the late Lāma Kazi Dawa-Samdup's *Guru* Norbu (of whom some account is recorded in *Tibetan Yoga and Secret Doctrines*, pp. 105–7), Lāma Lobzang Mingyur Dorje said to the Editor, in the year 1935:

I met him in Buxaduar more than twenty years ago, and found him to be a most excellent Lāma of the Kargyüd (*Dkar-brgyud*) Sect. The Director of Public Instruction of Bengal deputed me to inspect his monastic school, for the Government was making him a grant-in-aid. He had about twenty disciples. I remained with the *Guru* for two days, and made a very favourable report.

XVII. The Translating and Editing

In its original Block-Print form, the treatise translated as Book II consists of 143 lines of Tibetan text divided into 395 metrically constructed verses written on fifteen folios, or thirty pages counting the title-page, of Tibetan-made paper, each measuring 14½ by 3½ inches. Of the 395 verses, 389 are in a regular nine-syllable metre.[1] Of the other verses, consisting of *mantras*, three are of six, one of three, and two of two syllables each. There are, on an average, nine words in each of the 143 lines, or a total of about 1287 words. The metre of the 389 regular nine-syllable verses is illustrated by the following transliteration of verses 37 and 38:

> *Kri-yog bsnyen bsgrub mthah la zhen pas bsgribs.*
> *Ma-hā a-nu dbyings rig zhen pas bsgribs.*
> (*pron. Kri-yog nyen drub thah la zhen pe drib.*
> *Ma-hā ah-nu ying rig zhen pe drib*).

The translation is on page 206, following.

In order to make the words fit the metre, many of them throughout the text are abbreviated, like the first two here given, *Kri-yog* being a shortened form of the Sanskrit *Kriyā-Yoga*. Some of the verses are merely so many words or

---

[1] See *Tibetan Yoga and Secret Doctrines*, pp. 278–80, where Tibetan versification is discussed.

syllables without verbal or other connexion. Owing to this abbreviated style of diction and to the epigrammatic character of
the aphoristic text as a whole, all the skilled ability of the
two translators and of the Editor was required to produce a
rendering which would be true both to the highly philosophical and classical Tibetan, with its many technical and idiomatic expressions, and to the requirements of literary English.
No such translation can be expected to be entirely free from
error, more especially in our actual pioneering stage of Tibetan studies. The translators and the Editor believe, however,
that the rendering herein contained faithfully conveys the
real meanings which an educated *lāma* would derive from a
careful study of the treatise in its original form.

No attempt has been made in the English translation to
conform to the metrical structure of the Tibetan text. Nor
has a strictly literal rendering always been considered desirable; and frequently a rather free rendering has been found
necessary to bring out in the English the inner significance of
the Tibetan idioms, in particular those peculiarly Tantric.

The same methods were employed in translating the
excerpts from the Block-Print text of the Biography of
Padma-Sambhava by the late Sardar Bahādur S. W. Laden
La, ably assisted by Lāma Sonam Senge, a graduate in Tibetan
Grammar of the Sakya Monastery, Tibet, and by the Editor.
The work of translating these excerpts was begun in Darjeeling on 22 November 1935 and completed in Calcutta on
21 January 1936. The Block-Print which was used consisted
of 397 large folios, or 794 pages inclusive of the title-page.

The translation of the text of the 'Yoga of Knowing the
Mind in Its Nakedness' was started on 4 September 1935, the
forty-fourth birthday of the Lāma Karma Sumdhon Paul, in
the bungalow then occupied by the Editor, just outside the
entrance to the Ghoom Monastery, Darjeeling. The first
rough draft of the translation was in manuscript form on the
second day of the following month; and the various revisions
of the translation were completed, there in Ghoom, about five
weeks later.

Although the 'Yoga of Knowing the Mind in Its Nakedness',

like the '*Yoga* of the Great Symbol' set forth in *Tibetan Yoga and Secret Doctrines*, is not strictly a *Tantra*, it is, nevertheless, a product of Tantricism.

The Epitome of the Biography is, necessarily, a brief synopsis of the very extensive and frequently verbose mass of matter comprised within the 794 large pages of the original text, which contains not only textual inconsistences, such as are inseparable from a collection of semi-historical traditions, but much mythology, as in its first chapters, that has no more than remote bearing on the life-history of Padma-Sambhava. Thus, the Epitome opens with the Buddha's prophecy of Padma's birth, on folio 40, where-the Biography properly begins, and thence continues to the end of the Tibetan text. No critical examination of the material, historical or philosophical, has been attempted; for our purpose in presenting it is essentially anthropological. This task of criticism remains for scholars of the future, when a translation of the Biography as a whole will have been made.

The version of the *Guru* Phadampa Sangay's teachings contained in Book III is based upon a translation made by the late Lāma Kazi Dawa-Samdup in the year 1919, from a manuscript text, the history of which is given in the annotation on the title-page of Book III.

So far as is consistent with soundness of method, the use of square brackets has been avoided, especially in Book II. But wherever they appear they usually indicate an interpolation intended to bring out the meaning of an abbreviated or concise aphorism or phrase, or of an idiomatic, technical, or obscure expression. Sometimes they are used, in translated texts, parenthetically.

The examination of the textual matter of all three Books has been anthropological, in the strict sense of Anthropology, the Knowing, or Knowledge, of Man. Its critical examination from the viewpoint of history, philosophy, and philology remains for specialists in those respective fields of scholarship. As to the validity of the doctrines presented, the right attitude is that of the rationalist, so well stated by the Buddha when He admonished His disciples not to believe or accept anything, even though contained in Bibles and taught by Sages, until tested *yogically* and found to be true.

Up to the present time, occidental research concerning Padma-Sambhava and the very voluminous mass of material treating of him, chiefly in Tibetan, Mongolian, and Chinese, has been quite pioneer and limited. Save for our present treatise there is no work in English chiefly devoted to the Great *Guru*. Brief accounts concerning him are contained in *The Buddhism of Tibet*, by Dr. L. A. Waddell, to which frequent reference is made herein, in *Tibetan Literary Texts and Documents Concerning Chinese Turkestan*, by Dr. F. W. Thomas, and in works on Tibet by Sir Charles Bell and other writers, including the three preceding volumes of our own Tibetan Series.[1]

XVIII. ENGLISHING

The English language, itself an importation into Great Britain from the European Continent, has attained preeminence by virtue of its unsurpassed power of absorbing the words of other languages. Its original Anglo-Celtic vocabulary was fundamentally Germanic. Under the Romans, the long

---

[1] In German, the chief works concerning Padma-Sambhava are, by E. Schlagintweit, *Die Lebensbeschreibung von Padma-Sambhava, dem Begründer des Lāmaismus (Aus dem Tibetischen übersetzt)*, and by A. Grünwedel, *Padmasambhava und Verwandtes* (Leipzig u. Berlin, 1912) ; those concerning the *Padma-thaṅ-yig* are by A. Grünwedel, *Drei Leptscha Texte ; Mit Auszügen aus dem Padma-thaṅ-yig und Glossar* (Leiden, 1896), *Flucht des Padmasambhava aus dem Hause seines königlichen Pflegevaters Indrabhuti* (Leipzig, 1902), and *Ein Kapitel des Ta-se-sun* (Berlin, 1896). Other matter concerning Padma-Sambhava are: by A. Grünwedel, *Padmasambhava und Mandarava* (Leipzig, 1898) ; by S. H. Ribbach, *Vier Bilder des Padmasambhava und seiner Gefolgschaft* (Hamburg, 1917) ; by B. Laufer, *Die Bru-ža Sprache und die historische Stellung des Padmasambhava (T'oung Pao,* Ser. II, Vol. 9, 1908), and *Btsun-mo-bkai-thaṅ-yig* (Leipzig, 1911). In French, the outstanding work is *Le Dict de Padma* (Paris, 1933), a translation from the Tibetan of the *Padma Thang Yig MS. de Lithang*, by Gustave-Charles Touissaint, concerning the 'History of the Existences of the Guru Padma-Sambhava', the matter of which parallels in a general way although not in fullness of detail that of the *Unabridged Biography* epitomitized herein in Book I. Each of these two biographical works consist of 117 chapters and both have the same three titles in the colophons. The chapters of the one work do not, however, correspond with those of the other work as to content.

process of word-absorption from classical sources, more especially from Latin, began, and attained great momentum with the coming of Christianity. When the Norman conquerors made French the court language, fresh impetus was given to the latinization. The Renaissance brought in many more classically derived words. Then, after the discovery of America, generation by generation, as England became more and more the seat of empire, English laid under tribute all the languages of England's far-flung possessions. In modern times, the demand of the physical sciences for new terminologies has been satisfied by further recourse to the languages of Greece and Rome.

The words now anglicized are so numerous that they constitute at least three-quarters and perhaps four-fifths of the vocabulary of English as a whole. Eventually, if the ever widening process of word-absorption continues, as it appears destined to continue, English, by realizing in itself the at-one-ment of all the languages of mankind, will become the universal world language.

Ever since the British occupation of India, especially during the last quarter of the nineteenth century, and with accelerating rapidity since the beginning of the twentieth century, English has been absorbing an immense number of entirely new words expressive of the transcendent things of the spirit, from Sanskrit sources. Whilst Science, Commerce, and Techniques have been creating their own particular vocabularies chiefly from French, Latin, and Greek, the New Philosophy, based upon the Ancient Higher Psychology of the Sages, now reshaping the thought of the Occident far more profoundly than during the fifteenth-century Renaissance, has been establishing another vocabulary, of immeasurably greater value to Occidental man. Words such as *Buddha, Nirvana, karma, yoga, guru, rishi, tantra, mantra* are already fully naturalized and appear as English in the Oxford *New English Dictionary*. In order that this process of naturalization may be quickened, it is incumbent upon those who are students of the Supreme Science, the Divine Wisdom, rather than professional philologists (to whom philological exactitude is essential) to employ such transliterations from the Sanskrit as are most in keeping with vernacular English phonetics and therefore the easiest to anglicize. For illustration, *Nirvāṇa* appears in the *New English Dictionary* bereft of the two diacritical marks (which for the purpose of exact scholarship are indispensable) because it has become anglicized and is, strictly speaking, no longer Sanskrit.

Accordingly, the Editor has made choice of a middle path, which avoids the two extremes, of philological exactitude and of complete anglicization; and, therefore, all Sanskrit, Tibetan, and other transliterations from oriental and foreign languages have been italicized and diacritical marks have been added for the purpose of conforming to the parallel usage in the previous volumes of this Series. But, favouring the anglicization process, the Editor has preferred to write *Shiva* as an English word, rather than *Śiva* as a Sanskrit word; and, similarly, *Ashoka* and *Upanishad* rather than *Aṣoka* and *Upaniṣad*; the Bengali-Sanskrit *Sangsāra* (favoured, as, for instance, in *The Tantra of the Great Liberation*, p. cxvi, by the late Sir John Woodroffe) rather than *Saṇsāra* (or *Saṃsāra*), and so on. Preference has been given to such forms derived from the Tibetan as *Nyingma* instead of *Ñingma*, *Thī-Srong-Detsan* instead of *Thī-Sroṅ-Detsan*, and so on. The result being inconsistent with either of the two extremes is, of course, open to the criticism of scholars. It is, however, intended to represent a transitional stage in the anglicization process; and this is its justification in a popularly written treatise of this character.

After all, the chief social consideration is not phonetic exactness of the form anglicized, but its acceptance as a word symbol of very definite import. In the end, it is popular usage, not exactitude of spelling or pronunciation, that determines the formation of standard speech. Words being, as the Buddhas teach, merely *sangsāric* means of expounding the *Dharma*, it matters not how they are written or spoken so long as they convey the meaning intended, and thus assist mankind to attain the Great Liberation.

XIX. CRITICISM BY CRITICS

This Introduction is intended to serve as a commentary to the two chief texts upon which this volume is based, the text of the Biography, summarized in our Epitome, and the text of the '*Yoga* of Knowing the Mind In Its Unobscured Reality [or Nakedness]'. Book III serves as an independent commentary to Book II. The annotations to the texts are supplementary to this Introduction as a commentary. A certain amount of repetition, each time in a different context or from a different viewpoint, has been allowed, somewhat after the style employed by the *Gurus* to produce emphasis upon essentials; this appears to be quite necessary in presenting to the Occident these most recondite of oriental doctrines.

The *yogic* treatise itself, presented by Book II, is, essentially, and as critics may fairly point out, a series of suggestive deductions in aphorisms unaccompanied by proof. No treatise on Reality can be other than intellectually stated. Nevertheless, if it be, as it purports to be, based upon realizable truths, the proof must lie in the putting its teachings to the test of practical application in a strictly scientific manner. If one wishes to sustain his body he must eat and digest food for himself; no one else can do this for him. Or, otherwise stated, in keeping with the Piers Plowman philosophy of four-teenth-century England, 'It is not what a man eats, but what he digests that makes him strong'. Similarly, it is not what a critic may think or believe to be true which is always true, or necessarily true because he thinks it is; but only what he proves empirically to be true. Accordingly, if any one desires to criticize, let him do so only after having applied the '*Yoga* of Knowing the Mind in Its Nakedness' exhaustively.

Padma-Sambhava, to whom the authorship of the treatise is attributed, may be taken to be, on the basis of historically verifiable data concerning him, one who has proved for himself, by actual realization, the assertions therein contained. This is clear from the passage at the end of the treatise concerning the tasting of honey. A chemical formula, even one of the simplest, such as H_2O (or water), cannot be scientifically, or chemically, stated except in language common to all chemists, and none but chemists can interpret it fully. Likewise, recondite supra-mundane doctrines cannot be conveyed in written form without employing written words; and if written in the symbolical formulae of the esoteric science of alchemy, the transcendent chemistry, none but students of the occult sciences are fitted to study, much less interpret and criticize them.

XX. Conclusion

In concluding this Introduction there arises in the mind of him who writes these words the teaching, the most practically important of all the teachings of the *Gurus*, that whosoever hears and applies the *Dharma* must continually recollect that human life is transient and fleeting, and that the human body, although the 'Vessel of Salvation', is no more than a *karmic* aggregate productive of suffering. Attachment to life and form, and to *sangsāric* sensuousness will thereby be avoided. But, at the same time, the disciple must not fail to take good care of his or her bodily instrument, not for the purpose of enjoying worldly pleasures, but for the sole end of attaining the Great Liberation.[1]

Having obtained this pure and difficult-to-obtain, free, and endowed human body, it would be a cause of regret to die an irreligious and worldly man.

This human life in the Age of Darkness, the *Kali Yuga*, being so brief and uncertain, it would be a cause of regret to spend it in worldly aims and pursuits.

The mind, imbued with love and compassion in thought and deed, ought ever to be directed to the service of all sentient beings.[2]

---

[1] In similar language, the same teaching is set forth at more length in *Homeless Brothers*, based upon *Buddha, Truth and Brotherhood*, a translation from the Japanese of an epitomized version of a number of Buddhist Scriptures prepared by Prof. S. Yamabe of Kyoto, and incorporated in *A Buddhist Bible* (pp. 625–33), compiled and published by Dwight Goddard, at Thetford, Vermont, U.S.A. *A Buddhist Bible* will be found of much assistance to all students of our Tibetan Series.

[2] *The Precepts of the Gurus*, whence these three (I. 2–3; II. 9) come, contained in Book I of *Tibetan Yoga and Secret Doctrines*, are all-sufficient to guide the *yogin* and to serve as a *guru* to the *yogin* who desires a *guru*.

Nāgārjuna, one of the most illustrious of the Great *Gurus*, in his *Epistles* to his friend King De-chöd Zang-po, wrote:

There are those who pass from light to light, those who pass from darkness to darkness, those who pass from light to darkness, and those who pass from darkness to light. Of these four, be thou the first. . . .

The Teacher hath called Faith, Chastity, Charity, Learning, Sincerity united with Modesty, Avoidance of Wrong Action, and Wisdom the Seven Divine Riches. Know that other riches cannot aid thee. . . .

He who would misuse the boon of human life is far more stupid than he who would employ a gold vessel inlaid with precious gems as a receptacle for filth. . . .

The Buddha hath said that association with holy men is the root of all virtue. . . .

Right Views, Right Livelihood, Right Endeavour, Right Recollection, Right Meditation, Right Speech, Right Intentions, and Right Judgement are the Eight Parts of the Path. By meditating upon them one attaineth Peace.[1]

And, like the faithful folk of Tingri, Tibet, may each reader of this volume comprehend the full import of the words of their *Guru* Phadampa Sangay (whose Last Testament of Teachings is set forth herein, in Book III) when he sang,

Like the sunshine from a clear space twixt the clouds the *Dharma* is.
Know that now there is such Sunshine; use it wisely, Tingri folk.

[1] These excerpts are recensions from an English rendering of the *Epistles*, entitled in Tibetan *Bshes-pahi-hphrin-yig* (Skt. *Suttri* [da] *Lekha*, 'Friendly Letters'), prepared by the late Lāma Kazi Dawa-Samdup in the year 1919 and now in the Editor's possession.

PLATE V

THE EIGHT *GURUS*

Described on pages xxi–xxiv

BOOK I

AN EPITOME OF
THE LIFE AND TEACHINGS OF
TIBET'S GREAT *GURU*
PADMA-SAMBHAVA

ACCORDING TO THE BIOGRAPHY BY HIS CHIEF DISCIPLE
THE TIBETAN LADY YESHEY TSHOGYAL
INCARNATION OF SARASVATI
GODDESS OF LEARNING[1]

Based upon Excerpts rendered into English by the late
Sardar Bahādur S. W. Laden La, C.B.E., F.R.G.S.,
assisted by Lāma Sonam Senge

---

[1] The various titles given to the Biography are set forth herein, both in
Tibetan and English translation, in the Colophon, on pages 191–2. The more
general title, on the first folio of the Block-Print text, is as follows:
'Herein is contained the Unabridged Biography of the Urgyān *Guru*
Padma-Sambhava: "The Gold Rosary [of Teachings] Illuminating the
Path of Liberation" (*U-rgyān Guru Pad-ma Hbyung-gnas gyi Rnam-
thar Rgyas-pa Gser-gyi Phreng-ba Thar-lam Gsal-byed Bzhug-so*).'

A Fully Enlightened One

'Know, Vasettha, that from time to time a Tathāgata is born into the world, a Fully Enlightened One, blessed and worthy, abounding in wisdom and goodness, happy, with knowledge of the world, unsurpassed as a guide to erring mortals, a teacher of gods and men, a Blessed Buddha. He, by Himself, thoroughly understandeth, and seeth, as it were face to face, this Universe—the world below, with all its spiritual beings, and the worlds above, of Māra and Brahma—and all creatures, Samanas and Brāhmins, gods and men; and He then maketh His knowledge known to others. The Truth doth He proclaim, both in its letter and in its spirit, beautiful in its origin, beautiful in its progress, beautiful in its consummation; the Higher Life doth He reveal, in all its purity and in all its perfectness.'

The Buddha, *Tevigga Suttanta*, I, 46
(based upon the translation in *The Library of Original Sources*, i, edited by Oliver J. Thatcher).

THE INTRODUCTION

In this Book, Padma-Sambhava is presented as the divine personification of Tibetan idealism, a Culture Hero greater than even the Buddha Gautama. The wonders of oriental myth, the mysteriousness of the secret doctrines of the Mahāyāna, and the marvels of magic enhalo him. Like the Celtic Arthur and Cuchullain, the Scandinavian Odin and Thor, the Greek Orpheus and Odysseus, or the Egyptian Osiris and Hermes, the Lotus-Born One is of superhuman lineage, transcendent over the pomp and circumstance and the conventionalities of the world.

In the *Saga of Gesar*, the Iliad of Central Asia, Padma-Sambhava's heroic characteristics are similarly emphasized.[1] While Gesar, the supernormally gifted warrior-king puts down violence and injustice, the Great *Guru's* mission is to overthrow unrighteousness and establish the *Dharma*.

Probably nowhere in the sacred literature of mankind is there to be found a more remarkable parallelism than that existing between the accounts of the extraordinary characteristics attributed to Padma-Sambhava and to Melchizedek. Each was a King of Righteousness and a King of Peace, and a high priest. Each, as is said of Melchizedek, was 'without father, without mother, without genealogy, having neither beginning of days nor end of life' and 'abideth a priest continually'.[2] Both alike, being of the Succession of Great Teachers, founded an occult spiritual fraternity, that of Melchizedek traditionally dating from as early as the sixth century B.C., and that of Padma-Sambhava dating from the middle of the eighth century A.D. Nothing is known either of the origin or of the end of these two Heroes. According to tradition, both of them are believed never to have died.[3]

To the historian and student of religious origins, no less than to anthropologists, this Epitome of the Great *Guru's*

[1] Cf. *The Superhuman Life of Gesar of Ling*, by Alexandra David-Neel and Lāma Yongden (London, 1933).

[2] Cf. Hebrews vii. 2–3.

[3] Ibid. vi. 20; vii. 17.

Biography should prove to be of unique value. Not only does it illustrate the process of deification of one who undoubtedly was an historical character, but it also affords glimpses into the remarkable cultural state of India twelve centuries ago, and sets forth certain far-reaching deductions arrived at by a succession of Sages of the Mahāyāna School concerning the supreme problem of Reality.

Quite apart from the myths, the folk traditions, and the lore of the *Gurus*, the Biography contains much that should be of more than ordinary interest to Buddhists of all Schools. This is clearly indicated by the sections of the Epitome about the ordination of Padma by Ānanda, the story of the unfaithful monk, how Ānanda was chosen chief disciple, Ānanda's testimony concerning the Buddha and the Scriptures, and the remarkable account of the defeat of the non-Buddhists at Bōdh-Gayā in controversy and magic. Whether the Theravāda Buddhist sees fit to give credence or not to these Mahāyāna accounts relating to the life and teachings of the Buddha, they at least show that in Buddhism, as in Christianity and other religions, there is an apocryphal literature. In themselves, they are of value in the study of Buddhist origins.

Of the strange incidents and various doctrines described in the Epitome, each of its readers must be the judge. In it, undoubtedly, the rational and the irrational blend, and so do the esoteric and the exoteric. But underlying the Biography of the Great *Guru* when seen as a whole there is discernible the Right Intention of the illustrious Tibetan lady Yeshey Tshogyal, who, as the colophon of the Tibetan text records, compiled it in manuscript form some twelve hundred years ago, and then hid it in a cave in Tibet, where it remained until the time came for its recovery and transmission to our age. And each reader of the Epitome, which now follows, is indebted to her, as the faithful disciple is to the preceptor.

THE EPITOME OF THE GREAT *GURU'S*
BIOGRAPHY

THE BUDDHA'S PROPHECY OF THE BIRTH OF
PADMA-SAMBHAVA

When the Buddha was about to pass away at Kushinagara,[1] and His disciples were weeping, He said to them, 'The world being transitory and death inevitable for all livings things, the time for my own departure hath come. But weep not; for twelve years after my departure, from a lotus blossom on the Dhanakosha Lake,[2] in the north-western corner of the country of Urgyān,[3] there will be born one who will be much wiser and more spiritually powerful than Myself. He will be called Padma-Sambhava,[4] and by him the Esoteric Doctrine will be established.'

THE KING INDRABODHI

In the country of Urgyān (or Udyāna), westward from Bōdh-Gayā, there was the great city of Jatumati, containing a palace called 'Emerald Palace' wherein dwelt King Indra-bodhi. Although possessed of vast worldly wealth and power and blessed with five hundred queens and one hundred Buddhist and one hundred non-Buddhist ministers, Indra-bodhi was blind; and his subjects called him 'the wealthiest king without eyes'. When his only son and heir died and famine immediately thereafter weakened his kingdom, Indra-bodhi wept, overcome with misfortune. Consoled by a *yogī*, the King called together the priests, and they made offerings to the gods and read the sacred books. Then the King took oath to give in charity all his possessions; and his treasury

---

[1] Kushinagara, the place of the Buddha's *Pari-Nirvāṇa*, is about thirty-five miles east of the modern Gorakpur. Kushinagara means 'Town (or Place) of Kusha-Grass', a grass sacred to *yogins* (see p. 152[1]).

[2] According to some accounts, the Dhanakosha Lake, or, as it is otherwise called, the Lotus Lake (Tib. *Tsho-Padma-chan*), is placed near Hard-war, in the United Provinces of India, although it is usually stated to be in the country of Urgyān (or Udyāna).

[3] Urgyān (or Udyāna) is said to have corresponded to the country about Gazni, to the north-west of Kashmir. (Cf. L. A. Waddell, op. cit., p. 26.)

[4] Or the 'Lotus-Born'. See pp. 131, 173.

and granaries were emptied. In the end, his subjects were so impoverished that they were obliged to eat the young un-ripened crops and even flowers.

THE KING'S DESPONDENCY

Oppressed with the thought of being heirless, the King made offerings and prayers to the deities of all the prevailing faiths, but, no son being vouchsafed to him, he lost confidence in every religion. Then, one day, he went to the roof of his palace and beat the summoning drum; and, when all the people had come, he addressed the assembled priests thus: 'Hear me, each of you! I have made prayer to the deities and to the guardian spirits of this land and offerings to the Trinity,[1] but I have not been blessed with a son. Religion is, therefore, devoid of truth; and I command that within seven days ye destroy every one of these deities and guardian spirits. Other-wise, ye shall know my punishment.'

AVALOKITESHVARA'S APPEAL TO AMITĀBHA

The priests, in their consternation, hurriedly collected materials for the performance of a ceremony of burnt offer-ings. The deities and guardian spirits, filled with anger, sent storms of wind, hail, and blood; and throughout Urgyān the inhabitants were as frightened as fish are when taken from the water and placed upon dry sand. In great pity, Avalo-kiteshvara made appeal to the Buddha Amitābha, in the Sukhāvatī Heaven, to protect the suffering people.

AMITĀBHA'S RESPONSE AND EMANATION

Thereupon, the Buddha Amitābha thought, 'Let me take birth in the Dhanakosha Lake'; and there went forth from His tongue a ray of red light, which, like a meteor, entered the centre of the lake. Where the ray entered the water, there appeared a small island covered with golden-coloured grass, whence flowed three springs of the colour of turquoise; and from the centre of the island there sprang forth a lotus

---

[1] Namely, the Buddha, the *Dharma* (or Scriptures), and the *Saṅgha* (or Brotherhood of the Priests of the Buddhist Order).

PLATE VI

EMANATION
Described on pages xxiv–xxvi

blossom. Simultaneously, the Buddha Amitābha, with great radiance, emitted from His heart a five-pointed *dorje*,[1] and the *dorje* fell into the centre of the lotus blossom.

THE KING'S AND THE PRIESTS' DREAMS

Being appeased by this, the deities and guardian spirits ceased harming the people of Urgyān, and circumambulated the lake, making obeisance and offerings. The King dreamt that he held in his hand a five-pointed *dorje* which emitted radiance so great that all the kingdom was illuminated. Upon awakening, the King was so happy that he worshipped the Trinity; and the deities and guardian spirits appeared and made humble submission to him. The Buddhist priests, too, had an auspicious dream, which perturbed the non-Buddhist priests: they beheld a thousand suns illuminating the world.

THE PROPHECY OF AMITĀBHA'S INCARNATION

Then, whilst the King was piously circumambulating a *stūpa* of nine steps which had miraculously sprung forth from a pond in front of his palace, gods appeared in the heavens and prophesied: 'Hail! Hail! the Lord Amitābha, Protector of Mankind, shall take birth as a Divine Incarnation from a lotus blossom amidst the Jewel Lake;[2] and he will be worthy to become thy son. Suffer no harm to befall Him and give Him thy protection. Thereby, every good will come to thee.'

The King reported this prophecy to his minister of state Triguṇadhara and requested him to search for the promised

---

[1] The Tibetan *dorje* (Skt. *Vajra*), being one of the chief ritual objects of Tibetan Buddhism, has come to be called the *lāmas'* sceptre. Esoterically, the word *dorje* has many meanings. It is applied to Buddhas and deities, to Tantric initiates, to specially sacred places, to texts and philosophical systems. For instance, *Vajrayāna*, meaning 'Path of the *Vajra*', is the name of one of the most esoteric of the schools of Northern Buddhism. *Dorje*, or *Vajra*, is applied to anything of an exalted religious character which is lasting, immune to destruction, occultly powerful and irresistible. *Dorje Lopon*, referring to the high initiate presiding at Tibetan Tantric rites, is a further illustration of its usage. On the cover of this volume is depicted a double *dorje*, which is like a Greek cross. In *The Tibetan Book of the Dead*, facing page 137, appears an illustration of the single *dorje*, which, rather than the double *dorje*, is the form commonly used.

[2] Or the Dhanakosha Lake.

son. The minister went to the lake at once, and saw at the centre of the lake a very large lotus full blown and seated in its midst a beautiful boy child, apparently about one year of age. Perspiration beaded the child's face, and an aura encircled him. Doubtful of the wisdom of having the King adopt so unusual a child, that might not be of human origin, the minister decided to postpone reporting the discovery.

THE WISH-GRANTING GEM

The kingdom being impoverished, the King called his ministers together for advice. Some suggested increase of agriculture, some increase of trade, and others declared for the making of war and the plundering of the property of others. Rather than adopt any policy not in accord with the precepts of the *Dharma*, the King decided to risk his own life for the good of his people and obtain from the *Nāgas*, who dwelt beneath the waters of the ocean, a wondrous wish-granting gem. 'When I return with the gem', he said, 'I shall be able to feed all my subjects and all the mendicants.'

Then the King went to the palace of the *Nāgas*, and the wish-granting gem was presented to him by their princess. As soon as the gem was placed in the hand of the King he wished for sight in his left eye and the sight came.

THE KING'S DISCOVERY OF THE LOTUS-BORN CHILD

On his return to the Urgyān country, just as the minister Triguṇadhara approached and greeted him, the King noticed a rainbow of five colours over the Dhanakosha Lake, although there were no clouds and the sun was shining brightly. And the King said to the minister, 'Please go and ascertain what there is in that lake yonder'.

'How is it that thou, being blind, canst see this?' asked the minister. 'I appealed to the wish-granting gem and my sight was restored', replied the King. Thereupon the minister revealed his discovery of the wonderful babe, saying, 'I dared not report the matter to thee previously', and he begged the King to go to the lake and see for himself. 'Last night', responded the King, 'I dreamt that from the sky there came

into my hand a nine-pointed *dorje*, and before that I dreamt
that from my heart issued a sun, the light of which shone over
the whole world.'

The King and his minister went to the lake and, taking a
small boat, reached the place over which the rainbow shone.
There they beheld a fragrant lotus blossom, the circumference
of which exceeded that of one's body and circled arms, and
seated at the centre of the blossom a fair rosy-cheeked little
boy resembling the Lord Buddha, holding in his right hand a
tiny lotus blossom and in his left hand a tiny holy-water pot,
and in the folds of the left arm a tiny three-pronged staff.

The King felt much veneration for the self-born babe; and,
in excess of joy, he wept. He asked the child, 'Who are thy
father and mother, and of what country and caste art thou?
What food sustaineth thee; and why art thou here?' The
child answered, 'My father is Wisdom and my mother is the
Voidness. My country is the country of the *Dharma*. I am of
no caste and of no creed. I am sustained by perplexity; and
I am here to destroy Lust, Anger, and Sloth.' When the child
had ceased speaking, the King's right eye was no longer blind.
Overwhelmed with joy, the King named the child 'The Lake-
born *Dorje*', and he and the minister made obeisance to the
child.

THE CHILD IS TAKEN TO THE PALACE

The King asked the child if he would come to him, and the
child said, 'I will, for I have entered the world to benefit all
sentient creatures, to dominate those that are harmful, and
for the good of the Doctrine of the Buddhas'. Then the lotus
opened more fully and the child leapt, like a discharged arrow,
to the shore of the lake. At the spot where the child touched
the earth a lotus blossom immediately sprang up, and in it
the child seated himself, whereupon the King named him
'The Lotus-Born', and thought to himself, 'He will be my
heir and my *guru*'. Then the King severed the lotus blossom
from its stem and lifted it up with the child sitting therein and
with the minister set out for the palace.

The cranes and the wild ducks were overwhelmed with

grief at the loss of the child. Some perched on the child's shoulders. Some flew in front and bowed down their heads. Some fell to the earth and lay there as if dead. Some circled round and round the lake wailing. Some placed their beaks in the earth and wept. Even the trees and bushes bent over towards the child in their sadness. Magpies and parrots, peacocks and other birds flew to the fore of the procession and placed their wings tip to tip in an effort to halt the procession. Vultures and kites struck the King and the minister with their beaks. The small birds gave vent to their cries. Lions, tigers, bears, and other ferocious animals ran about on all sides in a threatening attitude trying to disrupt the procession. Elephants, buffaloes, and asses came out of the jungle and joined with the other animals in protest. The guardian spirits and the genii of the locality were greatly perturbed and caused thunder, lightning, and hail.

When the procession reached the villages all the villagers joined it. There happened to be an old man sitting by the wayside fishing; and the Lotus-Born One, seeing him, thought to himself, 'This is a sign that if I become the King of this country I shall suffer even as the fish do'. Shortly afterwards, the Lotus-Born One, upon seeing a crow chasing a partridge, which took refuge under a raspberry bush and escaped, thought to himself, 'The raspberry bush represents the kingdom, the crow represents the king, and the partridge represents myself; and the significance is that I must gradually abdicate from the kingship'.

THE LOTUS-BORN ONE AS PRINCE, ATHLETE, AND KING

When the procession reached the palace, the King took the wish-granting gem and wished a throne made of seven sorts of precious gems surmounted by a royal umbrella. The throne appeared instantaneously, and on it he seated the child and acknowledged him as son and heir. The Lotus-Born One became known as the *Bodhisattva*[1] Prince, and was proclaimed

---

[1] A *Bodhisattva*, or Enlightened Being, is one who is far advanced on the path to Buddhahood. Gautama, for example, was a *Bodhisattva* up to the moment of His supreme Illumination, attained while sitting in meditation under the Bodhi-Tree, whereupon he became a Buddha.

king. When he was thirteen years of age, as he sat on a throne of gold and turquoise and priests were performing religious ceremonies for the prosperity of the kingdom, the Buddha Amitābha, Avalokiteshvara, and the Guardian Gods of the Ten Directions[1] came and anointed him with holy water and named him 'The Lotus King'.[2]

The Lotus King established a new legal code based upon the Ten Precepts.[3] The kingdom prospered and the people were happy. He studied and became learned, and excelled in poetry and philosophy. In wrestling and sports none could equal him. He could shoot an arrow through the eye of a needle. He could send forth thirteen arrows, one directly after another, so quickly that the second arrow hit the first and forced it higher, and the third the second, and so on to the thirteenth. The force with which he discharged an arrow was so great that the arrow would penetrate seven doors of leather and seven doors of iron; and when he shot an arrow upward, no one could see how high it went. So the people called him 'The Mighty Athletic Hero-King'.

Once he picked up a stone as big as a yak[4] and threw it so far that it was barely visible. He could take nine anvils in a sling and cast them against a great boulder and overthrow it. With one breath he could run around the city thrice, with the speed of an arrow. He surpassed the fish in swimming. He

[1] These are the ten gods who, like door-keepers at an initiatory assembly, guard the world, one in each of the ten directions, which are the four cardinal and intermediate points of the compass, the nadir, and zenith.

[2] Tib. *Padma Gyalpo*, one of the eight manifestations, or personalities, assumed by the Great *Guru*, and described on page xxii.

[3] The Ten Precepts (*Dasha-Shila*), or Prohibitions, of the Buddhist Moral Code are: (1) Kill not; (2) Steal not; (3) Commit not adultery; (4) Lie not; (5) Drink not Strong Drink; (6) Eat no Food except at the stated times; (7) Use no Wreaths, Ornaments, or Perfumes; (8) Use no High Mats or Thrones [to sit or sleep upon]; (9) Abstain from Dancing, Singing, Music, and Worldly Spectacles; (10) Own no Gold or Silver and accept none. Of these the first five (the *Panca-Shila*) are binding upon the laity; the whole ten are binding upon members of the Order only, but sometimes laymen take a pious vow to observe, on certain fast days, one or more of those numbered 6 to 9. (Cf. L. A. Waddell, *The Buddhism of Tibet*, Cambridge, 1934, p. 134.)

[4] The *yak* is the Tibetan long-haired animal of the bovine family, the male being used as a beast of burden and in agricultural work, the female as a milch cow.

could lasso a flying hawk. He was also a master musician.
Now he was named 'The Undefeated Lion King'.

The Coming of the Arhants

One day he went unaccompanied to the 'Sorrowful Forest',
which lay about two miles from the palace, to meditate. As
he sat there in the Buddha posture, Arhants,[1] who were
passing by overhead in the firmament, descended and praised
him saying, 'Hail! Hail! Thou art the undoubted Lotus King,
Thou art the second Buddha, heralding a new era, who shalt
conquer the world. Though we were to possess hundreds of
tongues and go from kalpa to kalpa,[2] we would not be fortunate enough to enjoy even a fraction of thy vast learning.'
After circumambulating him seven times, they ascended and
disappeared.

The Plan to Fetter Padma by Marriage

The King Indrabodhi and the ministers, seeing the Prince's
inclination towards the meditative life, feared that eventually
he would renounce the kingdom, so they assembled in council
and decided to find for him a wife. The Prince knew that the
chief purpose of the plan was to fetter him to the household
state; and he refused to choose any of the many maidens who
were carefully selected from all parts of Urgyān. The King
Indrabodhi insisted that the Prince make choice and marry
within seven days. After due consideration, the Prince decided
not to disobey the old King who, like a father, had safe-
guarded and reared him, and he gave to the King in writing a
description of the sort of a maiden he would accept.

The written description was handed over to the minister

---

[1] An Arhant, literally 'Worthy One', is a Buddhist saint, often indistinguishable from a Bodhisattva, and comparable to the Hindu Rishi, who has
attained the goal of the Noble Eightfold Path, and, at death, is fitted for
Nirvāṇa. If the Arhant renounces his right to enter Nirvāṇa, in order to
work for the salvation of the unenlightened, he automatically becomes a
perfected Bodhisattva.

[2] A kalpa is a Day of Brahma, or the period of a thousand yugas, or
ages, in which the Cosmos endures before being dissolved again in the Night
of Brahma.

Triguṇadhara with the King's command to find such a maiden without delay. The minister immediately set out for Singala, where, at a religious festival in honour of the Lord Buddha, he saw a most attractive girl, one of a group of five hundred maidens. Questioning the girl, he ascertained that her name was Bhāsadhara ('The Light-Holder'), that she was the daughter of King Chandra Kumār and already betrothed to a prince.[1] The minister hurriedly returned to his King and reported that he considered Bhāsadhara entirely suitable.

The Choice of Bhāsadhara and the Marriage Ceremony

On the pretext that he wished to give them valuable gifts, the King Indrabodhi invited Bhāsadhara and her four hundred and ninety-nine companions to his palace. When the Prince saw Bhāsadhara he was pleased with her; he handed to her the wish-granting gem and she wished that she might become his queen. Bhāsadhara and all the maidens returned to Singala, and a letter was sent to King Chandra Kumār requesting that he give Bhāsadhara in marriage to the Lotus-Born Prince. King Chandra Kumār replied that although he would be glad to meet the request he was unable to do so, for even then Bhāsadhara's marriage to a prince of Singala was about to take place.

When informed of this reply, the Lotus-Born Prince said, 'She alone is suitable, and I must have her'. The King Indrabodhi, calling in a *yogī* and informing him of the matter, commanded him to proceed to Singala, saying, 'Go to the palace

---

[1] The late Gustave-Charles Toussaint in his *Le Dict de Padma* (Paris, 1933), p. 491, considers this reference to 'Singala' (commonly regarded as being synonymous with Ceylon) to refer to a continental country not far from Udyāna (or Urgyān) and substitutes for it the name 'Siṁhapura'. Dr. L. A. Waddell, in *The Buddhism of Tibet* (Cambridge, 1934), p. 381[4], being of like opinion, says: 'This is probably the Siṁhapura of Hiuen Tsiang, which adjoined Udayāna, or Udyāna; or it may be Sagāla.' The late Sardar Bahādur S. W. Laden La remarked, as we translated this passage, that 'Singala' may have been what is now the Gantour District of the Madras Presidency rather than Ceylon. All of this and very much more that the Biography will present, as we proceed, touch complex problems of geography and history, the detailed consideration of which is beyond the scope of our present essentially anthropological study.

where the marriage procession is to halt for a night, and place under the tips of the girl's finger-nails iron dust moistened with water'.[1]

After the *yogī* had set out on the mission, the King went to the roof of the palace and raising aloft, on a banner of victory,[2] the wish-granting gem and, bowing to the four cardinal directions, prayed that Bhāsadhara with all her attendant maidens should be brought there before him ; and, as if by a wind,they were brought.

The King ordered that preparations for the marriage of the Lotus-Born Prince and Bhāsadhara be made at once. Bhāsadhara was bathed, arrayed in fine garments and jewels, and placed on a seat beside the Lotus-Born Prince ; and they were married. One hundred thousand women of Urgyān proclaimed Bhāsadhara Queen.[3] Then the four hundred and ninety-nine other maidens were married to the Prince, for it was customary for a King of Urgyān to have five hundred wives. Thus for five years the Prince experienced worldly happiness.

THE RENUNCIATION

Then the Dhyānī Buddha Vajra-Sattva appeared and announced to the Prince that the time had come to renounce both the married state and the throne. And the King Indrabodhi dreamt that the Sun and Moon set simultaneously, that the palace was filled with lamentation and that all the ministers were weeping. When the King awoke, he was overcome with forebodings and sadness. Shortly afterwards, the Prince, with his ministers, went for a walk to the 'Sorrowful Forest' where he had been visited by the *Arhants* ; and there appeared in the southern heavens the various emblems of the Buddhist Faith, to signify that the Prince was about to become a world

---

[1] Iron, the world over, is commonly taboo to evil spirits, and prevents spells from taking effect. Its use here seems to be precautionary, neutralizing any magical power which might be exercised to prevent the spiriting-away of Bhāsadhara.

[2] Such a banner is shown in *Tibet's Great Yogī Milarepa*, opposite p. 30.

[3] In ancient India it was customary in some kingdoms, as in Urgyān, for women to proclaim the accession of a queen and for men to proclaim the accession of a king.

emperor. Accordingly, one after another, many kings made submission to him.

Thus having attained the heights of worldly power and of sensuous enjoyment, the Lotus-Born One realized the illusory and unsatisfactory nature of all worldly things. And, thinking of the Great Renunciation of the Lord Buddha, he announced to the King–Father his intention to abdicate and enter the Order. Faced by the King–Father's opposition, he said to him, 'If thou dost not permit me to embrace religion, I will die here in thy very presence'; and he struck his right side with a dagger, seemingly with intent to do away with himself. Fearful lest the Prince carry out the threat, the old King thought, 'It is preferable that I allow him to enter the Order than for him to die'. Neither the entreaties of the ministers of state, nor the special pleading of the King's bosom friend, 'Golden Light', who was fetched from Singala especially, nor the lamentations of the five hundred queens, moved the Lotus-Born One from his fixed purpose. Therefore he was named 'The Irresistible *Dorje* King'.

THE PARTING

The Queens, in tears, said to the Lotus-Born One as he was taking leave of them, 'Thou, our Lord, art like the eyes below our forehead. Not for a moment can we be parted from thee. Shalt thou abandon us as though we were corpses in a cemetery? Wherever thou goest, invite us to join thee; otherwise we shall resemble ownerless dogs. Hast thou no pity for us?'

The Lotus-Born One replied, 'This worldly life is transitory, and separation is inevitable. As in a market-place, human beings come together and then separate. Why, therefore, be troubled about separation? This is the Wheel of the World; let us renounce it and fix our thoughts upon attaining Liberation. I am determined to follow the religious career; and I will prepare the way for your own salvation, so that ye may join me hereafter. For the present, remain here.' Because, as he left, he promised to return to them when he had attained the Truth, they named him 'The King Who Keepeth One in Mind'.

The *Karmic* taking of Life

In another part of Urgyān, to which the Lotus-Born One went, there happened to be a man born with organs of genera-tion all over his body, because in his previous life he, having been a priest, violated the vow of celibacy by living with a courtesan. The courtesan was reborn as the son of a king; and the man, assuming the form of a fly, alighted on the infant son's forehead. The Lotus-Born One threw a pebble at the fly with such force that the pebble not only killed the fly but penetrated to the child's brain, carrying the fly with it; and both the fly and the child died.

When charged with the crime, the Lotus-Born One ex-plained that in a former life he had been a contemporary of the courtesan and been known as Gautama, that Padma Tsalag, the courtesan's paramour, in a fit of jealousy had killed her when informed, by her own maid-servant, of her secret acceptance of a rival who was a merchant named Hari, and that, Padma Tsalag having falsely accused Gautama of the murder, Gautama was put to death. Inasmuch as the fly was Padma Tsalag[1] and the king's son the courtesan, the Lotus-Born One was impelled by *karma* to commit the deed. He said, 'Had it not been for the *karma*, the pebble could not have killed both the fly and the child'. The Lotus-Born One requested the King Indrabodhi to allow the law of the realm to take its course, and was imprisoned in the palace.

The royal city was then besieged by ten thousand evil spirits who sought to prevent the Lotus-Born One from becoming a great and learned priest and destroying their prestige and power. The gates both of the city and palace being closely guarded because of the siege, the Lotus-Born One considered

---

[1] There are both the exoteric or vulgar interpretation of the rebirth doctrine, such as this folk-tale illustrates, and the esoteric interpretation of the initiates which does not sanction the wide-spread popular belief in transmigration from the human to sub-human forms. See *The Tibetan Book of the Dead*, pp. 39–61. While the many, the exotericists, may accept this strange folk-tale literally, the more spiritually advanced of the Great *Guru's* devotees interpret it symbolically, as they do very much else in the Biography as a whole, the fly being to them significant of the undesirable characteristics of the unbridled sensuality associated with Padma Tsalag.

how he might escape. And, putting off his garments, he placed
on his naked body magical ornaments made of human bone,
and, taking with him a *dorje* and a *trīshūla*,[1] went to the roof
of the palace and danced like a mad man. He let both the
trīshūla and the *dorje* fall below; the prongs of the *trīshūla*,
striking the breast of the wife of one of the ministers of state,
pierced her heart, and the *dorje*, striking the head of her
infant son, penetrated to the brain, and both died.

THE GOING INTO EXILE

The ministers advised that the Lotus-Born One be put to
death by hanging, but the King said, 'This son is not of human
origin; and, inasmuch as he may be an incarnate divinity,
capital punishment cannot be inflicted upon him. Accordingly, I decree that he be exiled.'

The King summoned the Lotus-Born One and told him that
the decree would come into force after three months. The
Lotus-Born One explained that, as in the case of the slaying
of the infant and the fly, there existed a *karmic* reason for the
slaying of the minister's wife and son. The minister's son had
been in that former life the courtesan's maid-servant who had
betrayed to Padma Tsalag the clandestine relationship between the courtesan and the merchant Hari; and the minister's wife was the reincarnation of this merchant Hari. Though
unrepentant, the Lotus-Born One bore no ill will towards
any one.

Different parts of India, also China, Persia, and the mysterious country called Shambhala were considered as places
of exile for the Prince, but the King told him that he might go
wherever he liked. 'To me', said the Prince, 'all countries are
pleasant; I need only undertake religious work and every
place becometh my monastery.'

Secretly, the King presented the Prince with the wish-
granting gem, saying, 'This will satisfy all thy wants'. The
Prince handed it back, saying, 'Whatever I behold is my

---

[1] The *trīshūla* is a three-pronged staff like that held by him in the
Frontispiece. It is employed in Tantric rituals, and symbolizes mastership
of occult powers.

wish-granting gem'; and when the King, in response to the Prince's request, extended his hand opened, the Prince spat in it, and instantaneously the spittle became another wish-granting gem.

Bhāsadhara, weeping, caught the Prince by the hand and pleaded to be allowed to go with him into exile. Then she appealed to the King not to let him be exiled. Meanwhile, the Prince departed and went to a garden whence he addressed the multitude that followed him:

'The body is impermanent; it is like the edge of a precipice.[1] The breath is impermanent; it is like the cloud. The mind is impermanent; it is like the lightning. Life is impermanent; it is like the dew on the grass.'

Then the Guardian Kings of the four cardinal directions with their attendant deities appeared and prostrated themselves before the Prince and praised him. The Four Ḍākinī[2] also came with music and song; and they placed the Prince on a celestial horse and he disappeared into the heavens, in a southerly direction. At sunset he descended to earth and went to a cave where he engaged in worship and prayer for seven days, and all the Peaceful Deities[3] appeared to him as in a mirror and conferred upon him transcendency over birth and death.

THE GOD OF THE CORPSES

Thence he proceeded to the 'Cool Sandal-Wood' Cemetery,[4]

[1] Even as the body leads one to death, so does the edge of a precipice.
[2] These are four chief ḍākinī, namely, the Divine (or Vajra) Ḍākinī, associated with the eastern direction, in a maṇḍala; the Precious (or Ratna) Ḍākinī, of the southern direction; the Lotus (or Padma) Ḍākinī, of the western; and the Action (or Karma) Ḍākinī, of the northern direction. The centre, or central position, is assigned to the Ḍākinī of Enlightenment, or the Buddha Ḍākinī.
[3] In Tantric cults the principal deities, including the Buddhas, are symbolically represented in the dualistic moods of peacefulness and wrathfulness, as illustrated throughout The Tibetan Book of the Dead.
[4] This cemetery (Tib. Bsil-ba-tshal), wherein the Buddha is said to have delivered some of His Mahāyāna teachings, is one of the Eight Cemeteries of ancient India, in all of which, one after another, the Lotus-Born One practised the yoga of sosānika. Sosānika (or 'frequenting of cemeteries') is one of the twelve observances incumbent upon a bhikṣhu. It is intended to impress upon him the three chief sangsāric phenomena, namely, transitoriness, suffering (or sorrow), and vacuity (or illusoriness), by witnessing the funerals,

about ten miles from Bōdh-Gayā. Using corpses for his seat, he remained there five years practising meditation. His food was the food offered to the dead[1] and his clothing the shrouds of the corpses. People called him 'The God of the Corpses'. It was here that he first expounded, to the *ḍākinī*, the nine progressive steps on the Great Path.

When a famine occurred, a multitude of corpses was deposited in the cemetery without food or shrouds; and Padma, as we shall now call the Great *Guru*, transmuted the flesh of the corpses into pure food and subsisted upon it, and the skin of the corpses served him for raiment. He subjugated the spiritual beings inhabiting the cemetery and made them his servitors.

The Overthrow of the Irreligious

Indrarāja, a petty king of the Urgyān country, having become inimical to religion, and his subjects, following his example, likewise, Padma went there in the guise of one of the Wrathful Deities and deprived the king and all the men among the unbelievers of their bodies, or means of sowing further evil *karma*; and, magically transmuting the bodies, he drank the blood and ate the flesh.[2] Their consciousness-principles[3] he liberated and prevented from falling into the hells.[4] Every woman whom he met he took to himself, in order to purify

the grieving relatives, the combats of beasts of prey for the remains, and by smelling the stench of the decaying corpses. The Buddha, too, is said to have practised *sosānika*. (Cf. L. A. Waddell, op. cit., p. 381[6].)

[1] It was then customary for the surviving relatives when depositing a corpse in a cemetery (or cremation ground, or place of corpses) to put with it a large earthenware pot full of cooked rice.

[2] Apparently this magical transmutation is to be regarded as being the reverse of that whereby, according to pagan beliefs of antiquity, wine may be transmuted into blood and bread into flesh.

[3] The term 'soul', as understood in the Occident, has no equivalent in Buddhist thought, Buddhism denying the existence of an unchanging personal entity. Here, as elsewhere, the term consciousness-principle (Tib. *pho*, and *nam-she*) is preferable. Cf. *The Tibetan Book of the Dead*, pp. 86[n], 92[3].

[4] This legend, in the eyes of the Tibetans, shows that it is right for a Great *Yogī* to cut short the career of an evil-doer by depriving him of his body and directing his consciousness-principle (which is quite different from the 'soul' in occidental theology) in such manner that it will be reborn in a religious environment. But to take life without the *yogic* power so to direct the consciousness-principle is a most henious sin.

her spiritually and fit her to become the mother of religiously minded offspring.[1]

THE YOUTHFUL ESCAPED DEMON

The queen of King Ahruta having died in pregnancy, her corpse was deposited in a cemetery where Padma was meditating. From the womb of the corpse, Padma recovered a female child which was still alive. As there existed a *karmic* relationship from a past life between the child and Padma, he decided to rear it. King Ahruta sent soldiers to attack Padma, and King Warma-Shrī sent a mighty warrior famed for prowess in arms to aid the attackers. Padma shot the warrior with an arrow and escaped; and thus he acquired the name, 'The Youthful Escaped Demon'.

After erecting a *stūpa*[2] of repentance, Padma took up residence in the 'Cemetery of Happiness', where the Wrathful *Ḍākinī* known as the 'Subjugator of Demons' came and blessed him. Afterwards, he sat in meditation in the Sosaling Cemetery, to the south of the Urgyān country, and received the blessings of the *ḍākinī* of the Peaceful Order.

THE SUBMISSION OF THE *ḌĀKINĪ* OF THE LAKE

Thence, going to the Dhanakosha Lake, where he was born, he preached the Mahāyāna to the *ḍākinī* in their own lan-

[1] Like many other Culture Heroes, Padma-Sambhava makes natural use of his masculinity, as in this instance, for eugenic good. It is pointed out in our General Introduction that conventional concepts of sex morality are completely ignored by him. Under other circumstances, that which has been called his Tantric dalliance with females, both human and of the *ḍākinī* order, is regarded by the Nyingmapas as being one of his many religious acts which has esoteric significance and results in benefit to the religion. The act itself is called in Tibetan *Dze-pa*.

[2] The Tibetan *Ch'orten*, literally meaning 'receptacle for offerings', corresponds to the *stūpa* (*caitya*, or *tope*) of Indian Buddhism. A *stūpa* is usually a conical masonry structure containing, like a tumulus, whence it was probably derived, a central chamber intended to hold reliques such as charred bits of bones from the funeral pyre of a saint, precious objects like images, and texts of scriptures. From a few of the ancient Indian *stūpas* authentic reliques of the Buddha have been recovered. As in this textual instance, a *stūpa* may be a *stūpa* of repentance. Other *stūpas*, like many at Bōdh-Gayā, are votive *stūpas*. Generally, a *stūpa* is a cenotaph in memory of the Buddha or a great Buddhist *Arhant* or *Bodhisattva*. See *Tibet's Great Yogī Milarepa*, wherein a *stūpa* is shown and its symbolism expounded, opposite p. 269.

guage.[1] He brought them and other deities of the locality under the sway of his *yogic* power; and they vowed to give to him their aid in his mission on Earth.

THE BLESSING BY VAJRA-VARĀHĪ

Padma's next place of abode was the 'Very Fearful Cemetery', where Vajra-Varāhī[2] appeared and blessed him. The four orders of male *ḍākinī* and the *ḍākinī* of the Three Secret Places—which are underneath, upon, and above the Earth— also appeared; and, after conferring upon him the power to overcome others, named him 'Dorje Dragpo'.[3]

THE DECISION TO SEEK *GURUS*

Padma now went to Bōdh-Gayā,[4] and worshipped at the Temple. Practising shape-shifting, he multiplied his body so that sometimes it appeared like a vast herd of elephants and sometimes like a multitude of *yogīs*. Asked by the people who he was and what *guru* he had, he replied, 'I have no father, no mother, no abbot, no *guru*, no caste, no name; I am the self-born Buddha'. Disbelieving him, the people said, 'Inasmuch as he hath no *guru*, may he not be a demon?'[5] This

---

[1] This is one of the secret languages of Tibet, which, as the late Lāma Kazi Dawa-Samdup told me, is nowadays known only by a very few highly initiated *Lāmas*.

[2] Vajra-Varāhī (Tib. *Dorje-Phag-mo*) is believed by the Tibetans to be incarnate successively in each abbess of the Yam-dok Lake monastery, Tibet. The name, literally meaning 'Indestructible (*Vajra*) Sow (*Varāhī*)', suggests, like other names of Vajra Deities of the Vajra-yāna School, high initiatory powers.

[3] Or 'Indomitable Wrathful One', a *Drag-po* being a demoniacal deity of the most terrific type, tantrically symbolizing nature's destructive forces. Members of the *Drag-po* (Skt. *Bhairava*) Order are chiefly defenders of Buddhism.

[4] Text: *Rdorje-gdan* (pron. *Dorje-dān*): Skt. *Vajrāsana*, meaning, with reference to the place, or seat, where the Buddha sat in meditation and attained Enlightenment, Indestructible (or Immutable, or Diamond-like) Throne. Bōdh-Gayā is also written, but incorrectly, Buddha-Gayā.

[5] This query would be put today by the pious multitudes of India to the millions in the Occident who pride themselves on having no *guru*, no wise guide to the science of life and the art of living and of dying. None in India or Tibet save the occidentalized are without religion; and today every boy and girl, even among the outcastes, still receives religious instruction and has a *guru*. Aware of the worldly effects of Westernization, so marked in America, the Tibetans, like the Nepalese, maintain a policy of watchful

remark aroused in Padma the thought, 'Although I am a self-born incarnation of the Buddha and therefore do not need a *guru*, it will be wise for me to go to learned *pandits* and make a study of the Three Secret Doctrines,[1] seeing that these people and those of coming generations need spiritual guidance'.

PADMA'S MASTERY OF ASTROLOGY, MEDICINE, LANGUAGES, ARTS, AND CRAFTS

Accordingly, Padma went first to a saintly *guru* who was a *Loka-Siddha*,[2] at Benares, and mastered astrology. He was taught all about the year of the conception of the Buddha, the year in which the mother of the Buddha dreamt that a white elephant entered her womb, the year of the Buddha's birth, and how these esoterically significant periods have correspondence with the Tibetan calendar. He was also taught how the Sun and Moon eclipse one another. And now he was called 'The Astrologer of the Kālachakra'.[3]

Having mastered astrology, Padma mastered medicine under the son of a famous physician, known as 'The Youth Who Can Heal'. Thus Padma became known as 'The Life-Saving Essence of Medicine'.

aloofness. The Tibetans have a proverb which may be rendered thus: 'Inasmuch as men and beasts are alike in eating, sleeping, and copulating, if men be without religion, which alone differentiates them from beasts, they become indistinguishable from beasts.' The applicability of this to present world conditions is self-evident.

[1] The Three Secret Doctrines are, briefly, the teachings conveyed by initiation, concerning the External (or Exoteric), the Internal (or Esoteric), and the Transcendental (or Non-Dualistic, i.e. Non-Exoteric and Non-Esoteric) aspects of Truth, or Reality. The essentiality of the Hīnayāna represents the first; the essentiality of the Mahāyāna, the second; and the Doctrine of the Voidness (Skt. *Shūnyatā*), as set forth in the *Prajñā Pāramitā*, represents the third.

[2] A *Loka-Siddha*, or 'World *Siddha*', is one who has attained all *yogic* accomplishments, or powers over human existence, both physical and psychical, and, as in this instance, is also an adept in the astrological sciences.

[3] Tib. *Dus-kyi-Khorlo*, or 'Circle of Time', one of the most esoteric of Tantric doctrines. (See p. xviii, above.) The Kālachakra Doctrine includes what the Lāma Sonam Senge designates as 'the science of all kinds of Astrology and Astronomy'. 'The Kālachakra Doctrine itself', he added, 'has been known in Tibet for a thousand years or more.'

Padma's next teacher was a *yogī*, the most learned in ortho-graphy and writing, who taught him Sanskrit and related vernacular languages, the language of demons, the meaning of signs and symbols, and the languages of gods and of brute creatures, and of all the other beings of the Six States of Existence.[1] Altogether, Padma mastered sixty-four forms of writing and three hundred and sixty languages. And the name he was given was 'The Lion *Guru* of Speech'.

Then, placing himself under the guidance of a great artist, named Vishvakarma, who was eighty years of age, Padma became expert in working with gold and gems, silver, copper, iron, and stone, in the making of images, in painting, clay-modelling, engraving, carpentry, masonry, rope-making, boot-making, hat-making, tailoring, and in all other arts and crafts. A beggar women taught him to mould and glaze clay pots. And the name given him was 'The Learned Master of All Applied Arts'.

THE *GURU* PRABHAHASTI (OR 'ELEPHANT OF LIGHT')

In his wanderings shortly afterwards, Padma encountered two ordained monks on their way to their *guru*. Making obeisance to them, he requested of them religious instruction. Frightened at his being armed and at his uncouth appear-ance, they took him to be one of the order of demons who eat human flesh, and ran away. He called to them, saying, 'I have relinquished evil actions and taken to the religious life. Be good enough to instruct me in religion.' At their request, he handed over to them his bow and quiver of iron arrows and accompanied them to their *guru*, Prabhahasti, an incarnate emanation of the Ādi-Buddha, who lived in a wooden house with nine doors.[2] After bowing down before the *guru*, Padma addressed him thus: 'Hail! Hail! be good enough to give ear to me, thou noble *guru*. Although I am a prince, born in the

---

[1] The Six States of Existence are the realms of the gods, of titans, of men, of brutes, of ghosts, and of dwellers in various hells.

[2] This passage is an example of the esotericism underlying many of the legends, the 'nine doors' being the nine apertures of the human body, namely, the two apertures of the eyes, the two of the nose, the two of the ears, the mouth, anus, and aperture of the organ of sex.

country of Urgyān, I sinfully killed the demon son of a minister and was exiled. I am without worldly possessions; and I fear that I have done wrong in coming here without a gift to offer to thee.[1] Nevertheless, condescend to teach me all that thou knowest.'

The *guru* replied, 'Hail! Hail! thou wondrous youth! Thou art the precious vessel into which to pour the essence of the religious teachings. Thou art the incarnate receptacle for the Mahāyāna; I will instruct thee in the whole of it.'

Padma responded, 'First of all, please confer upon me the state of *brahmacharya*.'[2] And the *guru* said, 'I understand the *yoga* systems; and if thou desirest instruction in them as forming a part of the Mahāyāna, I will so instruct thee, but I cannot confer upon thee the state of *brahmacharya*.[3] For this thou shouldst go to Ānanda at the Asura Cave. Meanwhile, and before I instruct thee in the Mahāyāna, receive my blessing.'

Accordingly, Prabhahasti taught Padma the means of attaining Buddhahood, of avoiding spiritual retrogression, of gaining mastery over the Three Regions,[4] and concerning the *Pāramitās*[5] and *yoga*. Although Padma could remember and master anything he had been taught once, this *guru*, in order to cleanse Padma of his sins, made him review each of the teachings eighteen times.

PADMA'S ORDINATION BY ĀNANDA

Afterward, at the Asura Cave, in the presence of Ānanda, Padma took the vow of celibacy and received ordination into

---

[1] It is customary for a disciple when first presenting himself to a *guru* to make the *guru* a gift, thereby signifying his desire for spiritual guidance. See *Tibet's Great Yogī Milarepa*, pp. 65, 68, 77, 103.

[2] The state of *brahmacharya*, or sexual continence, is one of the essentials for success in practically applied *yoga*.

[3] As will presently be seen, Padma was destined to take the vow of celibacy before Ānanda, the cousin and chief disciple of the Buddha, at the Asura Cave, and to receive from him ordination into the Order. The instructions which Prabhahasti gave to Padma appear to have been more or less exoteric or preliminary to those given by Ānanda later, and may, therefore, be called intellectual rather than applied. In this connexion, it is significant that Prabhahasti does not initiate, but merely blesses, Padma.

[4] See p. 205[1], following.   [5] See pp. 173[2], 234[3], following.

the Order; and Ānanda made Padma a regent of the Buddha. The Earth Goddess came carrying a yellow robe; and, as she robed Padma in it, all the Buddhas of past aeons appeared in the firmament from the ten directions and named Padma 'The Lion of the Shakyas, Possessor of the Doctrine'.

PADMA'S QUESTIONING CONCERNING ĀNANDA'S PRE-EMINENCE

Being a fully ordained monk, and possessed of the power of the Mahāyāna to destroy the evils of the world, Padma, like the previous Buddhas, went forth and taught the Doctrine and discussed it with *Bodhisattvas*. Then, having become a *Bodhisattva* himself, he returned to Ānanda; and, at a time when Ānanda was discussing the *Dharma*, asked him how he had become the Lord Buddha's chief disciple. Ānanda replied that his pre-eminence was due to his having faithfully practised the precepts; and, in illustration, told the following story:

THE STORY OF THE UNFAITHFUL MONK

A monk at Bōdh-Gayā, named 'Good Star' (*Legs-pahi-Skarma*) had memorized twelve volumes of the precepts, but practised none of them, so the Lord Buddha admonished him, saying, 'Although thou canst recite all these precepts from memory, thou failest to practise them. Thou canst not, therefore, be considered a man of learning.' At this, the monk grew exceedingly angry, and retorted, 'There are only three things that make Thee different from me: Thy thirty-two illustrious names, Thine eighty good examples, and Thine aura the breadth of Thine outstretched arms. I, too, am learned. Despite my having served Thee for twenty-four years, I have not discovered any knowledge in Thee the size of a *til*-seed.'[1] Then, the monk's temper increasing, he shouted at the top of his voice, 'I refuse to serve Thee any longer, thou worthless beggar; I am much superior to Thee in understanding of the Doctrine, Thou scoundrel who hath run away from Thine own kingdom'. And, still shouting angrily, the monk went off.

---

[1] The Indian *til*-seed, like a mustard seed, is very small.

How Ānanda was chosen Chief Disciple

The Lord Buddha called together the disciples and said to them, ' "Good Star" became very angry and left me. I desire to ascertain who will serve me in his stead.' All the disciples together bowed down and offered themselves, each one saying, 'I desire to serve; I desire to serve'. He asked, 'Why do ye desire to serve me, knowing that I am now grown old?' And the Lord Buddha not choosing any of them, they entered into silent meditation; and Moggallāna at once saw that Ānanda was the most suitable to select. Accordingly, the assembly, composed of five hundred learned monks, many of them *Bodhisattvas*, chose Ānanda. The Lord Buddha smiled, and said, 'Welcome!' and Ānanda said, 'Although I am quite unfitted to serve Thee, nevertheless, if I must serve Thee, I desire Thee to make to me three promises. The first promise is that I be allowed to provide mine own food and clothing; the second is, that Thou shalt give to me whatever [religious guidance] I may beg of Thee; and the third is, that Thou shalt not give out a [new] doctrine at a time when I am not present.'

The Buddha again smiled, and made reply, 'Very well; very well; very well'.

The Buddha Foretells the Unfaithful Monk's Death

Ānanda's first request of the Lord was for information concerning 'Good Star'; and, thereupon, the Lord prophesied that 'Good Star' would die within seven days and become an unhappy ghost in the monastic garden. When told of the prophecy by Ānanda, 'Good Star', somewhat perturbed, said, 'Occasionally His lies come true. If I am alive after seven days, I shall have some more things to say about Him. Meanwhile I shall remain here.'

On the morning of the eighth day Ānanda found 'Good Star' dead and his ghost haunting the garden. Thereafter, whenever the Lord Buddha was in the garden expounding the *Dharma*, the ghost turned its face away from the Lord and placed its hands over its ears.

ĀNANDA'S TESTIMONY CONCERNING THE BUDDHA

Ānanda said it was because of all these things that he had served the Lord faithfully for twenty-one years. Then he told how the Buddha had attained Buddhahood at Bōdh-Gayā in His thirty-fifth year; how He set the Wheel of the Law in motion at Sarnath, near Benares, by teaching to His disciples the Four Noble Truths: Sorrow, the cause of Sorrow, the Overcoming of Sorrow, and the method (or Path of Salvation) whereby Sorrow may be overcome. Ānanda also told how, continuing to preach at Sarnath for seven years less two months, the Buddha taught the Truths contained both in the twelve volumes of precepts which 'Good Star' had memorized and in ten other volumes. The contents of each of these ten volumes, Ānanda described as follows: volume 1 expounded the doctrine of good and evil; volumes 2, 3, 4, the one-hundred-dred religious duties; volume 5, the method of practising these duties; volume 6, the theories of self; volume 7, *yoga*; volume 8, recompense for kindness; volume 9, Wisdom; and volume 10, mind and thought. There were also a number of other teachings, concerning lust, anger and sloth, priestly precepts, *guru* and *shishya*, methods of preaching, the Voidness, the fruits of practising the precepts, and the method of attaining Deliverance.[1]

During the second period of His mission, extending over about ten years, the Lord preached the Mahāyāna in Magadha, at Gṛidhrakūta, Jetavana, and elsewhere. He also preached to Maitreya, Avalokiteshvara and other *Bodhisattvas* in heaven-worlds, and to gods and demons, the essence of the *Dharma* as set forth in various Scriptures; and told of His visit to Ceylon.

The third period of the Buddha's preaching extended over thirteen years, and was chiefly to gods, *nāgas*, *arhants*, and various orders of spiritual beings. During the fourth period, of seven years, He taught Tantric doctrines, but only exoterically.

---

[1] Tibetan Buddhists regard the teachings given out by the Buddha at Sarnath as being of the Hīnayāna (or Theravāda) and those delivered afterwards in other places as being of the Mahāyāna.

The Buddha directed and empowered Vajra-Pāṇi[1] to teach the esoteric aspects of the *Tantras*, and said to him, 'In the same country and epoch there cannot be two Buddhas of Bōdh-Gayā[2] preaching the Doctrine. If there be another Buddha, He can come only after the departure of the present Buddha.'

It was at this time and until His eighty-second year, when He passed away into *Nirvāṇa*, that the Lord Buddha preached the *Vinaya*, *Sūtra*, and *Abhidharma Piṭaka*,[3] and the *Getri*.[4]

PADMA'S STUDIES UNDER ĀNANDA

Padma was much pleased with this lengthy discourse of Ānanda's [which has here been summarized], and he remained with Ānanda for five years and mastered the twelve volumes of precepts comprising the *Getri*, which 'Good Star' had memorized.

When his studies under Ānanda were nearing completion, Padma, seeing the limitations of the exoteric exposition of the Doctrine, thought to himself, 'By means of the teachings concerning the Voidness and the Divine Wisdom I must discover a more perfect path'.[5]

[1] Vajra-Pāṇi (Tib. *Phyag-na-Rdo-rje*: pron. Chhak-na-Dorje; or *Phyag-Rdor*: pron. *Chhak-Dor*) 'Wielder of the *Vajra* (or Thunderbolt of the Gods)', is assumed to be a Tantric personification of the force personified as Indra by the Hindus, Zeus by the Greeks, Jupiter by the Romans, and Jehovah by the Hebrews. He is the spiritual son of Akṣhobhya, the second of the Five Dhyānī Buddhas. Cf. L. A. Waddell, op. cit., p. 356. As Chhak-Dor he is the ruling deity in the Tantric system.

[2] That is to say, there can be no two Buddhas incarnate at the same time who have attained Enlightenment as Gautama did at Bōdh-Gayā.

[3] These three *Piṭaka* (or collections) comprise the canon of Southern Buddhism. The *Vinaya Piṭaka* consists of rules for the government of the priesthood; the *Sūtra Piṭaka*, of discourses of the Buddha; the *Abhidharma Piṭaka*, of the psychology and metaphysics.

[4] See note 1 on p. 204, following. The Tibetan tradition here set forth concerning various periods of the Buddha's teaching suggests the theory formulated by the Chinese monk Chih-chē (who lived during the last half of the sixth century A.D.) that the sermons and utterances of the Buddha point to five great periods in His life. The student is referred to K. L. Reichelt, op. cit., pp. 43–45.

[5] The translated text of the 'Yoga of Knowing the Mind', contained herein in Book II, sets forth in epitomized form the results of this far-reaching decision of the Great *Guru* to discover the Ultimate Truth. The Scriptures of all religions are designed to guide the unenlightened multitude towards the

ĀNANDA'S TESTIMONY CONCERNING THE SCRIPTURES

He asked Ānanda, 'For how long have the *Sūtras* and *Mantras*[1] been recorded; and, if counted, how many volumes of them are there, and where are the texts to be had?' Ānanda replied, 'Ever since the Lord's passing away into *Nirvāṇa*, all that He said hath been recorded. If carried by the Elephant of Indra,[2] there would be five hundred loads of these writings.' A dispute arose between the *Devas* and the *Nāgas*, the *Devas* wishing to have the Scriptures in their world and the *Nāgas* to have them in theirs. The volumes of the *Boom*[3] were hidden in the realm of the *Nāgas*; the *Prajñā-Pāramitā* was hidden in Indra's heaven; most of the *Sūtras* were hidden in Bōdh-Gayā; the *Abhidharma Piṭaka* was hidden in the Nālanda Monastery; the greater part of the Mahāyāna texts were hidden in Urgyān. Other texts were deposited in the *stūpa* at Nālanda. And all of these writings were secured against the ravages of insects and of moisture.

PADMA'S TEACHINGS AND VARIOUS STUDIES

Upon completing his studies under Ānanda, Padma went to a cemetery, wherein dwelt the Tantric deity Mahākāla,[4]

Higher Teachings. Guidance by priests, even by the wisest *gurus*, is for the purpose of fitting the disciple to be a lamp and a refuge unto himself, as the Buddha taught. The Path may be pointed out, leading from the obscuring darkness of worldly existence to the unobscured radiance of the *Nirvāṇic* Goal. But the pilgrim must by his own efforts travel the route of the Pilgrimage to its very end; no one else can do it for him.

[1] The *Mantras* are the special Scriptures of the Mantrayāna School of Northern Buddhism.

[2] A mythical elephant of supernormal strength, commonly referred to in the literature of India, as here, figuratively, to emphasize oriental exaggeration.

[3] The *Boom*, or '*Bum* (Skt. *Sata Sahasrikā*), meaning '100,000 [shlokas of Transcendental Wisdom]', consists of the first twelve of the twenty-one volumes of the Tibetan canonical *S'er-p'yin* (pron. *Sher-chin*), as translated from the original Sanskrit *Prajñā-Pāramitā* (which corresponds to the *Abhidharma* of the Southern School of Buddhism). (See *Tibetan Yoga and Secret Doctrines*, pp. 343–9.)

[4] Mahākāla ('Great Black One') is the Tantric personification of the masculine, or *shakta*, aspect of the disintegrating forces of the Cosmos, of which Kāli ('Black Female One') is the feminine, or *shakti*, aspect. As such, Mahākāla is the Lord of Death, synonymous with Dharma-Rāja. And he is the wrathful manifestation of Avalokiteshvara (Tib. *Chenrazee*) of whom the Dalai Lāma is the incarnate representative on Earth.

who had the body of a yak, the head of a lion, and legs like serpents. The cemetery contained a *stūpa* made of precious gems, against which Padma was accustomed to rest his back as he expounded the *Dharma*; and there for five years he occupied himself with teaching the *ḍākinī*, and was called 'The Sun-rays One'.[1]

Desirous of finding a doctrine capable of being expounded in few words of vast import and which, when applied, would be immediately efficacious, even as the Sun once it has arisen is immediately efficacious in giving light and heat, Padma went to the Ādi-Buddha in the 'Og-min Heaven, and was taught the Doctrine of the Great Perfection.[2] And then Padma was called Vajra-Dhāra in the esoteric aspect.[3]

After this, Padma went to the Cemetery of 'Expanded Happiness', in Kashmir. There, for five years, Padma taught the *Dharma* to the demoness Gaurima and to many *ḍākinī*; and he was named 'The Transmitter of Wisdom to all Worlds'.[4] Thence he went to Vajra-Sattva in His heaven-world, and acquired proficiency in *yoga* and in Tantric doctrines;[5] and was named Vajra-Dhāra in the exoteric aspect.

Padma also dwelt for a period of five years in the 'Self-Created Peak' Cemetery in Nepal, where, after teaching and subjugating various classes of spiritual beings, including

---

[1] Tib. *Nyi-ma Hod-zer*, one of the eight forms, or personalities, in which Padma-Sambhava manifested himself. (See Illustration V and its description on p. xxii, above.)

[2] The Doctrine of the Great Perfection is the root doctrine of mystical insight of the Nyingma School founded by Padma-Sambhava. (See *Tibetan Yoga and Secret Doctrines*, pp. 277–8.)

[3] Vajra-Dhāra ('Holder of the Vajra, or *Dorje*') is the super-human Teacher of the Secret Doctrine upon which the Vajrayāna and Mantrayāna are based. He is associated with the Ādi (or Primordial)-Buddha, personification of the One Cosmic Mind, and with the *Dharma-Kāya* ('Body, or Essentiality, of the *Dharma* or Truth'), symbolical of Reality. As such, Vajra-Dhāra is the Divine *Guru* of the Nyingma School.

[4] Tib. *Lōden Chog-se*, another of the eight personalities in which Padma manifested himself.

[5] Vajra-Sattva is the *Sambhoga-Kāya* aspect, or reflex of the *Dharma-Kāya* aspect, of the Dhyānī Buddha Akṣhobhya associated with the Eastern Realm of Pre-eminent Happiness, as in *The Tibetan Book of the Dead* (p. 108). Exoterically He manifests the Universe, esoterically He comprises all deities. He, like Shiva, being the Great Master of *Yoga*, is, in this School, the Tutelary of all aspirants for success in *yoga*.

demons, and acquiring dominion over the Three Regions of
conditioned existence, he was called 'He Who Teacheth with
the Voice of a Lion'.[1]

In the heaven of the Ādi-Buddha, Padma was completely
instructed in the Nine Vehicles, or Paths,[2] in twenty-one
treatises on *Chitti-Yoga*,[3] and in everything appertaining to
the *Mantras*, and *Tantras*; and was called 'The Completely
Taught One'.

It was in the 'Lanka-Peak' Cemetery, in the Sahor country,
after he had preached to and disciplined many fearful demons,
that he was named 'The One Born of a Lotus'.[4]

In the 'God-Peak' Cemetery, of the land of Urgyān, Padma
remained five years, and received instruction from one of the
ḍākinī of the Vajra-Yoginī Order[5] on the secret Tantric
method of attaining liberation. It was after he had taught
the *ḍākinī* in the 'Lotus-Peak' Cemetery that Padma became
known as 'The Eternal Comforter of all [Beings]'.[6]

PADMA'S INITIATION BY A *ḌĀKINĪ*

Padma's next teacher was an ordained *ḍākinī*, who dwelt
in a sandal-wood garden, in the midst of a cemetery, in a
palace of skulls. When he arrived at the door of the palace
he found it closed. Then there appeared a servant woman

[1] Or *Seṅ-ge Dra-dog*, which is yet another of the names given to the
eight personifications, or forms, assumed by Padma.

[2] These consist of nine methods of attaining Enlightenment, such as those
represented by the *Mahāyāna*, *Hīnayāna*, *Vajrayāna*, *Mantrayāna*, and
Yogā-chāra (based upon the *Five Books of Maitreya*, the coming Buddha).
Similarly, in Hinduism there are the Six Schools (Skt. *Shad-Darshanas*) of
Philosophy, or Visions, or Means of attaining Liberation, namely, the
Nyāya, *Vaisheshika*, *Sānkhya*, *Mimāngsa*, *Yoga*, and the *Vedānta* systems.

[3] Or *Yoga* appertaining to the mind in its True Nature, as expounded in
our treatise.

[4] The Tibetans say that this cemetery was inhabited by many water-
born creatures who compared their birth with that of the lotus and correlatively with that of the Great *Guru*. Hence they named him 'The One Born
of a Lotus' (Skt. *Padma-Sambhava*).

[5] The order of Vajrayāna *devatas* is collectively personified in Vajra-
Yoginī, the chief tutelary goddess associated with many esoteric practices
of Tibetan Tantric *yoga*. (See *Tibetan Yoga and Secret Doctrines*, Illustration V and description of Vajra-Yoginī on pp. 173–5.)

[6] Or, more literally, *Dorje Drō-lō*, the name of another of Padma's eight
personalities. (See p. xxiii, above.)

carrying water into the palace; and Padma sat in meditation
so that her water-carrying was halted by his *yogic* power.
Thereupon, producing a knife of crystal, she cut open her
breast, and exhibited in the upper portion of it the forty-two
Peaceful Deities and in the lower portion of it the fifty-eight
Wrathful Deities.[1] Addressing Padma, she said, 'I observe
that thou art a wonderful mendicant possessed of great
power. But look at me; hast thou not faith in me?' Padma
bowed down before her, made apology, and requested the
teachings he sought. She replied, 'I am only a maid-servant.
Come inside.'

Upon entering the palace, Padma beheld the *ḍākinī* enthroned on a sun and moon throne, holding in her hands a
double-drum[2] and a human-skull cup,[3] and surrounded by
thirty-two *ḍākinī* making sacrificial offerings to her. Padma
made obeisance to the enthroned *ḍākinī* and offerings, and
begged her to teach him both esoterically and exoterically.
The one hundred Peaceful and Wrathful Deities then appeared overhead. 'Behold', said the *ḍākinī*, 'the Deities.
Now take initiation.' And Padma responded, 'Inasmuch as
all the Buddhas throughout the aeons have had *gurus*, accept
me as thy disciple'.

Then the *ḍākinī* absorbed all the Deities into her body.
She transformed Padma into the syllable *Hūm*.[4] The *Hūm*
rested on her lips, and she conferred upon it the Buddha-
Amitābha blessing. Then she swallowed the *Hūm*; and inside
her stomach Padma received the secret Avalokiteshvara initiation. When the *Hūm* reached the region of the *Kuṇḍalinī*,
she conferred upon him initiation of body, speech, and mind;

---

[1] These constitute the Tantric *maṇḍala* of One Hundred Deities. (See
The Tibetan Book of the Dead, p. 217.)

[2] The Tibetan *damāru*, or ritual drum. (See Illustration V.)

[3] Such as that held by Padma-Sambhava in the Frontispiece.

[4] The *mantra* syllable *Hūm* of the Tibetans, when properly intoned by an
initiate of the Mantrayāna, is said to be one of the most efficacious of all
mantras, like the *Aum* (or *Om*) of the Hindus. It plays a very important role
in all Tantric rituals of Tibet, and is associated with the psychic centres
(Skt. *chakra*) of the lower part of the body, and thus with the *Mūlādhāra-
chakra*, at the base of the spinal column, wherein the Serpent Power of the
Goddess Kuṇḍalinī resides, the awakening of which, under wise guidance, is
essential to successful initiation.

and he was cleansed of all defilements and obscurations. In secret, she also granted to him the Hayagrīva initiation,[1] which gives power to dominate all evil spiritual beings.

The Wisdom-Holder *Guru*

A Wisdom-Holder[2] of 'Og-min, the highest of the Buddha heavens, afterwards taught to Padma all that was known concerning magic, rebirth, worldly knowledge, hidden treasure, power over worldly possessions, and longevity, both exoterically and esoterically.

The Zen-like Methods of a Burmese *Guru*

This Wisdom-Holder directed Padma to Pegu,[3] in Burma, to acquire from Prince Shrī Singha, who dwelt in a cave, the essence of all Schools of Buddhism, without differentiating one teaching from another. When Padma requested the *guru* Shrī Singha to teach him this, the *guru* pointed to the heavens and said, 'Have no desire for what thou seest. Desire not; desire not. Desire; desire. Have no desire for desire; have no desire for desire. Desire and deliverance must be simultaneous. Voidness; voidness. Non-voidness; non-voidness. Non-obscuration; non-obscuration. Obscuration; obscuration.[4] Emptiness of all things; emptiness of all things. Desire above, below, at the centre, in all directions, without differentiation.' When all of this had been explained in detail, and the *guru* had assured Padma that he would realize the essentiality of all doctrines, Padma praised the *guru*.[5]

[1] This initiation consists in the transference of such occult power as will enable the initiate to employ with mastery the cosmic forces personified by the Tantric deity Hayagrīva (Tib. *Rta-mgrin*: pron. *Tam-ding*), the Horse-headed One, and manifested through evil spirits and otherwise as forces of destruction or disharmony.

[2] Tib. *Rig-hdzin* (pron. *Rig-zin*), a highly advanced being, such as a *Bodhisattva*.

[3] Text: *Ser-ling*, the ancient Pegu, in Burma, where Buddhism flourished in the ninth and tenth centuries A.D.

[4] Or Ignorance (Skt. *Avidyā*).

[5] This *guru's* method of teaching resembles that of the *gurus* of the Zen School, and is intended to stir the disciple to deep meditative introspection, to the end that he will be enabled to answer his own questions and solve his own problems. The Zen School, precisely like the '*Yoga* of Knowing the Mind in its Nakedness', teaches the futility of seeking outside oneself, in Scriptures or through *gurus*, deliverance from Ignorance.

Then Padma asked him, 'What is the difference between Buddhas and non-Buddhas?' And Shrī Singha replied, 'Even though one seek to discern a difference, there is no difference.[1] Therefore be free of doubt concerning external things. To overcome doubt concerning internal things, employ the perfect absolute Divine Wisdom. No one yet hath discovered either the Primary Cause or the Secondary Cause. I myself have not been able to do so; and thou, likewise, thou Lotus-Born One, shalt fail in this.'

THE SUPERNORMAL ORIGIN OF MAÑJUSHRĪ

Padma's next great *guru* was the *Bodhisattva* Mañjushrī, residing on the Five-Peaked Mountain, near the Sītā-sara River, in the Shanshi Province of China. Mañjushrī's origin, like that of Padma, was supernormal:

The Buddha once went to China to teach the *Dharma*, but instead of listening to Him the people cursed Him. So He returned to Gṛidhrakūta, in India.[2] Considering it to be useless to explain the higher truths to the Chinese, He decided to have introduced into China the conditional truths,[3] along with astrology. Accordingly, the Buddha, while at Gṛidhrakūta, emitted from the crown of His head a golden yellow light-ray which fell upon a tree growing near a *stūpa*, one of five *stūpas*, each of which was on one of the peaks of the Five-Peaked Mountain. From the tree grew a goitre-like excrescence, whence there sprang a lotus blossom. And from this

[1] Understanding of this paradoxical assertion implies understanding of the teaching that all living things, sub-human as well as human, are potentially Buddhas, or, in the Gnostic Christian sense, Christs. Accordingly, the *guru* goes on to suggest that what men call differences are merely differences of illusory external appearances. Innately all things are the One, and, thus, in essence, indistinguishable. Hui-neng, one of the Chinese teachers of the Zen School, similarly declares, 'The only difference between a Buddha and an ordinary man is that the one realizeth that he is a Buddha and the other doth not'. And as Bodhi-dharma, the first of the Zen teachers, taught, all things contain the Buddha nature from beginningless time.

[2] According to Tibetan tradition, it was at Gṛidhrakūta that the Buddha taught the Mahāyāna. Gṛidhrakūta, or the 'Vulture's Peak', is the highest of five mountains surrounding Rājagriha, where the first great Buddhist Council was held in 477 B.C.

[3] That is, the more exoteric aspects of the *Dharma*, which are preliminary or subordinate to the esoteric aspects.

lotus blossom Mañjushrī was born, holding in his right hand the Sword of Wisdom and in his left hand a blue lotus blossom, supporting the Book of Wisdom; and the people spoke of Him as having been born without a father and mother.

The Golden Tortoise and Mañjushrī's Astrological Systems

From Mañjushrī's head there issued a golden tortoise. The tortoise entered the Sītā-sara River, and from a bubble there came forth two white tortoises, male and female, which gave birth to five sorts of tortoises.[1]

At about this time the Lord Buddha emitted from the crown of His head a white light-ray which fell upon the Goddess of Victory. The Goddess went to Mañjushrī; and he, taking in his hand the golden tortoise, said, 'This is the great golden tortoise'. Then he instructed and initiated the Goddess in seven astrological systems; and she studied under him a total of 84,000 treatises. Of these, 21,000 treated of astrology as applied to living human beings, 21,000 of astrology as applied to the dead,[2] 21,000 of astrology as applied to marriage, and 21,000 of astrology as applied to land and agriculture.[3]

Padma Restores Mañjushrī's Astrological Teachings to Mankind

When these astrological teachings, known as the teachings which issued from the head of the most holy Mañjushrī, had

[1] The Chinese employ the tortoise, symbolical of the Cosmos, for purposes of divination, as suggested by the *Si-pa-Khor-lo* (*Srid-pa-Hkhor-lo*), a Tibetan astrological and divinatory chart of Chinese origin, presided over by Mañjushrī transformed into a tortoise, on the different parts of whose body Sanskrit letters are placed in a magical sequence.

[2] In Tibet, astrology is employed to ascertain the auspicious day and hour for a funeral, and the time, place, and circumstances of a deceased person's rebirth, the moment of death being made the basis of calculation. (See *The Tibetan Book of the Dead*, p. 193[n].)

[3] Throughout India, Ceylon, Tibet, China, and other lands of the Orient, all the chief activities of one's earthly career, all agricultural operations such as ploughing, sowing, and harvesting crops, and the determining of the characteristics of land and of places are subject to astrological calculations. In Ceylon, where horary astrology is still a flourishing science, the exact moment for initiating the construction of a house, a fence, or gate, for felling a tree, digging a well, and for all similar operations, is fixed by astrology.

spread all over the world, the people gave so much attention
to them that the *Dharma* of the Lord Buddha was neglected.
So Mañjushrī placed all the texts containing the teachings in
a charmed copper box and hid it in a rock on the eastern side
of the Five-Peaked Mountain. Deprived thus of astrological
guidance, mankind suffered dire misfortunes: diseases, short-
ness of life, poverty, barrenness of cattle, and famine.

Upon learning of these misfortunes, Avalokiteshvara went
to Padma-Sambhava and said, 'I have renovated the world
thrice; and, thinking that all beings were happy, returned to
Ripotāla.[1] But now, when I look down, I behold so much
suffering that I weep.' And Avalokiteshvara added, 'Assume
the guise of Brahma; and, for the good of the creatures of the
world, go and recover these hidden treasures [of texts]'.

Having assumed the guise of Brahma, Padma went to
Mañjushrī and said, 'Although not really a part of the *Dharma*
of the Lord Buddha, astrology is, nevertheless, of vast benefit
to worldly creatures. Therefore, I beg of thee to take out the
hidden texts and instruct me in them.' And Mañjushrī took
out the hidden texts and instructed and initiated Padma in
all of them.[2]

OTHER *GURUS* OF PADMA

After completing his training is astrology under Mañjushrī,
Padma received further instruction in religion from the Ādi-
Buddha. Then, by various human *gurus*, each of whom gave
him a new name, he was initiated in eight doctrines, concerning the Peaceful and Wrathful Deities, the demons of the
Three Realms of Existence, offering of hymns of praise, male-
dictions, the best of all religious essences, and the essentiality
of consecration; and the corresponding deities appeared
before him. He constructed a *stūpa* of thirteen steps and in it
hid the texts of these eight doctrines.

[1] Text: *Ripotāla*, the heavenly residence of Avalokiteshvara: Skt.
Potāla, the name by which the palace of the Dalai Lāma (The incarnation
of Avalokiteshvara) is known outside of Tibet.

[2] The many titles of these astrological treatises are given in a long list on
folios 105–6 of our Tibetan text.

PADMA'S RECOVERY OF HIDDEN TEXTS

Then there appeared to Padma a *ḍākinī* who, after having saluted him as 'the incarnation of the Mind of the Buddha Amitābha', declared that the time was ripe for him to take out the hidden texts of the Lord Buddha's teachings. And Padma gathered together the texts, some from the heaven-worlds, some from the *nāga*-world, and some from the human-world;[1] and, upon mastering their contents, Padma was called 'The Powerful Wealthy One of the World'.[2]

YOGIC ARTS MASTERED BY PADMA

Padma now went to Gṛidhrakūta and mastered the *yogic* art of extracting essences for producing health and longevity; the power of supernormal seeing, hearing, feeling, smelling, and tasting, by drinking only water and abstaining from food, and of retaining healthfulness and bodily warmth without wearing clothing;[3] and the method of acquiring clearness of mind, lightness of body, and fleetness of foot through breath-control, and of prolonging life and of acquiring learning as limitless as the sky through fasting and application of the teachings concerning the Voidness.[4] And by practising all penances, Padma became inured to all hardships. His name at this time was 'The Enjoyer of Greatest Bliss'.

Padma also mastered the *yogic* art of extracting elixir from pebbles and sand, and of transmuting filth and flesh of human corpses into pure food. Another accomplishment was expert-ness in acrobatics. He was then called 'The Kingly Enjoyer of Food'.

Other *yogic* arts in which Padma acquired proficiency were the prolonging of life by taking essence of gold, the preventing

[1] The names of these texts are given on folio 107 of our Tibetan text.

[2] As is the wise custom of the East, one is said to be powerful and wealthy not in worldly things, but in Wisdom. The name here applied to Padma is commonly applied to Avalokiteshvara.

[3] This suggests the practice of *Tummo*, a translated text of which is contained in Book III of *Tibetan Yoga and Secret Doctrines*.

[4] In this series of accomplishments (Skt. *siddhi*), *yogic* power over the Five Elements (earth, water, fire, air, ether) is symbolically implied. The essences symbolize earth; the drinking, water; the clothing, fire; the breath-control, air; the Voidness, ether.

of disease by taking essence of silver, the walking on water by taking essence of pearl, the neutralizing of poison by taking essence of iron, the acquiring of clear vision by taking essence of lapis-lazuli.[1] Now he was named 'The Lotus Essence of Jewels'.

Padma mastered the practice of one thousand such essences, and promulgated them for the benefit of mankind. The texts of some of them he wrote on paper and hid.

The Buddha of Medicine appeared before Padma, and, giving to him a pot of *amrita*,[2] requested him to drink of it. Padma drank one half of it for the prolongation of his life and the other half he hid in a *stūpa*; and now he was called 'Padma the One of Accomplishment'.[3]

Brahma, Lord of *Rishis*, accompanied by twenty-one Great *Rishis*, appeared before Padma, and showered flowers on him and sang his praises. Brahma addressed him, and said, 'Thou art an emanation of the mind of Amitābha, and wert born of a lotus. Thou hast mastered the arts appertaining to medicine, to the neutralizing of poison, to the Five Elements, and to the prolongation of life.'

PADMA'S DESTRUCTION OF THE BUTCHERS

There happened to be at one of the extremities of India a town inhabited by butchers; and Padma, in order to dominate and destroy them, incarnated as one of their sons named Kati, the Evil-Handed Outcaste. To Kati, being by profession a butcher, it made no difference whether he killed and ate a beast or a man; and so he began killing the butchers and eating their flesh. When he took to the habit of cutting off bits of his own flesh and eating it, the people cursed him and drove him away.[4]

---

[1] Text: *bai-dur-ya*: Skt. *vaidūrya*, referring to malachite or chrysolite, of which there are three varieties, the yellow, green, and white lapis-lazuli. The chief of the Medical Buddhas, the Bedūriya Buddha, is named after this curative mineral substance.

[2] *Amrita* is the nectar of the gods, which confers upon men the boon of long or immortal life.

[3] Or 'Padma the *Siddha*'.

[4] All living things being one's kin, the eating of the flesh of the lower animals is, to the strict Buddhist, essentially the same as eating one's own flesh.

Kati went off and made the acquaintance of a butcher named Tumpo,[1] who was quite as wicked as himself, and said to him, 'Both of us live the same sort of a life and we should be quite good company for one another.' Kati furnished Tumpo with bows and arrows and snares, and said to him, 'Now keep on killing the butchers with all thy might and I with all my might will send their consciousness-principles to the abodes of the gods'. In this way all the butchers were killed off.[2]

PADMA'S CONQUEST OF ALL EVILS AND OF ALL DEITIES

Padma's next exploit was the subjugation and conversion of heretics and demons, who vowed to give their life to help him establish the *Dharma*. He wrote a book on how to subjugate and convert demons, and hid it in a rock.

Then Padma thought, 'I cannot very well spread the Doctrine and aid sentient beings until I destroy evil'. He returned to the 'Cool Sandal-Wood' Cemetery near Bōdh-Gayā, and there constructed of human skulls a house with eight doors, and inside it a throne whereon he sat like a lion and entered into meditation. The god Tho-wo-Hūṃ-chen[3] appeared before Padma and making obeisance to him said, '*Hūṃ*! O thou, the *Vajra*-bodied One, Holder of the Shākya Religion, who, like a lion, sittest on thy throne, being self-born, self-grown, the conqueror of birth, old age, and death, eternally youthful, transcendent over physical weakness and infirmities, thou art the True Body.[4] Victorious thou art over the demon born of the bodily aggregates, over the demon of suffering and disease,

---

[1] This name refers to a fierce-looking individual who is a member of a barbarous tribe regarded as being outside of caste.

[2] Although this tale is, apparently, to be taken as a legendary fable to emphasize the Buddhist precept prohibiting, as the Emperor Ashoka did by law, the taking of life, whether human or sub-human, the Tibetans who accept it literally maintain that the Great *Guru*, by killing the butchers and sending their consciousness-principles to the heaven-worlds and thus saving them from the sufferings of the hells, wherein otherwise they would have fallen, acted wisely and humanely. The text goes on to say that he also closed the doors to their rebirth in states lower than human.

[3] A deity of the Wrathful Order under whose protection are placed temples and places of pilgrimage.

[4] That is, the Body of Truth, the *Dharma-Kāya*.

over death and the messenger of the Lord of Death,[1] and over
the god of lust. O thou Hero, the time hath come for thee to
subjugate all these evils.'

Then Padma came out of his meditation. Mounting to the
roof of the house, he hoisted eight victory-banners, spread
out human hides from the corpses of the cemetery and thereon
danced in wrathful mood various dances. He assumed a form
with nine heads and eighteen hands. He intoned mystic
mantras while holding a rosary of beads made of human bones.
In this wise he subjugated all these demons and evil spirits,
slew them, and took their hearts and blood in his mouth.
Their consciousness-principles he transmuted into the syllable
Hūṃ and caused the *Hūṃ* to vanish into the heaven-worlds.
He was now called 'The Essence of the *Vajra*'.

Transforming himself into the King of Wrathful Deities,
Padma, while sitting in meditation, subjugated the gnomes.
In the same manner he brought under his control all women
who had broken solemn vows, and, destroying their bodies,
sent their consciousness-principles to the heavens of the
Buddha.[2] Now he was called 'The Subjugator of Gnomes'.

Assuming the form of Hayagrīva, the horse-headed deity,
Padma performed magical dances on the surface of a boiling
poisonous lake, and all the malignant and demoniacal *nāgas*
inhabiting the lake made submission to him; and he was
named 'The Subjugator of *Nāgas*'.

Assuming the forms of other deities, he subjugated various
kinds of demons, such as those causing epidemics, diseases,
hindrances, hail, and famine. In the guise of the Red Mañjushrī,[3] Padma brought all the gods inhabiting the heavens
presided over by Brahma under his control, by uttering their

[1] Otherwise known as Dharma-Rāja, the Lord of Truth, Judge of the
Dead, King of the Lower Regions; and also as Yama, the Lord of Death.
(See *The Tibetan Book of the Dead*, p. 35.)

[2] Since these women had broken their vows and were, according to
Tibetan belief, *karmically* destined to be reborn among the gnomes, Padma
conferred immeasurable good upon them by saving them from their fate and
sending their consciousness-principles to Buddha realms.

[3] Mañjushrī is represented in many aspects, most of the countries where
Northern Buddhism prevails having their own special Mañjushrī. See
description of Illustration IV, p. xix, above.

mantras.[1] And, in other guises, Padma conquered all the most furious and fearful evil spirits, and 21,000 devils, male and female.

As Halā-halā,[2] Padma dominated all good and bad demons controlling oracles in Tibet.[3] As the Body of the Thirty-two Wrathful Swastikas, Padma dominated the Nine Planets, the Sun, Moon, Mars, Mercury, Venus, Jupiter, Saturn, Rahu, and Khetu,[4] and all things under their influence. As the six-faced Yama, the Lord of Death, Padma dominated all the Lords of Death under Yama. Similarly, Padma conquered Pe-har, the King of the Three Realms of Existence,[5] subdued all haughtiness, gained ascendency over Mahādeva,[6] Pashupatī,[7] and other deities of the Brāhmins, and also over the chief deities of the Jains. And the god Mahākāla,[8] and the goddesses Remati[9] and Ekadzati,[10] appeared before Padma

---

[1] Each living thing, in all states of existence, possesses a bodily form attuned to a certain frequency of vibration. A *mantra* is a syllable or series of syllables of the same frequency as the thing or being (usually an invisible spiritual being, god or demon) to which it appertains; and an expert magician who knows the *mantra* of any deity or order of lesser beings can, by intoning it properly, invoke the deity or dominate the lesser beings. (See *The Tibetan Book of the Dead*, pp. 220–2.)

[2] Halā-halā is a Tantric six-faced manifestation of Avalokiteshvara.

[3] Some of the demons of this order control the 'spirit-mediums' officially appointed as oracles in Tibet, and are believed to be vengeful spirits of deceased *lāmas* who, when in human bodies, practised black magic and thus failed spiritually. The Tibetans call them *Btsan*.

[4] The Nine Planets are described in *Tibetan Yoga and Secret Doctrines*, p. 287.

[5] It was Pe-har whom Padma afterwards made the guardian deity of the famous Monastery of Sāmyé.

[6] Text: *Wang-chuk Chen-po*: Skt. *Mahādeva* ('Great Deva'). Mahādeva, who in various forms and aspects is worshipped by Tibetans and by Hindus, dwells on Mount Kailās, the goal of the Pilgrimage, in western Tibet.

[7] Text: *Gu-lang*: Skt. *Pashupatī*, a goddess chiefly of the Nepalese. As Gulang, this deity is propitiated by all mothers in Tibet who have living children.

[8] Text: *Gon-po-Nag-po*: Skt. *Mahākāla* ('Great Black One'), or *Kālānātha* ('Black Lord'), a form of the Hindu Shiva, is one of the chief Tantric deities of the Tibetans.

[9] Text: *Re-ma-ti*, a form of the Hindu Kālī, and a deity of great significance both to the Reformed (or Gelugpa) and Unreformed (Ningmapa) sects of Tibetan Buddhism, is commonly chosen as the tutelary by highly advanced *yogins*, and is associated with Tantric secret doctrines.

[10] Text: *E-ka-dza-ti*, a one-eyed goddess of the mystic cults, the single-eye symbolizing the single (or non-dualistic) eye of Wisdom.

and praised him for thus having conquered all evils and all deities.

THE RESUSCITATION OF THE SLAIN EVIL BEINGS AND THE INCULCATION OF THE *DHARMA*

Padma so far had employed *mantras* and magic to conquer evil; but now, desiring to attain Absolute Knowledge of Truth, he went to Bōdh-Gayā to subjugate all untruth by employing the power of the *Sūtras*; and there he sat in meditation. By uttering the *Hrī-Hūṃ-Ah mantra*, Padma resuscitated all the evil spirits, *nāgas*, and demons he had slain, taught them the *Dharma*, initiated them,[1] and made them to serve the cause of religion. Returning to Gṛidhrakūta in order to ascertain if there were any more beings in need of special religious teachings, he found none.

After this, he preached the *Dharma*, both exoterically and esoterically, to the *ḍākinī*, especially to the four chief *ḍākinī*[2] at the Dhanakosha Lake where he was born. Vajra-Varāhī,[3] together with these *ḍākinī*, made submission to him. He likewise taught the gods of the Eight Planets.

THE BIRTH AND GIRLHOOD OF MANDĀRAVĀ

Padma went to the city of Sahor,[4] in the north-western corner of the country of Urgyān, where King Arshadhara reigned. The King had 360 wives and 720 ministers of state. Padma beholding the King and his principal wife, the Queen Haukī, in union, caused a light-ray to enter the Queen's

[1] That is, he gave them 'Power' (text: *Wang*). This *mantra* appertains chiefly to Avalokiteshvara.

[2] See *Tibetan Yoga and Secret Doctrines*, p. 306.

[3] The Tibetans sometimes call Vajra-Varāhī 'The Most Precious Power of Speech, the Female Energy of All Good' (cf. L. A. Waddell, op. cit., p. 275). Her association here with these *ḍākinī* of the lake indicates that she, too, is of their order.

[4] Sahor (or Zahor), signifying a city or town, is sometimes thought to have been situated in what is now Mandi, a small principality in the Punjab between the rivers Byas and Ravi, where there is a lake sacred as a place of Hindu pilgrimage. (Cf. S. C. Dās, op. cit., p. 1089.) Tibetan Buddhists also make pilgrimages to the lake, believing it to be the very lake which miraculously appeared on the site of the pyre underneath which Padma was tied to a stake and condemned to death by burning, as our narrative will presently tell.

womb, and she dreamt that one hundred suns rose simultaneously, that their heat parched the Sahor country, and
that from the crown of her head sprang forth a flower of
turquoise. Gods and goddesses overshadowed the Queen during her pregnancy. A daughter being born, to the consternation of the royal household, the Queen called in a *yogī* and
showed to him the girl and narrated the dream. The *yogī*
bathed the girl with perfume, placed her so that half her body
was in sunshine and half in shade. After having carefully
examined the babe, the *yogī* announced that she possessed
the 32 signs of a Buddha,[1] that she was the daughter of a god
and could not, therefore, be given in marriage, and that she
would renounce the world and become a *yoginī*; and he named
her Mandāravā.[2]

The girl grew up rapidly, growing as much in one day as a
normal child would in a month. By the time she was thirteen,
she was regarded by everybody as really being an incarnate
goddess. Chinese princes, Hindu, Moslem, and Persian kings
were among her forty royal suitors. When she refused all of
them, the King commanded her to choose one of them within
three days. Thinking over her past lives, she told the King she
must devote her life to religion. The King, much angered at
her decision, placed a guard of 500 servants over her and
refused her exit from the palace, and told the guards that he
would put all of them to death if they allowed Mandāravā to
commit suicide.

The Queen's own servants having failed to find meat such
as the Queen desired, the Queen secretly sent Mandāravā out
to find some. The markets were over for the day and Mandāravā found no meat for sale; so she cut off flesh from a child's
corpse which she discovered on her way back to the palace

[1] There are 32 signs of physical, moral, psychic, and spiritual potentialities of Buddhahood, which appear on the bodies of *Bodhisattvas* about to
become Buddhas.

[2] Mandāravā, whose full name was Mandāravā Kumāri Devi, is said to
have been the sister of the Indian monk Shānta-Rakshita, the family priest
of Thī-Srong-Detsan, King of Tibet, who, at the monk's suggestion, invited
Padma-Sambhava to Tibet to re-establish Buddhism. Padma-Sambhava
made Shānta-Rakshita the first abbot of Sāmyé Monastery. (Cf. L. A.
Waddell, op. cit., pp. 24[5], 28.)

and gave it to her mother, who ordered her to make a stew of it, and Mandāravā did so. Upon partaking of the stew, the King was levitated from his seat and felt as though he could fly; and taking the meat to be that of a Brāhmin seven times born,[1] sent Mandāravā to fetch the remainder of the corpse. The King took the corpse, had it turned into magical pills, and had these buried in a box in a cemetery under the guardianship of the *ḍākinī*.

MANDĀRAVĀ'S ESCAPE TO THE JUNGLE AND ORDINATION

Mandāravā, accompanied by a maid-servant, escaped from the palace through a secret passage-way and, going into the jungle, discarded her garments of silk and her jewellery, and prayed that she might become a sister of the Order and not a bride. She pulled out her hair and scratched her face with her finger-nails in order to destroy her beauty so that no suitors would desire her, and entered into silent meditation.

The maid-servant, in consternation, hurriedly returned to the palace and made report to the King. The King dismissed Mandāravā's suitors, saying that she had joined the Sister-hood; and he had her and her 500 maid-sevants ordained, and built for them a palatial monastery where they entered upon the religious life.

PADMA'S ARRIVAL AND INSTRUCTION OF MANDĀRAVĀ

Knowing that the time had come to instruct Mandāravā, Padma flew on a cloud from the Dhanakosha Lake to Man-dāravā's religious retreat. Mandāravā and her followers, who were out in their garden, beheld a smiling youth sitting in a rainbow. The air was filled with the sound of cymbals and the odour of incense. Overcome with joy and wonder, Mandāravā and her followers swooned. Padma revived them by emanating red, white, and blue light rays.[2] He landed in the garden and

---

[1] Text: *Kewa-dun*. The translator told me, as we translated this passage, that he recalled seeing, as a boy, a dried bit of such flesh brought to his mother and described as having been found by a *tertön* (or taker-out of hidden books and treasures) amidst a cache of hidden books in Tibet.

[2] The red ray symbolizes the speech-principle; the white, the body-prin-ciple; the blue, the mind-principle.

all the nuns bowed down before him. Then Mandāravā invited him into the monastery to expound the Doctrine.

Mandāravā having questioned Padma concerning his parentage and country, he replied, 'I have no parents. I am a gift of the Voidness. I am the essentiality of Amitābha and of Avalokiteshvara, born of a lotus in the Dhanakosha Lake; and, being of the same essence as the Ādi-Buddha, Vajra-Dhāra, and the Buddha of Bōdh-Gayā, I am the Lotus miraculously produced from all These. I will aid all beings. I am the master of the Eight Fathers of Generation, of the Eight Mothers of Birth, of the Eight Places of Travel, of the Eight Places of Abode, of the Eight Cemeteries for Meditation, of the Eight Kinds of *Gurus*, of the Eight Classes of Wisdom, of the Eight Highest *Lāmas* [or Directors of Religion], of the Eight Classes of Magical Illusion, of the Eight Sorts of Garments, of the Eight Tantric Deities Difficult to Propitiate, of the Eight Parts of *Yogic* Dress in Cemeteries, of the Eight Past and Eight Future [Events?], of the Eight Classes of Past Error and of the Eight Classes of Future Error. I have collected all perfection doctrines, and I know the past, present, and future in completeness. I will plant the banners of the Truth in the Ten Directions throughout this World. I am the matchless [Teacher] of all.'

Padma instructed Mandāravā and her 500 followers in the Three *Yogas*[1] first; and they practised these *yogas*.

MANDĀRAVĀ'S IMPRISONMENT AND PADMA'S BURNING AT THE STAKE

A cowherd having observed the coming of Padma and how he was taken inside the monastery by the nuns, went to the door and listened, and, hearing him talking to them, reported that Mandāravā was living with a youthful *brahmachāri* and was not so virtuous as they took her to be. When the King heard this accusation, he offered a reward for anyone able to prove it; and the cowherd claimed the reward. The King

[1] These comprise the *Ati*, *Anu*, and *Chitti* systems of *Yoga*, of the *Yogāchāra* (or 'Contemplative') School of the Mahāyāna, founded by Asaṅga, which developed into the *Mantrayāna*, or 'Path of the *Mantra*', about A.D. 700. (Cf. L. A. Waddell, op. cit., p. 128.)

ordered that the monastery be forcibly entered and that the youth be seized if found within; and Padma was taken and bound with ropes.

The King commanded, 'Collect *til*-seed oil from the villagers and burn the youth. To punish Mandāravā, confine her naked in a pit filled with thorns for twenty-five years. Put a cover over the pit so that she cannot see the blue sky. Imprison the two chief nuns in a dungeon; and confine all the other nuns to the monastery in such manner that they can never more hear the voice of a man.'

Soldiers took Padma, stripped him naked, spat upon him, assaulted him and stoned him, tied his hands behind his back, placed a rope around his neck, and bound him to a stake at the junction of three roads. The people to the number of 17,000 were ordered each to fetch a small bundle of wood and a small measure of *til*-seed oil. A long roll of black cloth was soaked in the oil and then wrapped around Padma. Then there were heaped over him leaves of the *tala*-tree and of the *palmyra* palm. Upon these the wood was placed and the *til*-seed oil poured over it. The pyre was as high as a mountain; and when fire was put to it from the four cardinal directions the smoke hid the sun and the sky. The multitude were satisfied and dispersed to their homes.

A great sound was heard as of an earthquake. All the deities and the Buddhas came to Padma's aid. Some created a lake, some cast aside the wood, some unrolled the oil-soaked cloth, some fanned him. On the seventh day afterwards the King looked forth and, seeing that there was still smoke coming from the pyre,[1] thought to himself. 'This mendicant may have been, after all, some incarnation;' and he sent ministers to investigate. To their astonishment, they saw a rainbow-enhaloed lake where the pyre had been and surrounding the lake all the wood aflame, and at the centre of the lake a lotus blossom upon which sat a beautiful child with an aura, apparently about eight years of age, its face covered with a dew-like perspiration. Eight maidens of the same appearance as Mandāravā attended the child.

[1] The pyre should have been already reduced to ashes.

When the King heard the ministers' report, he took it all to be a dream. He himself went to the lake and walked around it rubbing his eyes to be sure he was awake; and the child cried out, 'O thou evil King, who sought to burn to death the Great Teacher of the past, present and future, thou hast come. Thy thoughts being fixed upon the things of this world, thou practisest no religion. Thou imprisonest persons without reason. Being dominated by the Five Poisons—lust, anger, sloth, jealousy, selfishness—thou doest evil. Thou knowest naught of the future. Thou and thy ministers are violators of the Ten Precepts.' The King made humble repentance, recognized in Padma the Buddha of the past, present, and future, and offered himself and his kingdom to him. In accepting the King's repentance, Padma said, 'Be not grieved. My activities are as vast as the sky. I know neither pleasure nor pain. Fire cannot burn this inexhaustible body of bliss.'

Mandāravā refused to come out of the thorn-filled pit when the King sent for her. Not until the King in person went to her and explained everything did she return to the palace. Then she sang her *guru's* praises and Padma in his turn sang hers. The King clad Padma in royal garments, placed jewels upon him and a crown-like head-dress, and gave to him both the kingdom and Mandāravā.

PADMA'S METHOD OF PREVENTING WAR

The old suitors of Mandāravā made war against the King for giving Mandāravā to Padma. Mahāpāla brought up his army first. Obtaining from the demi-gods enormous all-victorious bows and arrows, Padma dispatched them on an elephant along with a message carried by two gigantic heroes. When Mahāpāla beheld the bows and arrows and learned that Padma and the two heroes could handle them, and fearing lest Padma had a thousand such heroes and arms, he withdrew his army. It being rumoured that no one could possibly use such mighty bows and arrows, Rāhula,[1] at Padma's command, took up one of the bows and arrows and hit a horn

[1] A personification of the God of the Planet Rāhula.

target at a distance from which a man would barely have been visible; and all the kings withdrew their armies.

THE SAHOR KING'S INITIATION

The Sahor King, taking Padma as his *guru*, begged him for adequate instruction in the doctrines of the *Mantras*, *Tantras*, and *Sūtras*, that he might attain *Nirvāṇa*; and Padma said, 'O King, difficult is it for thee when immersed in worldly affairs to practise the Precepts. Wert thou to be taught the secret doctrines appertaining to the *Mantras* and *Tantras* without initiation, it would be like pouring water into an earthen pot before the pot has been fired.'[1] But, after receiving the necessary *yogic* training, the King and twenty-one of his followers were duly initiated; and the King became a teacher of the *Dharma*.

MANDĀRAVĀ'S QUESTIONS AND PADMA'S ANSWERS

One day Mandāravā put to Padma a series of doctrinal questions, which, with Padma's replies, were as follows:

'How do the *Sūtras* differ from the *Mantras* and *Tantras*?'

'The *Sūtras* are the seed, the *Mantras* and *Tantras* are the fruit.'

'What difference is there between the Greater Path and the Lesser Path?'[2]

'The difference is twofold; that between the ordinary significance and the implied significance.'[3]

'What difference is there between the conditional and the unconditional truth?'

'The difference is that between the non-truth and the truth.'[4]

'What is the difference between ritual and Divine Wisdom?'[5]

---

[1] Even as an unfired earthen pot will not retain water, so the untrained and uninitiated disciple cannot retain Truth in its fullness. The Jungian interpretation would be that the Truth often produces an inflation and disruption of the personality.

[2] Or 'between the Mahāyāna and the Hīnayāna'.

[3] Or 'between the exoteric and the esoteric'.

[4] Or 'between the partial truth and the full truth'.

[5] Or 'between exoteric religious observances and intuitive insight'.

'The difference is that between non-having and having.'

'What is the difference between the *Sangsāra* and *Nirvāna*?'

'The difference is that between Ignorance and Wisdom.'

When Mandāravā asked Padma concerning her past and future lives, he replied that the answer would be too long to give then. To her query, 'Who was my father in my previous incarnation?' Padma answered, 'Thy father was the prince of a *yogī* king of Kalinga. He became an ordained monk of the Lord Buddha at Benares. He converted the Jains and Hindus to Buddhism. The monastery of Vikramashīla was under his jurisdiction. He fought the non-Buddhists and slew many, and because of this sin he returned to *sangsāric* birth, being conceived in the womb of the Queen of King Arti. The Queen died; and in the cemetery I cut open the womb and took out the child, which died and was reborn as your father the King.'

'What fate awaiteth my father in his next births?'

'He will first be born as Akara-mati-shīla in the Monkeyland of Tibet;[1] then in the country of the *Rākṣhasas*;[2] then as a prince of the King of Kotāla; then among the demi-gods, and I shall be his *guru*; then as Deva Akarachandra, son of a monk, in Nepal. Then, after being taught by Avalokiteshvara in His heaven, he will take birth as prince Lhaje, son of King Mu-thī-tsan-po of Tibet. He will encounter me in Tibet, and once more I shall tell him of his future. After twenty generations he will be reborn in the Sahor country, now as a virtuous king, now as a very learned man (or *pandit*), now in lower conditions, but through my kindness he shall never see the hell-worlds. All this thou shalt keep secret.' Padma instructed Mandāravā in the Precepts and the Doctrine. And

---

[1] When in ancient times travellers from India first visited Tibet, the Tibetans were in a state of barbarism, and observing their faces reddened, as today, with cold-resisting ochre-coloured ointment, their apparently ferocious mien, their bodies covered with hairy animal skins and their uncouth manners, the travellers took them to be a species of apes. There is also a legend of Tibetan origin, that the progenitor of the Tibetans was a monkey. Tibet is known to the people of Tibet as the *Bod-kyi-yul*, the Country of Bhot. Before it accepted Buddhism, Tibet was known as the country of the red-faced cannibals (or savages)—*Dong-mar-can-gyi-yul*.

[2] A non-human land, sometimes fancifully taken to be Ceylon.

he remained in the Sahor country for 200 years and established the Faith.

PADMA'S AND MANDĀRAVĀ'S MEDITATION IN CAVES

Thinking the time ripe to preach the *Dharma* throughout India, China, Tibet, Nepal, and non-Buddhist countries, Padma told Mandāravā of his imminent departure. She requested that he first instruct her in *Kuṇḍalinī Yoga*; and he said, 'I am going to Ripotāla to the east. On the third night after I am gone face the east and make earnest supplication to me, and I will come to thee.' Padma, sitting on a seat formed of crossed *dorjes*, was conveyed by four goddesses to the heavenly palace of Avalokiteshvara whence he went to a cave and sat in meditation.

Overcome with loneliness and sad at heart, Mandāravā fled weeping from the Sahor palace. Padma appeared before her and said, 'Thou canst not control thyself, yet askest all the doctrines of me. Renounce all worldly things and centre thy mind on religion.' Padma took her to the cave in Avalokiteshvara's heaven, and for three months and seven days made prayer and offerings to the Buddha of Long Life.[1] Then Amitāyus appeared, placed the urn of boundless life on the heads of Padma and Mandāravā, gave them to drink of the nectar of immortality, initiated them, and conferred upon them immunity from death and birth until the end of the *kalpa*. Padma was transformed into Hayagrīva and Mandāravā into Vajra-Vārāhī.[2] Both possessed the *siddhi* of transformation into a rainbow and of invisibility. After this, Padma and Mandāravā descended to the human world and dwelt in the Cave of the 'High Slate Mountains' in the country of Kotāla, between Sahor and the rest of India, where they remained for twelve years practising *yoga*, the King of Kotāla giving them maintenance.

---

[1] That is, Amitāyus ('The One of Boundless Life'), the Buddha invoked for the obtaining of longevity, especially in the celebration of the Tibetan eucharist. He is represented as holding on his lap a vase of life-giving ambrosia, the nectar of the immortals.

[2] See pp. 121[2] and 142[3], above.

THE PRINCESS GIVES HER BODY TO FEED THE
STARVING BEASTS

Padma, in a *yogic* vision, beheld a cemetery wherein the animals which fed on the flesh of the dead were starving because of a dearth of new corpses. Feeling great compassion for the animals, Padma went to the cemetery and offered to them his own body for food. But his body was a body of invisibility,[1] and the animals could not eat it.

[1] That is to say, a non-fleshy, subtle body, such as is attained by success in *yoga*. Psychic research in Europe and America has accumulated much data tending to support the hypothesis of an etheric body as being the normally invisible framework sustaining the body of flesh. Two American physicians found, by weighing a dying person before and a moment after death, that the death-process resulted in a loss of weight of from two to three ounces, which have been credited to the withdrawn etheric body. Colonel de Rochas, Professor of the Polytechnic at Paris, proved that when the etheric body is exteriorized by hypnotizing the subject, sensation no longer exists in the physical body, but is removed thence to a distance of two or three metres. Madame de Esperance, a trance 'medium', dematerialized her legs; and Baron de Meck also reports the case of a man who could dematerialize at will to such a degree that lights could be seen through his body. The Baron himself experimentally ascertained that where a physical limb had been amputated from a living human organism the etheric limb is still present. (Cf. Baron de Meck's Lecture as reported in *The Two Worlds*, London, 16 Dec. 1938, p. 794.) Similarly, as oriental masters of *yoga* maintain, when the fleshly form as a whole is amputated by the high surgery of death, the etheric counterpart (which the Tibetans call the 'rainbow body' because of its auric radiances) continues to exist, possessed not only of the normal sense faculties of the Earth-plane body, but also of the super-normal faculties of the body of the after-death plane (known in Tibetan as the *Bardo*, or state intervening between the complete dematerialization produced by the death-process and the complete rematerialization produced by the birth-process). The translated text in *The Tibetan Book of the Dead*, pp. 158–9, describes the *Bardo*-body of the after-death state as follows:

Addressing the deceased, the Officiant says, 'Thou mayst have been, when living, blind of the eye, or deaf, or lame, yet on this After-Death Plane thine eyes will see forms, and thine ears will hear sounds, and all other sense-organs of thine will be unimpaired and very keen and complete. . . . Thy present body being a desire-body—thine intellect having been separated from its seat [the human body]—is not a body of gross matter, so that now thou hast the power to go right through any rock-masses, hills, boulders, earth, houses, and Mt. Meru itself without being impeded. . . . Or thou canst instantaneously arrive in whatever place thou wishest; thou hast the power of reaching there within the time which a man taketh to bend, or to stretch forth his hand. . . . None is there [of the various psychic powers of illusion and of shape-shifting] which thou mayst desire which thou canst not exhibit. The ability to exercise them unimpededly existeth in thee now.'

The *lāmas* maintain that all these miraculous powers, if developed on the Earth-plane through *yogic* practices, can be exercised either in the fleshly or

In order to ascertain what he should do to save the animals, Padma entered into meditation; and discovering thereby that the late King of Sahor had reincarnated as the princess of the King of Kotāla, considered how the flesh of this princess might be given to the animals. Padma transformed himself into a pair of hawks, and they built a nest and laid eggs in it. The princess happening to go out to gather *kusha* grass,[1] saw the eggs, and placed leaves over the nest to shelter the eggs, and stones at the corners of the nest to prevent it from being blown away. The male hawk assisted her. Pity was thus aroused in her; and, deciding to adopt the religious life, she went to Padma and Mandāravā at the cave seeking religious guidance. Padma said to the princess, 'If thou desirest to become a woman of religion, realize first the sufferings of all the animals in the cemetery; then go and offer to them thy body. By devouring thy body, all these animals will be reborn as human beings, and become thy disciples when thou thyself, after some lives, shalt be born as King Srong-Tsan-Gampo in the Land of Snow.[2] He will send envoys to bring the image of Avalokiteshvara to Tibet. At that time the animals will take

in the *Bardo*-body at will, as they were by the Great *Guru*, to whom journeys in the subtle (or etheric) body to extra-terrestrial states of existence are reported in the Biography as having been as commonplace as journeys in the fleshly form are among ordinary men.

A 'body of invisibility', or, following our Tibetan text more literally, a 'body capable of vanishing', is a concept quite similar to that of the alchemist's *lapis* (or *corpus*) *invisibilitatis*', to which frequent reference is made by Dr. Jung in *Psychology and Alchemy* and other of his writings.

[1] A grass peculiar to India, used by *yogins* for making mats and cushions upon which to sit when meditating. It also affords feed for cattle. *Lāmas* make brooms of it for temple use and also employ it as an altar decoration, associated with the sacred peacock feathers, in holy-water vases. It is prized as a sacrificial grass by Hindus and by Buddhists on account of its having formed the cushion upon which the *Bodhisattva* Gautama sat under the Bodhi-Tree when He became the Buddha.

[2] Text: *Kha-wa-chen*, 'Land of Snow', a name given to Tibet. Srong-Tsan-Gampo, who flourished in the first half of the seventh century A.D. and died about 650, was the first Buddhist king of Tibet, and, being a great patron of learning, is justly the most famous and popular of Tibetan rulers. He was canonized as an incarnation of Avalokiteshvara, the Lord of Mercy and Compassion, and thus prepared the way for the line of Dalai Lāmas. He is believed to have reincarnated in 1077 as Dvag-po Lharje, the direct apostolic successor of Milarepa, and became known as the Great *Guru* Gampopa, dying in 1152.

human birth, some in the east of India, some in Singala; they
will build two hundred monasteries and be servitors of the
Buddha, the *Dharma* and the *Sangha*.[1] Then the image of
the eleven-faced Avalokiteshvara will be taken to Tibet, and
the Children of the Monkey shall have opportunity of worshipping Him.'

The princess at once handed over to Padma her garments
and ornaments, and, going to the cemetery, offered her body
to the animals and they devoured it.

When the King learned from Padma of the wondrous pity
of the princess, he, too, sought religious guidance of him; and
Padma went to the palace and preached the Mahāyāna of
self-sacrifice and universal altruism, for all living things.

PADMA'S CONDEMNATION BY KING ASHOKA

Then after having visited each of the Eight Great Cemeteries
of India, and other places, Padma went to Pataliputra,[2]
where lived King Ashoka,[3] who, after having incited feuds
between the older and younger monks, had the latter put to
death and the former beaten and left to die. The King had
also made war against a rival king and captured him, and
was now holding him prisoner.

In order to subdue Ashoka, Padma transformed himself
into a *bhikshu*[4] and went to Ashoka's palace and begged alms.
'This man', said Ashoka, 'is come to show contempt of me',
and he ordered Padma to be imprisoned. As a punishment,
Padma was cast into a vat of boiling oil. 'Boil him until he is
dissolved', commanded the King. On the following day the

[1] Literally, the Body, the Mind, the Speech, which are Tibetan equivalents for the Buddha, the *Dharma*, the *Sangha*.

[2] Pataliputra, 'The City of Sweet Scented Flowers', known to the ancient
Greeks as 'Palibothra', situated near the modern Patna on the Ganges, was
the capital of Ashoka's empire, where, during the ninth year of his reign, or
in 261 B.C., he adopted Buddhism as the state religion. (Cf. L. A. Waddell,
op. cit., p. xx.) Previously, in 245 B.C., a special Buddhist council was held
at Pataliputra, but, inasmuch as only the stricter wing of the monastic orders
was represented, the Chinese Buddhists do not recognize this council's
decisions. (Cf. K. L. Reichelt, op. cit., p. 23.)

[3] This legendary story concerns the Ashoka who, after his subsequent
conversion to Buddhism, became the famous Buddhist Emperor of India.

[4] A *Bhikshu* is an ordained monk of the Buddhist Order. *Bhikshu* is
Sanskrit, the Pāli form being *Bhikkhu* and the Tibetan, *Ge-long* (*Dge-slon*).

King went to the vat to see how well the sentence had been carried out ; and he beheld a lotus blossom growing out of the vat and the *bhikṣhu* sitting amidst the blossom. Overcome with wonder, Ashoka immediately recognized his error, and, bowing down before the *bhikṣhu* in repentance, said, 'Owing to sloth, I have committed a great sin ; O Lord, tell me how I may atone for it'. And Padma replied, 'If thou build ten million[1] *stūpas* in one night and make surpassingly great charitable gifts to the poor, only thus canst thou wipe away thy sin'.

The King said, 'It is easy to make such gifts to the poor, but difficult to build so many *stūpas* in one night. Perhaps thy words imply that I shall be unable to wipe away my sin.' Padma replied, 'Thou art come into the world in fulfilment of the Lord Buddha's prophecy.[2] If thou go and make prayer before the Bodhi-Tree at Bōdh-Gayā, thou shalt succeed in building so many *stūpas*.'

The King went to the Bodhi-Tree and prayed, 'If it be true that I am come into the world in fulfilment of the Lord Buddha's prophecy, may I be empowered to build so many millions of *stūpas* in one night'; and, to his astonishment, this came to pass. And in the City of Maghadha[3] the King gave surpassingly great alms to the poor.

Public Examination of Two Rival Princes in Medicine

Now Padma took up residence in a cemetery in the country of Baidha,[4] where lived a *yogī* King named Balin, who was

---

[1] This is a typical example of oriental exaggeration to emphasize greatness of number.

[2] This prophecy would refer to the historic fact that King Ashoka became the Great Buddhist Emperor of India. As such, he has been called the Buddhist Constantine. In order to signify his sincere conversion to Buddhism and his deep remorse at the appalling loss of human life and the widespread suffering which his bloody conquest of Kaliṅga, in southern India, had caused, he changed his name from Ashoka, or 'The Sorrowless One', to 'The Compassionate One' (*Piye-dasi* in the Indian vernacular and *Priya-darsin* in Sanskrit). In his edicts he is also called 'The One Beloved of the Gods', *Devanam-priya*. (Cf. L. A. Waddell, op. cit., p. xxi.)

[3] By some authorities the City of Maghadha is believed to have occupied the site of the modern Allahabad ; others have associated it with the modern Patna, or Patalipūtra.

[4] According to the *Kah-gyur* version, Baidha was the birth-place of the

very learned in medicine. Balin had two wives and each had given him a son. To the son of the elder wife, Balin secretly taught all of his medical knowledge, but to the son of the younger wife he taught nothing of it. One day, the King announced that he intended to ascertain by means of an examination which son had a better head for studying medicine. The mother of the younger son thinking that the King was planning thereby to choose one of the sons as heir to the throne, wept bitterly because her son knew nothing of medical science. Her son told her not to lament; and, going to Padma in the cemetery, mastered the five higher systems of medicine. When the time approached for the examination, the King made public proclamation that whichever son showed greater proficiency in medical knowledge would be chosen to succeed to the kingship.

Publicly the two sons were examined. The elder son showed proficiency in three hundred medical treatises; but the younger son showed much greater proficiency, and, in addition to his exposition of them, set forth the Doctrine of the Buddha so wonderfully that *devas*, *nāgas*, and demons appeared and made obeisance to him.

'Without having been taught, thou hast mastered everything', said the King, and he bowed down before the son and set the son's feet on his head. In anger, the elder wife cried, 'Although thou hast secretly instructed mine own son, to the son of the younger queen thou hast conveyed the very essence of medical science. Had they been taught together my son would have been the victor. And now thou hast disgraced him in public. Unless thou divide the kingdom equally between the two, I will put an end to my life here and now.' To this proposal of dividing the kingdom the King agreed, whereupon the younger son said, 'I will embrace the religious career'. And the victorious son, becoming Padma's disciple, mastered

Prince Vishantara, whose incarnation represents the last and greatest of the Ten Great [Former] Births (or *Mahājātaka*) preceding the birth in which the *Bodhisattva* Gautama attained Buddhahood. Tibetans believe Baidha (or Biddha) to be the ancient Videha, which they identify, probably erroneously, with the modern Bettiah is northern Bengal. (Cf. L. A. Waddell, op. cit., p. 543[8].)

the *Sūtras*, the *Tantras*, and the *Mantras*, and wrote many
treatises on religion and medicine, and was named Siddhi-
Phala.[1]

THE SUN *YOGI* SETS FIRE TO THE VIKRAMASHĪLA MONASTERY

During this epoch a Sun-*Siddha*[2] was preaching non-
Buddhist doctrines. He practised a *yoga* intended to draw the
Sun's vital energy into his own body, so that when he opened
his eyes fire came forth and set aflame the Buddhist monastery
of Vikramashīla [in Magadhā]. In the conflagration, many of
the *Abhidharma* scriptures were destroyed. As a result of this
destruction, the *nāga* King Muchilinda became very ill.[3]
Nanda, another King of the *nāgas*, foresaw that Muchilinda
would die unless a human physician were summoned at once.
Two *nāgas* fetched the *Bhikṣhu* Siddhi-Phala, who cured
Muchilinda. As a reward, the King presented the *bhikṣhu*
with the greater part of the text of the *Boom*, which Ānanda,
the chief disciple of the Buddha, had hidden in the realm of the
nāgas. The part of the *Boom* which the *nāga* King withheld was
his security for the *bhikṣhu's* promise to return to the *nāgas'*
kingdom. And this *bhikṣhu*, after his return to the human
world with the *Boom*, became known as Ārya Nāgārjuna.

THE SUPERNORMAL BIRTH OF ĀRYA-DEVA, DISCIPLE OF NĀGĀRJUNA

Padma now went to a cemetery in the country of Singala.
The King of Singala, Shrī Phala, became his patron and

---

[1] A Sanskrit appellation meaning 'Fruit of *Siddhi*', or 'Fruit of *Yogic* Accomplishments'.

[2] A Sun-*Siddha* (Skt. *Sūrya-Siddha*) is a *yogī* proficient in *yogic* practices relating to the Sun, as the matter which follows shows. The Editor recalls having encountered on the banks of the upper Ganges, near Rikhikesh, a *yogī* who practised similarly. Daily the *yogī* sat in practice with his gaze fixed on the unclouded disk of the tropical Sun, with no protection whatsoever to his eyes. If not done with utmost care, the practice may result in total blindness, but this practitioner enjoyed unusually keen vision and was in robust health. His exact purpose in so practising he never made quite clear to me.

[3] This illness was due to pollution of the air and water (which *nāgas* inhabit) by the burning of the monastery and scriptures (of which the *nāga* King had been made the custodian).

disciple. Padma by his supernormal vision beheld the non-Buddhists bring up their army, and complete the destruction of the Vikramashīla Monastery and re-establish the non-Buddhist religion. After Padma had seen this vision, the King's gardener noticed in a pond of the palace garden an immense lotus blossom which never folded its petals at night. When the King and Queen went to see the lotus blossom they beheld in it a beautiful child, apparently about eight years old, with perspiring face.[1] The King's chief priest, being called to explain what the child was, said, 'He is the incarnation of Shākya Mitra. He is destined to defeat Maticitra, the arch-enemy of Buddhism, whose tutelary deity is Mahādeva. Take him into the palace and care for him.' And the King took the child and cared for him; and Padma initiated the child and instructed him in the *Dharma*; and the child was called Ārya-Deva. The child begged Padma for ordination into the Order, but Padma, refusing to ordain him, said, 'Thou art to be ordained by Nāgārjuna.'[2] And Padma remained in Baidha and Singala nearly two hundred years,[3] and converted the people to Mahāyāna Buddhism.

THE ESTABLISHING OF BUDDHISM IN BENGAL

In eastern Bengal a youthful non-Buddhist King was ruling. His palace was surrounded by six moats and had eight doors.

---

[1] The appearance of the child following Padma's vision suggests that Padma exercised his *yogic* powers to bring about the lotus-birth of the child, and the parallelism between the perspiring face of this child and of Padma's when found in a lotus points to a spiritual relationship between them or may even imply that this child is one of the Great *Guru's* emanations.

[2] Nāgārjuna was the greatest of the Fathers of the Māhāyāna, having been (*c.* A.D. 150) the thirteenth, or according to some the fourteenth, in the direct succession of the Buddhist Patriarchs. He is believed to have been the reincarnation of Ānanda, the Buddha's illustrious disciple. As has been suggested above, Nāgārjuna was the transmitter of the *Prajñā-Pāramitā*. (See *Tibetan Yoga and Secret Doctrines*, pp. 344–6.) Ārya-Deva did receive ordination at the hands of Nāgārjuna and was his most learned disciple and successor to the Buddhist hierarchical chair at Nālanda, the Oxford of ancient India.

[3] This Biography represents the Great *Guru* as having flourished in India and elsewhere in the human world for many centuries. He, being a Master of *Yoga*, lived, as has been already suggested above, in a non-fleshy body, immune to illness, old age, and death. He is thus the idealized living exponent of Buddhism practically applied and, in this respect, a Buddha greater than the Buddha Gautama, as the Tibetan Buddhists believe.

He possessed a cat with a thousand eyes, and a magical light-giving gem. His subjects were many, his power great, but his rule was harmful.

Padma, upon setting out to subdue this King, placed Mandāravā on a main highway and directed her to transform herself into a cat-faced being. By means of magic, Padma collected an army of 81,000 men and armed them with bows and arrows. The King was slain and his kingdom conquered. The Five Goddesses of Sensual Pleasure, who were the King's chief deities, were converted. Assuming the guise of the Ādi-Buddha, Padma caused the consciousness-principles of all who had been killed in the war to go to the paradises. The living he converted to Buddhism. He aided the poor, and comforted the brute creatures. The country prospered and the people were happy.

The Vikramashīla Monastery having been rebuilt, King Houlagou of Persia came with a large army and destroyed the twelve buildings comprising the Monastery and a part of the *Abhidharma* scriptures of the Mahāyāna School. Two learned *bhikṣhus*, Thok-me[1] and Yik-nyen,[2] transformed themselves into ordained nuns; and they introduced and established the Five Doctrines of Maitreya, the Eight Kinds of *Prakaraṇa*[3] and the *Abhidharma-Kosha*.

PADMA ATTAINS TO BUDDHAHOOD AT BŌDH-GAYĀ

Padma went to Bōdh-Gayā and in the presence of the *Guru* Singha constructed the *Maṇḍalas* of the Wrathful Deities associated with *Ati-Yoga*, *Chitti-Yoga*, and *Yangti-Yoga*; and, by this means, demonstrated to the *Guru* the methods whereby, in virtue of doctrine and conduct, one may, step by step, attain *Nirvāṇa*.[4] When the verbal part of the exposition was

[1] This is the Tibetan equivalent of Āryasangha (or Asaṅga), the founder of the Yogāchāra School. He is also known as the Sage of Ajanta, with reference to the famous Caves of Ajanta, which in his day were known as Achintapuri Vihara. He is said to have lived 150 years.

[2] A Tibetan name meaning 'Precious-Stone Helper'.

[3] The Eight *Prakaraṇa* are eight metaphysical treatises appertaining to the Hīnayāna School.

[4] As this passage suggests, these three *yogas*, appertaining to the Yogāchāra School, are directly associated with the *Nirvāṇic* Path. (See p. 145[1], above.)

completed, Padma levitated himself and rose into the air so high that he could no longer be seen, and then reappeared in various supernormal forms and exhibited various supernormal powers. He returned to the earth and there constructed a *stūpa* of precious stones and consecrated it.

Many learned *pandits* who happened to witness Padma's magical performances, requested that he teach to them the Doctrine; and he expounded to them the *Sūtras, Tantras, Mantras, Vinaya Piṭaka, Abhidharma,* and medical sciences in detail; and they named him 'The Great *Pandit*'. Then Padma taught them the system of *Kriyā Yoga*[1] in its completeness; and they named him 'The *Dorje* without Imperfection' [or 'The *Dorje* Lacking in Nothing']. Everything that Padma taught to the *pandits*, they wrote down. Then they placed all the manuscripts in a box made of precious gems, tied the box to a banner of victory, and raised the banner over the ruins of the Vikramashīla Monastery. They now named Padma 'The Enlightened One [or Buddha], the Victory Banner of the Doctrine'. Immediately afterwards there was a fall of rain for seven days, all diseases disappeared, and the thirteen lucky signs appeared. Thus Padma really became a Buddha at Bōdh-Gayā; and from the roof of the palace there he roared like a lion. The non-Buddhists were much agitated; and he converted them; and they named him '*Guru* Sèng-ge-Dradog'.[2]

PADMA'S MISSION TO EIGHT COUNTRIES

Padma considered that the time had come to go on to eight other countries to establish the Doctrine, and he went first to the country of Jambu-mala to the east of Urgyān, where grew many *jambu* [*eugenia jambolans*] trees, and taught the *Vajrāyāna* form of Buddhism. Next he went to the country of Par-pa-ta, to the south, where the prevailing cult was of the Black Mañjushrī;[3] and there he taught concerning the

---

[1] See p. 206[2], following.

[2] That is, 'The Lion-roaring *Guru*', the name of one of the eight chief forms assumed by Padma. (See Illustration V and its description, p. xxiii.)

[3] Or Mañjushrī in wrathful aspect: Tib. *Dorje-Jig-je*: Skt. *Vajra-Bhairava*, 'Immutable Wrathful One', one of the most important deities of the

peaceful and the wrathful aspects of Mañjushrī. Then he went
to the country of Nāgapota, to the west, where the people
were devotees of Hayagrīva in Lotus Aspect; and to them
Padma taught concerning the peaceful and wrathful aspects
of Avalokiteshvara.[1] Thence he went to the country of Kasha-
kamala, to the north, where the cult of the *Phurbu*, or Magical
Dagger,[2] prevailed; and Padma amplified this worship. From
here, he went to the country known as Trang-srong,[3] to the
southeast, where the people worshipped the Mother Goddesses; and Padma amplified their worship by teaching them
how to invoke these goddesses. Going thence to the country
of the flesh-eating *Rākṣhasas*, to the southwest, ruled by a
king of the Ten-headed Dynasty of Lanka (or Ceylon), where
the people worshipped Vishnu, he taught the Kālachakra
Doctrine to convert them. Padma's next mission was to the
country of Lung-lha,[4] to the northwest, peopled by devotees
of Mahādeva; and to them he taught concerning *sangsāric*
offerings with hymns of praise.[5] In the eighth of the countries,
called Kekki-ling, or 'Place of Heroes', to the northeast, where
the people practised black magic, Padma introduced one of
the eight systems for propitiating deities.

Now Padma went to the Dhanakosha Lake, at the centre
of the Urgyān country,[6] and found the people prospering and
the Mahāyāna doctrines flourishing. He entered into meditation and ascertained that the time was not yet come to convert all other countries; and he returned to Bengal and lived
with Mandāravā in a cemetery, where the two practised *yoga*.

Gelugpa, or Established Church of Tibetan Buddhism. (See Illustration VI.)
Mañjushrī in peaceful aspect is the Guardian of Divine Wisdom. (See Illustration IV.)

[1] Avalokiteshvara represents the peaceful and Hayagrīva the wrathful
aspect of the Lord of Mercy, of whom the Dalai Lāma is the incarnate representative on Earth.

[2] The Tibetan *phurbu* is a symbolical dagger with a triangular-shaped
blade, used for the ceremonial exorcising, or slaying, of demons.

[3] A Tibetan place-name equivalent to the Sanskrit *Krisi*, or *Suni*, meaning 'Reciter of Sacred Hymns'.

[4] This Tibetan term, meaning 'Wind God' (Skt. *Marut*), refers to the
storm god presiding over the North-west Quarter of the heavens.

[5] Text: *Jik-ten Choe-toe*, with reference to the eight gods difficult to propitiate, of the Nyingma School. (See S. C. Dās, op. cit., p. 325.)

[6] As will be noted, each of the eight countries last above named was in

PADMA'S SUSPICIOUS FRIEND

One of Padma's friends having visited Padma and Man-dāravā in their cemetery retreat and suspecting that the two were living together as husband and wife, said to Padma, 'What a wonderful man thou art! Thou hast left thy lawful wife Bhāsadhara in thy palace in the Urgyān country; and this is quite disgraceful!' And notwithstanding that the friend slighted Padma by refusing to invite him to his home, Padma thought to himself, 'Inasmuch as this fellow is ignorant of the inner significance of the Mahāyāna and of the *yogic* practices appertaining to the three chief psychic nerves,[1] I should pardon him.'

THE ONE SEVEN TIMES BORN A BRĀHMIN

Transforming himself into the son of a Brāhmin, Padma went to the Khasar-Pāṇi[2] Temple and made obeisance before a Brāhmin possessed of divine prescience. 'Why dost thou make obeisance to me?' asked the Brāhmin. And Padma replied, 'In order that I may aid the creatures of the world, I require the flesh of one who hath been born a Brāhmin seven times successively.[3] If thou canst not provide me with any now, please do so at the hour of thy decease.'

The Brāhmin said, 'While in this world, one ought not to relinquish one's life before the time hath come; but as soon as I am dead thou mayst have my flesh'; and then Padma took leave of the Brāhmin.

Five years afterwards, the Brāhmin died. A great *pandit* named Dhombhi Heruka immediately appeared to claim the body. Many wolves attacked the *pandit*, but, exercising *yogic* powers, he drove them away by looking at them; and, placing

one of the Eight Directions, the Dhanakosha Lake in the Urgyān country being central to all of them. Thus they constitute a vast geometrical *maṇḍala*-like symbolic figure.

[1] These are, according to *Kuṇḍalinī Yoga*, the median-nerve, in the hollow of the spinal column, and the right and left psychic nerves coiled around the spinal column. (See *The Tibetan Book of the Dead*, p. 215.)

[2] Khasar-Pāṇi is a form of Avalokiteshvara.

[3] One so born is believed to possess the power of seeing into the future, as did this Brāhmin. Similarly, in the Occident, a seventh son is believed to be endowed with 'the sight'.

the body on his lap, mounted a tiger. He used serpents for the bridle, girth, and crupper of the tiger, wore on his body ornaments of human bone, and, carrying a three-pronged staff,[1] went to the Moslem city of De-dan. There he rode round about announcing that he would make a gift of the body to anyone who could come and take it.[2] A passer-by remarked, 'Look at this *yogī* who is talking nonsense. He would not be riding the tiger had he not given it honey, nor making use of the serpents had he not given them musk.'[3]

THE WINE-DRINKING *HERUKA* WHO PREVENTED THE SUN FROM SETTING

Then the *Heruka* went to a tavern kept by a woman named Vinasā and ordered wine. 'How much?' asked the woman. 'I wish to buy as much as thou hast', he replied. 'I have five hundred jars', she said; and the *Heruka* said, 'I will pay the price at sunset'.

The *Heruka* not only drank all the wine which the woman had, but kept her busy fetching wine from other shops. When the Sun was about to set, the *Heruka* placed his *phurbu*[4] half in sunshine, half in shadow, and the Sun could not set; and he kept it there so long that the country became parched, the grass dried up and the trees died. For seven days the *Heruka* sat there drinking wine, and all the while the *phurbu* remained half in sunshine, half in shadow, and the Sun continued shining.

The people complained bitterly to their King, saying that

[1] Such as that (shown in Illustration I) commonly held by Padma-Sambhava, of whom Dhombhi Heruka is an emanation or metamorphosis. The term *heruka* refers to the wrathful manifestations of the chief Tantric deity, Samvara (Tib. *Demchog*), and is applied only to great masters of Tantric *yoga*. One aspect of Demchog is believed to be successively incarnate in the hierarchical line of the Chief Lāma resident in Peking.

[2] *Yogīs* commonly practise gift-making, in order to accumulate spiritual merit, in accordance with the precept, 'It is better to give than to receive'.

[3] According to popular Tibetan belief, a tiger can be tamed by feeding it on honey, and a serpent kept at a distance by the odour of musk. As Tibetans are accustomed to carry musk on their person, it is said that they are never bitten by serpents. The translator told me he had never known of a Tibetan to die from snake-bite.

[4] A *phurbu* is usually carried by a Tibetan *yogin* concealed on his person for use in *yogic* ceremonial practices.

a mendicant who was sitting in a tavern drinking wine might be the source of their dire misfortune.[1] So, on the morning when the seven days of the *Heruka's* wine-drinking were ended, the King went to the *Heruka* and said, 'O thou mendicant who shouldst be doing good to all creatures, why art thou drinking in this fashion?' And the *Heruka* answered, 'O King, I am without money to pay for the wine which I have drunk'. And when the King promised to settle the account, the *Heruka* took up the *phurbu* and the Sun set.

After this, the *Heruka* went to the Cave of Kuru-kullā and made it his abode. Vinasā, the wine-seller, who had unbounded faith in the *Heruka*, paid a visit to him, taking with her, on an elephant, wine and food and presented them to him, and requested that he accept her as his disciple, which he did. He favoured her with full instructions in *yoga*; and she attained the *siddhi* of immunity to drowning in water, of flying through the air, and of passing through solid substances.

How the Urgyān King was Cured of Snake Bite

The King of the Urgyān country, having gone to a cemetery, was bitten by a venomous serpent. When the most learned Brāhmins, mendicants, and physicians failed to cure him, they decided that the only hope lay in water from the bottom of the ocean. Such water was speedily procured, but the bearer, while fetching it, encountered a youth weeping and, upon asking the youth why he wept, the youth said that the King was dead. Much perturbed, the bearer threw away the water and hurried to the palace and found the King still alive.[2]

Vinasā, now the learned disciple of the *Heruka*, was sent for; and she, succeeding in fetching water taken from the depths of the ocean, cured the King; and the King, in gratitude, made her his spiritual adviser.

---

[1] No *yogin* is expected to enter a tavern where intoxicants are sold, much less to drink alcoholic liquor; and seeing that the *Heruka* had not the least regard for these prohibitions, the people suspected that their misfortunes were the direct result of his evil actions.

[2] The serpent which bit the King was the incarnation of an evil *nāga*, and the youth was a form which this *nāga* assumed in order to prevent the cure of the King.

Vinasā being a woman of low caste, the wives of the King objected to her presence. Vinasā was quite willing to quit the post, but the King would not hear of it. Seeing how difficult it was for her to get away from the palace, Vinasā magically produced a child, and pretending that it had been born to her in the normal manner, presented it to the King, saying that it was to be his *guru* in place of herself. The King accepted the child and reared it, and the child became a most learned saint, known as Saint La-wa-pa.

PADMA AND MANDĀRAVĀ ARE BURNED AT THE STAKE IN URGYĀN

The time having come, as Padma foresaw, to discipline the people of Urgyān, four *ḍākinī* appeared with a palanquin and placed Padma and Mandāravā in it and transported them by air to the land of Urgyān. Appearing there as mendicants, Padma and Mandāravā begged their food from house to house. Eventually Padma was recognized, and when the ministers of the King heard of it they said, 'This is the man who ignored the Queen Bhāsadhara and killed the wife and son of the minister; and now he is living with a beggar woman. Formerly he broke the law of the realm; and he hath returned to do further harm to us.'

Without the King's knowledge, the ministers had Padma and Mandāravā seized. The pair were tied together, and then wrapped in oil-saturated cloth and fettered to a stake. Wood was piled around them, oil poured over the wood, and fire set to the pyre from each of the four cardinal directions. Even on the twenty-first day afterwards the pyre still gave off smoke,[1] and a rainbow enhaloed it. When the King inquired about the cause of the phenomenon, and no one volunteered an explanation, Bhāsadhara said, 'My husband, having entered the Order, abandoned me and the kingdom for the sake of religion. Then, having recently returned to live with a beggar woman, he was condemned by the ministers and burnt to death.' Angry at not having been consulted concerning the

---

[1] Usually such a pyre ceases smoking by the seventh day after having been fired.

condemnation, the King said, 'If he were an incarnation he could not have been burnt'; and, going to the place where the pyre had been, he beheld a lake, in the centre of which stood an enormous lotus blossom, and Padma and Mandāravā sitting together in the lotus blossom, enhaloed in auras so radiant that one could hardly look upon them. The Earth-Goddess, accompanied by other divinities, appeared, and in songs of praise told of Padma's deeds in the world. The King and the ministers and the multitudes also offered praise and asked Padma's forgiveness; and the King invited Padma to be his *guru* until the *kalpa* should end, and to diffuse the Doctrine. Padma said, 'The Three Worlds are a prison-house; even though one be born a *Dharma-rāja*,[1] one cannot escape from worldly pleasures. And even though one be possessed of the *Dharma-Kāya*[2] and know not how to govern one's own mind, one cannot break the chain of miseries of *sangsāric* existence. O King, make pure thy mind and attain clear vision; and thou shalt attain Buddhahood.'[3]

The King's mind was at once changed; and he and his ministers and followers entered the Order. Padma was escorted to the palace, and the King placed him upon the royal seat, and obeisance and offerings were made to him. For thirteen years Padma remained in the Urgyān land, disciplining the people and establishing the Faith.

MANDĀRAVĀ AND THE ABANDONED FEMALE BABE

Mandāravā went to the Sacred *Heruka* Cave of the *Ḍākinī*, and there became the *ḍākinī's* abbess. Sometimes she assumed the form of a *ḍākinī*, sometimes that of a jackal or tigress, sometimes that of a small boy or girl. By such means she advanced the Doctrine, and converted the various types of beings.

---

[1] A *Dharma-rāja*, or 'King of the *Dharma*', is the highest type of an ideal monarch.

[2] The *Dharma-Kāya*, or 'Body of the *Dharma*', symbolizes the *Nirvāṇic* state in which a Buddha exists. (See *The Tibetan Book of the Dead*, pp. 10–15.)

[3] This doctrine is strictly Buddhistic, the Buddha having emphasized that the whole aim of His teaching is to deliver the mind from its bondage to the *Sangsāra*. This, too, is the purpose of the teaching set forth in our treatise which follows. (Cf. *Tibetan Yoga and Secret Doctrines*, pp. 5–6.)

There lived in the City of Pal-pang-gyu a man and his wife who were weavers. The wife died in giving birth to a female child; and the father, thinking the child could not survive without a mother, deposited both the child and the mother's corpse in a cemetery. Mandāravā, in her tigress transformation, went to the cemetery to eat of the flesh of corpses and saw the child sucking the breast of the dead mother, and, feeling infinite compassion, suckled the child and nurtured it with her own milk. Day by day the tigress ate of the mother's corpse and fed bits of the flesh to the child.

When the child was sixteen, she was as pretty as a goddess, and Mandāravā left her to shift for herself. Padma, seeing that the hour had come to convert the girl, assumed the guise of a *bhikṣhu* and initiated her into the *Maṇḍala* of Vajra-Sattva.[1]

THE COWHERD *GURU*

A cowherd, who had been supplying the pair with milk, also became Padma's disciple, and, after having been initiated by Padma into the same *Maṇḍala*, attained the *siddhi* of Vajra-Sattva. There having appeared on the cowherd's forehead, as a result of this *siddhi*, the *mantric* syllable *Hūṃ*, Padma named him *Hūṃ-kāra*. Then Padma taught the cowherd the Doctrine of the Long *Hūṃ*;[2] and he also conferred upon him the *siddhi* of fast-walking,[3] so that he had the power of walking thus, levitated one cubit above the ground.[4] As a

---

[1] See *The Tibetan Book of the Dead*, pp. 108–10, 220.

[2] This Doctrine, which appertains to the Wisdom of the Five Dhyānī Buddhas, is set forth in detail in *Tibetan Yoga and Secret Doctrines*, Book VI.

[3] Text: *Rkang-mgyogs* (pron. *Kang-gyok*), literally meaning 'fast feet', or 'fleetness of foot'.

[4] The late Sardar Bahādur Laden La told me that he had once seen a Tibetan *yogī* transporting himself in this manner. It was in Tibet about the year 1931. 'I had sent him', he said, 'to carry a message to a great *lāma* named Pha-pong-kha living in Lhāsa; and he traversed a distance of twelve miles in about twenty minutes.' A master of this art of fast-walking, called in Tibetan a *lung-gom-pa*, was once encountered, while exercising this art, in the wilds of northern Tibet by Madame Alexandra David-Neel, the explorer of Tibetan mysticism. Apparently the man was in a meditative trance, his eyes wide open and gaze fixed on some invisible far-distant object; and she was told that to stop him in his fast-walking would probably

psychic result of so much progress in *yoga*, a protuberance resembling the head of the Horse-headed Hayagrīva appeared on the cowherd's head above the aperture of Brahma.[1] Then, as the cowherd progressed further in *yoga*, the outline of a single *dorje* appeared on his body over the heart and that of a double *dorje* on his forehead, and from each of his nine bodily apertures light radiated.[2]

After having attained these *siddhi*, the cowherd, driving his cattle home at nightfall, was seen by his master as Vajra-Sattva; and the master exalted the cowherd on a specially arranged seat and bowed down before him. 'Why', asked the cowherd, 'art thou bowing down before me, thy servant? People will look down upon thee for doing so.' And the master replied, 'Thou art Vajra-Sattva; canst thou tell me where my cowherd is?' And the master and the people assembled and declared the cowherd to be their *guru*; and the cowherd expounded the Doctrine and made many converts.

---

kill him. He did not run, but 'seemed to lift himself from the ground, proceeding by leaps. He looked as if he had been endowed with the elasticity of a ball and rebounded each time his feet touched the ground. His steps had the regularity of a pendulum. He wore the usual monastic robe and toga, both rather ragged. His left hand gripped a fold of the toga and was half hidden by the cloth. The right hand held a *phurbu* (magic dagger). His right arm moved slightly at each step, quite as though the *phurbu*, whose pointed extremity was far above the ground, had touched it and were actually a support.' Observed from a distance, he 'seemed as if carried on wings'. (Cf. A. David-Neel, *With Mystics and Magicians in Tibet*, London, 1931, pp. 201–4.) Reference to this art is also made above (on p. 137), where Padma is represented as having mastered the method of acquiring 'fleetness of foot'.

[1] This is the aperture whence the consciousness-principle departs from the body at death, called in Sanskrit the *Brāhmarandhra*. (See *The Tibetan Book of the Dead*, pp. xxix, 18, 87[3].)

[2] Thus the cowherd attained five perfections or *yogic* accomplishments (Skt. *siddhi*): the perfection of body, resulting in fast-walking (Tib. *Kang-gyok-thar-phyin-pa*); the perfection of speech, or vast *yogic* learning (Tib. *Sung-thar-phyin-pa*); the perfection of mind, or mastery of mental processes (Tib. *Thuk-thar-phyin-pa*); the perfection of efficiency in spiritual work, or mastery of the teachings (Tib. *Thin-le-thar-phyin-pa*); and the perfection of excellence, or adeptship in *yoga* (Tib. *Yon-ten-thar-phyin-pa*). As a result of the second perfection, the Hayagrīva-like protuberance appeared; of the third, the single *dorje*; of the fourth, the double *dorje*; of the fifth, the radiance from the nine bodily apertures (Tib. *Ne-gu*), which are the two apertures of the eyes, the two of the nose, the two of the ears, and those of the mouth, anus, and generative organ.

The Story of Shākya Shrī Mitra

A brief biography of Shākya Shrī Mitra is set forth as
follows: Dharma-Bhitti, daughter of King Dharma Ashoka,
was asleep in a garden and dreamt that a white-complexioned
man in a rainbow aura placed before her a vessel of *amrita*, and
poured holy water on her head so that it entered her body
through the aperture of Brahma and made her feel most tranquil. Ten months afterward she gave birth to a boy child.
Feeling great shame, she exposed the child, and it was lost in
the sand. A dog belonging to a vassal of the King of the Urgyān
country discovered the child, which was still alive, and
brought it to the King; and the child was reared in the royal
household. When the boy was five years old he expressed his
desire to become a *bhikṣhu*, but, being too young for ordination, was sent to the Shrī Nālanda Monastery, where, under
Padma-Karpo,[1] he became learned in the Five Classes of
Knowledge.[2] The great *Pandit* Shrī Singha named the youth
Vimala Mitra; and then the abbot of Nālanda named him
Shākya Shrī Mitra, and admitted him to the fellowship of the
five hundred *pandits* of Nālanda.

The Non-Buddhists' Defeat at Bōdh-Gayā in Controversy and Magic

Exercising his power of prescience, Padma saw that he
should return to Bōdh-Gayā. First he went to the Cemetery
of Jalandhar[3] to meditate. Meanwhile, a non-Buddhist King,
known as 'The All-pervading Demi-god', having collected his
army, sent four high non-Buddhist priests, each accom-

[1] Probably the Padma-Karpo who established Buddhism in Bhutan, and
became one of the *Gurus* of the Kargyütpa School. (See *Tibetan Yoga and
Secret Doctrines*, p. 251[5].)

[2] The Five Classes of Knowledge are: Knowledge of Medicine, of Languages, of Dialects, of Physics and Mechanical Arts, and of the *Tri-
Piṭaka*, comprising, as in the Southern School, the Buddhist Scriptures.

[3] At Jalandhar, in north India, about the end of the first century A.D.,
under the auspices of King Kanishka, the great Buddhist council was held
which caused the schism into what has come to be called 'Northern' and
'Southern' Buddhism. Today, Southern Buddhism prevails in Ceylon,
Burma, Thailand, and Cambodia, and Northern Buddhism in Tibet, Sikkim,
Bhutan, Nepal, Ladak, Mongolia, Tartary, China, and Japan.

panied by nine *pandits* and five hundred followers, to Bōdh-Gayā, to prepare the way for the overthrow of Buddhism. Each of the four high priests approached Bōdh-Gayā from one of the four cardinal directions and challenged the Buddhists there to public debate, saying, 'If ye be defeated by us, it shall be incumbent upon you to join our Faith; and, if ye defeat us, we will become Buddhists'. The four chief scholars of the Buddhists said among themselves, 'Although we can defeat them in controversy, we cannot overcome their occult powers'.

When the Buddhists were assembled in the royal palace at Bōdh-Gayā discussing the coming debate, a woman with a blue complexion, carrying a broom in her hand, suddenly appeared and said, 'If ye compete with the non-Buddhists, ye will not be successful. There is one, my brother, who can defeat them.' They replied, 'What is thy brother's name, and where doth he live?' She answered, 'His name is Padma Vajra,[1] and he is at present living in the Jalandhar Cemetery'. The Buddhists wishing to know how they might invite him, she said, 'Ye cannot invite him. Assemble at the Temple of the Bodhi-Tree,[2] make many offerings and prayer, and I will go and fetch him.'

The strange woman vanished as suddenly as she had appeared; and the Buddhists, doing as she had advised, made prayer to Padma Vajra to come and vanquish the non-Buddhists. Next morning at dawn, Padma arrived at the palace, coming down through the branches of the trees like a great bird, and at once entered into meditation; and, while Padma was meditating, the Buddhists sounded their religious drums. As the drums were sounding, the spies of the non-Buddhists listened to what the Buddhists were saying. The spy on the east side reported how the Buddhists said that the non-Buddhists, whose brains were like those of foxes, would be defeated. The spy on the south side reported the Buddhists

---

[1] Meaning 'Diamond (or Indestructible or Adamantine) Lotus'. The strange woman herself was a *ḍākinī* in disguise.

[2] Referring to the Temple of Bōdh-Gayā, built at the side of the Bodhi-Tree under which Gautama attained Buddhahood.

as having said that the followers of Ganesha and their army would be subdued. The spy on the west side reported having heard that the mischievous non-Buddhists with their followers would be annihilated, and the spy on the north side that all the black assembly would be crushed.

When the Sun rose, Padma assumed the guise of a *Dharma-Rāja* and flew over Bôdh-Gayā. The King of Bôdh-Gayā, seeing him thus manifesting magical power, doubted his intellectual ability, and said to him, 'O thou, a mere boy of eight years, pretending to be a *pandit*, thou art not fitted to defeat the non-Buddhists'. Padma replied, 'O my lord, I am an old man of three thousand years; and who is it that is saying I am only eight years of age? Thou brainless one, why presume to compete with me?'

The King made no response, but on his telling the non-Buddhists what Padma had said, they requested, 'O King, be good enough to call in now that inferior monk who caused our hairs to stand on end this morning. Should we fail to nip him in the bud our religion may suffer; we must subdue him.'

Then all the most learned non-Buddhists, possessed of magical powers, assembled. Padma emanated four personalities resembling his own personality, one in each of the four directions, while he himself remained in meditation; and these four personalities debated the religious subjects with the non-Buddhists; and the Buddhists, winning, clapped their hands, shouting that the non-Buddhists were defeated. Similarly, the Buddhists came off victorious in the miracle-performing contest which followed.

In the next competition, which consisted in producing magical fire, the non-Buddhists were better by ten flames; and, as the non-Buddhists were applauding, Padma cried, 'Wait! wait!' Then, placing his hand on the ground, a lotus blossom sprang up and from it went forth a flame that reached to the top of the world. Thereupon, the four chief priests of the non-Buddhists with a few followers flew up into the sky. Padma pointed at them, and fire went round and round and over them; and, filled with fear, they descended to their places, shouting to Padma, 'Thou hast defeated us, both in argumentation and in magic; prepare to meet thy death within seven days'. Going off into the jungle, they practised black magic in order to kill Padma. All their 500 followers, who were left behind, embraced Buddhism.[1]

Padma then made thank-offerings to the *ḍākinī*; and, next morning at dawn, the *ḍākinī* called 'Subduer of Evil' appeared and gave to him a leather box bound with iron nails, saying, 'Hold in check the demons and the non-Buddhists'. Upon opening the box, Padma found in it manuscripts of secret doctrines explaining how to produce thunder, lightning, and hail within seven days of commencing appropriate magical ceremonies.[2] No sooner had the four non-Buddhist priests completed the magical rites which were intended to cause Padma's death and had returned to their home city, than thunder and lightning came and killed them and set the city afire so that all its non-Buddhist inhabitants perished.

Padma went to the roof of the palace in Bōdh-Gayā and, exercising his power of roaring like a lion, all non-Buddhists who heard him fell down in great fear and embraced the Doctrine. Religious drums and gongs and conch shells were sounded from the palace roof. The chief Buddhists carried Padma aloft on their heads and named him 'The Most Exalted Lion Roarer'.[3] Neighbouring kings invited Padma to their kingdoms, and Buddhism spread widely. The converted non-Buddhists at Bōdh-Gayā called him 'The All-Subduing Victorious One'.

THE MARRIAGE OF THE DEFORMED PRINCE

In the non-Buddhist Ser-ling country there was born to the King a deformed prince. The child's face was bony and of a

---

[1] In similar fashion, on the Hill of Tara, Ireland, St. Patrick and the Druids, in the Irish King's presence, competed in producing magical fire and other of the phenomena herein described; and, St. Patrick, being victorious, converted the pagan Irish to Christianity even as Padma converted the non-Buddhists to Buddhism.

[2] Milarepa, too, studied these secret doctrines and practised them. (See *Tibet's Great Yogi Milarepa*, pp. 68, 77-79, 117-18.)

[3] Text: *Phak-pa Seṅg-ge Dradog*, 'Arya (or Most Exalted) Lion-Roarer'. Formerly Padma was given a similar but lesser appellation, Seṅg-ge Dradog; see p. 159, above.

bluish colour and very ugly, one eye was blind, the left leg
lame, the right hand crippled, and the body emitted an offensive odour like rotting hide. The King and Queen, ashamed of
the child, kept him secreted in the palace. When the prince
grew up and wished to marry and live as a layman, they said
to him, 'Thou art too deformed and ugly ; no bride would marry
thee. It would be better for thee to enter the Order and allow
us to supply thy needs.' The prince replied, 'Religion is empty
within and luxurious without. If ye, my parents, do not pro-
cure me a bride, I shall set the palace afire and then do away
with myself, or I shall kill both of you.' The prince, having
procured a lighted torch, came rushing at the King and
Queen ; so, in fear of the prince, they married him to the princess of the King of Baidha, relinquished the palace and lived
apart from him. The princess exhibited such great displeasure
of her royal husband that he was fearful lest she run away.

Padma, sitting in meditation, saw the trouble between the
newly married pair ; and, going to the court-yard of the palace
and exhibiting magical powers, produced many men and
women wearing ornaments of human bone, and dancing. The
princess wished to go out to see the magical performance, but
the prince would not allow her. Looking out of a window, she
caught sight of Padma, and exclaimed, 'Oh! if only I had a
husband like that man how happy I should be!'

Padma hearing her, replied, 'If a [married][1] woman love
another man, she suffereth such anguish of heart that the two
cannot be comrades. If a man love a woman [against her will],[1]
harm resulteth, as from evil spirits, and preventeth their
comradeship. If husband and wife be socially unequal, lack of
mutual respect, like that attributed to Ara,[2] ariseth, and this
also preventeth comradeship.'

The prince and princess were so deeply affected by these
remarks that they went out to Padma and bowed down and

[1] These two interpolations are necessary to bring out the sense implied
by the Tibetan, Padma's remarks here being in the nature of a reprimand
to the princess for expressing love for him, and to the prince for living with
the princess against her will.

[2] Ara was a famous bandit who had no respect for anybody, whether of
high or low birth.

made offerings before him, and embraced Buddhism. The King, recalling Padma's former exploits in the Baidha country, was much displeased, and said, 'This little beggar killed my priest and destroyed my palace.' Then Padma was seized and placed in an enclosure of bricks over which straw was heaped and set afire. Next morning, at the place where Padma had been enclosed and the fire set, there stood a *stūpa* of gold. And the King and Queen and all their subjects made public repentance and became Buddhists.

THE FORMAL GIVING OF THE NAME PADMA-SAMBHAVA

After this, Padma preached the *Dharma* to gods, *nāgas*, *ḍākinī* and demons in their own respective languages and realms; and to men in many parts of the human world—in China, Assam, Ghasha,[1] Trusha [near Simla], and elsewhere in India, and in Persia. He built many temples and monasteries, 824 of them in Tibet. In Devachān, the heaven of Avalokiteshvara,[2] he constructed a *stūpa* of crystal. Because

---

[1] Or Gharsha (*Gharsha-kha-dō-ling*, 'Country of the *Ḍākinī*'), the present Lahoul, above Kulu.

[2] Avalokiteshvara being the spiritual offspring of Amitābha, the Buddha of Boundless (or Immeasurable) Light, resides in Amitābha's Western Paradise, known to Tibetans as *Deva-chān* ('Abode of the *Devas*') and in Sanskrit as *Sukhāvatī* ('Realm of Happiness'). For the pious Mahāyāna Buddhist who is far below the evolutionary status of Buddhahood, Sukhāvatī is the heaven-world wherein he aspires to dwell during the interval between two incarnations. Sukhāvatī is attained as a *karmic* result of altruistic service done in the name of Amitābha and of Avalokiteshvara, the all-merciful *Bodhisattva* who has renounced the right to enter *Nirvāṇa* in order to help guide mankind to the Great Liberation. It is for making direct appeal to Avalokiteshvara that use is made of his *mantra*: *Om Maṇi Padme Hūṃ!* ('*Om!* The Jewel in the Lotus! *Hūṃ!*')

Esoterically, it is said that Amitābha, the fourth of the Five Buddhas of Meditation, represents the Buddha Essence innate in man, and that to be born in his paradise implies the awakening of this Buddha Essence; and that Avalokiteshvara, Amitābha's celestial *Bodhisattvic* reflex, is the 'personification of the self-generative cosmic force', the *Om* (or *Aum*) of his *mantra* being its symbol. (Cf. *A Brief Glossary of Buddhist Terms*, by the Buddhist Lodge, London, 1937, pp. 8, 14.)

Thus the Mahāyāna consists of three Paths. The first Path, trodden by the unevolved multitude, leads to the highest of the paradises. A second Path, that of the *Pratyeka* (i.e. self-evolved, or solitary non-teaching) Buddhas, leads to *Nirvāṇa*. The third and most glorious Path is that of the *Bodhisattvas*, leading to Perfect Buddhahood. On the first Path, the aspirant practises piety; on the second, philosophy; on the third, the Six *Pāramitā*

of having done all these things, he was given the name Padma-Sambhava.

The Brāhmin Boy that became the King of Bōdh-Gayā

While sitting in meditation in Avalokiteshvara's heaven, Padma perceived that Bōdh-Gayā had been taken and sacked by a non-Buddhist King named 'Vishnu of the *Nāgas*'. The temple and palace had been reduced to ruin, the monks set to doing worldly works and the people were suffering greatly because of the King's tyranny. And Padma foresaw that the son of a certain Brāhmin's daughter and a fish were destined to overthrow the King.

One day this Brāhmin's daughter was out watching her cattle when rain came on and she took shelter in a cave and fell asleep. She dreamt that Padma as a beautiful youth came and cohabited with her and initiated her. After some days she told her brother's wife about the dream, saying that she was pregnant and wished to kill herself. The brother, hearing of this, said he would look after the child; and the girl gave birth to a boy. The family astrologer declared that the child had been born under a good sign and the child was named 'Sambhāra of the Essence of Time'.

When the boy was about eight years old, he asked his mother, 'Who was my father?' The mother wept and said, 'Thou hast no father'. Then he asked, 'Who is the King of this country, and who is his priest [or *guru*]?' The mother replied, 'His name is "Vishnu of the *Nāgas*," and he hath many non-Buddhist priests'. The boy said, 'It is not right to support a son who hath no father. So permit me to go to Bōdh-Gayā.'

And the boy went to Bōdh-Gayā, and sought to enter a non-Buddhist monastery, but, being too young for admission, he found employment in the King's kitchen.

The King having the habit of eating raw fish, the boy transformed himself into a fish in a stream and was caught by a

(or Transcendental Virtues), and, delaying his own entrance into *Nirvāṇa*, the Supra-*sangsāric* State, dedicates himself to teaching a suffering world the means of crossing, in the Ship of the *Dharma*, the Sea of *Sangsāric* Existence to the Other Shore.

fisherman and given to the King to eat. As the King was
about to bite off a bit of the fish, it slipped from his grasp and
went into his stomach where it caused him severe pain. When
all the priests had been called to the palace to offer aid, the
boy reappeared in his natural shape, and, taking advantage
of the commotion, set fire to the palace, opened its windows
and locked its doors, and all who were within it perished.
Then the boy went to the city of Sahor and was ordained a
Buddhist priest, and attained many spiritual perfections.

Now that Bōdh-Gayā was once more under Buddhist control, the Buddhists there decided to rebuild the Temple and
the old palace and restore Buddhist rule. For a whole year
search was made for one suitable to become the king, and no
one was found.

The boy, assuming the guise of a beggar, went to the market-place and sat down there. That very day, the party of
Buddhists who were making search for a suitable candidate
for the kingship, took an elephant to the market-place and
announced that he to whom the elephant should go and offer
a vase as a crown would be regarded as the king. As soon as
the elephant was set free, it ran, with trunk and tail straight
out, direct to the boy and placed the vase on his head. And
the boy became the King of Bōdh-Gayā.

Later on, when the boy met his mother, she refused to
believe that he, the King, was her son, saying that her son
had died in the last Bōdh-Gayā fire. So the King made prayer
that a fish should be born under a wooden plank, saying to
his mother, ' If this prayer be granted, thou must believe that
I am thy son'. The fish was thus found and the mother
believed. And under this virtuous Buddhist King, ' Sambhāra
of the Essence of Time', the Faith spread and the country
prospered.

PADMA'S FURTHER EXPLOITS

Padma now revisited Bōdh-Gayā, consecrated the restored
Temple and palace, had many *stūpas* constructed and the lost
scriptures re-written, and revived the Faith as a whole. He
also went to the country of asafoetida in Khoten, where he

remained 200 years and established the *Sūtra*, the *Mantra*, and the *Mahāyāna* forms of Buddhism.[1] Then he proceeded to a hill on the frontier of India and Nepal and entered into meditation. Seven huntsmen came with barking dogs and Padma magically stopped the barking. The huntsmen, overcome with fear, reported this to the king and the king ordered Padma to quit the place.

THE MONKEY-REARED GIRL AND PADMA'S INTERRUPTED MEDITATION

Thence Padma went to the temple of Shankhu. The Queen of King Ge-wa-dzin of Nepal having died when giving birth to a female child, the child, along with the Queen's corpse, was deposited in the cemetery. A monkey, finding the child, adopted it; and the child grew up, feeding on fruits. When the girl was ten years old, her hands were webbed like the feet of a duck, but she was very beautiful. Padma went to the cemetery and initiated the girl and named her Shākya-devi. Then, taking her to a cave for further instruction, he formed a *maṇḍala* of nine lighted lamps; and, as he sat there with her in *yogic* meditation, three impediments arose. Firstly, in the evening, lightning interrupted their meditation, but ceased when they broke their meditation. As a result of this, drought prevailed for three years. Secondly, at midnight, the chief of the *māras*[2] appeared and, after disturbing the meditation, vanished. As a result of this, all over India and Nepal famine prevailed. Thirdly, in the morning before dawn a bird interrupted the meditation; and, as a result, the evil spirits of India, Nepal, and Tibet brought epidemics upon men and cattle.

Because of all these things, Padma sought advice of those who had been his *gurus*; and they consulted together and

---

[1] Khoten, or eastern Turkestan, as recent archaeological research confirms, was once a very flourishing centre of Mahāyāna Buddhism; and is commercially noted for its production of asafoetida, which Tibetans employ in treating colds and 'winds' in the heart.

[2] The *māras* are demons who seek to prevent human beings from attaining Enlightenment, as in the classic instance of the *Bodhisattva* Gautama when He sat under the Bodhi-Tree on the point of attaining Buddhahood.

advised him to study the *Dorje-Phurbu* teachings[1] under Pandit Prabhahasti.

Accordingly, Padma wrote to this *pandit* and the *pandit* dispatched to Padma a *phurbu* text, which was so heavy that a man could hardly carry it. As soon as the text reached Padma in the cave, the evil spirits that had caused the impediments disappeared and Padma and Shākya-devi were able to continue their *yogic* practices without molestation. And Padma said, 'I am like the lotus blossom. Although it groweth out of the mud, no mud adhereth to it'. Making a copy of the text, he secreted it in the cave. Vapour arose from the sea, clouds formed in the sky, rain fell, flowers blossomed and fruits ripened. All famine and disease disappeared and people were happy. And after Padma had established the Doctrine in the region of the cave he was called 'Padma, the Victorious Tutelary of the *Ḍākinī*'.[2]

PADMA'S MANY MAGICAL GUISES

Padma, assuming numerous guises, continued to subdue evil. Sometimes he appeared as a common beggar, sometimes as a boy of eight years, sometimes as lightning, or wind, sometimes as a beautiful youth in dalliance with women, sometimes as a beautiful woman in love with men, sometimes as a bird, an animal, or insect, sometimes as a physician, or rich almsgiver. At other times he became a boat and wind on the sea to rescue men, or water with which to extinguish fire. He taught the ignorant, awakened the slothful, and dominated jealousy by heroic deeds. To overcome sloth, anger, and lust in mankind, he appeared as the Three Chief Teachers, Avalokiteshvara, Mañjushrī, and Vajra-Pāṇi; to overcome arrogance, he assumed the Body, the Speech, and the Mind of the

---

[1] These teachings concern magical methods of dominating demons and overcoming their evil influences. The Tibetan *dorje* (or thunderbolt of the gods) and the *phurbu* (or magical dagger), being ritual objects used for controlling and exorcizing evil spirits, lend their names to the magical teachings.

[2] The *ḍākinī*, an exalted class of fairy-like spiritual beings, themselves commonly chosen as tutelaries by neophytes in Tibet, appear from this appellation to have chosen Padma as their own tutelary by virtue of his mastery over gods, demons, and men.

Buddha;[1] and, to overcome jealousy, the fifth of the 'Five Poisons',[2] he transformed himself into the Five Dhyānī Buddhas.[3] He was now called 'The Chief Possessor of Magical Dances [or of Shape-Shifting]'. In short, to accomplish his mission to all sentient creatures, human, super-human, and sub-human, Padma assumed the guise most suitable to the occasion.

TEXTS AND TREASURES HIDDEN BY PADMA

The many books which he wrote he hid in the world of men, in heaven-worlds, and in the realm of the *nāgas* under the waters of seas and lakes, in order that there might be preserved for future generations the original uncorrupted teachings. For this reason the *ḍākinī* called him 'The One Possessed of Power over Hidden Treasures [of Texts].' Many of these hidden texts were written on tala-palm leaves, on silk, and on blue [or lacquered] paper in ink of gold, silver, copper, iron, and malachite, and enclosed in gold-lined boxes, earthen pots, stone receptacles, skulls, and precious stones. All that he taught was recorded and hidden. Even the teachings of the Lord Buddha in their purity he hid, so that the non-Buddhists might not interpolate them. No one save the *tertöns* [or takers-out of hidden texts] would have power to discover and bring forth the secreted writings.[4]

[1] The Body of the Buddha is the *Dharma-Kāya*; the Mind, the *Sambhoga-Kāya*; the Speech, the *Nirmāṇa-Kāya*. These Three *Kāyas* are the three forms in which the Buddha Essence is mystically personified. The first is the True Body, wherein all Buddhas in *Nirvāṇa* are in inconceivable at-one-ment; the second is the Reflected Body of glory where dwell, in the heaven-worlds, the Dhyānī Buddhas and all Buddhas and *Bodhisattvas* within the *Sangsāra* when not incarnate on Earth; the third is the Body of Incarnation in which all Buddhas and *Bodhisattvas* dwell when working among men. (See *The Tibetan Book of the Dead*, pp. 10–17.)

[2] These are lust, hatred (or anger), stupidity (or sloth), egotism (or arrogance), and jealousy. (See *Tibet's Great Yogī Milarepa*, pp. 195[1], 260.)

[3] These, the Buddhas of Meditation, are Vairochana, Vajra-Sattva, Ratna-Sambhava, Amitābha, and Amogha-Siddhi. (See *The Tibetan Book of the Dead*, pp. 105–18.)

[4] These *tertöns*, some of whom have appeared, are said to be reincarnations of certain of Padma's disciples, or else emanations of Padma himself. The text of our present treatise, like that of the *Bardo Thödol*, is believed by the Tibetans to have been among these texts thus written and hidden by Padma and subsequently taken out by a *tertön*. (See *The Tibetan Book of the*

Padma placed the hidden texts under the guardianship of the *ḍākinī* and Wisdom-Holders; and he blessed the texts so that none of them should fall into the hands of one who, lacking the merit born of good deeds done in a past incarnation, was undeserving. Thus there could be no diminution of the Doctrine, nor of initiation, nor of priestly succession through reincarnation, nor of the practice of religion.

Between the Khang-kar-te-say Mountains [near the Nepal frontier in southern Tibet] and Tri-shi-trik in China, Padma hid 108 large works, 125 important images, five very rare essences [of secret doctrines], the sacred books of Buddhism and of the Bönpos,[1] and books on medicine, astrology, arts, and crafts. Similar caches were made by Padma in Nepalese caves and temples. Along with the texts, he buried such worldly treasures, magical weapons, and food as would afford support to the *tertöns* who should take out the texts and give them to the world. Altogether, Padma is credited with having hidden away texts and accessory objects to the number of ten million.[2]

The Hidden Treasures and Persons fitted to Discover them

After explaining to Shākya-devi, in answer to her question why, as already set forth above, so many texts and treasures had been hidden, Padma added, 'Ārya-devā and Nāgārjuna will take out one of the hidden treasures and thereby subdue the non-Buddhists'.

Then Shākya-devi asked, 'O Great *Guru*, if the number of the treasures is so great how did they originate, and why call them treasures? Who shall have the merit of a previous incarnation to profit by them? Who shall possess the power to take

---

Dead, pp. 75–77.) According to the Nyingma School, sacred texts have been found by *tertöns* in forty-nine different places in Tibet.

[1] The Bönpos are the followers of the pre-Buddhistic religion of Tibet called Bön, which Padma dominated, taking over certain of its teachings and incorporating them in his Tantric Buddhism, as illustrated in *Tibetan Yoga and Secret Doctrines*, Book V.

[2] This, of course, is another typical oriental figurative exaggeration, expressive of multitude, but without precise numerical significance.

out the treasures? And how will the discoverer of such a treasure take birth? Please explain all this to me.'

Padma replied, 'Be good enough to give ear, O thou, of
meritorious birth. It was after the destruction of the Demon
Thar-pa Nag-po[1] that the treasures originated. From his mind
sprang the Eight Cemeteries.[2] His skin represents the paper;
his hands and legs represent the pen; the watery fluid which
he exuded from the four apertures of his body[3] represents the
ink. Out of these three [the skin, bodily limbs, and watery
fluid] came the "Five Poisons"; and from the "Five Poisons"
came the alphabet of letters. His skull, mouth, and nose became the receptacles for containing the treasures. His internal
organs, toes, and fingers represent the places of the treasures.
The Six Receptacles of the Doctrine[4] will declare who shall
possess the power to discover the treasures. From the five
chief organs [the heart, liver, lungs, stomach, and intestines]
will come the Blessed Ones.[5] From the five sensory organs [the
tongue, nostrils, ears, eyes, and organs of touch including
those of sex] will come the "Five Powers",[6] and also the
"Five Elements";[7] and from the "Five Elements", the Body
[the *Dharma-Kāya*], the Mind [the *Sambhoga-Kāya*], and the
Speech [the *Nirmāna-Kāya*].'

'If classified, there would be eighteen kinds of treasures.
The mad finder[8] of the chief treasure shall be known as the

[1] A Tibetan name of a *rudra*, or demon, meaning 'Black Salvation', who
obstructed the progress of Buddhism in Tibet. Padma subjugated him and
enlisted his powerful services in the spread of the *Dharma*. After Thar-pa
Nag-po died he reincarnated as a *Mahākala*.

[2] These are the well-known Eight Great Cemeteries (or Cremation
Grounds) of ancient India in which Padma lived and meditated at various
times.

[3] These are the mouth, nose, anus, and sex organ.

[4] These are probably six of the chief patriarchs of the Mahāyāna such as
Nāgārjuna, Ārya-devā (mentioned by Padma above), otherwise known as
Kana-devā, and their immediate successors.

[5] The Teachers of the *Dharma*, the Buddhas, *Bodhisattvas*, and Great *Gurus*.

[6] The Five Powers are: the Power of religious faith, the Power of diligent
application, the Power of memory, the Power of profound meditation, and
the Power of ingenuity or wit.

[7] Namely, Earth, Water, Fire, Air, Ether.

[8] It is customary among *gurus* and *yogīs* to refer euphemistically to one
of high spiritual accomplishments as being mad. (Cf. *Tibetan Yoga and
Secret Doctrines*, p. 269.)

balls of the eyes, and those inferior *tertöns* shall be known as
the skin of the eyes. If any of the *tertöns* be called an eunuch,[1]
he shall be like the discharge from the nose [of the Demon];
one of higher life and blissfulness shall be like the consciousness and mind. Anyone who may be called a *tertön* of average
spirituality shall be like the liver and bile. And from all these
examples thou shouldst be able to recognize the discoverers.'

These hidden treasures, as Padma, at great length, proceeded to explain, cannot all be found simultaneously. One
after another, when needed for the advancement of mankind,
they will be discovered. Just as the *udambara*[2] is rare so are
tertöns. Whenever a *tertön* is born, the *udambara* will appear.
If the birth be among the *kshatriya*, the blossom's colour will
be white; if among *brāhmins*, the blossom will be red; if among
vaishyas, it will be yellow; and if among *shūdras*,[3] blue. The
birth of a *tertön* is immediately followed by the death of either
the mother or father of the *tertön*. Two or more *tertöns* cannot
be born simultaneously [or in the same generation], for only
one *tertön* incarnates at a time. The power to find the hidden
treasures will be given chiefly to six persons, who will be born
one after another and succeed each other; there will be five
tertöns of lesser degree.[4] Kings, persons of worldly fortune,
laymen, and those attached to property will not have this
power.

THE SCORPION *GURU*

After completing other missions, in the valley of Nepal,
and in Kosala,[5] Padma went to the Cave of Phūllahari where

[1] This whole passage being esoterically symbolical, the appellation
eunuch is symbolic also, and probably refers to a *yogin* who has made
himself, not literally, but figuratively in the Biblical sense, an eunuch to attain
righteouness.

[2] The *udambara* (*ficus clonerata*) is a mythical lotus of immense size which
is commonly represented in oriental literature as blooming only when a
great spiritual being like a Buddha is born on Earth.

[3] The *kshatriya*, or warrior class, the *brāhmins*, or spiritually learned
class, the *vaishyas*, or merchant class, and the *shūdras*, or labouring class,
constitute the four castes of the Hindu social organization.

[4] In Padma's *Abridged Testament*, the full Tibetan title of which is given
in *The Tibetan Book of the Dead*, on p. 76, Padma mentions eight *tertöns* who
are to be his own incarnations.

[5] Kosala was a part of the ancient Oudh.

Vajra-pāṇi appeared to him and foretold how Padma would attain a certain *siddhi* in the great cemetery near Rājagir. Padma, upon reaching the cemetery, beheld an enormous scorpion having nine heads and eighteen horns and three eyes on each head. Padma made obeisance to the scorpion, and it requested him to come on the morrow for the *siddhi*. Accordingly, Padma kept the appointment; and the scorpion took out from under a rock a triangular-shaped stone box containing manuscript texts of the *Phurbu* Doctrine,[1] and Padma at once understood the texts. And each of the eyes and each of the horns of the scorpion gave out one *yāna*.[2]

PADMA'S JOURNEY TO TIBET

Padma returned to Bōdh-Gayā at the request of the King Nyima Singha; and while he was there strengthening the Doctrine the thought came to Padma that the time had come for him to proceed to Tibet to establish Tibetan Buddhism more firmly than it had been established originally by King Srong-Tsan-Gampo and thereafter re-established by King Thī-Srong-Detsan, the incarnation of Mañjushrī.[3]

King Thī-Srong-Detsan had tried to build a monastery at Sāmyé, but the site not having been properly consecrated, evil spirits prevented the construction; no sooner was a wall built than it was thrown down.[4] Some of the King's priests declared that a priest of superior powers was needed to subdue the evil spirits; and the King dispatched messengers to India and to China to find such a priest. As a result, the Great *Paṇḍita Bodhisattva*, who was teaching in Nālanda, went to Tibet at the King's invitation; and the King met the *Bodhisattva* at Sang-phor [near Sāmyé]. Although the *Bodhisattva* conse-

---

[1] See pp. 160, 177[1], above, for explanation.

[2] A *yāna* is a doctrinal method or path for attaining spiritual powers.

[3] Srong-tsan-Gampo died in A.D. 650, and Thī-Srong-Detsan reigned from A.D. 740 to 786. During the ninety years separating the two reigns, Buddhism suffered a decline and almost disappeared, the immediate successors of Srong-Tsan-Gampo having apostatized to the old pre-Buddhist Bön religion.

[4] Although the external visible cause of this was probably earthquakes, the Tibetans considered the hidden cause to be demoniacal. At all events, according to Tibetan historical records, as soon as the site had been exorcized by Padma, no more walls were thrown down.

crated and exorcised the site of the Sāmyé Monastery, the evil spirits were not overcome; and he advised the King that Padma-Sambhava, then at Bōdh-Gayā, was the only one able to subdue the evil spirits, and the King invited Padma-Sambhava to come to Tibet.[1]

Padma, accepting the invitation, set out for Tibet on the fifteenth day of the eleventh month according to the Tibetan calendar.[2] On the thirtieth of the same month he reached Nepal. Padma said that he would proceed, stage by stage, as he subdued the demons of one place after another. He remained in Nepal three months as the guest of King Vasudhari, preaching the Doctrine. When he was about to quit Nepal, after having subdued many evils, the *ḍākinī* and other spiritual beings who had befriended and aided him, begged him not to go; and he said, 'I must go; the time hath come to subdue the evil spirits of Tibet'.

THE WATER MIRACLE

Padma then travelled on towards Tibet subduing demoniacal beings all along the route; and his first resting place was at Tod-lung [about twelve miles from Lhāsa]. The Tibetan King sent the two chief ministers of state to meet Padma, with letters and presents and 500 mounted followers. The King's own horse, saddled with a golden saddle, was sent to fetch Padma. When this numerous delegation met Padma

[1] Certain scholars in the Occident have stated that Padma-Sambhava was a professor in the Buddhist University of Nālanda at the time the Tibetan King invited him to Tibet (e.g. Dr. L. A. Waddell, op. cit., p. 24); and the Editor having accepted this statement repeated it in his own publications (as in *The Tibetan Book of the Dead*, p. 74). Now it appears from this original textual account that it was the Great *Paṇḍita Bodhisattva*, and not Padma-Sambhava, who was the professor in Nālanda; and, as our text shows later, the *Bodhisattva* was undoubtedly a personage quite distinct from Padma-Sambhava. The Tibetan King, for instance, on the occasion of Padma's public reception at Sāmyé, placed Padma on a golden throne and the *Bodhisattva* on a silver throne. Furthermore, the *Bodhisattva* is shown herein to have died at about the same time as the King Thī-Srong-Detsan. Apparently, therefore, because of erroneous reading of the Tibetan text, the *Bodhisattva* and Padma have been taken to be one and the same person.

[2] The Tibetan year, which is lunar, begins in February with the rise of the new moon. Thus the eleventh month would be December of the year A.D. 746. His arrival in Tibet was about three and a half months later, or in A.D. 747, at the beginning of springtime.

they were suffering from lack of water, and no water being available at the place, Padma, taking a long stick, struck a rock with it and water flowed forth, and men and beasts quenched their thirst. The place is called Zhon-pa-hi-lha-chhu.[1]

THE ROYAL RECEPTION OF PADMA AND THE FIRE MIRACLE

The King with his party went to Zung-khar, near the Haopori Pass [seven to eight miles from Lhāsa], to meet Padma. The people had assembled there in vast numbers to greet Padma; and he was taken in procession, to the accompaniment of music and dancing by masked dancers, to Lhāsa, where great festivity ensued.

When Padma and the King met, Padma failed to bow down before the King, and seeing that the King expected him to do so, even as the *Bodhisattva* at the time of his reception had done, Padma said to the King, 'Thou wert born of a mother's womb; I was born of a lotus, and am a second Buddha'. Then, after having referred to his *yogic* powers and learning, Padma said, 'O King, inasmuch as I have come for thy good, thou shouldst bow down before me'. And Padma pointed his fingers at the King and fire issued from the tips of the fingers and burnt the King's garments, and there came thunder and an earthquake. Thereupon, the King and his ministers and all the people bowed down before Padma.

THE CONSTRUCTION OF THE SĀMYÉ MONASTERY

On the first day of the eighth Tibetan month Padma visited Sāmyé. The King escorted Padma to the Palace at Sāmyé and placed him on a gold throne and the *Bodhisattva* on a silver throne and made religious offerings; and Padma foretold what he was to do in Tibet.

Padma cast treasures in the lakes to win the goodwill of the

[1] A Tibetan place-name meaning 'Nectar of the Gods for the Cavalry', with reference to the water which Padma miraculously produced there for the King's mounted followers. The late Sardar Bahādur S. W. Laden La, when we translated this passage, told me that he had visited the place and that the water still flows in a stream of about 1 inch out of solid rock at a height of approximately 8 feet from the ground.

nāgas. Little by little he subdued the gods and goddesses and evil spirits throughout Tibet ; and performed many miracles.

On the eighth day of the eighth month of the earth-male-tiger year the work of building the Sāmyé Monastery was begun, Padma having consecrated the site and appeased the evil spirits by teaching to them the Precepts.[1] Padma appointed Brahma and Indra directors-in-chief of the building operations, the Four Kings of the Four Directions he made overseers, and the gods and evil spirits and the local genii and guardian deities he employed as labourers. Men carried on the work by day and the spiritual beings carried it on by night, so that progress was rapid.

THE TALE OF PADMA'S SUBJECTION OF THE *NĀGA* KING

Padma, seeing that the King of the *Nāgas* remained unsubdued, went to the Chhim-phug Cave near Sāmyé and entered into meditation for the purpose of overcoming the *Nāga* King. Just at that time the King Thī-Srong-Detsan was having much difficulty in procuring lumber for the building of the monastery ; and the *Nāga* King, assuming the guise of a white-complexioned man, went to the Tibetan King and said, 'I will supply all the wood needed, provided thou breakest, as I request thee to do, Padma's meditation'.[2] The Tibetan King vowed to carry out the request, and the man promised to provide the lumber.

The Tibetan King went to the cave ; but instead of seeing

---

[1] Sāmyé, the first Buddhist monastery built in Tibet after the Potāla at Lhāsa, is situated about thirty miles southeast of Lhāsa, near the north bank of the Tsang-po River, at an altitude of about 11,430 feet. Its full name translated into English means 'Academy for Obtaining the Heap of Unchanging Meditation'. Sāmyé, as it is today, comprises a large temple, four important colleges, and several other buildings, enclosed in a lofty circular wall about a mile and a half in circumference with gates facing the four cardinal points. Its large image of the Buddha, over ten feet high, is called 'The King of Sāmyé'. The monastic library is said to contain many rare manuscripts which were brought from India. (For fuller details see L. A. Waddell, op. cit., pp. 266–8.)

[2] Tibet being a country of very scanty timber resources, one can imagine the problem of finding suitable and adequate lumber which faced the Tibetan King, and how great was the temptation to grant the *Nāga* King's request.

Padma he beheld a huge *garuḍa*[1] holding in its claws an enormous serpent which it had almost swallowed; only a small portion of the serpent's tail remained unswallowed. The King said, 'Be gracious enough to break thy meditation, for we are about to attain a great *siddhi*'; whereupon the serpent freed itself, and the *garuda* became Padma, who asked, 'What *siddhi* is it?'

After the King had made explanation, Padma said, 'Whereas I have completely subdued all other evil spirits, I have only subdued the *Nāga* King's body and not his mind. Had I subdued his mind, the lumber would have come of itself. Hereafter, owing to thine action, the *Nāga* King will dominate Tibet and send upon the people eighteen kinds of leprosy; and the wrathful *nāgas* will be thine enemies.'

The Tibetan King returned to Sāmyé to ascertain whether or not the white-complexioned man had kept his vow, and found the wood already there; and this wood was utilized in the construction of the monastery.

Now the Tibetan King inquired of Padma if there was not still some way by which to subdue the *Nāga* King; and Padma replied, 'The only way is for the King of Tibet and the King of the *Nāgas* to become friends'. So Padma went to the Malgro Lake, near Sāmyé, wherein the *Nāga* King dwelt. The Tibetan King with his ministers hid themselves in a valley, as Padma had advised; and Padma pitched a small white tent on the shore of the lake and meditated there for three nights.[2] On the third night, a beautiful maiden appeared before Padma and asked, 'What art thou doing here, and what dost thou

[1] A *garuḍa* is a mythical creature, with eagle head, human-bird body, two human-like arms, and eagle wings and feet, symbolizing energy and aspiration. It is analogous to the classical phoenix and to the thunder-bird of the North American Red Men. In a more esoteric sense, the Tibetans, like the Chinese, regard it as symbolizing the Earth and its cosmic environment, its head representing the heavens, its eyes the Sun, its back the crescent Moon, its wings the wind, its feet the Earth itself, its tail the trees and plants. Like the adjutant, or stork, popularly called by the Hindus *garuḍa*, it is the enemy and devourer of serpents, as in our text. (Cf. L. A. Waddell, op. cit., pp. 395–6.)

[2] During these three nights, as the pitching of the tent suggests, Padma probably celebrated a form of the *Chöd* Rite (which is fully expounded in Book V of *Tibetan Yoga and Secret Doctrines*).

seek?' Padma answered, 'I desire the King of Tibet and the King of the *Nāgas* to become friends. The treasury of the Tibetan King having become empty through the building of the monastery, I have come to ask for wealth from the *Nāgas*. And I wish thee to convey this message to thy King.'

Then the maiden disappeared; and next morning a very large serpent emerged from the lake and stirred up the water; and gold flooded all the shores. Thus the treasury was replenished and the building of the monastery continued. Some of the gold was applied to the making of images and frescoes for the monastery, which had thirty-two entrances and required five years to complete.

Padma placed the monastery under the guardianship of the Wrathful Deity Pe-har.[1] The monastery was consecrated on the fifteenth day of the eleventh month of the male-water-horse year. The *Bodhisattva* himself consecrated it thrice. Then Padma meditated for one day, and initiated the King of Tibet into the Doctrine of Sarasvati.[2]

THE MIRACLES ATTENDING THE CONSECRATION

Comprised within the monastery there were one hundred and eight temples [or shrines]; and Padma manifested him-

[1] Pe-har (usually pronounced *Pé-kar*) belongs to the kingly group of Wrathful Protectors, and is the chief of the Four Great Kings who guard the four quarters of the Universe. Although Pe-har appears to be a non-Hindu deity, he has sometimes been identified with the Hindu deity Veda, or the Chinese Wei-to, whom the Chinese Buddhists invoke as a protector of monasteries. Hence *Pe-har* is believed by some scholars to be a corruption of the Sanskrit *Vihar* ('Monastery'). It is believed that Pe-har successively incarnates in each of the living oracles represented by 'The Religious Noble' (*Ch'ö-je*), the actual State Oracle of Tibet known as the Nä-ch'uṅ Oracle. Pe-har is said to inspire also the Karma-s'ar Oracle in Lhāsa. (Cf. L. A. Waddell, op. cit., pp. 371, 478–81.) Each Tibetan monastery is under the guardianship of some such deity of the Wrathful Order of Tantric Guardians; and so are all Tibetan temples, sacred mountains, rivers, lakes, places of pilgrimage, and natural deposits of precious metals or gems. Similarly, each field and dwelling-house in Tibet is under the guardianship of a beneficent spiritual being, as are cattle and crops; and each individual Tibetan, man, woman, and child, has a tutelary, or directing and guardian deity, comparable to the guardian angel of Christians.

[2] Sarasvati, the Goddess of Learning, is sometimes, as she seems to be here, the *shakti*, or feminine complement, of Mañjushrī, the God of Divine Wisdom; and, accordingly, it appears that the King was initiated into the secret Tantric doctrines associated with the Sarasvati-Mañjushrī *maṇḍala*.

self in one hundred and eight bodies, each body like his own, and simultaneously performed the consecration ceremony. When, in three of these temples,, he was scattering the blossoms used in the ceremony, the images descended from the altars and circumambulated their own temples thrice. The images of the other temples came out of their temples and moved their hands. The King was afraid, and doubted that the images would go back to their temples. Padma snapped his fingers, and each of the images returned to its own place. From the painted flames of fire in the haloes of the frescoes depicting the Wrathful Guardian Deities by the doors, real flames of fire issued. Again the King was afraid; and Padma threw flowers on the flames and the flames subsided, and from the petals of the flowers sprang up lotus blossoms.

The deities assembled in the sky overhead, and witnessed the consecration ceremony; and there was a rain of flowers, accompanied by other phenomena. The thousands of people present were witnesses to all these miracles.

The Bönpos's Defeat in Public Debate and their Expulsion from Tibet

Later on, the Buddhists and Bönpos in Tibet publicly debated; and, the Bönpos being defeated, the King expelled most of those who would not embrace Buddhism, to the deserts of the north, to Nepal, Mongolia, and other sparsely populated countries. Buddhism was introduced into all parts of Tibet. The *Kanjur* and *Tanjur* and other Mahāyāna works were translated from the Sanskrit into Tibetan. So also were the exoteric and esoteric *Tantras* and *Mantras*, and treatises on medicine and astrology.

The Authoress and Origin of the Biography

Folio 288[b] gives an account of the origin of the incarnate *ḍākinī* Ye-she-Tsho-gyal,[1] who, having been one of Padma's

---

[1] A Tibetan name meaning 'Victorious [One] of the Ocean of Wisdom'. The late Sir John Woodroffe (Arthur Avalon) in an article entitled 'Origin of the *Vajrayāna Devatas*', reprinted from the *Modern Review* for June 1916 and based on work which he and the late Lāma Kazi Dawa-Samdup did together, states, on p. 2: '*Guru* Padma-Sambhava, the so-called founder of "Lāmaism", had five women disciples who compiled several accounts of

most intimate disciples from the age of sixteen, compiled the matter contained within the Biography.

THE HIDING OF THE MANUSCRIPT TEXT OF THE BIOGRAPHY

When Ye-she-Tsho-gyal had finished writing down, on yellow paper, at Padma's dictation, the matter of this Biography, Padma said to her, 'Before thou diest, bury this manuscript in the Cave situated about eighteen yards from a solitary tree growing over a rock shaped like a lion in Boom-thang.[1] The Cave, into which no light penetrateth, can be entered only from above, by sliding down a rope. I have already buried the *Long-sal-nyi-mai-gyud*[2] therein, and this manuscript should be preserved along with that.' He admonished her that if the hiding of the manuscript was not kept secret, the *ḍākinī* would trouble her.

TERTÖNS, DEATH OF THE BODHISATTVA AND THE KING, AND SUMMARY

From folio 303[b] to folio 332[a] directions are given for finding hidden texts and their accompanying treasures, together with the names of *tertöns*, and the auspicious times and omens which guide the *tertöns*.

Folios 332[b] and 333 contain accounts of the death of the *Bodhisattva* from Nālanda, who preceded Padma to Tibet, and of the passing of King Thī-Srong-Detsan, whose death occurred at about the same time as that of the *Bodhisattva*. To King Mu-thī-tsan-po, who succeeded to the Tibetan throne, Padma, speaking of himself, declared that he had been born

the teachings of their Master and hid them in various places for the benefit of future believers. One of these disciples, Khandro [or *Ḍākinī*] Yeshe Tshogyal, was a Tibetan lady who is said to have possessed such a wonderful power of memory that if she was told a thing only once she remembered it for ever. She gathered what she had heard from her *Guru* into a book called the *Padma Thangyig Serteng*, or Golden Rosary of the history of her *Guru*, who was entitled the Lotus-born (Padma-Sambhava). The book was hidden away and was subsequently revealed under inspiration some five hundred years ago by [a] *Tertön.*' *Padma Thangyig Serteng* is another title for the Biography of the Great *Guru* herein epitomized.

[1] Boom-thang is about fourteen miles northeast of Lhāsa.

[2] Text: *Klong-gsal-nyi-mahi-rgyud* (pron. *Long-sal-nyi-mai-gyud*), meaning 'A Clear Treatise on the *Tantra* of *Sūrya*, the Sun.'

in the eighth year after the passing of the Buddha, from a
lotus blossom in the Dhanakosha Lake.[1]

Afterwards comes a summarized account of Padma's activi-
ties and of the places he visited, which included Persia,
Sikkim, Bhutan, China, Ceylon, and all parts of Tibet and
India. And there is the statement that Padma remained in
Tibet one hundred and eleven years.

PADMA'S DEPARTURE FROM TIBET

Having decided to depart from Tibet, Padma said to the
King, 'The time is ripe to subjugate the *Rākshasas*; and only
the Lotus-Born can subjugate them. If I do not subjugate
them now, they will devour all mankind, and the Earth will
be devoid of human beings.' Of the country of the *Rākshasas*,
which is triangular like a shoulder blade, and contains five
large cities, Padma gives a lengthy description. 'These cities
are not far from the Urgyān country.'[2] Each of these five
cities is composed of five hundred villages. Padma's purpose
was not to destroy the *Rākshasas*, but to convert them to
Buddhism.

As Padma was about to depart from Tibet, he said, 'Hereafter, the Doctrine will be disseminated by Avalokiteshvara.'[3]

[1] If one were inclined to seek reconciliation between this account of
Padma-Sambhava having been born eight years after the passing of the
Buddha and that of the Buddha's prophecy given on p. 105, above, it would
be necessary to assume that Padma-Sambhava did not begin his active
mission in the world until his fortieth year; but a biography such as this of
the Great *Guru*, wherein historical facts and legendary stories are inex-
tricably interwoven, cannot be expected to exhibit correlation or common
unity of its many diverse parts.

[2] This passage, literally quoted from the text, recalls one theory among
other theories, advanced by the late Sardar Bahādur S. W. Laden La, that
Urgyān, Padma's native country, was probably in Southern India and not,
as is commonly assumed, 'the country about Ghazni to the northwest of
Kashmir' (cf. L. A. Waddell, op. cit., p. 26) or, as others have thought, a
part of what is now Afghanistan. The supposition that the country of the
Rākshasas is Ceylon, tends to support the theory. Sometimes, too, the
country of the *Rākshasas* has been supposed to be Java.

[3] This probably refers to the Dalai Lāma, the incarnation of Avalokiteshvara, as being the future guardian and teacher of the *Dharma* in Tibet, of
whom the first historical representative was the Grand (Dalai) Lāma
Geden-dub (A.D. 1391–1475), the nephew of Tsong-Khapa, the founder of
the Gelugpa Order. (Cf. L. A. Waddell, op. cit., pp. 38 and 233.)

The King and the ministers of state and the attendants, mounted on horses, accompanied Padma to Gung-thang-la,[1] where all the party halted for the night.

In the morning, after Padma had given his parting good wishes to the King and everyone present, there appeared out of the heavens, in the midst of rainbow radiance, a blue horse fully saddled. Celestial music was heard, and a concourse of deities also appeared. Padma mounted the horse and the horse rose upward. Then, after Padma had pronounced his final blessings, in the name of the Buddha, the *Dharma*, and the *Sangha*, he and the deities following him disappeared on the sun-rays.

PADMA'S ARRIVAL IN THE COUNTRY OF THE *RĀKSHASAS* AND THEIR SUBJECTION

Certain *lāmas* entered into deep *yogic* meditation and watched Padma pass over the Urgyān country and afterward come down in the country of Singala[2] and take shelter under a magnolia tree; and they saw the blue horse rolling in the golden sands of Singala. Later they beheld Padma surrounded by *Rākshasa* maidens, whom he was teaching, and then that he had transformed himself into the King of the *Rākshasas* and subjugated all the *Rākshasas*.

Here Chapter 116 ends on folio 393. Chapter 117 contains the Tibetan King's lamentations about Padma's departure.

THE COLOPHON OF THE BIOGRAPHY

On folio 394 the Colophon begins, and is as follows:

'This Book was written down [or compiled] by Ye-she-Tsho-gyal, the incarnation of Yang-chen,[3] in order to benefit the creatures of coming generations and to prevent its contents from being lost to their memory.

'The name of this Book is *Padma Ka-ḥi-thang-yig* [or *Padma's Precepts*].[4] It is also called *Ke-rap Nam-thar Gye-pa*

---

[1] Gung-thang-la, meaning 'High Plain Pass', is in Mangyul, on the northern confines of Tibet.

[2] Text: *Singa-la*, is here presumed to refer to Ceylon.

[3] Or, in Sanskrit, Sarasvati, Goddess of Learning.

[4] Tib., *Padma-bkaḥi-thang-yig*.

[or *Complete Birth-History*].[1] Another of its titles is *Thī-Srong-Detsan Ka-chem* [or *Thī-Srong-Detsan's Testament*].[2]

'This well-detailed [account of the Book's] origin has been recorded in writing and buried [along with the Book] like a precious gem.

'May this [Book] be met with by persons of great meritorious deeds.

'This hidden treasure was taken out from the large Mirror Cave of Pourī by the *Guru* Sang-gye Ling-pa.

'[It was in the form of] a scroll written in Sanskrit,[3] and translated into Tibetan without the omission of a word.

'For the good of the beings of the world, the Nam-gyal-Duk-pa[4] carved the blocks of type under the supervision of the reigning Pum-thang family of Bhutan, by command of Ngag-ki-Wang-po.'[5]

The last folio, 397, ends with good wishes to all sentient beings and with praises of Padma.

[The translation, of which this Epitome is the fruit, was completed on the twenty-first day of January 1936.]

[1] Tib., *Skyes-rabs-rnam-thar-rgyas-pa*.

[2] Tib., *Khri-srong-ldehu-btsan-gyi-bkaḥ-chems* (or *kha-chems*).

[3] According to Tibetan tradition, Ye-she-Tsho-gyal had acquired from Indian *pandits* a sound knowledge of Sanskrit before she compiled this Biography.

[4] Meaning 'Ever Victorious Bhutanese'.

[5] Meaning 'The One Powerful of Speech', probably the name of a *Dharma-Rāja* (or 'Religious King') of Bhutan.

PLATE VII

THE *TRI-KĀYA* OR THREE DIVINE BODIES

Described on pages xxvi–xxvii

BOOK II

HERE FOLLOWS THE [*YOGA* OF] KNOWING THE MIND, THE SEEING OF REALITY, CALLED SELF-LIBERATION, FROM 'THE PROFOUND DOCTRINE OF SELF-LIBERATION BY MEDITATION UPON THE PEACEFUL AND WRATHFUL DEITIES'[1]

ACCORDING TO LĀMA KARMA SUMDHON PAUL'S AND LĀMA LOBZANG MINGYUR DORJE'S ENGLISH RENDERING

[1] Text: ZAB-CHŎS ZHI-KHRO DGONGS-PA RANG-GRŎL LAS RIG-PA NGO-SPRŎD GÇER-MTHONG RANG-GRŎL SHES-BYA-WA BZHUGS-SO (pron.: ZAB-CHŎ SHI-HTO GONG-PA RANG-DŎL LAY RIG-PA NGO-TŎD CHER-THONG RANG-DŎL SHAY-JHA-WA ZHUG-SO).

Another rendering might be: HEREIN IS CONTAINED THE [ART OF] KNOWING THE MIND, THE SEEING OF [MIND IN ITS] NAKEDNESS, CALLED SELF-LIBERA-TION, FROM 'THE PROFOUND DOCTRINE OF SELF-LIBERATION BY MEDITATING UPON THE PEACEFUL AND WRATHFUL DEITIES'.

Wakefulness

'Wakefulness is the path to immortality; heedlessness is the path to death. Those who are wakeful die not; the heedless are as if dead already.

'The wise, those who have realized this efficacy of wakefulness, rejoice in wakefulness, and are drawn to such spheres of activity as engage the Noble Ones.

'Such sages, ever meditative, ever putting forth strong effort, attain the incomparable security of *Nirvāṇa*.

'Continually increasing is the glory of him who is wakeful, who hath aroused himself and is ever alert, who performeth blameless deeds, and acteth with becoming consideration, who restraineth himself, and leadeth a righteous life.

'Let such an one, rousing himself to wakefulness by self-restraint and self-subjugation make for himself an island which no flood can overwhelm.

      *   *   *   *

'As a man of discernment, standing on a rocky eminence, beholdeth those who are below and in distress, so doth the sage, who by his wakefulness hath put to flight his ignorance, look down upon suffering mankind from the Heights of Wisdom which he hath attained.

'Wakeful amidst the heedless, keenly vigilant amidst the sleeping ones, the wise man forgeth ahead, even as a charger outdistanceth a horse of lesser strength.'

The Buddha, from the *Dhammapada*, vv. 21–25, 28–29
(based upon N. K. Bhagwat's Translation).

PLATE VIII

BODHIDHARMA

Described on page xxvii

INTRODUCTION

As the Biography in the preceding Book has shown, Padma-Sambhava spent many years as a disciple under various wise teachers in India, Burma, Afghanistan, Nepal, and other lands. He practised the different *yogas*. Having lived in India at a time when India was still comparatively free from disrupting foreign influences and the good life was that of the philosopher, he was able to collect, like a honey-bee, the nectar from the rarest of blossoms in the Orient's vast garden of philosophical and psychic research. And here, in this *yogic* treatise, he has transmitted to us the results, which are, intrinsically, of more value than all the gold and precious gems of the world.

Even as Bodhidharma, the twenty-eighth of the Buddhist Patriarchs, was the great pioneer teacher of the Dhyāna School of Buddhism to the people of China, where he went by sea from India and arrived in Canton in A.D. 527[1] and gave direction to the enlightening spiritual influences that made Buddhism an integral part of Chinese culture, so was Padma-Sambhava the great pioneer teacher of the Tantric School of Buddhism to the people of Tibet, where he arrived from India in A.D. 747, by invitation of the Tibetan King, and, under royal patronage, made Tibet Buddhistic. Both teachers taught that Right Meditation is the indispensable means of attaining the Goal of the Buddha's *Nirvāṇic* Path. Accordingly, Bodhidharma founded the Meditation (Skt. *Dhyāna*) School in China known as the Ch'an, whence arose the Zen School of Japan; and Padma-Sambhava founded in Tibet the Nyingma School, of which the more esoteric teachings are set forth in the Ādi-Yoga System, otherwise known as the Doctrine of the Great Perfection (Tib. *Rdzogs-Ch'en*), whence arose the Western Branch of the Chinese Esoteric Sect known as the Tibetan Esoteric Sect (Chinese, *Tsang Mi Tsung*) or the Lotus Division (Chinese *Lien Hua Pu*). Although

---

[1] Cf. J. Blofeld, *The Jewel in the Lotus* (London, 1948), p. 128. The exact date of Bodhidharma's arrival in China is uncertain. Other dates, e.g. A.D. 520 and 526, have been assigned to the event.

the Eastern Branch of this Sect arose in China independently of the direct personal influence of Padma-Sambhava, it was inspired by the same Yogāchāra School of India that inspired his teachings in Tibet, and its founders, Vajrabodhi and Amoghavajra, who reached China together in A.D. 719, had been his fellow students in Bengal.[1]

Our present treatise, attributed to Padma-Sambhava, which expounds the method of realizing the Great Liberation of *Nirvāṇa* by *yogic* understanding of the One Mind, appertains to the Doctrine of the Great Perfection of the Dhyāna School. Between it and the *Treatise on Achieving Pure Consciousness* (Chinese, *Ch'eng Wei Shih Lun*), upon which the Pure Consciousness Sect (Chinese, *Wei Shih Tsung*) of China is based,[2] there is a very close doctrinal relationship. Research may even establish direct historical relationship. Both treatises alike set forth the doctrine that the only reality is mind or consciousness and that no living thing has individualized existence but is fundamentally in eternal and inseparable at-one-ment with the universal all-consciousness.

Of the Doctrine of the Great Perfection itself, the *Guru* Marpa says to the neophyte Milarepa (who subsequently became Tibet's most beloved *Mahātma*) as he is about to initiate him into it,

It is excellent alike in its root, in its trunk, and in its branches. . . . He who meditateth upon it in the day is delivered in the course of that day; and the like happeneth to him who meditateth upon it in the night. . . . This is a doctrine for those intellects that are most highly developed.[3]

This introductory eulogy by the *Guru* Marpa may also, very fittingly, be applied to 'The *Yoga* of Knowing the Mind'.

In order to grasp intellectually the significance of this *yoga* of *yogas*, the student should make careful study not only of occidental psychology, but, more especially, of the psychologically-based philosophy of the Orient; and no better guidance therein can be found than the teachings concerning

---

[1] Cf. J. Blofeld, *The Jewel in the Lotus* (London, 1948), pp. 150–1.

[2] Ibid., pp. 161–2.

[3] Cf. W. Y. Evans-Wentz, *Tibet's Great Yogi Milarepa*, pp. 4, 85–86, and *Tibetan Yoga and Secret Doctrines*, pp. 277–8.

the Illusory Body and Dreams, forming part of *The Six Doctrines*, in *Tibetan Yoga and Secret Doctrines*, together with Dr. Jung's Psychological Commentary, the Foreword of this volume. It will also be found helpful, in this connexion, to re-read Sections IV and V of our General Introduction above.

This *yogic* treatise, like the Gospel of St. John, teaches that one needs only to look within oneself to find Truth, for Truth is not—as the mind in its true state is not—a subject of the Kingdom of Time and Space and *Māyā*. The ancient teaching that the Universe is the product of thought, that Brahma thinks the Universe and it is—as Jehovah thought light and there was light—will, when meditated upon, lead the meditant to the realization that the only reality is Mind, the One Mind, of which all the microcosmic minds throughout the Cosmos are illusorily parts, that everything conceivable is, at root, idea and thought, and thus the offspring of Mind.

The idea and the thought and the object are inseparable; and all three have their origin in mind. It was Plato's belief that ideas pre-exist in the mind, and that, being transcendent over all mundane concepts relating to past, present, and future, they are of that timelessness to which our text makes reference.

Tibetan Masters of *Yoga*, by projecting a mental image, and, through *yogic* power of will, giving to it a form as palpable as that which builders give to the blue-print of an architect, have demonstrated how all external appearances, even the most solid-appearing objective things, are mind-made. This *yogic* method of materialization is referred to at some length above, on page 29[1].

We must not think of mind as something tangible, as the misguided materialists do when they confuse brain substance with mind. In its human manifestation, mind is an invisible energy capable of setting into activity the visible physical brain, just as an invisible vibration sets into activity a radio. The brain thus activated gives off thought, and the radio sound. The sound is merely the product of the vibratory impulse to which the radio responds. Likewise, the thought produced by the brain is the product of the vibratory impulse

imparted to the brain by an invisible consciousness, which is
per se unknowable. If Brahma fails to think the Universe,
there is no Universe; and if there be no thought, there cannot
be such a thing as that which men call a material object. Unless an inventor thinks, and then gives substance to an invention, there will be no invention. As taught in our text, the One
Mind, the cosmic focus of consciousness, is all-in-all; there is
nothing other than it, no thought other than its thought, no
object or universe independent of it.

According to *The Six Doctrines*, all states of consciousness
—the waking, the sleeping, the hypnotic, that at death and
after death and at rebirth—are not, primordially viewed, true
states, being only illusory emanations of the microcosmic
mind. Our apparently solid planet is, accordingly, no more
solid or real than the world of the dream-state. A stone is as
hard in a dream as in the waking-state, because the stone
and the hardness are mental concepts. Thus, substance *per se*
having no existence apart from mind, the thesis of materialism is fallacious.

Wherever there is law, as there is in every manifested
aspect and kingdom of nature, from the atom to the cosmos,
there is mind. Mind itself, having neither place nor form, is
measureless. As our text repeatedly emphasizes, mind is of the
uncreated, timeless, spaceless, all-embracing Reality.

Evolution is a purely mental process. The microcosmic
mind of man fashions for itself ever new mansions; and, in the
process of evolution, there is continuous expansion of mind
until at-one-ment with the One Mind has been attained.
The many illusorily re-become the One, the One illusorily
re-becomes the many; and thereby is made manifest the heart-
throb of the cosmos, the pulsation of existence, the inbreath-
ing and the outbreathing by Brahma of the cosmic Whole, the
eternal tidal rhythm of the Great Ocean. Just as we speak of
an expanding physical universe when the tide in the Great
Ocean is rising, so must we think of an expanding human
mind during this Day of Brahma. From the reservoir of Cosmic Consciousness there now flows through the microcosmic
mind of man a tiny trickle. As evolution proceeds, this trickle

will grow into a rivulet, the rivulet into a deep broad river, and, at last, this river will become an infinite sea. The rain-drop will have been merged in its Source.

The Conquerors of Life and Death vow not to enter *Nirvāṇa* until all things are restored to the divine at-one-ment; for They know it is only when They and all beings have awakened from the Earth-Dream and from the dreaming in the after-death and rebirth states that Complete Buddhahood can be attained. Though They themselves have gained the Goal, it cannot be fully enjoyed until all other sentient creatures, who, along with Them collectively form the Whole, have gained the Goal also.

Mind may be regarded from our human viewpoint as being composed of concepts, or ideas, its function being to think, and its products being thoughts; and, correlatively, we may mentally resolve the visible Universe into ideas, and these into mind, the One Mind, which our Teachers assert is the Sole Reality. So viewed, life is no more than an experience of mind.

When we know mind, we also know matter, for matter is mind; and there is nought else conceivable save mind, as this *yoga* postulates. In the One Mind is the summation of the whole of consciousness, the ineffable at-one-ment of all the One Mind's microcosmic aspects. In transcending the micro-cosmic mind of the human ego, man transcends himself; he becomes a conscious participator in the all-embracing Univer-sal Mind, the Over-Mind, the Cosmic Consciousness.

The Dream of Existence is for the purpose of enabling the dreamer to attain the Wisdom born of the Full Awakenment of Buddhahood. Ignorance gives way to understanding, illu-sion to disillusion, the state of sleep to the state of waking, the unreal to the real. *Sangsāric* consciousness is compounded of dualities; and beyond the dualism of the dreaming and the waking lies That which is beyond both.

Through knowing the microcosmic self, his own illusory little self, man attains knowledge of the selfless self, beyond self, the Self of All, the One Mind, beyond mind. This supreme attainment, being possible only when existence itself, as man knows existence, has been transcended, must forever remain, for the unenlightened, mentally incomprehensible, as our text suggests when enumerating the various names men apply to it.

So it is that the paths of the lower *yogas* merge into the Great Path, whereon the pilgrim relinquishes ego and self and even life. The Masters of the Mahāyāna declare that all verbal and symbolic methods of transmitting their teachings are directed to the one end of leading the disciple to that Great Path itself. Nevertheless, the disciple must first have exhausted the lesser paths; initially there must be the seed, then the growth, then the blossoming, and then the fruition. The acorn is not an oak as soon as it sprouts.

In this supreme system of realizing Truth in its undivided unity, by the aeon-old method of knowing the self in the sense implied by the Ancient Oracles and Mysteries, all the ordinary *yogic* practices or techniques, postures, breathings, exercises, and use of concentration-points are transcended. The 'Yoga of Knowing the Mind in its Nakedness' is, in fact, as the text proclaims, 'the most excellent of *yogas*'.

Those who are treading any of the lesser paths are unaware, unless under the guidance of a perfected *guru*, that they are on a lesser path. With very rare exceptions, the various teachers of *yoga* have unknowingly deemed some particular system of conventionalized *yoga* to be all-sufficient in itself, whereas it is, according to our text, no more than a preparation for the truly *Mahāyāna* or Great Path.

Thus the teachings herein set forth are presented as being the very quintessence of all *yogas*; and the Great Path leads from the mundane to the supramundane, from that which is formed and manifested to that which is beyond form and manifestation, from the created, the mind-projected, to the uncreated, the mind-contained, from the phenomenal to the noumenal, from the many to the One, from the *Sangsāra* to *Nirvāṇa*.

Similarly, the *Bhagavad-Gītā* teaches that the *yoga* of divine understanding is paramount, and leads to liberation. Since man, as the Greek Sages declared, is the measure of all things, he sees beyond the illusion of the world and of the self once he has attained understanding of what he intrinsically and transcendentally is.

This *yoga* teaches that mind and the world are inseparable, that without mind there would be no world, that the world is the child of mind, that, as the *Rishis* taught ages ago, Mind is the source of all that man perceives as time and space and the Universe. The *Sangsāra* being the dream-product of the One Mind, its illusory reality is entirely relative; when the One Mind no longer sustains its Creation, its Creation ceases to be.

The time approaches rapidly when occidental scientists, too, will realize that all their so-called exact knowledge is knowledge not of reality, but of an ever-changing, evanescent mirage. Instead of studying the real, they are studying the unreal, the phenomenal instead of the noumenal, appearances rather than the cause of appearances. In the True State of the One Mind, the pluralistic Universe has no existence; and therein man, as man, together with his mind-begotten world of sensuousness and all his mundane sciences, will have vanished into the Voidness.

[PART I. THE INTRODUCTORY PRELIMINARIES]

[*THE OBEISANCE*]

To the Divine Ones, the *Tri-Kāya*,[1] Who are the Embodiment of the All-Enlightened Mind Itself, obeisance.

[*THE FOREWORD*]

This treatise appertains to 'The Profound Doctrine of Self-Liberation by Meditating upon the Peaceful and Wrathful Deities'.[2]

It expounds the *Yoga* of Knowing the Mind, the Seeing of Reality, Self-Liberation.

By this method, one's mind is understood.

[*THE* GURU'S *FIRST CHARGE TO THE DISCIPLES AND THE INVOCATION*]

O blessed disciples,[3] ponder these teachings deeply.

Samayā; gya, gya, gya.[4]

E-ma-ho![5]

---

[1] Text: *Sku-gsum* (pron. *Kū-sūm*), the three states in which the Buddhas, the All-Enlightened Ones, exist, namely (1) the humanly incomprehensible, transcendent at-one-ment of the *Dharma-Kāya* ('Divine Body of Truth'), the primordial, unmodified, unshaped Thatness, beyond the realm of descriptive terms, and knowable solely by realization; (2) the celestial state of the *Sambhoga-Kāya* ('Divine Body of Perfect Endowment'), the reflex or modified aspect of the *Dharma-Kāya*; and (3) the state of divinely pure human embodiment, the *Nirmāna-Kāya* ('Divine Body of Incarnation'). The personifications of the *Tri-Kāya* vary according to sect or specialized doctrine. Amitābha, the Dhyānī Buddha of Boundless Light, Who presides over the Western Paradise of Sukhāvatī, very often personifies the *Dharma-Kāya*. In the *Bardo Thödol* series of texts, to which this text belongs, Samanta-Bhadra, the Primordial Buddha of the Nyingma School, personifies the *Dharma-Kāya*, Avalokiteshvara the *Sambhoga-Kāya*, and Padma-Sambhava the *Nirmāna-Kāya*, as in Illustration VII.

[2] By comparing this title with that of the translated text of *The Tibetan Book of the Dead*, known as the *Bardo Thödol*, it will be observed that both texts belong to the same *yogic* doctrine concerning self-liberation, or the attaining of *Nirvāna*.

[3] Literally '[spiritual] sons', i.e. disciples of a *guru*, or spiritual preceptor. According to the Mahāyāna School, Mañjushrī, Avalokiteshvara, Vajra-Pāni, and other Great *Bodhisattvas* are spiritual sons of Gautama the Buddha.

[4] This *mantra* indicates that the teachings about to be given are too profound and esoteric to be taught to, or comprehended by, any save *yogically*

---

[5] See p. 203.

[*SALUTATION TO THE ONE MIND*]

All hail to the One Mind[1] that embraces the whole *Sangsāra* and *Nirvāṇa*,

That eternally is as it is, yet is unknown,

That although ever clear and ever existing, is not visible,

That, although radiant and unobscured, is not recognized.

[*THESE TEACHINGS SUPPLEMENT THOSE OF THE BUDDHAS*]

These teachings are for the purpose of enabling one to know this Mind.

All that has been taught heretofore by the Buddhas of the Three Times,[2] in virtue of Their having known this Mind, as

purified and disciplined disciples. The reference to the disciples as being blessed, or *karmically* fortunate, confirms this. The treatise before us may, therefore, be regarded as appertaining to the Secret Lore of the *Gurus*. In the eyes of initiated Tibetans of this School, the *mantra* itself is equivalent to a seal of secrecy placed upon these teachings. Sometimes, in some of the esoteric manuscripts, the seal of secrecy takes the form of a carefully drawn double *dorje*, perhaps in colour, such as appears on the cover of this volume. A text like the text here translated ought never to be given publicity without authoritative permission, such as the late Lāma Kazi Dawa-Samdup obtained from his *guru* and then gave to the Editor, with respect to the *Bardo Thödol* series of texts as a whole. (See *Tibetan Yoga and Secret Doctrines*, pp. 105–7; also *The Tibetan Book of the Dead*, pp. 79–80.) The Sanskrit *Samayā* of our text corresponds to the Tibetan form *Tog-pa* (*Rtogs-pa*), meaning 'thorough perception', 'infallible knowledge', 'complete realization of Truth'. It also means 'self-realization', or 'self-knowledge'. *Tog-pa* cannot be thoroughly comprehended without practice of *yoga*. The first step consists in comprehending *Tog-pa* intellectually; the second, in deepening or expanding this comprehension by study; the third, in meditating upon *Tog-pa*; and the fourth, in fully comprehending it, such complete comprehension being equivalent to the realization of Buddhahood, or *Nirvāṇa*. The thrice-repeated *gya* (*rgya*) is a Tibetan expression literally translatable as 'vast'. The *mantra* may, therefore, be rendered as 'Vast, vast, vast is Divine Wisdom'.

[5] *E-ma-ho!* is an interjection, commonly occurring in the religious literature of Tibet, expressive of compassion for all living creatures. In this context, it is to be regarded as being the *guru's* invocation addressed to the Buddhas and *Bodhisattvas* in super-human realms that They may telepathically bestow upon the disciples Their divine grace and guidance. The Christian doctrine of divine grace is similar. An interesting illustration of this is supplied by the Latin inscription round the arched entrance of the chapel of the Editor's College in Oxford: *Ascendat Oratio; Descendat Gratia.*

[1] Text: *Sems-gchik-po* (pron. *sem-chik-po*), 'One Mind'.

[2] The Buddhas of the Three Times are: Dīpaṃkara ('The Luminous

recorded in 'The Door of the *Dharma*', consisting of the Eighty-Four Thousand *Shlokas*,[1] and elsewhere, remains incomprehensible.[2]

The Conquerors[3] have not elsewhere taught anything concerning the One Mind.

Although as vast as the illimitable sky, the Sacred Scriptures contain but a few words relating to knowledge of the mind.

This, the true explanation of these eternal teachings of the Conquerors, constitutes the correct method of their practical application.

[*THE* GURU'S *SECOND CHARGE TO THE DISCIPLES*]

Kye![4] *Kye! Ho!*
Blessed disciples, harken.

One'), of the past time-cycle; Shākya Muni ('The Sage of the Shākya Clan'), of the present time-cycle; and Maitreya ('The Loving One'), of the future time-cycle.

[1] These 84,000 *shlokas* contain the essentials of Buddhist teachings, and are, therefore, commonly known among Tibetan Buddhists as 'The Door of the *Dharma*', or 'Entrance into the *Dharma*', or, vernacularly, as the *Getri*.

[2] That is to say, incomprehensible by one of *yogically* untrained mind, as are all fundamentally esoteric teachings.

[3] The Conquerors (Skt. *Jina*) are the Buddhas, Who are the Conquerors of *sangsāric*, or conditioned, existence. In the Occident there prevails the view that oriental ascetics who renounce the world invariably do so to escape the burdens of social existence. Although this may be true of certain orders of monks in the Occident who do not accept the doctrines of *karma* and rebirth, it is not true of those Hindu and Buddhist monks who, sincere in their renunciation, look forward to the time, even though it be after numerous lifetimes on Earth, when they, too, like the Buddhas, shall have won the spiritual power to live in the midst of society, and, in helping men towards Liberation, shall conquer the world. To those who hold to the one-life-on-Earth theory and renounce the world in the hope of escaping from it for ever into a paradisal after-death state, there can be no desire or opportunity to return to the world to work for social betterment; and they alone may rightly be regarded as escapists. On the other hand, the candidates for Buddhahood, like the Gnostic candidates for Christhood, are the ones of iron will and indomitable purpose, who, like an athlete in training, bide the hour of their Victory. Such an ideal as that exemplified by the *Bodhisattva* cannot but make for greater and greater strength of mind and a desire to meet face to face and conquer every evil of human society in the glorious spirit of a Saint George, whose spear of righteousness transfixes the Dragon.

[4] Text: *Kye*, a vocative, known in Tibetan as the word of invocation or calling (or, as here, charge to the disciples), which may be translated as 'O!'

[THE RESULT OF NOT KNOWING THE ONE MIND]

Knowledge of that which is vulgarly called mind is widespread.

Inasmuch as the One Mind is unknown, or thought of erroneously, or known one-sidedly without being thoroughly known as it is, desire for these teachings will be immeasurable. They will also be sought after by ordinary individuals, who, not knowing the One Mind, do not know themselves.

They wander hither and thither in the Three Regions,[1] and thus among the Six Classes of beings,[2] suffering sorrow.

Such is the result of their error of not having attained understanding of their mind.

Because their suffering is in every way overpowering, even self-control is lacking to them.

Thus, although one may wish to know the mind as it is, one fails.

[THE RESULTS OF DESIRES]

Others, in accordance with their own particular faith and practice, having become fettered by desires,[3] cannot perceive the Clear Light.[4]

[1] The Three Regions (Tib. *Khams-gsum*: Skt. *Trailokya*) into which Buddhists divide the *Sangsāra*, or realm of conditioned existence, known to men as the Cosmos or Universe, are: (1) The Region of Desire (Skt. *Kāma-dhātu*), which is the lowest, comprising the six heavens of the *devas*, or gods, and the Earth; (2) the Region of Form (Skt. *Rūpa-dhātu*), comprising the purer heavens, wherein form is free from sensuality, called the sixteen worlds of Brahma, which are divided into four realms of meditation (Skt. *dhyāna*); (3) the Region of Formlessness (Skt. *Arūpa-dhātu*), comprising the four highest Brahma heavens, whence the Fully Awakened One passes into the unconditioned state of *Nirvāna*. (Cf. L. A. Waddell, op. cit., pp. 84–85.)

[2] These are: (1) the Gods (Tib. *Lha*: Skt. *Sura* or *Deva*); (2) Titans (Tib. *Lha-ma-yin*: Skt. *Asura*); (3) Man (Tib. *Mi*: Skt. *Nara*); (4) Beasts (Tib. *Du-dō*: Skt. *Tiryak*); (5) Ghosts (Tib. *Yi-dvag*: Skt. *Preta*); (6) Dwellers in Hells (Tib. *Nyal-kham*: Skt. *Naraka*). Thus the Six Classes of sentient beings are those of the Six States of Existence within the *Sangsāra*. The various Hells or states of *karmic* purgation, unlike the Hell of the Semitic Faiths, are, for the fallen ones who enter them, of but limited duration, like all other *sangsāric* states, the unconditional supra-*sangsāric Nirvānic* State alone being eternal, and transcendent over time.

[3] Commonly, unsound religious beliefs and practices result in increased

[4] See p. 206.

They are overwhelmed by suffering, and are in darkness because of their suffering.

Although the Middle Path contains the Twofold Truth,[1] because of desires it finally becomes obscured.

Desires likewise obscure *Kriyā-Yoga*[2] and *Seva-Sādhanā*,[3] and even the greatest and sublimest states of mind.

[*THE TRANSCENDENT AT-ONE-MENT*]

There being really no duality, pluralism is untrue.[4]

Until duality is transcended and at-one-ment realized, Enlightenment cannot be attained.

---

sangsāric bondage. There may be, for instance, strong desire to escape distasteful duties which are inseparable from the station in life assigned to one by *karma*, and, in consequence, an overpowering longing for death and for some after-death paradise. This merely results, as the *Bardo Thödol* teaches, in exchanging one state of illusion for another. *Karma* cannot possibly be escaped; it must be faced eventually and, no matter how terrible, experienced, if not in one lifetime then in another. There is no place to which one can go to get away from oneself, or from the results of one's actions. Very often, too, prayer may be made for purely worldly benefits rather than for emancipation from the bondage to appearances.

[4] For those who are attracted to religions which, not affording true guidance, tend to enhance the *karmic* predilections of the unenlightened to create ever new fetters, the Clear Light of Reality remains obscured by the darkness of *Avidyā* (Ignorance of Truth).

[1] Text: *Bden-gnyis* (pron. *Den-nyi*), 'Two Truths', or 'Twofold Truth': namely, the ordinary truth, such as that of science, which concerns all things and phenomena observable in nature; and the transcendental, or metaphysical, truth, as set forth in the teachings of the Buddha.

[2] Text: *Kri-yog*, an abbreviated form of the Sanskrit *Kriyā-Yoga*, the *yoga* concerned with religious observances and worship (*kriyā*).

[3] *Seva-Sādhanā*, the Sanskrit equivalent of the Tibetan *bsnyen-bsgrub* (pron. *nyen-drub*) of the text, literally means 'Service-Worship', with reference to a *yogic* practice of regarding all one's duties to society and the world as sacred, to the end that every act of life on Earth shall be performed with religious reverence.

[4] In the words of Plotinus, 'The Primordial [or First Principle] is neither all things that imply duality, nor any of them; it containeth no duality whatsoever' (v. vi. 6). It is said that Plotinus attained ecstatic realization of the divine at-one-ment, here symbolized by the One Mind. At the age of 39 he followed in the wake of the army of the Roman Emperor Gordian III in the expedition against Persia, and came into direct contact with Persian and Hindu *gurus*. We have, therefore, made Plotinus our chief occidental witness to the Truth expounded in this Mahāyāna text. In essentials, the Platonic philosophy, which Plotinus greatly enriched, is an efflorescence in the Occident of the more ancient Brāhmanical philosophy; and this accounts for the remarkable parallelisms, set forth in annotations, between the two Schools.

The whole *Sangsāra* and *Nirvāṇa*, as an inseparable unity, are one's mind.[1]

[THE GREAT SELF-LIBERATION]

Owing to worldly beliefs, which he is free to accept or reject, man wanders in the *Sangsara*.[2]

Therefore, practising the *Dharma*, freed from every attachment, grasp the whole essence of these teachings expounded in this Yoga of Self-Liberation by Knowing the Mind in its Real Nature.

The truths set forth herein are known as 'The Great Self-Liberation'; and in them culminates the Doctrine of the Great Ultimate Perfection.[3]

[1] This aphorism expounds most succinctly the ultimate teaching of the Mahāyāna. To comprehend it intellectually, a thorough understanding of the doctrine of the Voidness, the *Shūnyatā*, is necessary. (In our General Introduction, pp. 1–4, the doctrine has been set forth at some length.) The One Mind being the Cause of All Causes, the Ultimate Reality, every other aspect of the Whole, visible and invisible, and all states or conditions of consciousness, are inseparably parts of the One Mind. Every duality, even the Final Duality, the *Sangsāra* and *Nirvāṇa*, is, in the last analysis, found to be a unity. Therefore, both pluralism, or the belief that the Cosmos is primordially and eternally a plurality rather than a unity, and dualism, or the belief that all things conceivable are divided into indissoluble dualities, are untrue.

[2] Many of human kind believe in animism, in a 'soul', as being a principle of personal consciousness separately existing, apart from all other 'souls', eternally. Some animists believe that such a 'soul' repeatedly incarnates. Others hold that it dwells in a fleshly body on Earth only once prior to its final reincarnation at the time of a general resurrection and judgement of the dead, and thereafter for an endless eternity continues to exist as a personal entity either in a *sangsāric* state of sensuous blissfulness or in a *sangsāric* state of suffering of the most terrible character humanly imaginable. Again, there are vast multitudes who maintain that no part or principle of man survives death; and such as these, not having developed by *yogic* training that intuitive insight innately common to all men, are spiritually asleep and fettered by Ignorance (Skt. *Avidyā*). Inasmuch as all beliefs of this character fetter man to the *Sangsāra*, he is, so long as he remains unawakened to Truth, chained Prometheus-like to the Wheel of Life. Ignorance of human law cannot be used as a plea to escape the law's penalty; and ignorance of the Law of Truth (Skt. *Dharma*) causes man to suffer interminably, or until he breaks his fetters and claims his birthright to Freedom.

[3] Text: *Rdzogs-pa ch'en-po* (pron. *Dzog-pa ch'en-po*) = *Rdzog-ch'en*, 'Most Perfect', or 'Most Complete', or 'Great Ultimate Perfection', with reference to the chief doctrine known as the Great Perfection of the Nyingma School founded by Padma-Sambhava. In this doctrine, of which our present

[*THE* GURU'S *THIRD CHARGE TO THE DISCIPLES*]

Samayā; gya, gya, gya.

[*THE NATURE OF MIND*]

That which is commonly called mind is of intuitive[1] Wisdom.

Although the One Mind is, it has no existence.[2]

Being the source of all the bliss of *Nirvāṇa* and of all the sorrow of the *Sangsāra*, it is cherished like the Eleven *Yānas*.[3]

[*THE NAMES GIVEN TO THE MIND*]

The various names given to it are innumerable.

Some call it 'The Mental Self'.[4]

Certain heretics[5] call it 'The Ego'.[6]

treatise is the quintessence, all doctrines reach their culmination, or fruition, which is emancipation from *sangsāric*, or conditioned, existence and the attainment of the non-conditioned supra-*sangsāric* state of *Nirvāṇa*.

[1] Or literally, 'quick-knowing'. Intuitive Wisdom is known to the Mahā-yāna as *Prajñā*, the awakening of which, by practice of meditation, in relation to the doctrine of Enlightenment, is the aim of Zen Buddhism. As taught in the *Saddharma-Pundarika*, the *Dharma*, 'the true law understood by the Tathāgata, cannot be reasoned, is beyond the pale of reasoning'. Cf. D. T. Zuzuki, *Essays in Zen Buddhism* (New York, 1949), p. 71.

[2] Or, 'it has no existence [*sangsārically*]', that is to say, 'it has no conditioned existence'. As Plotinus teaches, 'above existence, therefore, is the One' (v. i. 10).

[3] Text: *Theg-pa bchu-gchig* (pron. *Theg-pa chu-chig*), 'Eleven *Yānas* (or Paths)', with reference to eleven schools of Buddhist philosophy or doctrine, of which the Mahā-Yāna and Hīna-Yāna are the two chief primary divisions. There is also a threefold primary division: (1) the Hīna-Yāna, or Shravaka-Yāna; (2) the Pratyeka-Buddha-Yāna, or Pradecika-Yāna; and (3) the Bodhisattva-Yāna, which is the Mahā-Yāna or Eka-Yāna. Then, again, the Mahā-Yāna has been sub-divided into the Mantra-Yāna and the Vajra-Yāna, which expound an esoteric Buddhism. The Mantra-Yāna is itself divided into the Hetu-Yāna, based on the Doctrine of Cause (Skt. *Hetu*) and the Phala-Yāna, based on the Doctrine of Effect (Skt. *Phala*); and each of these Schools is sub-divided into four, as illustrated by the Great Perfection sect of the Nyingma School of Padma-Sambhava. (Cf. S. C. Dās, op. cit., pp. 585–7.) Taking, with some uncertainty, the ten sub-divisions of the Mahā-Yāna here enumerated together with the Hīna-Yāna as a whole, we arrive at the Eleven *Yānas* of our text.

[4] Text: *sems-nyid* (pron. *sem-nyi*), literally, 'mind-self', or 'mental self'.

[5] According to the Mahāyāna, heresy, or the holding of wrong views concerning Truth, is of two sorts: (1) denial of reincarnation, denial that charity,

[6] See p. 209.

By the Hīnayānists it is called 'The Essentiality of Doctrines'.[1]

By the Yogāchāra[2] it is called 'Wisdom'.[3]

Some call it 'The Means of Attaining the Other Shore of Wisdom'.[4]

Some call it 'The Buddha Essence'.[5]

Some call it 'The Great Symbol'.[6]

Some call it 'The Sole Seed'.[7]

Some call it 'The Potentiality of Truth'.[8]

Some call it 'The All-Foundation'.[9]

Other names, in ordinary language, are also given to it.

self-sacrifice, and righteousness produce good *karma*, and denial both of unrighteousness and of Divine Wisdom; (2) the assertion that happiness and misery are arbitrarily allotted to human beings by a deity rather than as a direct result of the individual's past deeds, and that all things are either permanent or real, and that there is no *Nirvāṇic* Reality as their root or essentiality.

[6] Text: *bdag* (pron. *dag*), 'self', 'ego', 'I': Skt. *ātman*.

[1] Text: *gdams-ngag gdams-ngag* (pron. *dam-ngag dam-ngag*), literally 'precept (or religious teaching) precept', or 'precept of precepts', i.e. essentiality of doctrines (or teachings).

[2] The Yogāchāra is a system of Mahāyāna metaphysics, based on *yoga*, and developed by Āryasangha.

[3] Text: *sems* (pron. *sem*), 'mind', 'consciousness', 'Wisdom', &c.

[4] Text: *Shes-rab pha-rol phyin-pa* (pron. *Shay-rab pha-rol chin-pa*) = the short form, *Sher-phyin* (pron. *sher-chin*): Skt. *Prajñā-Pāramitā*, 'Divine Wisdom', known to Tibetan Buddhists as 'the means of arriving at the Other Shore of Wisdom'. It is also referred to as 'the Ship of Salvation', or 'the Vessel which conducts man to *Nirvāṇa* (or the Other Shore)'.

[5] Text: *Bde-gshegs snyings-po* (pron. *De-sheg nying po*), 'Sugatas' (i.e. Buddhas') Essence'.

[6] Text: *Phyag-rgya Ch'en-po* (pron. *Chag-gya Chen-po*): Skt. *Mahā-Mudrā*, 'Great Hand-Gesture', or 'Great Symbol'. The technical *yogic* meaning of *Mahā-Mudrā* is *Anuttara*, the highest and final doctrine. *Mahā-Mudrā*, the method of practically applying the *Dharma*, is also known as *Dharma Karma*. *Phyag* refers to knowledge of the Shūnyatā, or Voidness, and *rgya* conveys the meaning of liberation from worldliness; and *Ch'en-po* signifies the at-one-ment of these two all-important teachings. (Cf. S. C. Dās, op. cit., p. 831.) The *Yoga* of the Great Symbol is set forth in detail in *Tibetan Yoga and Secret Doctrines* (pp. 115–54).

[7] Text: *Thig-lé nyag-gchig* (pron. *Thig-lé nyag-chig*), 'Sole (or Unique) Seed'. *Thig-lé* = Skt. *Bindu*, 'Seed', 'Point', &c.

[8] Text: *Chös-kyi-dvyings* (pro. *Chö-kyi-ing*): Skt. *Dharma-Dhātu*, 'Seed (or Potentiality) of Truth', equivalent to the *Dharma-Kāya*, the Shape (which is Shapelessness) of the Divine Body of Truth regarded as the all-pervading Voidness. (See *The Tibetan Book of the Dead*, pp. 10–15.)

[9] Text: *Kun-gzhi* (pron. *Kun-zhi*), 'All-Foundation'.

[PART II. THE PRACTICAL APPLICATION]
[*THE TIMELESSNESS OF MIND*]

If one knows how to apply in a threefold manner[1] this knowing of the mind, all past knowledge lost to memory becomes perfectly clear, and also knowledge of the future, thought of as unborn and unconceived.

In the present, when the mind remains as it is naturally,[2] it is ordinarily comprehended by its own time.[3]

[1] It is customary among Tibetan Buddhist *gurus* to assign to all things a threefold aspect. The Cosmos itself is divided into the Three Regions; the Voidness, into the Three Voids; the Buddha Essence is manifested in the Three Divine Bodies; the chief perfections are threefold, namely, of the body, speech, and mind; there are three principal psychic centres, namely, of the brain, of the throat, and of the heart. Doctrines themselves are threefold, those of the two extremes and those of the Middle Path. Accordingly, this *Yoga* of Knowing the Mind is to be applied in a threefold manner to the end that the *yogin* may, like the Buddhas, become a Master of Everything—of the Three Regions, of the Three Divine Bodies, of the Three Perfections, of the Three Psychic Centres, and of all doctrines. To the one who thus attains understanding of his or her own limited *sangsāric* and illusory self, the 'soul' of animists, and correlatively realizes the True Essence of Mind, which is 'soul'-less and impersonal, there is no past and future, but only timelessness, as the next aphorism sets forth.

[2] Mind *per se*, in its true or natural state, is unmodified, primordial quiescence. By virtue of successful application of such *yogic* practices as are expounded in the text of the Great Symbol, in *Tibetan Yoga and Secret Doctrines* (Book II), the current of the thought-process, born of *sangsāric* existence, is inhibited and the True State realized. Then, there being no longer past or future, mind *per se* is comprehended by its own time, which is timelessness. As the great Buddhist Patriarch Ashvaghosha taught, during the first century A.D., 'While the essence of mind is eternally clean and pure, the influence of ignorance makes possible the existence of a defiled mind. But in spite of the defiled mind the mind [*per se*] is eternal, clear, pure, and not subject to transformation. Further, as its original nature is free from particularization, it knows in itself no change whatever, though it produces everywhere the various modes of existence. When the one-ness of the totality of things (*dharmadhātu*) is not recognized, then ignorance as well as particularization arises, and all phases of the defiled mind are thus developed. But the significance of this doctrine is so extremely deep and unfathomable that it can be fully comprehended by Buddhas and by no others.' (Cf. Prof. Suzuki's translation of Ashvaghosha's *The Awakening of Faith*, Chicago, 1900, pp. 79–80.)

[3] The sense here may be brought out by making comparison with the well-known aphorism in Milton's *Paradise Lost* (I. 254–5):

> The mind is its own place, and in itself
> Can make a Heaven of Hell, a Hell of Heaven.

Paraphrasing Milton, one may say that the mind is its own time, and of itself can make the past the present and the future the present. In other

[MIND IN ITS TRUE STATE]

When one seeks one's mind in its true state, it is found
to be quite intelligible, although invisible.

In its true state, mind is naked, immaculate; not made of
anything, being of the Voidness; clear, vacuous, without
duality, transparent; timeless, uncompounded, unimpeded,
colourless; not realizable as a separate thing, but as the
unity of all things, yet not composed of them; of one taste,[1]
and transcendent over differentiation.[2]

words, mind, in its pure, primordial, unmodified, natural condition, is
transcendent over what *sangsāric* man calls time. As implied above, in the
aphorisms that the One Mind embraces the whole *Sangsāra* and *Nirvāṇa*
and all other dualities, mind *per se* also transcends space. For, as the
Mahāyāna teaches, space is merely a mode of particularization. Therefore,
space *per se* has no existence any more than has time *per se*, it being impossible to think of space apart from the variety of things illusorily existing in
space. In this sense, then, space and objects of space are merely another
dualism. Time *per se* being timelessness, space *per se* is spacelessness. Neither
time nor space, *sangsārically* conceived, exists apart from relationship to the
sangsāric particularizing consciousness; and thus both have only a relative,
not an absolute existence.

Mind, being in its abstract or potential condition non-*sangsāric*, has innate
power (while it 'remains as it is naturally', that is, in its unmodified, or
primordially *Nirvāṇic*, true state) to view, by its own standard of timelessness, the past, the present, and the future as an inseparable homogeneous
unity. And this *yogic* power can be made operative in this world or in any
region of the *Sangsāra* by the devotee who masters the *yoga* herein expounded. In this connexion, reference may very profitably be made to *An
Experiment with Time* and *The Serial Universe*, by J. W. Dunne.

The One Mind, as Eternity, is the eternal present, but is neither past nor
future. Time, as Plotinus teaches, is the measure of movement. In its
naturalness, the One Mind, as the Quiescent, is the Immutable, the Motionless. Time begins with motion, with the initiation of thought; when the
mind attains the transcendent at-one-ment, by concentration upon unity,
and the thought-process is inhibited, simultaneously with the cessation of
thought, time ceases, and there is only timelessness.

[1] The expression, 'of one taste', occurs throughout Buddhist literature
to indicate, as here, homogeneity, undifferentiated at-one-ment, qualityless
or supramundane unity. The Buddha frequently uses it in this sense when
speaking of the single purpose of the Doctrine, which is to lead mankind to
Freedom, to *Nirvāṇa*. Even as the Great Waters are of one taste, the taste
of salt, so the One Mind is really One, and incapable of being divided, or of
being differentiated from any of the microcosmic aspects of the Thatness,
the Ultimate Reality.

[2] In similar language, Plotinus teaches that the One, 'possessing no
[geometrical] magnitude, is indivisible in its power. . . . We must also
insist that the One is infinite, not as would be a mass of a magnitude which

Nor is one's own mind separable from other minds.

To realize the quintessential being of the One Mind is to realize the immutable at-one-ment of the *Tri-Kāya*.

The mind, being, as the Uncreated and of the Voidness, the *Dharma-Kāya*, and, as the Vacuous and Self-Radiant, the *Sambhoga-Kāya*, and, as the Unobscured, shining for all living creatures, the *Nirmāṇa-Kāya*, is the Primordial Essence wherein its Three Divine Aspects are One.[1]

If the *yogic* application of this Wisdom be thorough, one will comprehend that which has just been set forth above.

[*MIND IS NON-CREATED*]

Mind in its true nature being non-created and self-radiant, how can one, without knowing the mind, assert that mind is created?

There being in this *yoga* nothing objective upon which to meditate, how can one, without having ascertained the true nature of mind by meditation, assert that mind is created?

Mind in its true state being Reality, how can one, without having discovered one's own mind, assert that mind is created?[2]

could be examined serially, but by the incommensurability of its power. Even though it be conceived as being of intelligence or divinity, it is still higher. If it be thought of as being the most perfect unity, it is still higher. Shouldst thou form for thyself an idea of a divinity by rising to what in thy comprehension is most unitary [the One is still simpler]; for it dwelleth within thee, and containeth nothing which is dependent' (VI. ix. 6).

[1] Plotinus's doctrine of the ultimate Unity parallels this doctrine of the At-one-ment of the *Tri-Kāya*: 'Inasmuch as Unity is the nature that begetteth all things, Unity cannot be any of them. It is, therefore, neither any particular thing, nor quantity, nor quality, nor intelligence, nor soul, nor what is movable, nor what is stable; nor doth it partake of place or time. But it is the uniform in itself, or rather it is the formless; for it is above all form, movement, and stability' (VI. ix. 3). 'The One cannot be enumerated along with anything, nor even with uniqueness, nor with aught else. The One cannot be enumerated in any way because It is measure without itself being measured' (V. v. 4).

[2] In the True State, the State of Reality, mind and matter in their *sangsāric*, or mundane, or temporally illusory aspects are inseparably one. Ashvaghosha teaches, 'there is no distinction between mind and matter; it is on account of the finite in the round of life and death that these distinctions appear [*sangsārically*]'. Eternally all things 'are neither mind nor matter, neither infinite wisdom nor finite knowledge, neither existing nor

Mind in its true state being undoubtedly ever-existing, how can one, without having seen the mind face to face, assert that mind is created?[1]

The thinking-principle being of the very essence of mind, how can one, without having sought and found it, assert that mind is created?

Mind being transcendent over creation, and thus partaking of the Uncreated, how can one assert that mind is created?

Mind being in its primordial, unmodified naturalness non-created,[2] as it should be taken to be, and without form, how can one assert that it is created?

Inasmuch as mind can also be taken to be devoid of quality, how can one venture to assert that it is created?[3]

non-existing, but are after all inexpressible'. Although words must be employed to convey thought, so that mankind may be led to discover Reality for themselves, 'the best human thought of all things is only temporary and is not Truth Absolute'. (Cf. Ashvaghosha's *Awakening of Faith*, as translated by the late Rev. Timothy Richard, Shanghai, 1907, pp. 26–28.) It is only quite recently that occidental scientists have discovered, as the Sages of the Mahāyāna did very many centuries ago, that matter, formerly believed by a now obsolete materialism to be inert, is, as indicated by the electronic character of the atom, the very quintessence of energy. Moreover, Western Science is beginning to suspect that the Universe is wholly a mental phenomenon; or, as the Wise Men of the East teach, that it is the product of One Cosmic Mind; or, in a theological sense, that it is the Thought of an Incommensurable Intelligence.

[1] Mind or consciousness in its true state being Reality, and ever-existing, is of the Uncreated; and, being uncreated, is primary in Nature. Accordingly, matter is derived from mind or consciousness, and not mind or consciousness from matter.

[2] Literally rendered, this passage would read, 'Mind being in its own place [i.e. in its primordial, unmodified naturalness] non-created'. This is one more illustration of the desirability of departing from a strictly literal rendering.

[3] Although the mind, in its mundane aspect, is the root of all quality, in its natural or true state of primordial non-createdness it is *per se* devoid of all quality and thus beyond the realm of predication. Being undifferentiated voidness, vacuity, or *no thing*, it transcends *sangsāric* attributes. As Ashvaghosha teaches, all phenomena throughout the *Sangsāra* are mind-made. 'Without mind, then, there is practically no objective existence. Thus all existence arises from imperfect notions in our mind. All differences are differences of the mind. But the mind cannot see itself, for it has no form. We should know that all phenomena are created by the imperfect notions in the finite mind; therefore all existence is like a reflection in a mirror, without substance, only a phantom of the mind. When the finite mind acts, then all kinds of things arise; when the finite mind ceases to act, then all kinds of things cease.' (Cf. Ashvaghosha's, *The Awakening of Faith*,

The self-born, qualityless mind, being like the Three Voids[1] undifferentiated, unmodified, how can one assert that mind is created?

Mind being without objectivity and causation, self-originated, self-born, how can one, without having endeavoured to know mind, assert that mind is created?

Inasmuch as Divine Wisdom dawns in accordance with its own time,[2] and one is emancipated, how can opponents of these teachings assert that it is created?

Mind being, as it is, of this nature, and thus unknowable,[3] how can one assert that it is created?

[*THE* YOGA *OF INTROSPECTION*]

The One Mind being verily of the Voidness and without any foundation, one's mind is, likewise, as vacuous as the

Richard's translation, p. 26.) The object of our present *yoga* is to arrive at that right understanding of mind which is attainable only when the finite activities, the thought-processes, of the mundane mind are stilled. Then the world of objectivity vanishes. When an electric current is cut off, the external or visible manifestation of electricity as kinetic energy ceases and no longer exists; there is then only electricity *per se* in its natural or unmodified state of potentiality. To know mind, one must know it in its true state.

[1] Apart from its threefold aspect, the Voidness is further divided by the *lāmas* into eighteen degrees, which may be extended to seventy. (Cf. L. A. Waddell, op. cit., pp. 125–6.)

[2] The Divine Wisdom, or the *yogic* knowing of mind, is attained in the true state of timelessness, which is the mind's or Divine Wisdom's own time. The One Mind, not having had an origin at any time, will not have an ending at any time; being really eternal, it cannot be known or conceived in terms of time.

[3] Mind in its finite or mundane aspect cannot know mind in its infinite, supramundane aspect. By virtue of *yogic* discipline the finite mind is purged of Ignorance (Skt. *Avidyā*). 'As Ignorance is thus annihilated, the mind [i.e. the *ālaya vijñāna*] is no more disturbed so as to be subject to individuation. As the mind is no more disturbed, the particularization of the surrounding world is annihilated. When in this wise the principle and the condition of defilement, their products, and the mental disturbances are all annihilated, it is said that we attain to *Nirvāṇa* and that various spontaneous displays of activity are accomplished.' (Ashvaghosha's *The Awakening of Faith*, Suzuki's translation, op. cit., pp. 86–87.) The same passage in Richard's rendering (op. cit., p. 17), is as follows: 'As Ignorance disappears, then false ideas cease to arise. As these false ideas do not arise, the former objective world also ends. As the forces cease to exist, then the false powers of the finite mind cease to exist, and this [state] is called *Nirvāṇa*, when the natural forces of the True Reality alone work.' These passages suggest the *yogic* process of transmuting the finite aspect of mind into the infinite, supramundane aspect.

sky.[1] To know whether this be so or not, look within thine own mind.

Being of the Voidness, and thus not to be conceived as having beginning or ending, Self-Born Wisdom has in reality been shining forever, like the Sun's essentiality,[2] itself unborn. To known whether this be so or not, look within thine own mind.

Divine Wisdom is undoubtedly indestructible, unbreakable, like the ever-flowing current of a river. To know whether this be so or not, look within thine own mind.

Being merely a flux of instability like the air of the firmament, objective appearances are without power to fascinate and fetter.[3] To know whether this be so or not, look within thine own mind.[4]

All appearances are verily one's own concepts, self-conceived in the mind, like reflections seen in a mirror.[5] To

---

[1] The finite aspect of mind being a microcosmic reflex of the One Mind, and, in the last analysis, inseparable from the One Mind, it partakes of its vacuous and foundationless nature. Only in the highest trance state of *samādhi*, or divine at-one-ment, is the truth of this realizable; it cannot be demonstrated intellectually, in the state in which mundane mind acts. This *yoga* is the *yoga* of introspection.

[2] Text: *snying-po* (pron. *nying-po*), pith, heart, essence, or essentiality, with reference to the secret essence of the Sun as known to the occult sciences, and thus suggestive of doctrines concerning the Sun *per se*, which, like the Mind *per se*, is of the Unborn, Unshaped, Unmodified Thatness, synonymous with the Voidness.

[3] As a result of successful practice of the *yoga* of knowing the mind in its true state, the *yogin*, having realized the wholly illusory and unsatisfactory nature of all mundane things, is no longer fettered by them. Mechanical gadgets, bodily luxuries, fashionable clothing, worldly conventionalities, the pomp and circumstance of men, even the intellectualisms of the world, have lost their hypnotic power to fascinate and fetter him, as they still do the ignorant multitudes, who, like long-immured prisoners rejoicing in their bondage, consider themselves 'progressive' and the *yogin* an unpractical visionary, and desire not Freedom.

[4] Again Plotinus's teaching is parallel: 'We must advance into the sanctuary, penetrating into it, if we have the strength to do so, closing our eyes to the spectacle of terrestrial things. . . . Whoever would let himself be misled by the pursuit of those vain shadows, mistaking them for realities, would grasp only an image as fugitive as the fluctuating form reflected by the waters, and would resemble that foolish youth [the ravishingly beautiful Narcissus] who, wishing to grasp that image of himself [seen in a stream], according to the fable, disappeared, carried away by the current' (I. vi. 8).

[5] Ashvaghosha and many other of the expounders of the esotericism of the Mahāyāna employ this simile of images seen reflected in a mirror to

known whether this be so or not, look within thine own mind.

Arising of themselves and being naturally free like the clouds in the sky, all external appearances verily fade away into their own respective places.[1] To know whether this be so or not, look within thine own mind.

[*THE* DHARMA *WITHIN*]

The *Dharma*[2] being nowhere save in the mind, there is no other place of meditation than the mind.

explain, as far as it is possible to do so in words, the unreality of all phenomenal appearances, the sum total of which constitutes the *Sangsāra*. Similarly, occidental science has arrived at the assumption that the true essence of things is not visible phenomena, but invisible noumena. The abstract and the potential manifest themselves as the concrete and kinetic. Behind the abstract and potential there is what Plato has called the realm of Ideas, and what the Mahāyānists call the One Mind, the homogeneous at-one-ment of all things conceivable, abstractly or concretely, potentially or kinetically, the undifferentiated, unpredicable *Shūnyatā*, or Voidness. 'The True Reality is originally only one, but the degrees of Ignorance are infinite. . . . There are unruly thoughts more numerous than the grains of sand of the Ganges, some arising from ignorant conceptions and others arising from ignorance of senses and desires. Thus all kinds of wild thoughts arise from Ignorance ; and have, first and last, infinite differences, which the Tathāgata alone knows.' (Cf. Ashvaghosha's *The Awakening of Faith*, Richard's translation, op. cit., p. 18, upon which our version is based.)

[1] This philosophical assertion is in amplification of the last. The comparing of the arising and passing away of appearances, born of unruly mental concepts, to that of clouds is very apt. As has been already suggested in our annotations and introductions, when the darkness of Ignorance is dissipated by the light of Divine Wisdom, all appearances vanish as does the fog of the night after the Sun has risen. It is the false concept in the mundane mind that the world is real which gives to the world its illusory aspect of being real. When this concept is transcended by realization of the true nature of mind, and the at-one-ment of the microcosmic mind with the Macrocosmic Mind is attained, the Universe and all apparent things of the phenomenal realm of the *Sangsāra* vanish, and there is only undifferentiated, primordial Vacuity, which is the natural, or native, place of every thing and of every appearance. And here, again, the testimony from realization by the recently deceased Sage of Tiruvannamalai, Sri Ramana Mahārshi, parallels this of the Great *Guru*: 'After all, the world is merely an idea or thought. When the mind ceases to think, the world vanishes, and there is bliss indescribable. When the mind begins to think, immediately the world reappears and there is suffering.' (Cf. *Who Am I?* p. 12.)

[2] According to the Mahāyāna, the *Dharma*, the Law of Being, the Truth, the Divine Wisdom, the Guide to the Science and Art of Living, is in its true nature the unpredicable Voidness.

The *Dharma* being nowhere save in the mind, there is no other doctrine to be taught or practised elsewhere.

The *Dharma* being nowhere save in the mind, there is no other place of truth for the observance of a vow.

The *Dharma* being nowhere save in the mind, there is no *Dharma* elsewhere whereby Liberation may be attained.

Again and again look within thine own mind.[1]

[1] Herein is set forth in a Buddhistic manner the ancient aphorism which Christianity, too, adopted and expressed: 'And the light shineth in darkness; and the darkness comprehended it not. . . . That was the true Light, which lighteth every man that cometh into the world.' St. John, i. 5, 9.

To serve as a Gnostic commentary to this '*Yoga* of Knowing the Mind', there is here added the following excerpts from a translation made by the late G. R. S. Mead of the original Greek of the Proem of the Gospel of St. John, and contained in *The Gnostic John the Baptizer* (published by John M. Watkins, London, 1924), pp. 123–6:

1. In the Beginning was Mind; and Mind was with God.
2. So Mind was God. This was in Beginning with God.
3. All kept coming into existence through it; and apart from it came into existence not a single [thing].
4. What hath come into existence in it was Life; and Life was the Light of the [true] Men.
5. And the Light shineth in the Darkness; and the Darkness did not emprison it. . . .
6. It was the True Light, which enlighteneth every Man who cometh into the world.
7. It was in the world; and the world kept coming into existence through it.
8. And the world did not know it. It came unto its own; and its own did not receive it.
9. And as many as received it, to them it gave power to become children of God,—
10. To those who have faith in his name,—Who was brought to birth, not out of [blending of] bloods,
11. Nor of urge of flesh, nor urge of a male,—but out of God.
12. So Mind became flesh and tabernacled in us,—
13. And we beheld its glory,—glory as of [? an] only-begotten Father,— full of Delight and Truth.

The following comments are made: To verse 4, 'The true Men who have the Light of Life are the Prophets and Perfect'. To verse 5, 'emprison' may otherwise be rendered, 'hold back', 'detain'. Between verses 5 and 6 comes a paragraph which 'seems clearly to be an interpolation into, or overwork-ing of, his original "source" by the writer, or perhaps part-compiler, of the fourth gospel': 'There was a Man sent by God,—his name Yōánes. This [Man] came for bearing witness, that he might bear witness about the Light, in order that all [men] might have faith through it. That [Man] was not the Light, but [came] in order that he might bear witness about the Light.' To verse 6, 'Man' is equivalent to 'Prophet' or 'Divine Messenger'. Verse 10,

When looking outwards into the vacuity of space,[1] there is no place to be found where the mind is shining.[2]

When looking inwards into one's own mind in search of the shining, there is to be found no thing that shines.

One's own mind is transparent, without quality.[3]

Being of the Clear Light of the Voidness, one's own mind is of the *Dharma-Kaya*; and, being void of quality, it is comparable to a cloudless sky.

It is not a multiplicity, and is omniscient.

Very great, indeed, is the difference between knowing and not knowing the import of these teachings.

[*THE WONDROUSNESS OF THESE TEACHINGS*]

This self-originated Clear Light, eternally unborn,[4] is a parentless babe of Wisdom. Wondrous is this.

Being non-created, it is Natural Wisdom.[5] Wondrous is this.

'his name' refers to the 'Mystic Name', or 'Mind', or 'Primality of Great Life'.

The translator of these verses of St. John's Gospel was a modern follower of the Gnosis, and England's outstanding scholar in the field of Gnosticism; and the Editor claimed him as a friend. The authorized version contained in the New Testament was made by men who considered Gnosticism 'heretical'. Owing to their anti-Gnostic bias, they failed to translate the Greek text in such manner as to bring out in English the real sense of the original, which is one of the few fragments in the present-day canon of exoteric Christianity that escaped the iconoclastic zeal of those who anathematized the Gnostics and destroyed all the invaluable manuscripts of esoteric Christianity they could lay hands on. Fortunately, a few manuscripts escaped; and among them are the *Bruce Codex*, now carefully treasured in the Bodleian Library, Oxford, and the *Berlin Codex*, in Berlin.

[1] This reference to the vacuity of space is to be taken figuratively only; for space, although apparently vacuous in the eyes of men, is actually the pleroma, or fullness, of all things, and the womb whence they come forth from latency, or abstractness, into the concrete, visible Universe.

[2] That Light, innate in every living thing, shines neither in nor from any place, for it is transcendent over place (or spatial differentiation), as over time; it shines only in the secret sanctuary of the aspirant's heart. Nor is there, as the next aphorism teaches, any *thing* that shines.

[3] This passage may be otherwise rendered: 'One's own mind is transparent, colourless (i.e. without *sangsāric* characteristics).

[4] All things which are born, or come into existence, being *sangsāric*, are transitory, illusory, unreal. Only the Thatness, transcendent over form, birth, being, existence, is non-*sangsāric*.

[5] Likewise, the Real, the True, the Thatness, knows no shaping, limitation

Not having known birth, it knows not death.[1] Wondrous is this.

Although it is Total Reality, there is no perceiver of it.[2] Wondrous is this.

Although wandering in the *Sangsāra*, it remains undefiled by evil. Wondrous is this.

Although seeing the Buddha, it remains unallied to good.[3] Wondrous is this.

Although possessed by all beings, it is not recognized.[4] Wondrous is this.

Those not knowing the fruit of this *yoga* seek other fruit.[5] Wondrous is this.

conditionality, creation. As the Unconditioned or Non-Created, Mind or Wisdom is simple, primordial, natural, but not of Nature, being non-*sangsāric* and beyond Nature. That which can be generated, formed, created, can also be dissipated, dispersed, destroyed; only that which is beyond generation, form, and creation, can be transcendent over them. Thus the Thatness, or Natural Wisdom, being superior to existence, is the Non-Existent At-one-ment of All Existences.

[1] Whatever manifests itself in time, or comes into *sangsāric* existence through being shaped or born, must inevitably go out of manifestation in time, or, in other words, suffer dissolution and death. The Real, the That-ness, must therefore be transcendent over both birth and death, as over all other dualities.

[2] There can be no percipient of Reality, for percipiency implies a doctrine of 'soul', or of an eternally individualized *sangsāric* entity. The One Mind cannot see itself, for it is not a self, or a thing, or an object of perception; it can only know that it is. Its nature is to know, not to be known.

[3] These two aphorisms express the doctrine that good and evil are merely a pair of *sangsāric* opposites, a duality, which, like all dualities, is in at-one-ment in the True State. (See General Introduction, pp. 35–57, where the theory of good and evil is discussed.)

[4] In the words of Plotinus, 'The One is not separated from other things, nor is It in them: there is nothing that possesseth the One; on the contrary, it is the One that possesseth all' (v. v. 9).

[5] 'Fruit' (Text: *ḥbras-bu*; pron. *dra-bu*) in this context, as elsewhere throughout this treatise, is a technical term, implying the *yogic* result of the successful application of this *yoga* concerning the knowing of mind. Being ignorant of the wondrous fruit thus obtainable, the unenlightened seek elsewhere than within themselves for spiritual guidance, as the next aphorism indicates. Sarat Chandra Dās (*Tibetan–English Dictionary*, Calcutta, 1902, p. 929) defines *ḥbras-bu* as being the fruit or reward resulting from passing successively through the three stages of ascetic meditation, and as the results of *karma*. There are four distinguishable 'fruits' of progressive perfection: (1) the ability to enter the stream of progressive perfection, which conveys one from *sangsāric* Ignorance to *Nirvānic* Wisdom; (2) the exhaustion of all *karmic* need of rebirth save the final rebirth in this

Although the Clear Light of Reality shines within one's own mind, the multitude look for it elsewhere. Wondrous is this.

[THE FOURFOLD GREAT PATH]

All hail to this Wisdom here set forth, concerning the invisible, immaculate Mind!

This teaching is the most excellent of teachings.

This meditation, devoid of mental concentration, all-embracing, free from every imperfection, is the most excellent of meditations.

This practice concerning the Uncreated State, when rightly comprehended, is the most excellent of practices.

This fruit of the *yoga* of the Eternally Unsought, naturally produced, is the most excellent of fruits.

Herewith we have accurately revealed the Fourfold Great Path.[1]

This teaching without error, this Great Path, is of the Clear Wisdom here set forth, which, being clear and unerring, is called the Path.

This meditation upon this unerring Great Path, is of the Clear Wisdom here set forth, which, being clear and unerring, is called the Path.

This practice relating to this unerring Great Path is of the Clear Wisdom here set forth, which, being clear and unerring, is called the Path.

The fruit of this unerring Great Path is of the Clear Wisdom here set forth, which, being clear and unerring, is called the Path.[2]

world, preparatory to entrance into *Nirvāṇa*; (3) the experiencing of this final birth; (4) the supramundane state of the *arhant*, or saint, who has conquered Ignorance. The Tibetan canonical *Kanjur* describes five classes of 'fruits', or results: (1) the 'fruit' born of mental, moral, and spiritual education; (2) a 'fruit' not consequent on what men call education; (3) the spiritual precedence attained by a *Pratyeka*, or Non-Teaching, Buddha; (4) the spiritual precedence of a *Bodhisattva*, a candidate for Buddhahood; (5) the final stage of omniscience to which a Buddha attains.

[1] Or the fourfold Mahāyāna. The four preceding aphorisms reveal the four parts of this Great Path of the 'Yoga of Knowing the Mind', which are (1) the actual teaching, (2) the actual meditation, (3) the actual practice, or practical application, and (4) the actual fruit, or result attained.

[2] These four aphorisms concern the four progressive stages in the 'Yoga

[THE GREAT LIGHT]

This *yoga* also concerns the foundation of the immutable Great Light.

The teaching of this changeless Great Light is of the unique Clear Wisdom here set forth, which, illuminating the Three Times,[1] is called 'The Light'.

The meditation upon this changeless Great Light is of the unique clear Wisdom here set forth, which, illuminating the Three Times, is called 'The Light'.

The practice relating to this changeless Great Light is of the unique Clear Wisdom, here set forth, which, illuminating the Three Times, is called 'The Light'.

The fruit of this changeless Great Light is of the unique Clear Wisdom here set forth, which, illuminating the Three Times, is called 'The Light'.[2]

---

of Knowing the Mind', which are common to all *yogas*. The teaching, or the sowing of the seed of Truth, is the first stage; the meditation, or the intellectual comprehension of the teaching, is the second; the practice, or the practical application of the teaching, is the third; and the fruit, or the harvest born of the seed sown by the teaching, watered by the meditation and cultivated by the practice, is the fourth. What appears to the occidental as redundancy of expression, or unnecessary repetition, in these and the aphorisms which immediately follow, appears to the oriental as poetical emphasis; and this literary style, which is typically oriental, is found in the scriptures of all Schools of Buddhism, being particularly characteristic of the Pāli Canon of the Southern School. In ancient times, when all sacred and *yogic* teachings were commonly conveyed orally, this repetitive style of expression was adopted in order to ameliorate, as it did, the task of memorizing the words of the Teachers. Then, in later times, when the teachings were committed to writing and crystallized into canons and orthodox treatises at the dictation of those in whose memory the teachings were preserved, the old repetitive style was retained unchanged. As an instance of the repetitive style in occidental religious literature, one may take the 'Hail Mary' of the Roman Catholic Church.

[1] This phrase may be otherwise rendered: 'being explanatory [or illuminative] of the Three Times'—which are the past, the present, and the future.

[2] This epitomized *yoga* of the Light consists of four stages of perfection in devotion: (1) the initial glimpsing of the Light (the Divine Wisdom concerning Reality); (2) the progressive increase in the perception of the Light; (3) the comprehension of the essentiality of the Light, or of Truth; (4) the power to prolong meditation indefinitely and so enter into *samādhi*.

[*THE DOCTRINE OF THE THREE TIMES*]

The essence of the doctrine concerning the Three Times in at-one-ment will now be expounded.

The *yoga* concerning past and future not being practised, memory of the past remains latent.[1]

The future, not being welcomed, is completely severed by the mind from the present.

The present, not being fixable, remains in the state of the Voidness.[2]

[*THE* YOGA *OF THE* NIRVĀṆIC *PATH*]

There being no thing upon which to meditate, no meditation is there whatsoever.

There being no thing to go astray, no going astray is there, if one be guided by memory.[3]

Without meditating, without going astray, look into the True State, wherein self-cognition, self-knowledge, self-illumination shine resplendently. These, so shining, are called 'The *Bodhisattvic* Mind'.[4]

---

[1] Or, literally, 'is relinquished'.

[2] As has been set forth above, on pp. 7–9, 210[3], mind, in its true nature, takes no cognizance of *sangsāric* time, and is, therefore, as timeless as it is conditionless. By not practising the *yoga* of introspection whereby, as in modern psycho-analysis, all memories of past experiences are recoverable when brought under the purview of the present, latent memories remain latent, the past remains separated from the present. By not welcoming the future, or by ignorantly regarding it as not being realizable in the present, it is hidden, or cut off, from the present. And the present, being *sangsārically* unstable, is perceived by man as a constant flux of instability, or as an ever-moving point separating past from future. The present, and its two companion *sangsāric* concepts, the past and the future, are, in the primordial, unmodified, non-created state of the Voidness, realized by the master of this *yoga* to be homogeneous, or undifferentiated timelessness. To realize time *per se* is to realize the unpredicable at-one-ment of the Three Times.

[3] For countless aeons the microcosmic mind has been wandering in the *Sangsāra* and experiencing existence. Therefore, if the memories of the past be recovered by successful application of the *yoga* of introspection, they will be found to constitute invaluable stores of Wisdom, born of experiences during other ages and lifetimes when one had entered upon and trodden the Path, and adequate to guide and prevent one from going astray now.

[4] 'The *Bodhisattvic* Mind' is a symbolic term signifying the supernormally enlightened mind of one who, being a candidate for the complete enlightenment of Buddhahood, had taken the vow of a *Bodhisattva* ('Enlightened

In the Realm of Wisdom, transcendent over all meditation, naturally illuminative, where there is no going astray, the vacuous concepts,[1] the self-liberation, and the primordial Voidness are of the *Dharma-Kāya*.

Without realization of this, the Goal of the *Nirvāṇic* Path is unattainable.

Simultaneously with its realization the *Vajra-Sattva* state is realized.[2]

These teachings are exhaustive of all knowledge,[3] exceedingly deep, and immeasurable.

Although they are to be contemplated in a variety of ways, to this Mind of self-cognition and self-originated Wisdom,

Being'), not to relinquish *sangsāric* existence, by entering into *Nirvāṇa*, until all Ignorance has been transmuted into Divine Wisdom. In language which is astonishingly similar, Plotinus teaches of this same Divine Illumination, which he himself realized and of which he thus has right to speak: 'When one shall see the divine resplendence of virtue within onself; when one shall dwell within oneself wholly; when one shall cease to meet within oneself any obstacle to unity; when nothing foreign any longer altereth, by its admixture, the simplicity of thine inner essence; when within thy whole being thou shall be a veritable light, immeasurable, uncircumscribed, unincreasable, infinite, and entirely incommensurable because transcendent over all measure and quantity; when thou shalt have become such, then, having become sight itself, thou mayst have confidence in thyself, for thou wilt no longer have need of a guide. Thereupon, thou must discern with great care, for only by means of the eye that will then open itself within thee shalt thou be able to perceive the Supreme Beauty. To obtain this vision of the beautiful and of the divineness within, one must begin by rendering oneself beautiful and divine' (I. vi. 9).

[1] All concepts, as our text later teaches, are in their essentiality vacuous. In the True State, as in the Platonic realm of ideas, concepts *per se* are devoid of form or *sangsāric* content. Being of the Voidness, they are, as the unshaped, unformed, non-created, the supra-*sangsāric* unpredicable seed of thought of the Supra-*sangsāric* Mind, whence they are sown throughout space to produce shaped, formed, *sangsāric* universes of illusory appearances.

[2] *Vajra-Sattva* ('Immutable Being'), the *Sambhoga-Kāya* reflex of Akṣhobhya, the Dhyānī Buddha presiding over the Eastern Realm of Pre-eminent Happiness, is a personification of vast esoteric significance in the Mahāyāna. (See *The Tibetan Book of the Dead*, pp. 9[n], 108–10.) Vajra-Sattva is sometimes conceived as being equivalent to the Ādi (or Primordial)-Buddha, and he then symbolizes the *Dharma-Kāya*. Accordingly, realization of this state, when He is in this aspect, is equivalent to the realization of Perfect Buddhahood, or *Nirvāṇa*.

[3] Text: *mthah-drug* (pron. *tha-trug*), literally, 'six directions', namely, the four cardinal points, the zenith and nadir; here taken in a figurative sense as implying completeness, or exhaustion, of all knowledge.

there are no two such things as contemplation and contemplator.

When exhaustively contemplated, these teachings merge in at-one-ment with the scholarly seeker who has sought them,[1] although the seeker himself when sought cannot be found.[2]

Thereupon is attained the goal of the seeking, and also the end of the search itself.

Then, nothing more is there to be sought; nor is there need to seek anything.

This beginningless, vacuous, unconfused Clear Wisdom of self-cognition is the very same as that set forth in the Doctrine of the Great Perfection.[3]

Although there are no two such things as knowing and not knowing, there are profound and innumerable sorts of meditation; and surpassingly excellent it is in the end to know one's mind.[4]

There being no two such things as object of meditation and meditator, if by those who practise or do not practise meditation the meditator of meditation be sought and not found, thereupon the goal of the meditation is reached and also the end of the meditation itself.

There being no two such things as meditation and object of meditation, there is no need to fall under the sway of deeply obscuring Ignorance; for, as the result of meditation upon

---

[1] Literally, 'these teachings seek the scholarly seeker who has sought them', in the sense of their seeking to become one, or in at-one-ment, with the *yogin*, within whose mind they, being Truth or *Dharma*, are innate, awaiting the hour when he shall call them forth to seek and sanctify and awaken him.

[2] This paradoxical phrase implies that the seeker *per se*, the mind in its natural state of the Voidness, has no individualized, personal existence; and that, therefore, the seeker himself, although sought, cannot be found.

[3] See p. 207[3], above.

[4] Here, as above, and again in the aphorisms which are to follow, the language is paradoxical, and should be interpreted in terms of the doctrine of the Voidness. The aphorisms of this section are constructed with reference to the three aspects of treading the Path: (1) meditation, or thorough intellectual comprehension of the teachings after having heard them; (2) practice, or practical application of the teachings; (3) realization, or attaining the fruits, or results, of the practice.

the unmodified quiescence of mind,[1] the non-created Wisdom instantaneously shines forth clearly.[2]

Although there is an innumerable variety of profound practices, to one's mind in its true state they are non-existent; for there are no two such things as existence and non-existence.[3]

There being no two such things as practice and practitioner, if by those who practise or do not practise the practitioner of practice be sought and not found, thereupon the goal of the practice is reached and also the end of the practice itself.

Inasmuch as from eternity there is nothing whatsoever to be practised, there is no need to fall under the sway of errant propensities.[4]

The non-created, self-radiant Wisdom here set forth, being actionless,[5] immaculate, transcendent over acceptance or rejection,[6] is itself the perfect practice.

[1] Mind in its natural state may be compared to a calm ocean, unruffled by the least breath of air. Mind in its reflex (or *sangsāric*) aspect may be likened to the same ocean ruffled into waves by wind, the wind being the thought-process, the waves the thoughts.

[2] As similarly expounded in *Tibetan Yoga and Secret Doctrines*, Book II, 'The *Nirvāṇic* Path', p. 119, when the thought-process has been *yogically* inhibited 'There will undoubtedly arise the Simultaneously-born State'.

[3] Inasmuch as 'existence and non-existence' are a duality, existence *per se* and non-existence *per se* are merely meaningless *sangsāric* concepts; and, therefore, cannot be applied either to the practices or to the unpredicable Mind, which, being of the Voidness, of the Thatness, is transcendent over both existence and non-existence. The Absolute Reality can be realized, but it cannot be described by use of words, for words are only symbols representing mundane, or *sangsāric*, concepts. As Ashvaghosha teaches, 'the best human thought of all things is only temporary and is not Truth Absolute'.—*The Awakening of Faith*, Richard's translation (op. cit., p. 28).

[4] As will be seen later, every term of mankind's *sangsārically* conceived languages employed in an effort to lead the neophyte to the discovery of Truth *per se* must be, in the final analysis, rejected. If accepted as being other than *sangsāric*, all dualistic terms, imperfect similes, metaphors and phrases, such as the *guru* must perforce employ in the transmission of these teachings, become the source of error and errant propensities, which fetter the disciple.

[5] Wisdom, or Mind in its native condition, being unmoved by the process of *sangsāric* thought, is the All-Quiescent, the Motionless, the Immutable, the Actionless.

[6] Truth transcends the duality of acceptance and rejection, and is forever unaffected by man's opinion. 'When men consider and realize that the Absolute Mind has no need of thoughts like men's, they will be following the right way to reach the Boundless.'—Ashvaghosha's *The Awakening of Faith*, Richard's translation (op. cit., p. 15).

Although there are no two such things as pure and impure, there is an innumerable variety of fruits of *yoga*, all of which, to one's mind in its True State, are the conscious content of the non-created *Tri-Kāya*.[1]

There being no two such things as action and performer of action, if one seeks the performer of action and no performer of action be found anywhere, thereupon the goal of all fruit-obtaining is reached and also the final consummation itself.

There being no other method whatsoever of obtaining the fruit, there is no need to fall under the sway of the dualities of accepting and rejecting, trusting and distrusting these teachings.

Realization of the self-radiant and self-born Wisdom, as the manifestation of the *Tri-Kāya* in the self-cognizing mind, is the very fruit of attaining the Perfect *Nirvāṇa*.[2]

[THE EXPLANATION OF THE NAMES GIVEN TO THIS WISDOM]

This Wisdom delivers one from the eternally transitory Eight Aims.[3]

[1] The *Tri-Kāya*, or Three Divine Bodies, are the three aspects through which the Buddha Essence, the Thatness, manifests Itself. All true *yogas*, when conscientiously practised, assist the *yogin*, in varying degrees, to attain the One Goal; and although their immediate fruits or results *sangsārically* appear to be differentiated, in the *Tri-Kāya*, which is of Truth itself, they are in undifferentiated at-one-ment, because they are its conscious content. Though the rays of the Sun are innumerable and of varying effects, according to environment, receptivity, and conditions of perception, they are of one source and, therefore, ultimately of one homogeneous nature.

[2] Text: *Ye-sangs-rgyas-pa* (pron. *Ye-sang-gay-pa*). In this interesting compound, *Ye* = Eternal, or Beginningless, *Sangs* = Purification, and *Rgyas-pa* = Complete, or Full. Complete Purification (*sangs-rgyas-pa*), a Tibetan term synonymous with *Nirvāṇa*, which is here qualified as Eternal (*Ye*), is, consistently with the implied sense, translatable as 'the Perfect *Nirvāṇa*', in contradistinction to lesser degrees of *Nirvāṇic* enlightenment or of incomplete purification from *sangsāric* Ignorance. *Sangs-rgyas-pa* may also be taken as referring to the Buddha as the completely Purified One, or to Buddhahood as the Completely Purified State (i.e. *Nirvāṇa*). (See page 228[2], following.) There are three states of *Nirvāṇic* enlightenment recognized by the Mahāyāna: (1) conditional, or imperfect, *Nirvāṇa*; (2) Unconditional, or perfect, *Nirvāṇa*; (3) unlocalized, or absolute *Nirvāṇa*, wherein the *sangsāric* limitations of time and space are no longer existent.

[3] Text: *Mthaḥ-brgyad* (pron. *Tha-gay*), 'Eight Limits', or 'Eight Frontiers (or Ends)', with reference to the Eight Worldly Aims, which, taken in

Inasmuch as it does not fall under the sway of any extreme, it is called 'The Middle Path'.

It is called 'Wisdom' because of its unbroken continuity of memory.

Being the essence of the vacuity of mind, it is called 'The Essence of the Buddhas'.

If the significance of these teachings were known by all beings, surpassingly excellent would it be.

Therefore, these teachings are called 'The Means of Attaining the Other Shore of Wisdom [or The Transcendental Wisdom]'.

To Them who have passed away into *Nirvāṇa*, this Mind is both beginningless and endless; therefore is it called 'The Great Symbol'.[1]

Inasmuch as this Mind, by being known and by not being known, becomes the foundation of all the joys of *Nirvāṇa*[2] and of all the sorrows of the *Sangsāra*, it is called 'The All-Foundation'.

four pairs, are: gain and loss, good name and bad name, praise and defamation, happiness and misery. In other words, as already set forth, these teachings, when practised and realized, confer transcendence over all opposites, as over all transitory conditions to which *sangsāric* mind is fettered.

[1] As shown in *Tibetan Yoga and Secret Doctrines*, Book II, the Great Symbol occultly signifies complete spiritual enlightenment, or *Nirvāṇa*, or the realization of Mind in the True State.

[2] As otherwise set forth in *Tibetan Yoga and Secret Doctrines* (pp. 7–9), *Nirvāṇa* is a state beyond, or transcendent over the *Sangsāra*, or over the Realm of Birth, Illness, Old Age, and Death; it is emancipation from conditionedness and transitoriness, from existence as man knows existence. *Nirvāṇa* is not, therefore, as some misinformed writers have assumed, synonymous with total annihilation of being; it is a transcendence over *Māyā*, over Ignorance, over the Realm of Phenomena and of Transitory Appearances, a blowing out, by an act of will, of the flame of sensuous existence, an emergence from a lower into a higher consciousness, a triumph over the *sangsāric* animal mentality, the attaining of the Higher Evolution, of True Beingness. Sarat Chandra Dās (op. cit., p. 978), in referring to *Myan-hdas*, a Tibetan synonym for the Sanskrit term *Nirvāṇa*, quotes the canonical Tibetan *Kah-gyur* (sometimes, but less correctly, written, *Kang-gyur*, and *Kanjur*) as follows: 'The state of *Nirvāṇa* is supreme peace and bliss; it is freedom from illusive thoughts, egotism, and suffering; there is nothing of the three states of the damned, the sensations of heat and cold or hunger and thirst in it. Misery and transient transmigration having been exhausted, the emancipated one works for the good of others and achieves miracles inconceivably great.'

The impatient, ordinary person when dwelling in his fleshly body[1] calls this very clear Wisdom 'common intelligence'.

Regardless of whatever elegant and varied names be given to this Wisdom as the result of thorough study, what Wisdom other than it, as here revealed, can one really desire?

To desire more than this Wisdom is to be like one who seeks an elephant by following its footprints when the elephant itself has been found.

[*THE* YOGA *OF THE THATNESS*]

Quite impossible is it, even though one seek throughout the Three Regions, to find the Buddha[2] elsewhere than in the mind.[3]

Although he that is ignorant of this may seek externally or outside the mind to know himself, how is it possible to find oneself when seeking others rather than oneself?

He that thus seeks to know himself is like a fool giving a

---

[1] Or, literally, 'when dwelling in his stronghold' (or castle), which is the fleshly body.

[2] Text: *Sangs-rgyas* = *Sangs-rgyas-pa*, 'Completely Purified One (or State)', i.e. the Buddha (or Buddhahood). In the Mahāyāna sense, a Buddha is one who has become completely awakened from the slumber of the obscuring ignorance of Truth, i.e. from what in Sanskrit is known as *Avidyā*; or one thoroughly purged of all the *karmic* effects born of the wrong actions arising from *Avidyā*. *Sangs-rgyas* (pron. *Sang-gay*) also signifies 'being liberated from the beginning and by nature full of knowledge' (cf. S. C. Dās, op. cit., p. 1265), as implied by the doctrine of knowing the mind in its nakedness. Buddhahood is not to be realized externally, but internally, as being from beginningless time a natural characteristic of mind; one need not seek outside oneself, for Buddhahood is already innate in one, and only awaits the removal of *avidyā* to shine forth like the Sun when the clouds are dissipated. *Rgyas-pa* (pron. *Gay-pa*) by itself signifies one abounding in understanding, like a Buddha.

[3] This rendering of the aphorism was preferred by the Lāma Karma Sumdhon Paul. His collaborator in the translation of our present treatise, the Lāma Lobzang Mingyur Dorje, preferred the following rendering: 'Quite impossible is it, even though one seeks throughout the Three Regions, to find [or attain] Buddhahood without knowing the mind.' The parallel between this Buddhist teaching and the Christian teaching, of the *Christos* being within, is as remarkable as it is obvious; and lends added support to the contention that in essentialities the teachings of the Anointed One, in their original and Gnostic form, if not in their Church-Council form, are in at-one-ment with those of the Enlightened One.

performance in the midst of a crowd and forgetting who he is and then seeking everywhere to find himself.[1]

This simile also applies to one's erring in other ways.

Unless one knows or sees the natural state of substances [or things] and recognizes the Light in the mind, release from the *Sangsāra* is unattainable.

Unless one sees the Buddha in one's mind, *Nirvāṇa*[2] is obscured.[3]

Although the Wisdom of *Nirvāṇa* and the Ignorance of the *Sangsāra* illusorily appear to be two things, they cannot truly be differentiated.

It is an error to conceive them otherwise than as one.

Erring and non-erring are, intrinsically,[4] also a unity.

By not taking the mind to be naturally a duality, and allowing it, as the primordial consciousness, to abide in its own place, beings attain deliverance.[5]

The error of doing otherwise than this arises not from Ignorance in the mind itself, but from not having sought to know the Thatness.

Seek within thine own self-illuminated, self-originated mind whence, firstly, all such concepts arise, secondly, where they exist, and, lastly, whither they vanish.[6]

[1] Inasmuch as the Buddha-nature is innate in man, he need not seek salvation outside himself. If we search for what we already have, we are, indeed, like this fool. The same Zen-like doctrine was taught by the Mahārshi of Tiruvannamalai in the treatise entitled *Who Am I ?* referred to above.

[2] Text: *Myang-Ḥdas* (pron. *Nyang-day*) = *Mya-ngan las Ḥdas-pa* (pron. *Nya-ngan lay day-pa*) = Skt. *Nirvāṇa. Mya-ngan* = 'affliction', 'misery', 'sorrow'; *las* = 'from'; *Ḥdas-pa* = 'to pass from'; and the whole term = 'to pass from (or surmount) sorrow'. This is additional evidence that *Nirvāṇa* does not imply annihilation, but transcendence over the Realm of Sorrow, which is the *Sangsāra*.

[3] Here, again, the Lāma Lobzang Mingyur Dorje suggests an alternative rendering: 'Unless one realizes the Buddhahood [innate] in one's mind, *Nirvāṇa* is obscured.'

[4] Or, in other words, 'in their final *yogic* analysis'.

[5] In the words of Plotinus, 'Then, indeed, hath he attained at-one-ment, containing no difference, neither in regard to himself, nor to other beings' (VI. ix. 11).

[6] The *Yoga* of the Great Symbol (expounded at length in Book II of *Tibetan Yoga and Secret Doctrines*), which propounds a parallel analysis of the arising, existing, and passing away of mental concepts, will here be found very helpful. Concerning this *yoga* of introspection, upon which our

This realization is likened to that of a crow which, although already in possession of a pond, flies off elsewhere to quench its thirst, and finding no other drinking-place returns to the one pond.[1]

Similarly, the radiance which emanates from the One Mind, by emanating from one's own mind, emancipates the mind.

The One Mind, omniscient, vacuous, immaculate, eternally, the Unobscured Voidness, void of quality as the sky, self-originated Wisdom, shining clearly, imperishable, is Itself the Thatness.

The whole visible Universe also symbolizes the One Mind.[2]

present treatise is chiefly based, the late Mahārshi of Tiruvannamalai taught, in language surprisingly parallel to that of our own text, 'it is only when the subtle mind projects itself outwards through the brain and the senses that names and forms of the grosser world come into existence. When the mind lies absorbed in the *Hridaya* [the mind's Spiritual Centre or Source], these names and forms vanish. When the outgoing tendencies of the mind are suppressed and, with all its attention turned on itself alone, the mind is retained within the *Hridaya*, that condition is called introspection, or the subjective vision [Skt. *antarmukha-drishti*]. When the mind emerges from the *Hridaya* and busies itself with the creation of the gross world, that condition may be termed extrospection, or the objective vision [Skt. *bahirmukha-drishti*]. When the mind resides within the *Hridaya*, the primal thought of ego, or the "I", gradually vanishes and what remains is the Transcendent Self or *Ātman* [the Brāhmanical equivalent to the One Mind of the Mahāyāna]. It is that state, wherein there exists not the slightest trace of the notion "I", which is called Real Vision [Skt. *Swarūpa-drishti*], and, also, Silence [Skt. *Maunam*]. This Silence is spoken of as the Vision of Wisdom [Skt. *Jñāna-drishti*] in Vedānta. Thus quiescence is nothing but that state when mind remains merged in the Self, the *Brahman* [Skt. *Ātma-swarupam*].' (See *Who Am I ?* pp. 6–7, upon which our more clearly expressed version is based.)

[1] The Mahārshi employed a similar illustration: 'A man wandering in the sun retires to the shade of a tree and enjoys the cool atmosphere there. But after a time he is tempted to go into the hot sun. Again finding the heat unbearable, he returns to the shade. Incessantly he thus moves to and fro, from the shade into the sun and from the sun into the shade. Such a man, we say, is ignorant. A wise man would not quit the shade.' (Cf. *Who Am I ?* p. 12.) In this simile, the wise man is one who, having realized the true nature of mind, goes forth no longer into Ignorance; and the ignorant man is one who, not having attained Wisdom, is still not proof against the hypnotic glamour of appearances, and continually oscillates between the higher and the lower tendencies *karmically* innate within himself. As the *Upanishads* teach, the ignorant go from death to death; or, as the *Bardo Thödol* teaches, like a feather they are tossed about by the Wind of *Karma*.

[2] As a homogeneous whole, the Universe symbolizes the undivided One Mind.

By knowing the All-Consciousness in one's mind, one knows it to be as void of quality as the sky.

Although the sky may be taken provisionally as an illustration of the unpredicable Thatness, it is only symbolically so.[1]

Inasmuch as the vacuity of all visible things is to be recognized as merely analogous to the apparent vacuity of the sky, devoid of mind, content, and form, the knowing of the mind does not depend on the sky-symbol.[2]

Therefore, not straying from the Path, remain in that very state of the Voidness.

[THE YOGIC SCIENCE OF MENTAL CONCEPTS]

The various concepts, too, being illusory, and none of them real, fade away accordingly.

Thus, for example, everything postulated of the Whole, the *Sangsāra* and *Nirvāṇa*, arises from nothing more than mental concepts.

Changes in one's train of thought[3] [or in one's association of ideas] produce corresponding changes in one's conception of the external world.

Therefore, the various views concerning things are due merely to different mental concepts.[4]

[1] As suggested by the aphorism which follows, the sky, although in reality a plenum and not a vacuum, illusorily appears to be vacuous; and only by reason of its apparent vacuousness is it figuratively, or symbolically, employed as an illustration of the vacuity of all visible or perceptible things, and then merely as a means to an end.

[2] The sky-symbol is employed merely to help mankind to discover Truth itself. As Ashvaghosha teaches, the Buddha 'only provisionally makes use of words and definitions to lead all beings, while His real objective is to make them abandon symbolism and directly enter into the true reality [Skt. *tattva*]. Because, if they indulge themselves in reasonings, attach themselves to sophistry, and thus foster their subjective particularization, how could they have the true wisdom [Skt. *tattva-jñāna*] and attain *Nirvāṇa*?' (Cf. Suzuki's translation, op. cit., p. 113.)

[3] Text: *sems-rgyud* (pron. *sem-gyüd*), 'mind-chain', 'mind-connexion (or link)', 'mind-disposition', 'mind-association'; and, accordingly, the 'association of ideas' of occidental psychology.

[4] These aphorisms, and those which follow, having been composed long before the rise of occidental science, tend to weaken the assumption of our own psychologists that oriental thinkers are neither entitled to be called

The six classes of beings respectively conceive ideas in different ways.[1]

The unenlightened externally see the externally-transitory dually.[2]

The various doctrines are seen in accordance with one's own mental concepts.

As a thing is viewed, so it appears.[3]

To see things as a multiplicity, and so to cleave unto separateness, is to err.

psychologists nor is their science psychological. The same oriental psychology of mental concepts is elaborately developed in *The Tibetan Book of the Dead*.

[1] Concerning the six classes of beings, see p. 205[2], above. This, too, is sound psychology; and concerns not only human, but all other beings throughout the various *sangsāric* states of existence. Western psychologists know little enough as yet about man *per se*, less about sub-human creatures, and nothing whatsoever about beings in non-human worlds.

[2] Or, in other words, the unenlightened (literally, 'the heretics') being by heredity and environment fettered to dualism, see good and evil, Heaven and Hell, God and Devil, Wisdom and Ignorance, *Nirvāṇa* and the *Sangsāra* as dualities, incapable of that transcendent at-one-ment of all dualities.

[3] A man in good health sees the world in a manner quite different from one who is ill. Or, again, any given individual will interpret an experience, a book, a work of art, or view an object differently at different times according to the mood in which he or she happens to be. Similarly, the unenlightened, who are the spiritually unfit, guided by delusive *sangsāric* stimuli and thus unable to transcend appearances, view whatever is sensuously perceptible as being real, whereas the enlightened, who are the spiritually fit, view the same phenomena as being unreal. Correlatively, a chemist knows by experimental proof that water is not really what it appears to be, for it is the product of the proportional combination of two gases, oxygen and hydrogen, which are invisible. In other words, the unenlightened look upon the *sangsāra* with what is popularly known as 'a jaundiced eye', whereas the enlightened view it with the clear healthy eye of Wisdom, as an illusion or phantasmagorial dream, which is as hypnotically attractive to the lost travellers in the desert of *sangsāric* existence as a mirage of water is to the camel dying of thirst in the midst of the Sahara. Thus the unreality of appearances is demonstrated by their complete dependence upon ever-changing mental concepts, the concepts being in their turn the products of mind in its *sangsāric* mood, and this mood being due to the mental disorder called illusion or self-deception. The unenlightened are, in fact, the *sangsārically* insane; and the enlightened are those who, having been cured, have transcended the realm in which such insanity is endemic and highly contagious. Viewed in this manner, the '*Yoga* of Knowing the Mind in Its Nakedness' is a transcendental system of psychotherapy, intended to cure mankind of the hallucination that they are immortal 'souls', existing in a valid Universe composed of real worlds, everlasting hells, and eternal heavens.

Now follows the *yoga* of knowing all mental concepts.

The seeing of the Radiance [of this Wisdom or Mind], which shines without being perceived,[1] is Buddhahood.

Mistake not, by not controlling one's thoughts, one errs.

By controlling and understanding the thought-process in one's mind, emancipation is attained automatically.[2]

In general, all things mentally perceived are concepts.

The bodily forms in which the world of appearances is contained are also concepts of mind.[3]

'The quintessence of the six classes of beings' is also a mental concept.[4]

'The happiness of gods in heaven-worlds and of men' is another mental concept.

'The three unhappy states of suffering', too, are concepts of the mind.

'Ignorance, miseries, and the Five Poisons' are, likewise, mental concepts.

'Self-originated Divine Wisdom' is also a concept of the mind.

---

[1] As has been already taught, there is neither any perceiver nor any objectiveness of Reality. Here, as elsewhere, the *Yoga* of the Great Symbol will serve as a very helpful commentary.

[2] This teaching, too, parallels that of the *Yoga* of the Great Symbol. (See *Tibetan Yoga and Secret Doctrines*, p. 139.)

[3] All objective things are born of mental concepts, and, in themselves, or apart from mind, have no reality. As has been shown above (on p. 229[6]), when the *sangsāric* or finite mind is active, objectivity arises; when it ceases its activity, when the thought-process is *yogically* inhibited, objectivity ceases. Of this, Ashvaghosha, in *The Awakening of Faith*, says, 'All phenomena are originally in the mind and have really no outward form; therefore, as there is no form, it is an error to think that anything is there. All phenomena [or phenomenal, or objective, appearances] merely arise from false notions in the mind. If the mind is independent of these false ideas [or concepts], then all phenomena disappear.' (Cf. Richard's translation, op. cit., p. 26.)

[4] Everything *sangsārically* conceivable, whether it be, as here, 'the quintessence of the six classes of beings', or any of the things named in the aphorisms which follow, is merely a concept of the finite mind. The degree of a concept's reality, if any, can be ascertained only by *yogic* introspection, by knowing mind in its natural state. The *Bardo Thödol* text expounds the same psychology, and repeatedly asserts that all deities or spiritual beings seen by the percipient in the after-death state have no real individualized existence any more than have human or other beings or objective appearances. (See *The Tibetan Book of the Dead*, pp. 32–33.)

'The full realization of the passing away into *Nirvāṇa*' is also a concept of mind.

'Misfortune caused by demons and evil spirits'[1] is also a concept of mind.

'Gods and good fortune'[2] are also concepts of mind.

Likewise, the various 'perfections'[3] are mental concepts.

'Unconscious one-pointedness'[4] is also a mental concept.

The colour of any objective thing is also a mental concept.

'The Qualityless and Formless'[5] is also a mental concept.

'The One and the Many in at-one-ment' is also a mental concept.

'Existence and non-existence', as well as 'the Non-Created', are concepts of the mind.

[*THE REALIZATION AND THE GREAT LIBERATION*]
Nothing save mind is conceivable.[6]

---

[1] Like Jesus and His disciples and the early Christians as a whole, the Tibetans believe that invisible beings, commonly called demons and evil spirits, inflict upon men and beasts many sorts of bodily and mental disorders and other misfortunes. (See *Tibetan Yoga and Secret Doctrines*, pp. 287–9.)

[2] Even as demons and evil spirits are believed to be the authors of certain forms of bad fortune among mankind, so gods are believed to be the authors of certain forms of good fortune.

[3] The various 'perfections' are such as those classified as the Six *Pāramitā* ('Transcendental Virtues'): Charity, Morality, Patience, Industry, Meditation, Wisdom. Four others are sometimes added: Method, Prayer, Fortitude, Foreknowledge. (See L. A. Waddell, op. cit., p. 138.) There are also particular doctrines known as 'perfections', for example, the Doctrine of the Great Perfection of the School of Padma-Sambhava; and our present treatise is a similar doctrine of perfection.

[4] This technical expression is purely *yogic*. It refers to the state of *samādhic* trance, in which there is unconsciousness of the external world of appearances, and profound one-pointedness of mind.

[5] This technical expression refers to the Voidness.

[6] Or, otherwise rendered, 'There is nothing conceivable that is not mind'. This aphorism is perhaps the most paradoxical and profound of our present treatise; and to comprehend its significance even intellectually requires meditation and careful thinking. Inasmuch as all conceivable things are, in the last analysis, mind, there is nothing other than mind. Every objective thing, the world of appearances as a whole, the *Sangsāra* and *Nirvāṇa*, are, in their essentiality, mind. Apart from mind they are inconceivable, and cease to have even relative, or illusory, existence. So it follows that there is in fact nothing conceivable save mind. As the preceding aphorisms have emphasized, all conceivable terms descriptive of conditions and things are

Mind, when uninhibited, conceives all that comes into existence.[1]

That which comes into existence is like the wave of an ocean.[2]

The state of mind transcendent over all dualities brings Liberation.[3]

no more than symbols of mental concepts. The conditions or things themselves have their illusory being because they are the externalized products of mind. In the True State, neither the *Sangsāra* nor *Nirvāṇa* are differentiated, for they have no existence *per se*; there is only the Thatness. There being thus nothing conceivable which is real apart from mind, it may be helpful to apply to the Mind *per se* some such term as the Ultimate, or Sole, Concept. In doing so, however, we must remember that this is merely one more *sangsāric* term, and, as Ashvaghosha would say, is not Truth Absolute. The finite mind *per se* can never know the Infinite Mind *per se*. Only when the finite mind is annihilated, is blown out like a flame of a candle by the breath of Divine Wisdom, and *Nirvāṇa* is realized, can there be true knowing of mind. Here we have reached the frontier of the realm of terms; and progress beyond it is for the fearless, for those who are prepared to lose their life that they may find it. Mind (*sems*) in this context must not, however, be identified with the illusory *sangsāric* aspect of mind, which is, as this *yoga* emphasizes, merely a reflex of the Supra-mundane Mind, even as the moonlight is a reflex of the Sun's light, and no more real, in itself, than an image reflected in a mirror. It is in the mundane manifestation of mind that there arise the mental modifications, or concepts, which, as Patanjali teaches, the *yogin* aims to neutralize. The materialist, who denies that there is supramundaneness, knows no consciousness save that centred in the unenlightened human mind.

[1] The mind's natural function is to think, to visualize, to conceive. This is true both of the mundane and of the supramundane mind. The Cosmos is as much the product of the thought of the One Mind, the Great Architect, as St. Paul's Cathedral in London is the product of the thought of the mind of Sir Christopher Wren. What a dream is to the dreamer, the world of appearances is to the mind. Whatever dawns or becomes perceptible in the *Sangsāra* has been conceived in the womb of the mind.

[2] When the ocean is undisturbed, it appears in its natural state as a motionless homogeneous mass of water. When affected by external things, such as winds and earthquakes, it loses its naturalness; motion is imparted to it and waves arise on its surface. The ocean in its naturalness, as has been explained elsewhere (on p. 225[1]), symbolizes mind in its naturalness; the external things symbolize the thought-process, and the motion and waves symbolize the products of the thought-process. It is in order to know mind in its naturalness that the processes of thought, visualization and mental conception, are to be *yogically* inhibited. It is easier to know the ocean when it is in its natural condition. Then it is completely tranquil; and, its waters being pellucid, the *yogin* may look into their depths; the mud and debris which are poured into it by the floods of rivers of thought are absent. In this connexion, the *Yoga* of the Great Symbol is of immense assistance to the student.

[3] This aphorism parallels that previously given on p. 229, above. So long

It matters not what name may carelessly be applied to mind; truly mind is one, and apart from mind there is naught else.

That Unique One Mind is foundationless and rootless.[1]

There is nothing else to be realized.[2]

The Non-Created is the Non-Visible.

By knowing the invisible Voidness and the Clear Light through not seeing them separately—there being no multiplicity in the Voidness—one's own clear mind may be known, yet the Thatness itself is not knowable.[3]

Mind is beyond nature, but is experienced in bodily forms.[4]

The realization of the One Mind constitutes the All-Deliverance.

Without mastery of the mental processes there can be no realization.[5]

as man is fettered to appearances he cannot transcend appearances; he remains bound to the Wheel of Existence and, like a feather tossed about by the wind, goes from death to death incessantly. Emancipation and the attainment of Divine Wisdom are synonymous.

[1] Reality, to be real, must be devoid of foundation or dependence upon something external to itself. Similarly, the One Mind, to be real, must be devoid of root or source or origin.

[2] This parallels the aphorism, 'Nothing save mind is conceivable'; and might be phrased, 'Nothing save mind is realizable'.

[3] Were the Thatness knowable, dualism would be true; for there would then be an ultimate duality, the Thatness and the knower of the Thatness. The Absolute Truth is that the Thatness and the Knower of the Thatness are indistinguishably one; to know the Thatness, the knower must become the Thatness and cease to be the knower, even as one who would know existence must cease to exist.

[4] Even as the rays of the Sun are experienced millions of miles away by beings on the Earth and in conditions unlike those on the Sun, so the microcosmic aspect or radiance of the One Mind is experienced in myriads of bodily forms into which the One Mind, like a Sun, shines.

[5] Before there can be realization of the One Mind in its True State, there must be indomitable control of all the faculties and processes of the finite mind in order to inhibit them at will and thereby to experience the True State. Correlatively, the physical organism as a whole must be *yogically* disciplined. (See *Tibetan Yoga and Secret Doctrines*, Book II.) Plotinus likewise teaches that not until all thought and thinking are transcended can the Thatness be realized: 'If the primordial Principle thought, it would possess an attribute; consequently, instead of occupying the first rank, it would occupy only the second; instead of being One, it would be manifold and would be all the things which it thought; for it would already be manifold even if it limited itself to thinking itself. . . . Inasmuch as that is multiple which thinketh, the principle which is not multiple will not think. And as this Principle is the first, then intelligence and thought are entities

Similarly, although sesamum seed[1] is the source of oil, and milk the source of butter, not until the seed be pressed and the milk churned do the oil and butter appear.

Although sentient beings are of the Buddha essence itself, not until they realize this can they attain *Nirvāṇa*.

Even a cowherd [or an illiterate person] may by realization attain Liberation.[2]

[III. THE CONCLUDING SECTIONS]
[*THE GENERAL CONCLUSION*]

Though lacking in power of expression, the author has here made a faithful record [of his own *yogic* experiences].

To one who has tasted honey, it is superfluous for those who have not tasted it to offer an explanation of its taste.[3]

Not knowing the One Mind, even *pandits* go astray, despite their cleverness in expounding the many different doctrinal systems.

To give ear to the reports of one who has neither approached nor seen the Buddha[4] even for a moment is like harkening to flying rumours concerning a distant place one has never visited.

Simultaneously with the knowing of the Mind comes release from good and evil.[5]

---

later than the first. . . . As the Good must be simple, and self-sufficient, it hath no need to think. . . . That which thinketh is not thought, but what possesseth thought. Thus is there duality in what thinketh, but no duality is there in the First' (v. vi. 2–4, 6).

[1] Sesamum seed is one of India's chief sources of edible oil.

[2] The implication here is that literacy, or what we call 'culture', is not essential to realization of the highest spiritual experiences, for even an illiterate cowherd may attain Liberation. If, as assumed and as the colophon states, Padma-Sambhava composed this aphorism, he very probably had in mind as he formulated it his own cowherd pupil, Hūṃ-kāra, who attained such mastery of the occult sciences that he became a *guru* in his own right. (See the Epitome of the Biography, pp. 166–7.)

[3] There is an overabundance of men who are prepared to explain, most elaborately, all things in heaven and in earth without really knowing anything about them. They become *gurus*, collect disciples, and pose as 'Masters of the Far East'. The Christ called them blind leaders of the blind, for they mislead no one save the blind. To one who has himself realized Truth, their explanations of it are quite unnecessary.

[4] Or, in a freer translation, 'the Buddha within'.

[5] Such a release is from all other dualities as well, the duality of good and

If the mind is not known, all practice of good and evil results in nothing more than Heaven, or Hell, or the *Sangsāra*.[1]

As soon as one's mind is known to be of the Wisdom of the Voidness, concepts like good and evil *karma* cease to exist.[2]

Even as in the empty sky there seems to be, but is not, a fountain of water, so in the Voidness is neither good nor evil.[3]

When one's mind is thus known in its nakedness, this Doctrine of Seeing the Mind Naked, this Self-Liberation, is seen to be exceedingly profound.

Seek, therefore, thine own Wisdom within thee.[4]

It is the Vast Deep.[5]

[*THE FINAL GOOD WISHES*]

All hail! this is the Knowing of the Mind, the Seeing of Reality, Self-Liberation.

For the sake of future generations who shall be born during the Age of Darkness,[6] these essential aphorisms, necessarily brief and concise, herein set forth, were written down in accordance with Tantric teachings.[7]

evil being here regarded as the root duality whence all other dualities spring, even the ultimate duality, *Nirvāṇa* and the *Sangsāra*.

[1] So long as man is fettered to appearances, to dualism, his thoughts and actions result in nothing more than after-death states of heavenly happiness or hellish miseries to be followed repeatedly by return to the human state. Thus he remains bound to the ever-revolving Wheel of the *Sangsāra*.

[2] This aphorism succintly summarizes the *yogic* doctrine of concepts expounded above.

[3] The fountain refers to rain, which has its ultimate source in the Great Waters. Similarly, good and evil seem to be other than they are; they, like all dualities, all concepts of the *sangsāric* mind, are inconceivable apart from their ultimate source in the One Mind. In the Voidness of the One Mind they cease to exist, as do all other dualities; for there, as in the Great Waters, is undifferentiated homogeneity.

[4] This aphorism may be otherwise phrased: 'Seek, therefore, this Wisdom within thine own mind'; or, more literally, 'Therefore, thine own Wisdom, this [knowing of] mind, seek ye'.

[5] Text: *Zab-rgya* (pron. *Zab-gya*): *Zab* = Deep, *gya* = vast. This abbreviated expression may be rendered in fuller form as, 'Deep and vast is Divine Wisdom [or this Doctrine]': or more concisely, 'It is the Vast Deep'.

[6] Text: *snyigs-mahi* = *snyigs-mahi-dus* (pron. *nyig-mai-dü*), the 'degenerate age of evil' now prevailing: Skt. *Kali-Yuga*, 'Black [or Dark, or Iron] Age'.

[7] Text:⁻*rgyud-lung*⁻ (pron. *gyüd-lung*), which may be rendered either as

Although taught during this present epoch, the text of them was hidden away amidst a cache of precious things.¹

May this Book be read by those blessed devotees of the future.

[*THE* GURU'S *FINAL CHARGE TO THE DISCIPLES*]

Samayā ; *gya, gya, gya.*
[Vast, vast, vast is Divine Wisdom.]²

[*THE COLOPHON*]

These teachings, called 'The Knowing of the Mind in Its Self-Identifying, Self-Realizing, Self-Liberating Reality', were formulated by Padma-Sambhava,³ the spiritually-endowed Teacher⁴ from Urgyān.⁵

'Tantric prophecy' or as 'traditional precept'. We may, therefore, otherwise render the phrase as 'in accordance with Tantric [or traditional] teachings'.

¹ This treatise, like the whole of the *Bardo Thödol* Cycle, was recovered, when the time was ripe, by the *tertöns*, or Tibetan takers-out of hidden texts, all more or less of an occult or esoteric character. (See *The Tibetan Book of the Dead*, pp. 75–77.)

² Cf. pp. 202⁴, 238⁵, along with pp. 15–20 of the General Introduction.

³ Text: *Pad-ma-ḥbyung-gnas* (pron. *Pe-ma Jūng-në*: Skt. *Padma-Kāra*), the ordinary Tibetan name of the Great Master of the Tantric occult sciences, popularly known outside of Tibet as Padma-Sambhava. As Sarat Chandra Dās, in the *Tibetan–English Dictionary* (Calcutta, 1902, p. 779), has written: 'Throughout Tibet, Padma Jungnas may be asserted to be more popular than Gautama the Buddha; and [where he is known] as *Guru* Padma, Urgyān Padma, and Lopön Hūṃkara, his votaries are full of belief in his present might and powers of assistance.' Among the Great *Guru's* many names there are two others much used by Tibetans: *Guru* Rinpoch'e ('Precious *Guru*') and Urgyān Rinpoch'e ('Precious One of Urgyān'). They also call him simply '*Lo-pön*', the Tibetan equivalent of the Sanskrit '*Guru*', and of the English 'Teacher', or, 'Spiritual Preceptor'. Our Epitome of his Biography gives a number of other names, mostly initiatory.

⁴ Text: *mkhan-po* (pron. *khan-po*), a Tibetan appellation suggesting honour and prestige, applicable to a professor employed to teach, or to the head of a monastery, and, in general, to spiritually-endowed men of learning. 'In Tibet, the head of a particular college attached to a monastery, high priests who give vows to the junior or inferior *lāmas*, and professors of sacred literature, are called *mkhan-po*; also learned men, who as such are endowed with spiritual gifts [inherited] from their spiritual ancestors, are called *mkhan-po*. Again, learned men such as are sent to China are also styled *mkhan-po*.' (Cf. S. C. Dās, op. cit., p. 179.)

⁵ Text: *O-gyan* (pron. *U-gyān*), ordinarily transliterated into English as Urgyān, the country of Odiyāna, sometimes, but probably incorrectly,

May they not wane until the whole *Sangsāra* is emptied.[1]

[Here the text ends.]

taken to be (as in the Tibetan *Lam-yig*) the modern Gaznee, in Cabul. (See S. C. Dās, op. cit., p. 1352.)

[1] This is a Mahāyānic technical expression referring to the vow of a *Bodhisattva* not to enter into *Nirvāṇa* finally until all sentient beings are liberated and the whole *Sangsāra* shall thus be emptied of them.

Self-Salvation

'Therefore, O Ānanda, be ye lamps unto yourselves. Be ye a refuge to yourselves. Betake yourselves to no external refuge. Hold fast to the Truth as a lamp. Hold fast to the Truth as a refuge. Look not for refuge to any one besides yourselves.'—The Buddha.

The Book of the Great Decease, ii. 33

(after T. W. Rhys Davids' Translation).

PLATE IX

MAITREYA THE COMING BUDDHA

Described on pages xxvii–xxviii

BOOK III
THE LAST TESTAMENTARY
TEACHINGS OF THE *GURU* PHADAMPA
SANGAY

ACCORDING TO THE LATE LĀMA KAZI
DAWA-SAMDUP'S ENGLISH RENDERING

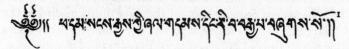

I. THE INTRODUCTION

ACCORDING to the late Lāma Kazi Dawa-Samdup, Phadampa
Sangay (or, as the Lāma otherwise called him, Kamalashīla)
appears to have flourished contemporaneously with Milarepa,
Tibet's Great *Yogī*. This name Kamalashīla is the same as

¹ This title, in Tibetan script, photographically reproduced from that of
our manuscript copy of the text, is in the late Lāma Kazi Dawa-Samdup's
own handwriting. Its English rendering is, 'Herein are Contained the Profound Manifold Teachings of Phadampa Sangay'. The late Lāma preferred
as an English title that which is placed here at the head of this Book,
because, as the introductory portion of the treatise states, the teachings
were Phadampa Sangay's last testamentary teachings to the people of
Tingri. A xylograph version of this work, examined by Lāma Lobzang
Mingyur Dorje, bears the title, 'The One Hundred Essential Teachings of
Phadampa Sangay to the People of Tingri (*Pha-dham-pa Sangs-rgyas kyis
Zhal-gdams Dhing-ri Brgya-rtsa-ma*)'.

A first-draft English translation of our text was made by the late Lāma
Kazi Dawa-Samdup shortly before the Editor became his disciple. Owing to
the passing away of the Lāma, the translation failed to receive the final
revision which he and the Editor had planned for it. When the manuscript
of the translation, accompanied by the original text, recently came into the
Editor's possession, its last page, or pages, were missing. In its entirety the
work appears to have consisted of approximately one hundred stanzas,
most of which are couplets, a few being of three verses. The xylograph text
referred to above consists of 102 stanzas. It is from our incomplete manuscript translation that the seventy-two stanzas herein given, in recension,
were selected. Their serial order corresponds to that of the Tibetan text, the
first being the first and the last the ninety-second therein. The Editor preferred to record the translated aphorisms, in keeping with the poetical
character of the original Tibetan text, in a metrical rather than a prose
form, although in some instances a prose version might have resulted in
greater clarity of expression.

that of the Indian *Bhikṣhu* Kamalashīla, who, like the Great *Guru* Padma-Sambhava, went from India to the Land of the Snowy Ranges and taught the *Dharma*. He is said to have been of the Sva-tantra Mādhyamika School of Buddhism, and the author of a number of treatises which are now extant in the Tibetan canonical commentary called the *Tanjur*. There is also attributed to him a work (*Tarka*) expounding the different philosophical systems of India.[1] A traditional belief, cited by the late Lāma, that Phadampa Sangay (or Kamala-shīla) lived for seven hundred years may possibly suggest that Phadampa Sangay was, in the eyes of his disciples, the Kamalashīla of the *Tanjur*, who was alive some three centuries prior to the time of Milarepa (A.D. 1052–1135). Or, otherwise, it may imply that Phadampa Sangay was believed to be a reincarnation of the said Kamalashīla.

Phadampa Sangay is said to have established the Shibyepa (*Shi-byed-pa*) School of Tibetan Tantricism. According to legendary accounts, he paid seven visits to Tibet, and on one occasion was miraculously transported to China. The foundation of the Tingri (or Dingri) Langgor Monastery, near Tingri, a town in Southern Tibet about fifty miles north-east of Lapchi (*Lab-phyi*), the Mount Everest of European geographers, is attributed to him;[2] and it was to the people of Tingri that his final teachings were delivered.

Phadampa Sangay established in Tibet a system of *yoga*, nowadays little known elsewhere, called Chö.[3] His chief disciple was Ma-chik-lap-dön. The Apostolic Succession of the first twelve of the Great *Gurus* of this School is as follows: (1) Dorje Chang, the super-human *Guru*, (2) Padma-Sambhava, (3) Tilopa, (4) Naropa, (5) Jam-yang-ma-way Seng-ge, (6) Kha-do Sukha Siddha, (7) Thok-me, (8) Nāgārjuna, (9) Ārya Devā, (10) Saraha, (11) Birūpa, and (12) Phadampa Sangay.

Inasmuch as Phadampa Sangay's *yogic* system parallels that of Padma-Sambhava, the first of the human Apostolic *Gurus* of the Chö School, an epitome of it is here presented

---

[1] Cf. L. A. Waddell, op. cit., p. 31.   [2] Cf. S. C. Dās, op. cit., p. 815.
[3] Tib. *Gchod* (or *Spyod*): pron. Chö.

to serve as an independent commentary, derived from Tibetan sources, on the 'Yoga of Knowing the Mind in Its Nakedness' expounded above in Book II.

The Introduction as contained in the text itself represents the *guru* as being near the time of his passing beyond sorrow, and these teachings, which he uttered extemporaneously, as being his last. Its translation is as follows:

'May blessings rest upon this [Book]!

'Dhampa Tsharchhen [the disciple] approached Phadampa Sangay [the *guru*] and supplicatingly said, "O Reverend Phadampa, thou thyself art growing old and going on from bliss to bliss, but what are we ourselves to do, or to whom can we look for protection and guidance?"

'The *guru* was overwhelmed with sadness; and his voice was broken with weeping as he gave utterance to the following verses, which were his last testamentary teachings to the people of Tingri.'[1]

II. THE *GURU'S* TEACHINGS

'To give oneself, body, speech, and heart, to the cause of
   Holy Truth,
Is the best and highest occupation, O ye Tingri folk.

'Wealth and riches are illusory, loaned for the moment's use;
Show not over-fondness for them, neither hoard them,
   Tingri folk.

'One's kindred are alluring visions, glamorous mirages;
Break the tie, sever the knot of sentiment, O Tingri folk.

[1] After the manner of Milarepa, who delivered his teachings in songs and hymns, Phadampa Sangay sings these precepts. In Tibet, and commonly throughout India and the Orient, poetry is still considered to be the most appropriate literary vehicle for the expounding and recording of religious lore, as it was in the culturally golden days when the Ancient Mysteries and the Greek drama flourished. But, in the Occident, poetry has become unfashionable, and the use of language, both in literature and everyday life, is controlled by a utilitarian commercialism. As in the United States of America, where the ears of the many no longer hear the ever-present music of Nature, even the majestic sonorousness of the language of the Authorized Version of the Bible has ceased to be in popular favour, and Bibles called 'modern', in unmusical vulgar English, have appeared in many versions.

'Fatherland and homes are transient, even as a nomads' camp;
Let not fondness bind you to them; renounce all things, O Tingri folk.

'Even on one's birthday morning, omens of one's death appear;
Ever be alert and watchful; waste no time, O Tingri folk.

'One-pointedly devote yourselves to the Sacred *Dharma* Path;
It shall be, in the hour of death, your Guide and Boat, O Tingri folk.

'Infallible is *karmic* law, ever impartial, just, and sure;
Abstain from even the smallest wrongful act, O ye Tingri folk.

'In a dream-state are all actions, however righteous they may seem;
Transcend deeds, and seek ye knowledge of the Real, O Tingri folk.[1]

'Ever transient is this world of ours; all things change and pass away;
For a distant journey even now prepare, O Tingri folk.

'The rhinoceros, deep in a jungle, thinketh he's immune from harm;
But look, the jungle is afire! is he safe now, Tingri folk?[2]

'Over the sea of birth and illness, age and death there is no bridge;
Build even now the Vessel that can cross it, O ye Tingri folk.

'Narrow is the ambuscade of birth and death and the dread *Bardo*;

[1] All *sangsāric* states of consciousness are to be regarded as being illusory dream-states; and, therefore, even though one is performing actions in what men call the waking-state, the actions are as unreal as are actions performed in what men call the dream-state. Equally illusory are all *sangsāric* states of after-death consciousness. The Great Liberation is dependent upon transcending the *Sangsāra* and becoming a Fully-Awakened One, as was the Buddha. The True State, the Real, is the State of Quiescence, wherein there are no *sangsāric* thoughts or actions.

[2] The jungle is the jungle of worldliness, aflame with the fires of lust, hatred, and Ignorance, where man, like the rhinoceros, thinks himself immune from harm.

The Five Passions,[1] like armed bandits, oft waylay one on the
    Path:
Seek the sacred *Guru*; he'll conduct you safely, Tingri folk.[2]

'Once when found, the sacred *Guru* never afterward is lost;
Visualize him overhead,[3] and worship him, O Tingri folk.

'Should the *Guru* will to do so, he can reach one anywhere;[4]
Firmly fix your faith and reverence on your *Guru*, Tingri folk.

'He that hath the most of money may have most of avarice;
Impartially, to every one, give ye alms, O Tingri folk.

'He that hath the most of power may have most of evil deeds;
Hanker not for worldly power, O ye folk of Tingri land.

'Hesitate not, neither tarry, lest ye fail to gain the Goal;
Be brave of heart and of fixed mind, even now, O Tingri folk.

'None can tell when Death, that grim and spectral enemy,
    will come;
Even now make preparations for his coming, Tingri folk.

'None can help one on the morrow after Death hath cut one
    off;
Hasten onward, ever goalward; win the Race, O Tingri folk.

'Surely, like the shades of evening slowly merging into night,
Grim Death, pausing not a moment, cometh nearer hour by
    hour;
Even now prepare the means to baffle him, O Tingri folk.

'Fair are the flowers in summer, then they fade and die in
    autumn;
Likewise doth this transient body bloom and pass, O Tingri
    folk.

---

[1] The Five Passions are hatred, pride, lust, jealousy, and stupidity.

[2] In Tibet, and in India, it is generally believed that a competent *guru*
can direct the spiritual progress of a disciple not only through the human
state but also through any of the after-death states.

[3] As in other texts of our Tibetan Series, and especially in *Tibetan Yoga
and Secret Doctrines* (pp. 262 ff.), the *Guru* when meditated upon is to be
visualized as seated in *yogic* posture above the crown of the disciple's head.

[4] The *Guru*, here impersonally referred to, is the *Guru* Phadampa
Sangay, who teaches of the ability of a truly great *Guru* to respond, telepathically and psychically, to a call for spiritual aid and guidance by a
disciple anywhere, distance being no barrier.

'Glorious is this human body when illumined by life's light;
Fearful, like the demon hosts, is the sight of it when dead;
Perfidious its allurements ever are, O Tingri folk.

'Men meet in a mart, and then, when all their trading's done,
   they part;
So from kindred and from friends shall ye be parted, Tingri
   folk.

'Know for certain that Illusion's shaky building will fall
   down;
Even now prepare efficient safeguards, O ye Tingri folk.[1]

'The Eagle of the Mind is sure to take its flight with wings
   spread free;
Train yourselves to fly as freely, even now, O Tingri folk.[2]

'All the beings of the Six Realms have been our loving parents;
Meditate with loving-kindness towards each one, O Tingri
   folk.[3]

'Harmful foes inciting wrong thoughts are illusions *karma*-
   wrought;
Thoughts of vengeance, harm, and hatred cast away, O Tingri
   folk.[4]

[1] The shaky building is the precarious human body. In the hour of Full
Enlightenment, the Buddha proclaimed that Illusion would never build the
house for Him again.

[2] This *yogic* training, to fly as freely before death as the Eagle of the
Mind does when the fleshly body dies, is in the practice of projecting the
'astral' body, set forth in *Tibetan Yoga and Secret Doctrines*, pp. 246–76.

[3] During the course of the infinite evolutionary outpourings of life, every
living creature in every state of existence has been, at some time or another,
a loving parent to every other sentient being. All living things, being
ultimately one, are entirely interdependent in their relationships; and, when
this is realized, the *yogin* ceases to have hatred for any, no matter how harmful or inimical they may illusorily appear to be and are *karmically*. Nor will
he do harm to the least of them. This, then, is the *yogic* science of harmless-
ness (Skt. *ahimsa*). (Cf. *Tibetan Yoga and Secret Doctrines*, p. 77[2].)

[4] This teaching supplements that of the preceding stanza. Foes are the
outcome of one's own actions. It is, therefore, folly to rebel against enemies.
The right course to pursue is to transmute enemies into friends, by the all-
conquering power of divine love. As the Buddha teaches, the more there is
of hatred from others, the more should there be of love from the hated.
Until mankind practise such wisdom as that set forth in the Sermon on the
Mount, they will, by returning hatred for hatred rather than by returning
love for hatred, continue to be fettered to Ignorance, and incessantly sow
and harvest hatred, revenge, unbrotherliness, and war.

'Pilgrimage and doing reverence purge the body of its faults;
Worldly business put aside; it is never finished, Tingri folk.

'Chanting of the prayers of refuge purgeth foulness from
  the tongue;
Waste no time in foolish talking; chant your prayers, O
  Tingri folk.

'Humble faith and pure devotion purge the mind of wrongful
  thoughts;
Meditate the gracious *guru* overhead, O Tingri folk.

'Bones and flesh, though born together, in the end must
  separate;
Think not your life a lasting good; soon it endeth, Tingri folk.

'Seek the True State, firm and stable, of the Pure Mind; hold
  it fast;
That is forever the Enduring, and the Changeless, Tingri folk.

'Grasp the Mind, the holy treasure, best of riches of man's
  life;
That is the only lasting treasure, O ye folk of Tingri land.

'Seek and enjoy the sacred elixir of meditation;
Once *samādhi* hath been tasted, hunger endeth, Tingri folk.

'Drink ye deeply of the nectar of the Stream of Consciousness;
'Tis perennial, thirst assuaging, cool and pure, O Tingri folk.

'Seek as your son the ever fair, immortal Child of Wisdom;
That is the best and noblest offspring, never dying, Tingri
  folk.

'Brandish the Spear of Reason aloft in the Voidness of space;
Aspiration hath no frontier, nor obstruction, Tingri folk.

'Keep alert the Unrestricted, as a guard against distraction;
Be calm of mind, but never slothful, O ye folk of Tingri land.

'Draw strength from the Unobstructed; let the Stream flow
  naturally;
No suppression, no indifference, should there be, O Tingri
  folk.[1]

  [1] In other words, the *yogin* is warned against forcible suppression of

'Seek in your minds the Bodies that are fourfold and inseparable;
Neither hoping, neither fearing for results, O Tingri folk.[1]

'The *Sangsāra* and *Nirvāṇa* have their source in the One
Mind;
But that Mind itself hath neither form nor substance, Tingri
folk.

'Likes and dislikes leave no traces, like the flight of birds
through air;
Cling not to experiences; ever changing are they, Tingri folk.[2]

'Unborn Truth, the *Dharma-Kāya*, like the Orb that giveth
day,
Waxeth not nor ever waneth in its radiance, Tingri folk.[3]

'Rebellious thoughts are a house abandoned wherein robbers
prowl;
Hidden gold they seek within it, but they find none, Tingri
folk.[4]

undesirable or lower tendencies, passions, or thoughts. They are to be
analysed in a psycho-analytical manner in order that their origin and characteristics may be thoroughly understood. Then, when their unsatisfactory
and illusory nature is comprehended, but not before, the *yogin* is to transmute and transcend them. It is not by fearing, or trying to run away from,
an evil that one progresses, but by facing it boldly and conquering it. Nor
is one to go to the other extreme of weakly giving way to it, or of being
indifferent to it. As set forth in the *Yoga* of the Great Symbol, there are
various progressive steps in controlling, and, finally, in inhibiting the
thought-process. One of them consists in allowing thoughts to flow naturally;
thereby, little by little, the *yogin* attains psychic strength. (See *Tibetan Yoga
and Secret Doctrines*, pp. 129–30.)

[1] The fourfold Bodies which are to be realized by the 'Yoga' of Knowing the Mind in Its Nakedness' as being an inseparable unity, are the three
Divine Bodies, the *Tri-Kāya*, and the illusory human body of the *yogin*.
There should never be hopes and fears concerning *yogic* success; for the
result is inevitable if the practice be right.

[2] Strictly speaking, likes and dislikes are *karmically* traceable, although,
practically speaking, they are, for the neophyte, as trackless or untraceable
as the airpaths of birds. Since, as this stanza implies, they are the results of
actions, or experiences, the *yogin* is advised not to cling to or hanker after
worldly experiences or sensuousness.

[3] The Truth, the *Dharma-Kāya*, the Thatness, is said to be the Unborn,
the Unshaped, the Unbecome; that which is born, shaped, and become, is
the Illusory, the *Sangsāric*.

[4] This teaching is similar to that concerning enemies. Rebellious thoughts
must not be fostered; they are as empty of good as the deserted house is
empty of gold.

'Sensuousness is ever-fleeting, like the ripples on a pond;
Seek ye not the ever-fleeting; 'tis delusive, Tingri folk.

'Though desires remembered charm one, as a rainbow's colours do,
No need is there to cling to them; show not weakness, Tingri folk.

'Bright and effulgent is the Mover, like the Sun when free from clouds;
In your own mind, [in its darkness], place no trust, O Tingri folk.[1]

'Like the zephyr is the Free Mind, unattached to any thought;[2]
For no object have attachment; transcend weakness, Tingri folk.

'The seeing of Reality, like a dream by one that's dumb,
Cannot be described in language to another, Tingri folk.[3]

'Blissful is the dawn of Wisdom, like the virgin's wedding night;
Till experienced none can know it as it is, O Tingri folk.

'Forms objective and the Voidness, in their essence, know as one;
Without circumference, and without centre are they, Tingri folk.

'Uncontrolled thoughts, like the gazings of a belle into her mirror,
Lead not to spiritual insight; know this truth, O Tingri folk.

'Like the frame and mounts of a violin are illusive bliss and pain;

[1] The 'Mover' appears to be synonymous with the One Mind, as the source of motion and of all *sangsāric* things. Its brightness and effulgence are contrasted with the darkness of the unenlightened microcosmic mind.
[2] The 'Free Mind', or Mind in its True State, is calm yet unimpeded, like a zephyr or gentle breeze, and transcendent over the thought-process.
[3] It is only by realization that the indescribable, unpredicable Thatness can be known; it cannot be described in any language, for all languages are entirely dependent upon *sangsāric* concepts born of *sangsāric* experiences.

From the primary come the secondary causes, Tingri folk.

'All creation, within and without, is contained in one's own
mind,

Like the water in the ice; seek to know this truly, Tingri folk.

'The erring Wheel of Ignorance, like the moisture in a
meadow,

Never can be checked, though one trieth every means, O
Tingri folk.[2]

'This human life, endowed and free, is indeed the greatest
boon;

Piteous are they who waste it aimlessly, O Tingri folk.

'Like the magic *Chintāmani* is the Great Path of the Truth,

Hard indeed to find, though sought for everywhere, O Tingri
folk.[3]

'Life-maintaining food and raiment in some manner will be
found;

So devote yourselves, most earnestly, to the *Dharma*, Tingri
folk.[4]

---

[1] Both bliss and pain are the results of primary causes; they are an
illusory duality. The one is inconceivable apart from the other, even as is
good apart from evil. From the frame and mounts of a violin as the primary
causes are produced as secondary causes harmonious sounds; but, as the
Mahāyāna teaches, no sound is other than illusory.

[2] In spite of the doctrine that eventually, in the course of inconceivable
aeons, all sentient beings will transcend Ignorance, one creation period
meanwhile succeeds another, apparently interminably; and, from this
practical viewpoint, there is no stopping the erring Wheel of Ignorance.
The few attain deliverance from it; the many remain bound to it, and so
pass from one state of existence to another incessantly, meeting death after
death in this world and in other worlds. Foolish it is to count upon salvation
by stoppage of the Wheel; one must save oneself by one's own efforts. The
wise tarry not in pleasure-grounds of the senses; they enter the Path and
attain Liberation.

[3] The Great Path, the Mahāyāna, leads to the Great Liberation. Like the
magic wish-granting gem, known in Sanskrit as the *Chintāmani*, it grants
all right desires and petitions of those who are fortunate enough to have
found it.

[4] This suggests the command of the Christ: 'Take no thought for your
life, what ye shall eat, or what ye shall drink; nor yet for your body, what
ye shall put on' (St. Matthew vi. 25). And, in Chanakya's *Nītidarpana*, or
'Mirror of Morals' (xii. 20), according to the translation by Durga Prashād
(Lahore, 1905), it is said: 'The wise should think of religion only, and not of
bread; for one's livelihood is ordained from one's very birth.'

'Practise hardships and endurance in your youth and in your
  prime;
Difficult to change is habit when one's old, O Tingri folk.[1]

'If when any passion dawneth there be sought the antidote,
Infallibly all the symptoms will be cured, O Tingri folk.[2]

'Evermore bear in your hearts the pain and sorrow of the
  world.
Faith thereby regaineth vigour; trim your Lamps, O Tingri
  folk.

'Life is transitory, like the morning dewdrops on the grass;
Be not idle, nor give time to worthless works, O Tingri folk.

'Like the sunshine from a clear space twixt the clouds the
  Dharma is:
Know that now there is such Sunshine; use it wisely, Tingri
  folk.

[1] It is anthropologically interesting to know that man's experiencing of
life in Tibet as in Europe and the Americas results in the same deductions,
as is here suggested by the *Guru*'s saying, 'Difficult to change is habit when
one's old', and by other universally human sayings elsewhere in the treatise.
This evidence of mankind's mental at-one-ment gives added support to the
thesis set forth in our General Introduction, on pp. 12–14, that the microcosmic minds of men are like single cells in a multicellular organism, symbolized by the macrocosmic One Mind. In observing this self-evident
platitudinousness of a number of the precepts, we should remember that
Phadampa Sangay is not addressing a group of learned *lāmas* in a monastic
college but a group of simple-minded peasants in a Tibetan village, to whom,
as he well knew, the commonplace rather than the philosophically abstruse
deductions from life's experiences make the greatest appeal.
  Platitudes when cut and polished become the precious gems of literature.
They are then known as proverbs, elegant sayings, golden precepts,
aphorisms of the *gurus*, and, in Bibles, beatitudes. So viewed, platitudes are
expressive of the very quintessence of mankind's experiences throughout
the ages; they set forth the principles and common denominators of life.
Accordingly, the platitudes of our treatise ought not to be dismissed merely
because they are commonplace. If made the bases for various exercises in
meditation, as the *Guru* intended that they should be, they will be found
productive of much spiritual fruit.
  [2] The antidote for passions is Divine Wisdom, which teaches of their
illusory and unsatisfying nature. When the antidote is applied *yogically*,
through knowing the Mind, as taught above in Book II, passions are dominated; they are not to be forcibly suppressed, as is sometimes erroneously
taught, but analysed, understood, and transmuted, and then applied to
higher than mundane ends.

'Though one thinketh joys and sorrows come of causes opposite,

Yet within oneself are found their roots and causes, Tingri folk.

'If excess of faith should lead you to contempt of truth at times,

Meditate *karmic* results in the *Sangsāra*, Tingri folk.

'Associates whose acts are wrong tend to make one's own like theirs;

Keep yourselves detatched from friendships that mislead one, Tingri folk.

'Associates whose acts are right help one on the Virtuous Path;

In the Wise and Holy have unwavering trust, O Tingri folk.

'Delusions born of Ignorance are the root of every ill;

Keep the Knower ever watchful, and controlled, O Tingri folk.

'By neutralizing all the Poisons, ye shall cut the Journey short;

Keep in your hearts the antidote; e'er apply it, Tingri folk.[1]

'Not from effort that's half-hearted cometh Perfect Buddhahood;

Evermore be clad in Wisdom's armour, O ye Tingri folk.

'Propensities long entertained give direction to one's acts;

Deeds that have been done in past time recollect not, Tingri folk.[2]

'If ye fail to grasp a meaning, [to the *Guru*] make ye prayer;

Doubt ye not that understanding then will come, O Tingri folk.'[3]

[1] The Poisons are sloth, anger, lust, arrogance, and jealousy; the antidote for sloth is diligence, for anger, love, for lust, self-control, for arrogance, humility, for jealousy, selflessness.

[2] In Chanakya's *Nītidarpana* (xiii. 2), according to Durga Prashād's rendering, above cited, occurs the following parallel maxim: 'Bewail not the dead past, nor think of the future; the wise think of the present only.'

[3] The prayer is to be made either to a superhuman *guru* in a heaven world, such as a Dhyānī Buddha or a *Bodhisattva*, or to a human *guru*, who may be physically far distant. Apparently it is not necessary in Tibet to

III. CONCLUDING THOUGHTS: POWER, CONQUEST, SECURITY

It is by the practical application of such *yoga* of introspection as is set forth in this Book III by Phadampa Sangay, and, more fully, in Books I and II above by Padma-Sambhava, and in the three preceding volumes of this Tibetan Series, that the Journey from the mundane to the supramundane becomes realizable—without dependence upon any *guru*, god, or saviour. The Buddhas do no more than chart the course over which They Themselves have journeyed; salvation is not to be won through the grace and will of some supreme deity, but in virtue of self-directed effort. If man thinks himself to be insignificant and weak and helpless, he will be so; for man is what man thinks. 'All that we are is the result of what we have thought.'[1] When man recognizes that his limitations and bondage are of his own making, automatically he will become universal and free; when he knows that he is Buddha, he will cease to be man, and, mightier than Brahma and Indra, he will be Lord of Lords, God of Gods.

The greatest conqueror is the Conqueror of Self. The dominion of such a One is not over this world alone, but over all worlds and beings, over those who are not yet men, over those who have grown to manhood, and over those who are gods.

It is by looking within, in true oriental manner, not by looking without, that the Highway to Universality and Omnipotence and Freedom is discoverable. The eyes of the mundane see only the mundane, the transitory, the powerless, the insecure, the unreal; the supramundane, the non-transitory, the all-powerful, the all-secure, the real, can be perceived only by the inner vision.

Thus, for as long as the Occident continues to fix its gaze

---

conduct para-psychological experiments to ascertain if there be telepathy; for telepathy is recognized by all classes of Tibetans, whether learned *lāmas* or unsophisticated peasants, as being a quite ordinary outcome of a disciple's *yogic* training.

[1] The Buddha, in the *Dhammapāda*, i. 1, Irving Babbitt's translation (Oxford University Press, New York and London, 1936), p. 3.

upon appearances, it will suffer disillusionment; the youthful enthusiasm of pioneer epochs, the mature pride born of worldly achievements in architecture, art, science, commerce, government, and then the hopeless despondency of national decadence foreshadowing inevitable fall, will continue to follow each other in an orderly and monotonous sequence, age after age.

Today, in France and all of Europe, as in the United States of America and Soviet Russia, the quest is for Security. But occidental man remains fettered to the evanescent and the insecure. Not until he has grown old enough and wise enough to cast aside his many toys and relinquish desire and ambition and greed will he be prepared to adopt the sole technique which can assure Security. Not until he has grown weary of the Insecure, to which he now so fondly clings, although with an increasing sense of misgiving, will he renounce it. Not until he has ascertained by bitter experience that his utilitarianism, his machines, his animal comforts, his technocracies, his various ideologies and schemes looking to social well-being and a Utopia here on Earth are no more than will-o'-the-wisps of the mundane mind, to lead him farther astray in the morass of sensuous existence, will he transcend the Illusory, and, entering upon the Wisdom-Path, attain the unshakeable and everlasting Security of *Nirvāṇa*.

Here endeth the fourth volume
of the teachings of the
Gurus concerning the
Yoga Path that
leadeth to
the Great
Libera-
tion.

May this Book assist Mankind to transmute Ignorance into Divine Wisdom.

INDEX

Black-type figures indicate the chief references, most of which may be used as a Glossary.

Buddhas of Meditation,
178³.
Buddhas of the Three
Times, 203, 203².
Buddhism, 104, 182³.
— Bengal and, 157–8.
— *Dhyāna*, 195.
— Esoteric, 54.
— Exoteric, 54.
— Flesh-eating and,
138⁴.
— *Mantrayāna*, 129¹.
— Northern, 3, 107¹,
168³.
— Nyingma School of,
81, 130², 195, 207³,
208³.
— Pali and Tibetan
Canons of, 53–54.
— Salvation and, 76.
— Schools of, 208³.
— Southern, 3, 53, 128³,
168³, 220².
— Tantric, 26, 31, 54,
58–63, 59¹, 195: see
Tantricism.
— Tibetan, 15, 25 ff.,
59–63, 127¹, 141⁹,
142⁴, 182, 188, 195,
210¹.
— Zen, 73–74, 133⁵,
134¹, 195, 208¹.
Buddhist Bible, A, 99¹.

Castes, Four Hindu, 181³.
Chakra, 132.
Chanakya's *Nītidarpana*,
250⁴, 252².
Chintāmani, 250, 250³.
Chitti-Yoga, 131, 131³.
Christ (*Christos*), xxxi,
20, 26¹, 34¹, 250⁴.
Christianity, xxxvi–
xxxviii, xlii–xliii,
218¹, 227¹.
— Buddhism and, 26¹,
228³.
— Esotericism and, 33–
35.
— Exotericists and, 33–
35.
— Sexuality and, 62.
Concepts, 80–81, 82,
223¹.
— *Yogic* Science of,
231 ff., 232³, 233³,⁴,
238²: see Ideas.
Consciousness, Cosmic,
6, 198–9.

— Ego and, xxxviii–
xxxix.
— Individual, xxxiii.
— *Sangsāric*, 8, 199,
244¹.
— Universal, 1.
Consciousness-principle,
119, 119³,⁴, 140, 158.
Culture, Four Methods
for, 24.

Daemons (Demons), 60,
139–42, 142³, 176²,
177¹, 234¹: see *Māras*;
Spirits.
Ḍākinī (Fairy), xxv,
119, 130, 142, 164,
165.
— Four, 118, 118², 121,
142, 171, 177².
— Padma - Sambhava
and, 120–1, 131–3,
137, 171, 177, 177².
— Peaceful and Wrath-
ful, 120; see Ye-she-
Tshogyal.
Dās, Sarat Chandra, 91,
219⁵, 227², 239³.
David-Neel, Madame
Alexandra, 29¹, 166⁴.
Death, 44–45.
— After-death state, 80,
82.
Desires, lii–liii.
Deva-chān, 173, 173².
Dharma, lxi–lxii, 4, 30,
31, 36, 39, 56, 88, 99,
134², 173, 208¹, 216–
18, 216², 224².
— Wisdom and, 15–16.
— Door of, 204, 204¹.
Dharma-Kāya, xxvi, 3,
4, 139⁴, 165, 165²,
178¹, 180, 202¹, 212,
223², 248³.
Dharma-Rāja, 140¹,
165, 165¹: see Mahā-
kāla.
Dhyānī - Bodhisattvas,
xxvi.
Dhyānī-Buddhas, 4, 17,
178, 178¹,³.
Dionysus Zagreus, 36.
Dorje, xv, xxiii, 107,
107¹, 117, 167, 177¹,
202⁴.
— Double, xxvii.
Drag-po, 60, 121³.
Dream-states, 3, 8, 45.

— *Sangsāra* and, 3,
244¹.
Dualism, liii–liv, 5, 37,
44, 199, 232², 237⁵,
238³.
— Mind and, 2.
— Ultimate, 4.
Dunne, J. W., lix, 211ⁿ.

Earth Goddess, 125,
165.
Education, Occidental,
21–23.
Eight Aims, 226, 226³.
Eight Cemeteries, 180,
180².
Esoteric Sect, Tibetan,
195–6.
Esotericism, xvii, 46¹,
58, 59, 105, 123², 186¹,
195, 202⁴, 208³, 215⁵,
223².
— Exotericism and, 32,
33–35, 54, 116¹.
— *Kālachakra* Doctrine
and, xvii–xix.
Essence, True, 3, 4.
— Three Aspects of,
3–4: see Mind.
Evil: see Good and Evil.
Existence, Six States of,
123, 123¹, 205².
Extraversion, xxxv ff.,
xlvii.

Five Elements, 180⁷.
Five Passions, 245¹.
Five Poisons, 147.
Five Powers, 180⁶.
Four Noble Truths, 127.
Freud, Introversion
and, xxxv.

Gaṇesha, 59.
Garuḍa, 186, 186¹.
Gelugpa School, 25.
Getri, 128, 128⁴, 204¹.
Gnosticism, 33–35, 33¹,
217¹.
— Canon of, 53.
Gods of the Ten Direc-
tions, 111, 111¹.
Good and Evil, 35–57,
219³, 238³.
— Buddhist Tantricism
and, 37.
— *Yogic* Doctrine of,
38: see Māra.
Great Crown Sutra, 30.

Great Perfection Doctrine, 130, 130[2], 195, 196, 207, 207[3], 234[3].

Gṛidhrakūta, 134, 134[2], 137.

Guru, vii, xxi–xxiv, 16, 18, 24, 40, 70, 98, 136, 242, 245[2,3,4].
— Dorje Drŏlŏ, xxiii.
— Lŏden Chog-se, xxii.
— Norbu, 92.
— Nyima Hodzer, xxii.
— Padma Gyalpo, xxii.
— Padma Jungnay, xxi–xxiv.
— Prabhahasti, 123–4, 124[3], 177.
— Prince Shri Singha, 11.
— Scorpion, 181–2.
— Seng-ge Dradog, xxiii.
— Teaching of, 50, 62, 80, 99–100.
— Wisdom - Holder, 133–4: see Hūṃ-Kāra.

Hathayoga, xxxix, xl.
Hayagrīva, 133, 133[1], 140, 160, 160[1].
Heruka, 161–3, 162[1], 163[1].
Hīnayāna, 127[1], 208[3].
Hinduism, Six Schools of, 131[2].
Hridaya, 16, 229[6].
Hui Ming Ch'ing, lix[3].
Hui-neng, 134[1].
Hull, R. F. C., viii.
Hūṃ, 132, 132[4], 140, 166.
— Long, 166, 166[2].
Hūṃ-Kāra, 20, 166–7, 167[2], 237[2].

Ideas, 199.
— Pre-existence of, 197: see Concepts.
Ignorance (Avidyā), xxxix, 13, 37, 39, 42, 43, 73, 76, 77, 81, 85, 214[3], 228[2].
— Wheel of, 250, 250[2].
Illiteracy, 20–24.
Introversion, xxxv, xlvi.
— Extraversion and, xxxv ff.

Iron and Evil Spirits, 114[1].

Jñānam, 72.
John, St., Gospel of, 4, 217[1].
Jung, Dr. C. G., viii, xlv[1], lviii[1], 79.
— Psychic Energy Essay of, lviii. Psychological Commentary, xxix–xliv, 197.

Kālachakra, 59, 60–61.
— Doctrine of, xvii–xix, 122, 122[3].
Kalpa, 30, 112, 112[2].
Kamalashīla, 242.
Kama Shastra, 52.
Kanjur, 15, 28, 220[n].
Karma, 72, 206[n].
— Karmic Pattern, 36.
— Taking of Life and, 116.
Kāyas, 178[1], 202[1].
— Three, xv, xxi, xxiv, xxvi–xxvii, 3–4.
Khorva, 29[1].
Khoten, 176[1].
Knowledge, 18.
— Five Classes of, 168, 168[2].
— Wisdom Contrasted with, 15–20.
Kriyā-Yoga, 206, 206[2].
Kuṇḍalinī Goddess, 33[n], 132[4].
Kusha Grass, 152, 152[1].
Kushinagara, 104[1].

La Fuente, Madame Marguerite, viii.
Lāma, 141[3], 152[2], 191.
— Dalai, 85[2], 87–88, 129[4], 190[3].
— Geden-ḍub, 190[3].
— Karma Sumdhon Paul, vii, xvii, xviii, 85[2], 89–91, 93, 193, 228[3].
— Kazi Dawa-Samdup, vii, 26[1], 28[1,2], 92, 94, 121[1], 241, 241[1].
— Lāma-tulkus, 85, 85[2].
— Lobzang Mingyur Dorje, vii, xviii, 91, 92, 193, 228[3], 229[3].
— Ngag-pa, 62, 62[1].
— Sherab-Gyatsho, 89, 91.

— Sonam Senge, 93, 122[3].
— Tashi, xvii–xviii, 86, 88, 90.
Last Testamentary Teachings of Phadampa Sangay, 94, 98, 241–54.
— History of Text of, 94, 241–3.
Learning, Eight Treasures of, 15.
— Higher, 24: see Culture; Knowledge.
Lévy-Bruhl, lx, lx[2].
Liberation, The Great, 6, 37, 71, 84, 85, 99, 196, 207, 234–7, 244[1]: see Buddhahood; Nirvāṇa.
— Self-, xxxvi, xlvi, li, lv–lvi, 193–240.
— Tantra of, 32[1], 161.
— Tantric Yoga and, 131: see Book of the Great Liberation; 'Yoga of Knowing the Mind'.
Life, 36 ff.
— Good and Evil and, 36, 55.
Light, Clear, lii, 11, 205, 205[4], 218.
— Great, lxiii–lxiv, 221: see Yoga of the Light.
Loka-Siddha, 122, 122[2].
Lounsbery, Miss Constant, viii.
Loyola, Ignatius, lii.

Mādhyamika (Middle Path), 2, 3, 14, 42, 43.
Magic, 141, 170–1.
Mahābhārata, 36.
Mahādeva, 141, 141[6].
Mahākāla, 129–30, 129[4], 141, 141[8].
Mahā-Mudra, 209[6].
Mahārshi, Sri Ramana, 12, 12[1], 23, 38, 38[1], 40[1], 71, 216[1], 229[1,6], 230[1].
Mahāyāna (Great Path), vii, xx, lxiii, 1 ff., 5, 6, 12, 13, 15–16, 31 ff., 58, 70, 77, 101, 104 ff., 119, 120, 125, 127, 127[1], 153, 173[2], 176, 176[1], 188, 200, 207[1], 208[3,5], 220, 250, 250[3], et passim.

'As long as the sky endureth, so long will there be no end of sentient beings for one to serve ; and to every one cometh the opportunity for such service. Till the opportunity come, I exhort each of you to have but the one resolve, namely, to attain Buddhahood for the good of all living things.'

Milarepa, from his last exhortation to his disciples, in *Tibet's Great Yogī Milarepa*, page 271.